# Transition of Secondary Students with Emotional or Behavioral Disorders

## Current Approaches for Positive Outcomes

### SECOND EDITION

Edited by Douglas Cheney

**Research Press**   2612 North Mattis Avenue, Champaign, Illinois 61822

(800) 519-2707   www.researchpress.com

Published by Research Press on behalf of the Council for Children with Behavioral Disorders and the Division on Career Development and Transition

Copyright © 2010 by the Council for Children with Behavioral Disorders and the Division on Career Development and Transition

## About the Council for Children with Behavioral Disorders (CCBD)

 CCBD, a division of the Council for Exceptional Children, is an international and professional organization committed to promoting and facilitating the education and general welfare of children and youth with behavioral and emotional disorders. CCBD actively pursues quality educational services and program alternatives for persons with behavioral disorders, advocates for the needs of such children and youth, emphasizes research and professional growth as vehicles for better understanding of behavioral disorders, and provides professional support for persons who are involved with and serve children and youth with behavioral disorders.

## About the Division on Career Development and Transition (DCDT)

 DCDT is a division of the Council for Exceptional Children. Its mission is to promote national and international efforts to improve the quality of and access to career/vocational and transition services, increase the participation of education in career development and transition goals, and influence policies affecting career development and transition services for persons with disabilities.

Copies of this book may be ordered from Research Press at the address given on the title page.

Composition by Jeff Helgesen
Cover design by Linda Brown, Positive I.D. Graphic Design, Inc.
Printed by Seaway Printing

ISBN-13: 978-0-87822-626-9
Library of Congress Control Number 2010920532

# Contents

**SECTION IV**
TRANSITION APPROACHES FOR STUDENTS WITH EBD
IN JUVENILE JUSTICE

# Figures and Tables

## FIGURES

## TABLES

# *Foreword*

Forewords are tricky things to write. Who reads the foreword, and what should be, or could be, the goal of the foreword? In writing this foreword for the second edition of this book, I am trying to provide some metaphors the readers might find helpful to guide their reading. I want to propose three metaphors—hurricanes, universal flappers, and swamps—to frame your reading.

Working with youth who have behavioral problems is probably the most difficult work in special education. Addressing transition to adult life is possibly the most perplexing work of all. Attempts to find the most effective one or two approaches have so far been largely unsuccessful. This lack of success is due, I think, to the complexity of the issues surrounding youth with behavioral disabilities. There is much fallibility in our work.

Atul Gawande (2002) has proposed a provocative idea about the nature of fallibility. Citing Samuel Gorovitz and Alasdair MacIntyre, he reviews the three basic possible causes of error:

> Why would a meteorologist, say, fail to correctly predict where a hurricane was going to make landfall? They saw three possible reasons. One was ignorance: perhaps science affords only a limited understanding of how hurricanes behave. A second reason was ineptitude: the knowledge is available, but the weatherman fails to apply it correctly. Both of these are surmountable sources of error. . . . The third possible cause of error the philosophers posited, however, was an insurmountable kind, one they termed "necessary fallibility." There may be some kinds of knowledge that science and technology will never deliver. (p. 120)

Gawande goes on to argue:

> Although all hurricanes follow predictable laws of behavior, each one is continuously shaped by myriad uncontrollable, accidental factors in the environment. To say precisely how one specific hurricane will behave would require a complete understanding of the world and all its particulars—in other words, omniscience. It's not that it's impossible to predict anything; plenty of things are completely predictable. Gorovitz and MacIntyre give the example of a random ice cube in a fire. Ice cubes are so simple and so alike that you can predict with complete assurance that an ice cube will melt. But when it comes to inferring exactly what is going on in a particular person, are people more like ice cubes or like hurricanes? (pp. 120–121)

I believe youth with behavioral disabilities are far more like hurricanes than ice cubes. We are faced with fallibility in our work. How do we proceed if this is true, and what does this book add to the existing literature? Well, at least two things, I think.

First, several "big ideas" run through these chapters—ideas that are worthy of unpacking into practical strategies that others might try, or at least start with, in their attempt to improve the life chances of youth with disturbing behaviors. These ideas include the core idea of individualization, the importance of context, and the use of assessment to determine interventions and to evaluate their effectiveness.

Second are the ideas about persevering and working through difficult times that the authors of this book test through their ongoing work.

The keystone of special education is individualization. Probably starting with Itard and his work with Victor, the "wild boy of Aveyron," the notion of developing programs that are matched to the individual needs of a specific person has permeated special education. Over time, individualization has been minimized, even despaired, but it has withstood all attempts to push it aside. The authors of this book once again emphasize the importance of keeping this notion in the forefront of our thinking.

I am reminded of the story of the "universal flapper." Several years ago, I had a toilet that was always "running." The flapper was not engaging appropriately. In my house, my wife is the chief mechanic and fixer so she set out to repair the "running commode." She made several trips to the hardware store to buy parts and get advice. Despite her best efforts, the problem exceeded her skill level. Finally, we called in a plumber. He was a typical plumber—large, loud but friendly, with pants sagging low under the weight of his tool belt and exposing parts of his body best left to your imagination. He took one look at the tank and immediately diagnosed the problem. "You have a 'universal flapper' in there," he declared, "and they never work. You need to match the flapper to the specific brand of commode." Aha, I thought! Yet another case of individualization. One flapper never fits the needs of all toilets, nor, for that matter, does one approach work for all kids.

Context is important. That statement may sound trite, but it is true and is often overlooked. Race, social class, family, culture, and community are all-important aspects of individualizing. The more we can understand (and appreciate) context, the better we can plan with the individual client. "All things being equal" is never a good way to start a sentence. They *never* are. Ecological analysis, listening carefully to the youth with disability, respecting parental concerns, and being aware of the racial, cultural, linguistic, and social aspects of our society are all aspects of understanding context. Individualization can only take place in context.

Assessment is the starting and ending points—the bookends—of individualization. We carefully determine the beginning point of our treatment (in terms of the individual and the context of their lives), we measure our interventions along the path, we adjust when outcomes are not as desired, and we celebrate our success at the end. Assessment is the tool we use to do this.

Some of the problems faced by professionals and practitioners in the field lend themselves to technical solutions, but most problems require reflection in context. This point is best exemplified by Donald Schön's story of the swamp:

> In the varied topography of professional practice, there is a high, hard ground overlooking a swamp. On the high ground, manageable problems lend themselves to solution through the application of research-based theory and technique. In the swamp lowland, messy, confusing problems defy technical solution. The irony of this situation is that the problems of the

> high ground tend to be relatively unimportant to individuals
> or society at large, however great their technical interest may
> be, while in the swamp lie the problems of greatest human
> concern. (1987, p. 3)

Our work is in the swamp. Theory seldom holds true here because things are messy. This requires us to use reflection. Reflection can be defined as the process an individual or group uses to make decisions when a problem continues despite attempts to resolve it. Multiple possible alternative solutions need to be considered, and one chosen. Developing individualized education programs (IEPs) and transition plans, matching services to needs, and selecting a particular program are all examples of when reflection might be used. The skills required for reflection are listening with respect, open sharing of ideas, keeping a "beginner's mind" (Suzuki, 1970), and being open to all possibilities. Important in reflection are the dispositions of respect and responsibility—respect for the ideas of others and responsibility to commit to the ideal of teamwork, because reflection is best practiced in teams.

The chapters in this book are chock full of examples of these ideas. The readers, whether teachers, parents, or agency workers, will come away with many good ideas to add to their repertoire of ideas. Their knowledge will be increased.

As important as the knowledge and skills in this book is the development of dispositions ("the habits of the heart") that are required to do this work. Our work requires passion and the gumption to continue, even when things aren't going well. This field is full of passionate people—teachers and parents, caseworkers and vocational counselors, mental health workers and juvenile justice workers. Without passion there would be none of the work described in this book.

Passion, however, can sometimes create secondary problems associated with a lack of collaboration, especially when passion is combined with optimism ("The world will be what I will it to be," "My agenda will triumph," "I can overcome any obstacle and win," "I am sure I am right") as opposed to hope ("I believe that whatever is best should happen"). Hope is the humble confidence that good will prevail. Hope defers to the basic principles of community, truth, honesty, democracy, deliberation, and justice. Hope is trust in the process and a commitment to support the process (Michaud, 1999).

As we wander through the swamp in the middle of a hurricane, I wish for you—and even more, I wish for myself—less optimism and more hope.

Eugene Edgar
College of Education
University of Washington, Seattle

## REFERENCES

Gawande, A. (2002). Final cut. In S. J. Gould (Ed.), *The best American essays: 2002* (pp. 111–123). New York: Houghton Mifflin.

Michaud, T. (1999). An ethic for the public scholar. In D. W. Brown (Ed.), *Higher education exchange, 1999* (pp. 16–23). New York: The Kettering Foundation.

Schön, D. (1987). Preparing professionals for the demands of practice. In D. Schön (Ed.), *Educating the reflective practitioner: Toward a new design for teaching and learning in the professions* (pp. 3–31). San Francisco: Jossey-Bass.

Suzuki, S. (1970). *Zen mind, beginner's mind.* New York: Weatherhill.

## CHAPTER 1

# An Overview of Transition Issues, Approaches, and Recommendations for Youth with Emotional or Behavioral Disorders

**Douglas Cheney**

This book was written for teachers who have looked into the angry eyes of an adolescent who, having had enough of the classroom lesson at hand, stormed out of the classroom, leaving a few choice words in his or her wake. It is written for teachers and transition specialists who have prepared and delivered countless lessons on social skills, vocational education, or community living skills that were received by their students with little interaction, a "whatever" attitude, and unknown outcomes. It is also for those interagency teams of teachers, vocational specialists, mental health specialists, and other community agency representatives who have developed educational, vocational, or residential placements for adolescents, only to see their efforts dissolve into lost opportunities. It is also intended for parents who have seen their sons and daughters make many positive improvements and then backslide due to unforeseen incidents that occur during a difficult day at school or work or during a reckless weekend when they were picked up by police or involved in a senseless tragedy. This book is intended to offer new hope and successful strategies and supports to students, providers, and parents who face these challenges and barriers.

This first edition of this book was conceptualized at the April 2001 conference of the Council for Exceptional Children (CEC) during discussions among the leadership of the Division on Career Development and Transition (DCDT) and the Council for Children with Behavioral Disorders (CCBD). Several of us discussed the need for a book that focused on transition issues and recommendations for youth with emotional or behavioral disabilities (EBD). The first edition was written and subsequently published by the two divisions through the Council for Exceptional Children. The book was received well by the professional community, and the divisions agreed at the 2008 CEC conference to support the revision and publication of a second edition. For this second edition, the authors have either revised their chapters, or, in a few cases, new authors have written chapters. The leadership of DCDT and CCBD believe that their members have much to gain by reading the work of the authors in this book. By presenting these transition approaches, we hope that a broader audience of practitioners and parents will be able to improve the educational, vocational, and community outcomes of youth with emotional or behavioral disabilities.

## TRANSITION OUTCOMES OF YOUTH WITH EMOTIONAL OR BEHAVIORAL DISABILITIES

### The National Longitudinal Transition Studies

As a result of the national focus on transition in the 1980s (Edgar, 1987, 1988; Hasazi, Gordon, & Roe, 1985; Will, 1984), the U.S. Office of Special Education Programs funded the National Longitudinal Transition Study (NLTS). SRI International conducted this 5-year study of a national sample of 8,000 youth ranging in ages from 13 through 21 who had been special education students in 1985 and 1986. Data on these students were collected from phone interviews with their parents, from a survey of educators in their schools, and from the students' school records. Within the larger sample, contacts with 1,321 students with EBD were attempted; 584 interviews were completed and data on an additional 89 students were obtained through the surveys and record reviews. Numerous analyses have been conducted on the NLTS data, and the major findings have been in areas of employment, education, social experiences, and affiliation with community-based agencies.

For students with EBD, 2 years after leaving school, 59% of them were employed, with the figure dropping to 52% 3 to 5 years after students left school. Their median hourly wage 3 to 5 years after high school was $3.35 (D'Amico & Blackorby, 1992). By comparison, 41% of students with disabilities, and 31% of young adults without disabilities, were unemployed 3 to 5 years after high school.

During high school, only 58% of students with EBD were enrolled in some form of vocational education, compared with 65% of all students with disabilities (D'Amico & Blackorby, 1992). Furthermore, 59% of the students with EBD dropped out of school, compared to 37% of all students with disabilities (Wagner, Blackorby, Cameto, & Newman, 1993). Postsecondary enrollment was also difficult for young adults with EBD. Only 17% of participants with EBD enrolled in postsecondary education programs 2 years after leaving high school. In the 3 to 5 years after participants left high school, this index rose to 26% and was comparable to the number of students with learning disabilities entering postsecondary programs. In comparison, 53% of students in the general population were enrolled in postsecondary education 2 years after high school, rising to 69% 3 years after high school.

Most students with EBD had a difficult time achieving independent living status in the first 5 years after high school. During that period, 40% of them were living independently, compared to 37% of all participants with disabilities (Newman, 1992). Additionally, 26% of youth with EBD became parents, almost 50% were arrested while in high school (Wagner & Shaver, 1989), and 58% were arrested within the 3- to 5-year period after leaving high school (Wagner, 1991). Finally, only 6% of participants with EBD received services from vocational rehabilitation compared to 13% with disabilities (Marder, Wechsler, & Valdes, 1993).

To assess the status of youth with disabilities in the early 21st century, the U.S. Office of Special Education Programs funded the second National Longitudinal Transition Study (NLTS-2). NLTS-2 compared the post–high school progress of youth with disabilities from the NLTS cohort in 1987 with a second cohort of students in 2003. Once again, data were collected on high-school completion, employment, postsecondary school involvement, living arrangements, and social engagement. Youth with EBD in the second cohort showed a substantial improvement in high-school completion (from 39% to 55%, a 16%

increase) but few other gains. Postsecondary enrollment increased to 22%, and most of this enrollment was in 2-year colleges, which increased nearly 10%. There was no better improvement in employment when compared to other disability categories, while prosocial, organized community group activities showed a slight increase to 18% (Wagner, Cameto, & Newman, 2003; Wagner, Newman, Cameto, & Levine, 2005).

Another change for the second cohort was an increased likelihood to receive negative consequences in the school and community (from 56% of the first cohort to 89% of the second), which included disciplinary actions at school, being fired from a job, or being arrested. Overall, although some functional areas improved in NLTS-2 for students with EBD, there were still major concerns about their ultimate ability to succeed in education, employment, and adult adjustment.

The reader is directed to other excellent reviews regarding NLTS-2 for a more fully elaborated discussion of these issues (see Wagner & Davis, 2006; Wagner, Kutash, Duchnowski, & Epstein, 2005), as well as to the NLTS-2 website (www.nlts2.org).

## Federal Legislative Priorities Since 1990: The Individuals with Disabilities Act (IDEA)

The findings regarding the poor secondary outcomes of youth with EBD had a significant impact on language in the 1990 IDEA. For the first time since the passage of this special education law in 1975, priority was assigned to emotional disturbance and transition issues. In IDEA 1990, Congress added a discretionary program focusing on research and demonstration projects in the area of emotional disturbance and increased the funding to the U.S. Office of Special Education and Rehabilitative Services to fund these projects throughout the 1990s. IDEA 1990 also mandated a planning process involving individuals with disabilities; parents; professionals; and representatives of state and local educational agencies, private schools, institutions of higher education, and national organizations with interest or experience in the program (Osher & Hanley, 1996). The planning process led to the development of the National Agenda to Improve Results for Children and Youth with Serious Emotional Disturbance (U.S. Department of Education, 1994). The national agenda had seven strategic targets that cut across three themes of prevention, cultural sensitivity and respect, and empowerment for providers and parents alike. These targets and themes have been instrumental in shaping research and demonstration efforts nationally since their inception.

IDEA 1990 provided clear definitions for our work in transition services for youth beginning at age 16. The 1990 Individuals with Disabilities Education Act defined transition services as

> a coordinated set of activities for a student, designed within an outcome-oriented process that promotes movement from school to post-school activities, including post-secondary education, vocational training, integrated employment (including supported employment), continuing and adult education, adult services, independent living, or community participation. The coordinated set of activities must be based on the individual student's needs, taking into account the student's preferences and interests, and must include instruction, community experiences, the development of employment and other post-school adult living objectives, and, if appropriate, acquisition of daily living skills and functional vocational evaluation. (20 U.S.C. Section 1401(a)(20) Individuals with Disabilities Education Act of 1990 (October 10, 1990), Public Law 101–476)

Some modifications have been made during the past two reauthorizations, but the definition of transition services is similar in the 2004 reauthorization of IDEA:

> Transition services means a coordinated set of activities for a child with a disability that—
>
> (1) Is designed to be within a results-oriented process, that is focused on improving the academic and functional achievement of the child with a disability to facilitate the child's movement from school to post-school activities, including post-secondary education, vocational education, integrated employment (including supported employment), continuing and adult education, adult services, independent living, or community participation;
>
> (2) Is based on the individual child's needs, taking into account the child's strengths, preferences, and interests; and includes—
>
> (i) Instruction;

(ii) Related services;

(iii) Community experiences;

(iv) The development of employment and other post-school adult living objectives; and

(v) If appropriate, acquisition of daily living skills and provision of a functional vocational evaluation. (§300.43)

Although the 1997 amendments to IDEA required that the individualized education program (IEP) include a statement of transition services (updated annually) for all students beginning at age 14, the age was set at 16 in the 2004 amendments to IDEA. Transition services must now delineate specific student needs under the applicable components of the IEP to explain and focus the courses of study (academic or vocational classes). Transition requirements under IDEIA 2004 include four main points: (1) an assessment that identifies one or more postsecondary goals, (2) listing of postsecondary goals in the areas of education and training, employment, and, when appropriate, independent living, (3) annual goals to assist students in meeting their postsecondary goals, and (4) specification of transition services including instructional activities and community experiences designed to help the student in his or her transition from school to anticipated postschool environments and to help achieve identified postsecondary goals (see Chapter 7 of this book).

IDEA 1997 required the transition plan to include, if appropriate, a statement of interagency responsibilities or needed linkages with community agencies. The requirements state that the student with a disability must be invited to participate in this planning process so that his or her interests in school, work, and community will be taken into consideration in developing the transition plan (U.S. Department of Education, 1999). This requirement was continued in the 2004 reauthorization. Additional mandates have included an emphasis on prevention research in the area of EBD, functional behavioral assessments for the most severe and challenging of student behavior, increased reporting by states on postsecondary outcomes of students, and reporting of graduation rates for students with disabilities.

The present requirements for transition services as mandated in IDEIA 2004 make it imperative that special educators and transition service providers have the knowledge and skills to address these legislative requirements. Fortunately, an extensive knowledge base has emerged over the past 10 years from research and demonstration projects in EBD. Because the law and research findings occurred concurrently, it became apparent that a book focusing on successful practices, models, programs, and directions for students with EBD and practitioners working with them was needed. The contents of this book have resulted from work of the authors over the past decade. These approaches have achieved some very positive results and hold promise for improving educational and transition services for youth with EBD.

## ORGANIZATION AND CONTENT OF THE BOOK

The book is organized in four major sections. Although some content from each section may overlap, the sections serve as organizers for the book. Gene Edgar's comments in the foreword to this book set the stage for these chapters by emphasizing the importance of individualization and context—and of acknowledging our own fallibility. Dr. Edgar uses metaphors to present these important concepts. Novices to the concept of transition for students with EBD will benefit by reading Dr. Edgar's seminal work on this topic (Edgar 1987, 1988).

The first section presents information regarding the overall context of transition for youth with EBD. From an ecological perspective, youth interact with their friends, live with their families or in another residential arrangement, participate in schools and agencies, and live in communities that are defined by a variety of cultural norms. In this first section, the authors present information on many of these areas, particularly the role that families, culture, providers, and friends play in the lives of these youth. The authors also present recommendations on how self-determination might be used in planning effective programs for youth with EBD in transition.

In the second section, authors address approaches for assessing the vocational, personal, and academic strengths of youth in transition and provide precise directions and examples for developing IEPs and transition plans. This section concludes with examples of how positive behavior supports can be implemented in high schools and coordinated at the school, classroom, and individual levels to improve outcomes for all youth in the school, including those with EBD.

The third section is devoted to comprehensive programs that have had success working with youth with EBD. The programs presented are from Ohio, New Hampshire, and Florida, and they share many characteristics related to integrating the youth's interests into effective service supports in the areas of academics, vocational training, job placement, and community living.

In the fourth section, our focus switches from community-based programs to programs in the juvenile justice system. Given the high rates that youth with EBD experience with arrests, and given that few successful programs have been reported on reintegrating youth with EBD into their communities, two chapters are presented in this section

In the final chapter of this book, Michael Bullis provides concluding thoughts on the school-to-community transition of students with EBD.

## Overview of Section I

In Chapter 2, Festus Obiakor and Lynn Wilder discuss issues and practices related to culturally and linguistically diverse (CLD) learners with EBD. The authors note that when CLD learners with EBD choose to strive for adult outcomes that involve interaction with and acceptance by the dominant culture, they are faced with the challenge of learning to work within the mores of the dominant culture (Sue & Sue, 2002). They must be willing to practice and use expected social skills, explore realistic job interests and opportunities, and refine their skills so employers or other adults in the community will appreciate them. Obiakor and Wilder suggest that this is a challenge for all learners with EBD, as well as for their teachers and employers.

Long-standing issues with racism, discrimination, bias, assessment, and community integration are barriers for CLD youth with EBD in transitioning successfully from school to community. Transition activities for CLD learners is perhaps more work intensive because learners and providers need to focus on developing supportive environments that empower learners, parents, and guardians in the transition process. Furthermore, transition services must be individualized according to the student's culture and disability (Wilder, 2001; Wilder et al., 2007), and learners must consider all potential career paths and have ample opportunities to explore various jobs in the transition process. The authors conclude their chapter by discussing the four essential pillars of a multicultural transition model: (1) the learner's career interests; (2) the learner's cognitive, academic, vocational, and social-emotional aptitude; (3) the learner's disability; and (4) the learner's culture.

Studies related to CLD youth and to adolescents with EBD in transition are scarce. Therefore, the effectiveness of the strategies and model discussed in the second chapter are extrapolated to CLD youth with EBD in transition based on findings of studies of CLD youth, youth with disabilities, and youth with EBD. Given this scarcity of research, the authors note that there will be variation from one CLD group to another and from one student to the next. Finally, the authors state that there may be variation in the behavior and aptitude for social competence of different students within the EBD group.

In Chapter 3, Erik Carter provides a definition of self-determination, links it to the transition process, and then discusses how self-determination approaches can be used with youth with EBD. The promotion of skills and opportunities that enhance self-determination are now often included as key components of model secondary and transition programs for youth with, or at risk for, EBD. The author provides a review of research to explain what is known about the self-determination skills and capacities of youth with EBD, the extent to which schools provide opportunities for youth to learn and practice these skills, and the potential influence on postschool outcomes. A section on promising approaches and avenues for equipping youth with EBD with the skills and experiences to enhance their self-determination should be very well received by teachers wishing to increase their emphasis on self-determination. Carter's use of a case study for applying these approaches makes this portion of the chapter useful and practical.

Finally, Chapter 3 offers methods for including students in their IEP development, for offering more authentic learning opportunities in the school and community, and for including parents and caregivers in more culturally responsive ways. By providing the structures and strategies for improving instructional, curricular, and other learning opportunities to promote student self-determination, this chapter addresses critical issues and approaches to promote the lifelong skills to shape the trajectories and outcomes of youth throughout high school and into adulthood.

In Chapter 4, Amy Pleet and Donna Wandry examine the important area of building partnerships with families during the transition process. This period is difficult and stressful for any family, but stressors can become extreme for families of youth with EBD. The authors note that current literature reveals that outreach to families, family therapy, ongoing communication with families, and including parents in IEP planning are essential components of transition programs for this population, but parents often have less involvement with transition planning than they would like.

The authors of Chapter 4 review content related to the inclusion of parents and families in the IEP process, present strategies that transition personnel can implement to build partnerships with parents of students with emotional or behavioral disorders, examine the changing context of family participation in educational programs, and discuss five roles for family members in the transition process. Because the authors believe that professionals' effectiveness in forming parent partnerships will increase with information, specific strategies, and an awareness of parent perspectives on these issues, they address the topic of parent views and how the parents perceived they were or were not supported during transition.

In Chapter 5, Francie Murry and Michael Todd Allen provide four specific strategies to create more positive outcomes for youth with EBD. This chapter is included in the context of service delivery because it presents the firsthand experiences of many of youth, parents, and service providers in educational and vocational settings. The four strategies discussed are ways to (1) promote students' engagement with school, (2) promote self-advocacy and self-regulation skills, (3) collaborate between school personnel and community service providers, and (4) establish mentorship programs for students' educational and transitional processes. The author describes these strategies and then gives examples of how youth and parents benefited from the strategies in transition programs. Differing facets of services and practices are provided and help to explain how effective transition programs for youth with EBD can improve transition outcomes.

## Overview of Section II

In Chapter 6, Larry Kortering, Patricia Braziel , and Patricia Sitlington review current approaches to vocational assessment and planning for youth with EBD. Their chapter is testimony to the weight that Edgar

(1987, 1988), Hasazi et al. (1985), and Will (1984) put on achieving employment as a priority for young adults. Kortering, Sitlington, and Braziel, however, believe the cart is employment—and the horse is an effective assessment and understanding of a youth's interests and skills in employment. As they note early in the chapter, school completion should be directly linked to preparation for suitable employment. Youth wonder about the relevance of schooling. In particular, youth who are disadvantaged, disenfranchised, or alienated from mainstream programs and college preparation question the relevance of English, math, or science in their employment pursuits. Kortering and his coauthors therefore provide an array of vocational assessments that are accessible to teachers, are efficient in their use, received adequate reviews, and yield important results to students, educators, and parents when planning vocational programs and placements for youth with EBD. The authors have used or observed these tools in practice and present two case studies that demonstrate effective assessment procedures with high-school-aged students.

James Shriner, Anthony Plotner, and Chad Rose have gone beyond the call of duty in preparing a very detailed and informative chapter on developing IEPs for youth with EBD. The authors of Chapter 7 discuss the current requirements and major concepts in law (IDEIA, 2004) for IEPs and then give clear examples of how teachers can meet these requirements when they write their IEPs for students who are 16 years of age or older. Specifically, they give us clear examples of how to integrate transition assessment into a student's present level of academic achievement and functional performance; how to write postsecondary goals that are linked to education, employment, and independent living; how to use functional behavioral assessment to write behavioral intervention plans (BIP); how the BIP should include social-emotional goal statements; how the student's course of study should lead directly to transition planning; and how the essential ingredient of cross-agency linkages is needed to fully implement the IEP. Throughout the chapter, the authors use an example of a specific IEP to explain how a model IEP can be developed and implemented in the high school and community.

In Chapter 8, Cinda Johnson and Hank Bohanon review schoolwide positive behavioral supports (PBS) at the secondary school level and provide examples of how high schools are implementing schoolwide PBS to improve school climate and student behavior. There is no doubt that

PBS has had a major impact on schools and that we will continue to see more high schools using this approach. This chapter provides information on how transition issues and PBS can be integrated to improve post-secondary outcomes of students with EBD. The high-school example describes how PBS was implemented and included the whole school staff in generating a plan to teach prosocial expectations to all students, acknowledging and reinforcing student use of prosocial behavior. The evaluation of the program found decreases in discipline referrals and improvements on the schoolwide evaluation tool. At the classroom level, an example demonstrates how tardies were decreased and how goal setting and self-determination were addressed. The authors explain how individual students have worked with IEP teams in schools that practice PBS to integrate content from their personal future plans into their IEP and transition plans. The authors also offer an example of how an integrated plan was developed to address school, community, and personal goals of one student. The authors conclude with timely recommendations for integrating PBS into high-school settings to improve the outcomes not only for students with EBD but for all students in the school.

## Overview of Section III

Thomas Valore, Claudia Lann Valore, Dennis Koenig, James Cirigliano, Patricia Cirigliano, and Steven Cirigliano present in Chapter 9 an innovative program for adolescents with EBD that has been in use since 1999 at the Positive Education Program (PEP) at the Midtown Center for Youth in Transition, in Cleveland, Ohio. PEP has been identified as a model treatment program for children and youth with EBD for many years, and this discussion of the Midtown program demonstrates PEP's commitment to enhancing their work whenever possible to meet the needs of families and youth. The Midtown Center is based on the principles of re-education developed by Hobbs (1982), and youth programs are individually designed to focus on three primary domains: education, employment, and empowerment. Midtown translates each domain into pathways that accommodate individual needs in learning and growing. In its first 7 years, Midtown served 321 youth from 24 school districts in an off-campus, downtown setting. The authors discuss how youth have addressed the three domains of education, employment, and empowerment, and then describe how one student was able to matriculate through Midtown and attain success in each of these domains. The student's parents also give a description of how Midtown was able to meet the broader needs of the family in the community, giving testimony to the necessity of a broad ecological model for transitioning youth from school to community.

In Chapter 10, JoAnne Malloy, Jonathan Drake, Kathleen Abate, and Gail Cormier describe Project RENEW, a community-based, alternative education and employment program in New Hampshire that focuses on high-school completion and positive transition to adulthood for youth with EBD. The transition process was designed by staff and an interagency team to incorporate best practice models and strategies from a variety of disciplines, including child welfare (wraparound), school-to-work (innovative crediting using work-based learning strategies), and developmental disabilities (personal futures planning), and created a comprehensive model that was built around five principles, four goals, and seven strategies. Their chapter highlights how these principles, goals, and strategies have been used to produce positive results for youth and young adults participating in the program. The authors give examples of how the RENEW intervention process has been applied with participants over the past 10 years, and how the positive outcomes have been achieved with youth in several cohorts in education, employment, and community living.

In Chapter 11, Hewitt Clark, Sarah Taylor, and Nicole Deschênes discuss their work with the transition to independence process (TIP) that has been evolving over the past 10 years. TIP empowers youth through personal choice making and social responsibility, and ensures that a safety net of support is available when youth face challenges and failures. The authors describe how one youth was able to turn his life around from arrests and school failure to positive relationships, employment, and educational success. The student benefited from many TIP principles and guidelines for program development, including strength-based assessments and plans, along with strong relationships with all constituents. Person-centered planning and individualized programs based on youth interests and respecting the youth's cultural background are framed by the authors as critical. Constant review of outcomes helps youth and their support team evaluate progress and maximize use of natural supports—all hallmarks of the TIP process. The chapter provides examples from the personal life stories of youth to describe how these practices change the outcomes for youth with EBD as they enter adulthood.

## Overview of Section IV

As the NLTS and state studies have demonstrated, youth with EBD are in jeopardy for engaging in juvenile offenses and being arrested for these offenses. Because of this risk factor, this book contains two chapters on this topic. The first—Chapter 12, by Deanne Unruh, Miriam Waintrup, and Tim Canter—presents the development and implementation of Project STAY OUT. In their introduction to the chapter, the authors note that an unsuccessful transition from the juvenile justice facility to the community has personal and societal costs. Successful transitions to the community reduce recidivism; support positive, long-term outcomes for formerly incarcerated people; and reduce additional costs to taxpayers, the community, and future victims. Project STAY OUT is a continuation of Project SUPPORT (Service Utilization Promoting Positive Outcomes in Rehabilitation and Transition for Incarcerated Adolescents with Disabilities), which began in 1999 as a statewide service effort managed by the Oregon Department of Education, Oregon Youth Authority, Oregon Office of Vocational Rehabilitation Services, and University of Oregon. The project has two broad goals: (1) to develop a systemwide service delivery model resulting in lower rates of recidivism and more positive rates of employment and education outcomes for incarcerated youth with EBD, and (2) to embed the program model within the existing community and state agencies to maintain sustained support for this targeted population. The chapter describes how transition specialists in Oregon have been able to coordinate services with vocational rehabilitation, mental health, corrections, and educational agencies to transition youth and young adults from corrections facilities into communities.

In Chapter 13, Heather Griller-Clark and Sarup Mathur continue the focus on transition for youth in the juvenile justice system. In this chapter, the authors clarify the process of transition for youth within the juvenile justice system and provide a definition of transition. Then, they discuss some of the challenges in providing transition services relating to school, work, and the community to youth in the juvenile justice system. They provide a review of 18 promising practices to improve transition services for youth with EBD in the juvenile justice system, which can be grouped into the broad categories of programming, institutional policy, coordination and collaboration, and evaluation. Finally, the authors present a comprehensive, six-component corrections–community transition system for youth with EBD in the juvenile justice system. The chapter provides a clear framework, with components and practical ideas for those in states and communities who are attempting to improve their transition services for incarcerated youth with disabilities.

We conclude this book with a chapter from Michael Bullis. Dr. Bullis, currently dean of education at the University of Oregon, dedicated his research career to improving transition services for youth with EBD. Beginning as a rehabilitation counselor and continuing as a professor at the university, Dr. Bullis has conducted research that has increased our knowledge base regarding assessment, effective strategies, and policy over the past three decades. He reviews his own history and interest in transition issues for these students and then provides his perspective on several tough questions regarding (1) the complicated issue of who should be served under the label of EBD due to differing procedures in psychiatry/psychology and education for identifying and labeling these youth for services, (2) where services should be provided and how to coordinate these services, and (3) how we determine the duration, intensity, and components of our services. As we have come to expect from Dr. Bullis, his questions are based on findings from recent research, and his major goal is to improve our understanding of components of transition for adolescents with EBD. His work has shaped and solidified the theoretical foundations of transition services and enhanced community and school practices for youth with EBD and their service providers.

## SUMMARY

The reader of this book should find many similar suggestions and cross-cutting themes for transitioning youth with EBD from school to community. Foremost is the inclusion of youth in the development of their program goals and activities. Findings from the work of this book's authors, as well as many others, confirms the importance of self-determined transition goals and activities in normative settings in the community as critical features for success. We have evolved from a culture that once suggested that best placement for young adults with EBD was in sheltered workshops with adults who had chronic mental health problems. Our best practices now suggest that early involvement in school-based vocational programs that are linked with competitive employment in the community leads to greater success and learning by youth with EBD. Further, the more these placements take into consideration the interests and skills of the individual student, the more likely he or she is to succeed in employment.

Across the educational programs discussed in this book, it is clear that flexible educational programs, which may be located on or off campus, are needed to provide youth with alternative modes of earning school credits. Requiring youth with EBD to take existing classes in a rigid high-school curriculum is a formula for disaster. It is highly recommended that youth be able to choose from an array of classes that are school, community, or work based. The IEP should include statements about classes that are to be taken and how they meet the educational and curriculum needs of the student.

For students who have been adjudicated in the juvenile justice system, a concentrated effort must be made to engage school, vocational rehabilitation, mental health, and other agencies providing social services for these youth when the youth reenter the community. These youth will need a highly involved transition specialist to work with them, as found in the project in Oregon. Furthermore, they will need more than just a placement with a family or living facility in the community. These youth will need extensive and ongoing supervision and support in their work and education in the community. Social support as well as educational or vocational support will be necessary to fulfill the employment and life goals of these youth.

Finally, a multicultural and familial perspective is required to improve upon our outcomes with youth. We must truly be able to reach these youth as individuals and use respectful methods that are culturally responsive. Too often, the institutional demands of school and work override the individual needs of ethnically diverse learners. A sound transition plan will include culturally competent practices and consider the role that family members might take in the plan. Family networks and support have been found to be important in the cases presented throughout this book.

By following these suggestions, it should be possible for educators and social service providers to improve transition services for youth with EBD. Although barriers and challenges will continue to surface for these youth, their service providers, and their families, the lessons learned to date are that unconditional care and a zero-reject model is the bottom line for service provision. This bottom line always emphasizes what we have known for years—caring, individualized services provided by authoritative adults can lead to successes for youth with EBD in employment, education, and community living. With this suggestion, I hope you enjoy this book and find it useful in your life and your work.

## REFERENCES

D'Amico, R., & Blackorby, J. (1992). Trend in employment among out-of-school youth with disabilities. In M. Wagner, R. D'Amico, L. Marder, L. Newman, & J. Blackorby. (Eds.), *What happens next? Trends in postschool outcomes of youths with disabilities* (pp. 4-1-4-47). Menlo Park, CA: SRI International.

Edgar, E. (1987). Secondary programs in special education. Are many of them justifiable? *Exceptional Children, 53,* 555–561.

Edgar, E. (1988). Employment as an outcome for mildly handicapped students. *Focus on Exceptional Children, 21,* 1–8.

Hasazi, S. B., Gordon, L. R., & Roe, C. A. (1985). Factors associated with the employment status of handicapped youth exiting high school from 1979 to 1983. *Exceptional Children, 51,* 445–469.

Hobbs, N. (1982). *The troubled and troubling child: Re-education in mental health, education, and human services programs for children and youth.* San Francisco: Jossey-Bass.

Individuals with Disabilities Education Act of 1990, Pub. L. No. 101–476 (1990).

Individuals with Disabilities Education Act of 1997, Pub. L. No. 105–17 (1997).

Individuals with Disabilities Education Improvement Act of 2004, Pub. L. No. 108–446 (2004).

Marder, C., Wechsler, M., & Valdes, K. (1993). *Services for youth with disabilities after secondary school.* Menlo Park, CA: SRI International.

Newman, L. (1992). A place to call home: Residential arrangements of out-of-school youth with disabilities. In M. Wagner, R. D'Amico, C. Marder, L. Newman, & J. Blackorby (Eds.), *What happens next? Trends in postschool outcomes of youth with disabilities* (pp. 5–1–5–35). Menlo Park, CA: SRI International.

Osher, D., & Hanley, T. (1996). Implications of the National Agenda to Improve Results for Children and Youth with or at Risk of Serious Emotional Disturbance. In R. J. Illback and C. M. Nelson (Eds.), *Emerging school-based approaches for children with emotional and behavioral problems: Research and practice in service integration* (pp. 7–36). New York: The Haworth Press.

Sue, D. W., & Sue, D. (2002). *Counseling the culturally different: Theory and practice* (4th ed.). New York: Wiley.

U. S. Department of Education. (1994). *The national agenda for achieving better results for children with serious emotional disturbance.* Washington, DC: Author. (ERIC Document Reproduction Service No. ED376690.)

U. S. Department of Education. (1999). *Twenty-first annual report to Congress on the implementation of the Individuals with Disabilities Education Act.* Washington, DC: Author.

Wagner, M. (1991). *The benefits associated with secondary vocational education for young people with disabilities.* Menlo Park, CA: SRI International.

Wagner, M., Blackorby, J., Cameto, R., & Newman, L. (1993). *What makes a difference? Influences on postschool outcomes of youth with disabilities. The third comprehensive report from the National Longitudinal Transition Study of Special Education Students.* Menlo Park, CA: SRI International.

Wagner, M., Cameto, R., & Newman, L. (2003). *Youth with disabilities: A changing population. A report of findings from the National Longitudinal Transition Study (NLTS) and the National Longitudinal Transition Study-2 (NLTS-2).* Menlo Park, CA: SRI International.

Wagner, M., & Davis, M. (2006). How are we preparing students with emotional disturbances for the transition to young adulthood? Findings from the National Longitudinal Transition Study-2. *Journal of Emotional and Behavioral Disorders, 14*(2) 86–98.

Wagner, M., Kutash, K., Duchnowski, A., & Epstein, M. (2005). The Special Education Elementary Longitudinal Study and the National Longitudinal Transition Study: Study designs and implications for children and youth with emotional disturbance. *Journal of Emotional and Behavioral Disorders, 13,* 25–41.

Wagner, M., Newman, L., Cameto, R., & Levine, P. (2005). *Changes over time in the early postschool outcomes of youth with disabilities. A report of findings from the National Longitudinal Transition Study (NLTS) and the National Longitudinal Transition Study-2 (NLTS-2)*. Menlo Park, CA: SRI International.

Wagner, M., & Shaver, D. (1989). *Educational programs and achievements of secondary special education students: Findings from the National Longitudinal Transition Study*. Menlo Park, CA: SRI International.

Wilder, L. K. (2001). Success in college for students with disabilities. *Theories and Practices in Supervision and Curriculum, 12*, 31–34.

Wilder, L. K., Shepherd, T. L., Murry, F., Rogers, E., Heaton, E., & Sonntag, A. W. (2007). Teacher ratings of social skills across ethnic groups for learners with mild disabilities: Implications for teacher education. *Curriculum and Teaching, 22*(1), 47–66.

Will, M. (1984). *OSERS program for the transition of youth with disabilities: Bridges from school to working life*. Washington, DC: Office of Special Education Rehabilitative Services.

# The Cultural, Familial, and Personal Context of Transition Services for Students with EBD

## CHAPTER 2

# Transitioning Culturally and Linguistically Diverse Learners with Emotional or Behavioral Disorders

**Festus E. Obiakor and Lynn K. Wilder**

Culturally and linguistically diverse (CLD) learners continue to endure multidimensional problems in general and special education. For instance, they experience misidentification, misassessment, miscategorization, misplacement, and misinstruction because they look, learn, talk, and behave differently (Cartledge, 2004; Obiakor, 1999, 2001b, 2004, 2007; Obiakor, Algozzine et al., 2002; Obiakor, Grant, & Dooley, 2002). Coupled with these problems, they are faced with transitional challenges from grade to grade, school to school, school to work, work to school, school to jail, jail to school, work to jail, and jail to work (Bakken & Aloia, 1999; Bakken & Obiakor, 2008; Wilder, Ashbaker, Obiakor, & Rotz, 2006). As a result, transitioning CLD learners with emotional or behavioral disorders (EBD) into adult life in the majority culture requires strategically planned processes. Understandably, some of these learners have failed at critical junctures, by dropping out of school or being confined in the juvenile or adult justice systems. However, many of them have been quite successful at adjusting to universally accepted appropriate behaviors within the dominant culture. As Bakken and Obiakor (2008) noted, learners who have been successful at postsecondary school life have usually expended great effort in the transition process. Life following secondary school might include independent living/self-survival, college or vocational/technical school graduation, meaningful employment, financial solvency, home ownership, family responsibilities, civically responsible behavior, civic and religious involvement, and satisfying social relationships (Bakken & Obiakor, 2008; D'Amico & Maxwell, 1995).

For many CLD learners, the pressure to survive in mainstream dominant society is enormous. Learners who are closely tied to their home cultures might have difficulty accepting the Eurocentric tenets of a majority and dominant culture (Obiakor 2001b, 2004, 2007; Wilder, Jackson, & Smith, 2001). Therein lies one of the many problems confronting transition experts and professionals. It is important that professionals help learners clarify their own preferences and assist them in identifying probable outcomes of their decisions when choosing postsecondary goals. Once learners choose goals, transition professionals should offer the proper mentoring, career counseling and job exploration, vocational and academic education, and social skills training to help them reach their goals (Wilder, 2001). Given the realities of prejudice or racism sometimes expressed in schools toward CLD learners and the antisocial behavior displayed by most students who are classified as EBD, achieving learners' goals may be difficult. Perhaps the most important teaching and learning that can occur between transition professionals and these learners is to view transition realistically. Adult support, encouragement, and teaching must occur at every stage of the transition process so that acquired skills may not be lost and the potential of learners may be maximized.

When CLD learners with EBD choose to adapt and accept the dominant culture, they are faced with the challenge of learning to work within the mores of that culture. In addition, they are forced to demonstrate consistently the expected social skills, explore realistic job interests and opportunities, and refine their talents so that their skills will be appreciated and utilized by employers. Although all learners with EBD must accomplish most of these adaptations, transition is perhaps more work-intensive for CLD learners because they also must "buy into" and then learn the nuances of the dominant culture (Bakken & Aloia, 1999). Some social skill competence within the dominant culture is vital to the overall success of learners with EBD. Realistically, some social skills will remain problematic for them—after all, difficulty with social skills is part of the EBD category. General and special education teachers and service providers might assume that CLD learners with EBD know and accept the social tenets of the dominant culture, but that is a precarious and probably erroneous assumption. Indeed, this assumption reveals the complexity of transitioning these learners into a world of work. For children and youth to advance from one stage of their lives to a new stage, they must be prepared for proper independent living in a heterogeneous, competitive society like the United States (Bakken & Aloia, 1999; Bakken & Obiakor, 2008; Wilder, Jackson, & Smith, 2001; Wilder, Ashbaker, Obiakor, & Rotz, 2006; Wilder et al., 2007).Yet this society or this new stage must be ready to provide avenues of survival for these learners, especially when they come from different cultural, racial, and socioeconomic backgrounds. In this chapter, we focus on how to transition CLD learners with EBD into the world of work.

## CRITICAL ISSUES IN THE TRANSITION PROCESS

Many critical issues revolve around the transition process for CLD learners with EBD. These issues include (1) the EBD classification of learners, (2) the disproportionate placement of CLD youth in the EBD category, (3) bias in the transition process, and (4) discrepant cultures of transition professionals and youth with EBD.

### EBD Classification of Learners

Several issues affect the transition outcomes of CLD learners with EBD. One issue concerns how emotional or behavioral disorders are defined, because this definition determines who has access to special education transition services. According to the federal definition as outlined by the Individuals with Disabilities Education Act (IDEA) of 1990, learners with conduct disorders are excluded from services, and the label given to those students who qualify is "seriously emotionally disturbed" (SED). A coalition of more than 30 professional groups that work with individuals with EBD proposed a definition that is broader than the federal definition. The definition by the coalition includes "children or youth with schizophrenic disorders, affective disorders, anxiety disorders, or other sustained disturbances of conduct or adjustment" (Forness & Knitzer, 1992; Young, Marchant, & Wilder, 2004).

Although every school district conducts a comprehensive assessment determine whether a learner qualifies for special education services under the category of EBD (now "emotional disturbance," based on IDEA reauthorization), this process differs across districts and states. Thus, the number of students who receive special education transition services may vary considerably because states identify as many as 2% or as few as 0.5% of learners in schools as EBD (Kauffman, 2001). In fact, the selection process tends to be less than scientific and objective and racial bias may enter into it in many cases. The reauthorization of IDEA as the Individuals with Disabilities Education Improvement Act (IDEIA) of 2004 recognized that culture, race, and language are connected to behavioral misinterpretations. The fact remains, however, that transition services available to CLD learners in special education programs may be different from or inferior to transition opportunities available to other students.

Although some scholars and educators (for example, Braaten, et al., 1988; Kauffman, 2002, 2003a, 2003b; Kauffman & Hallahan, 1995; Kauffmann, Mock, & Simpson, 2007) may feel that special education placement improves student chances for positive outcomes, others (such as Hilliard, 1992; Obiakor, 1999, 2001b; Obiakor & Ford, 2002; Obiakor et al., 2002) may be less enthusiastic. Logically, because general and special education practitioners are human beings, it is unrealistic to presume that their classification of learners will be errorless.

## Disproportionate Placement of CLD Youth in the EBD Category

The EBD category has come under fire recently because of the large numbers of CLD learners placed in it. The 1997 IDEA reauthorization required that, beginning with the 1998–99 school year, states must report the race/ethnicity of students served under each category of disability. For instance, according to the U. S. Department of Education (2001), African Americans account for 14.8% of the general population of students 6 to 21 years of age, yet they are classified as EBD about twice as often as would be expected. Overrepresentation of African Americans occurred in 10 of the 13 IDEA disability classifications. Earlier, Artiles and Trent (1994) revealed that African Americans are placed into special education more often than any other CLD group. In an analysis of 250 documents used to synthesize research studies, Coker, Menz, Johnson, and McAlees (1997) found that adult outcomes for any student with EBD are poorer than for other groups of individuals with disabilities and that African American youth with EBD usually have lower grade point averages, miss more school, and are employed less often than are other students with EBD. Coutinho, Oswald, and Forness (2002) discovered in their study of the 1998 U. S. Department of Education Office of Civil Rights data that, in addition to African Americans, other ethnic groups were also at greater risk of EBD classification than Whites. African American females were 1.4 times more likely than White females to be identified as EBD, African American males were 5.5 times as likely as White females to be identified, and Native American males were identified more often than their incidence in the normal population would suggest. Native American males were especially vulnerable to an EBD label if they lived in rural areas. However, Coutinho et al. acknowledged that race alone does not determine outcomes and that "disproportionality is, in part, a result of differential susceptibility" (2002, p. 120). In other words, CLD youth may be disproportionately placed and served due to factors other than or in addition to race, such as low socioeconomic status (SES).

Poverty, which is positively correlated with EBD for all CLD groups, adds to the disproportionate placement of CLD learners. Low socioeconomic status has been shown to be one predictor of mental illness in children and youth before age 18 (Werner & Smith, 1992). Students with low SES consistently perform lower than other students at all grade levels in academic achievement, and they are more likely to be identified with behavior problems, to be suspended from school, and to be referred for special education services than are students with middle socioeconomic status (Grossman, 1991). Coutinho et al. (2002) found that EBD identification increased for African American females and males and for Hispanic males with low socioeconomic status. To a large extent, poverty and race together constitute "dual minority status" and may multiply a student's chances of poor adult outcomes (Dooley & Voltz, 1999).

In addition, dropout rates are higher for students with EBD than for students with other disabilities: At least one of every two students with EBD leaves school early (Wagner, 1991). Migrant students have also had higher dropout rates than nonmigrants (Sitlington, Clark, & Kolstoe, 2000).

Students with low SES have less access to technology than students from middle and higher socioeconomic groups; this gap has negative outcomes for students with less access (Wilder, 2002a). Is it then any surprise that there is a myth of socioeconomic dissonance in general and special education programming? This myth frequently results in the retrogressive supposition that poverty means "poor" intelligence, "poor" self-concept, and "poor" zest to succeed in school and life (Obiakor, 2001b). It is generally accepted that children and youth are differentially resilient, even with risk factors for EBD placement, and their outcomes range from very successful to unsuccessful in terms of the dominant culture's view of social competence.

In addition to poverty and race factors, CLD learners are sometimes unfamiliar with social expectations of the dominant culture and may lack perfection using them, thus affecting their susceptibility to EBD classification. A logical extension is that trying to make numbers fit a normal distribution may be unrealistic when other factors interfere with the development of social competence in the dominant culture.

## Bias in the Transition Process

Racial disproportionality in special education programs for students with EBD frequently reflect inaccuracies in assessment, classification, and instruction processes (Dooley & Voltz, 1999; Obiakor, 1999, 2001b, 2007; Obiakor, Algozzine et al., 2002). Test bias has been recognized for many years as problematic in a comprehensive EBD assessment with CLD learners (Cartledge et al., 2002). Earlier, Valenzuela and Cervantes (1997) stated that "it is unethical to use standardized test scores as a basis for comparing CLD students to the normative population for diagnostic and placement purposes. These test scores should not be interpreted as indicative of a nondominant culture student's abilities or potential for learning or achievement" (p. 180).

As a consequence, tests used to determine EBD placement as well as tests used to make vocational decisions for EBD youth should be suspect. The norming procedures for some instruments still do not report reliability and validity in their technical manuals or in journal article studies that would justify their use for CLD learners. A study by Wilder and Sudweeks (2003) discovered that the Behavior Assessment Scale for Children (BASC), often used to assist to determine EBD placement, had poor reliability scores for African American and Hispanic learners. Furthermore, traditional deficit-based behavioral rating scales used in most school districts to assess social and emotional skills of students highlight only their problems and do not spotlight strengths, skills, or competencies. Braaten (2002) and Epstein (1999) agreed that such instruments convey an extremely negative view of students that is rarely useful for communicating with colleagues and parents, and for placement or transitional planning purposes. This negative view may increase parent, student, teacher, and administrator expectations for negative outcomes for CLD learners with EBD (see Obiakor, 1999, 2001b, 2007; Obiakor et al., 2002; Obiakor, Algozzine et al., 2002; Obiakor & Beachum, 2005b).

The manner in which school personnel assess the social competence of CLD learners with EBD and the information gleaned from the instruments they use, both for initial classification and placement and for transitional evaluation, consistently affects learner placement and, eventually, their adult outcomes. Interestingly, once CLD learners are identified as EBD, another factor that may affect their postsecondary outcomes is placement—that is, differences have been demonstrated regarding *where* adolescents with EBD are placed and served. CLD adolescents who display problematic behaviors are frequently placed into the juvenile justice system. White adolescents with similar difficulties are more likely to be placed in private psychiatric facilities, where they receive adequate counseling and treatment. Despite federal legislation passed in 1988 to require states to address the issue of disproportionate placement for CLD learners within the juvenile justice system, some states still have not responded, and disproportionate placement remains a serious problem (Hsia & Hamparian, 1998; Osher, Woodruff, & Sims, 2002). For instance, Osher et al. revealed that the percentage of African American youth "ultimately arrested and adjudicated into the juvenile correctional system is far greater than comparable percentages for White youth" (p. 1). As they pointed out, "there are multitude of factors contributing to this problem, including the presence of risk factors both at school and in the community; misinformed decisions and judgments by education, mental health, and juvenile justice professionals; and the impact of race, class, and culture across multiple social fields including school" (p. 1). Apparently, bias in the juvenile justice system exposes the failure of general and special education professionals to reach CLD learners.

## Discrepant Cultures of Transition Professionals and CLD Youth with EBD

Teachers and service providers tend to hold different expectations for certain groups of students (for example, students with low SES or those who come from cultures unlike their own). These expectations ultimately contribute to students' poor academic performance and maladaptive social behavior (Ford, Obiakor, & Patton, 1995; Obiakor, 1999, 2001a, 2007; Obiakor & Beachum, 2005b; Obiakor & Ford, 2002; Sue & Sue, 1999). Stinnett, Bull, Koonce, and Aldridge (1999) conducted a study of 363 undergraduate future general educators and found that most had negative expectations for students with SED and/or EBD labels, regardless of race, before they even had teaching jobs. These lowered expectations frequently influence career counselors, vocational education specialists, and special education teachers and service providers, especially when recommending occupations for CLD students with EBD. It is important to note that these lowered expectations are results of negative perceptions, illusory conclusions, prejudicial judgments, and deficit views of CLD group members. Artiles (1998), more than a decade ago, argued that

> the deficit view of minority people might often mediate White people's cognitive, emotional, and behavioral reactions to minority individuals, phenotypes, interactive styles, language proficiency, and world views. This is probably why, for instance, a police officer in Miami stops a Black man when driving in a predominantly White neighborhood, or why a security person in a department store in Virginia closely monitors a Black woman. This might also explain why a Chicano man in Los Angeles could not obtain a passport because he did not persuade the Immigration and Naturalization Service that he was born in the United States even after providing them with the required documentation, or why people in Seattle speak louder or slower to a Latino who speaks with an accent. Indeed, these are routine events in the daily lives of minority people. We need to acknowledge, therefore, that human difference has been seen as problematic in our society, that ethnic minority groups have been traditionally seen as "problem people," and that discrimination, prejudice, and racism are subtly and openly enacted every day in our country. (p. 33)

It is common knowledge that linguistic difference is an additional factor that can affect adult outcomes for CLD learners. Individuals with EBD who speak and learn differently find themselves over-identified, misassessed, mislabeled, and misinstructed by general and special education professionals (Obiakor, 1999, 2001b, 2007; Ortiz, 2001; Utley & Obiakor, 2001). As a consequence, they are provided with limited opportunities for postsecondary education and jobs. Earlier, Winzer and Mazurek (1998) observed that it takes students with normal cognitive abilities to develop language approximately 5 to 7 years to learn English well enough to understand vocabulary used for teaching and learning specific academic subjects in schools. CLD students get behind in their academic achievement if they are not taught academics and/or given transitional training in their own language as they learn English (Baca & Cervantes, 1998). Additionally, English language learners (ELLs) who speak nonstandard English may have difficulty with job placement as well as acceptance in the social context of the world of work.

For ELLs and other CLD youth with EBD, parents can play a vital role in the transition process. However, students' parents may have had negative experiences with schools in the past and therefore may be wary about working with school personnel on their child's behalf (Cartledge et al., 2002; Obiakor et al., 2002). This is unfortunate because parental involvement positively impacts student outcomes. Family involvement has been correlated with (1) an increase in appropriate social behavior, (2) better attitudes toward school, (3) strong attendance rates, (4) higher academic achievement and cognitive development, (5) fewer suspensions, (6) higher grades and test scores, (7) more homework completion, (8) better graduation rates, and (9) more enrollment in higher education (Campbell-Whatley & Gardner, 2002). General and special education teachers and service providers must be sensitive to parents of CLD learners, especially those with low SES in single-parent, largely female-headed households. Single parents often have grueling schedules that limit participation in their children's educational opportunities. Sometimes, parents' low educational levels, limited language proficiency, or linguistic differences may cause them to be uncomfortable collaborating and consulting with school personnel.

Regardless of parents' fears and reluctance to participate, school personnel have an ethical obligation to (1) shift their paradigms on how they define "good" or "bad" behavior (2) have realistic expectations for

CLD learners with EBD whose parents do not participate, (3) work to empower their students' parents, and (4) refrain from assuming that uninvolved parents do not care about their children. In many cases, students and their families from CLD backgrounds have limited social networks that lead to meaningful employment (Glover & Marshall, 1993); therefore, family involvement is of absolute importance. CLD learners may benefit from mentors from their home communities who have been successful in postsecondary environments (Guetzloe, 1997).

Despite the usual correlations between race, socioeconomic status, and EBD, a study of 2,258 students at multiple sites across several years in the Marriott Foundation's Bridges from School to Work program found that factors related to family involvement did not necessarily predict outcomes for learners in the structured, school-based internship program. What predicted positive outcomes were work-related behaviors, such as hours worked or internship completion (Fabian, Lent, & Willis, 1998). Although race and SES are related to poor outcomes in many instances, a lack of understanding of mainstream culture and inadequate vocational and academic preparation are also factors. The critical question, therefore, is, If schools and communities do not welcome people from diverse cultures, how can adequate preparation be possible? Cultural prejudice surely confounds the transition process, especially when the process inhibits the voices of those the process is supposed to help.

## TRANSITIONING CLD LEARNERS WITH EBD: FUTURE PERSPECTIVES

To adequately transition CLD learners with EBD, general and special education practitioners and service providers must (1) respond to cultural disconnections, (2) empower students and parents, (3) engage students in career counseling and job exploration, and (4) infuse transitional programs into the general curriculum.

### Responding to Cultural Disconnections

It is critical that general and special education professionals prepare CLD learners with EBD for the world of work. This preparation must include social skills of the dominant culture as well as academic, vocational, and language needed for survival in postsecondary environments and communities in which students are likely to be involved. Transition services must be individualized according to the student's culture and disability (Wilder et al., 2001; Wilder et al., 2007). Initially, the assessment and career counseling process must be as free from cultural bias as possible. Learners must consider all potential career paths, given their strengths and limitations, and they must have ample opportunities to explore various jobs in the transition process. Adults must serve as mentors for CLD youth with EBD who are in transition. Ideally, these mentors must belong to the student's own ethnic/cultural community and be successful in their adult roles. Frequent communication with parents—as well as parent and youth involvement in the entire assessment, individualized education program (IEP), and transition processes—are vital to the success of students.

Singh (1998) suggested selecting assessment instruments that have proven to be cross-culturally equivalent for use with students from diverse cultures. However, he noted "the likelihood of finding an instrument that has already been proven to be cross-culturally equivalent is very slim at this time" (p. 438). Leaders in the field of educational testing and measurement (see Thompson & Vacha-Haase, 2000) have called on researchers to collect reliability data for tests and rating scales normed for specific CLD groups and have recommended that future studies of tests include reliability data for specific study populations. To make this information available to diagnosticians, Thompson and Vacha-Haase recommended using reliability generalization as a technique for the meta-analysis of reliability estimates of scores across studies. The reliability of test scores for specific populations should then be made available in test manuals. Reliability generalization has merit for determining whether a particular rating scale measurement is reliable for CLD populations; if not, the use of that instrument for certain learners for eligibility and/or instructional planning purposes should not be warranted.

Another assessment practice useful with CLD learners with behavioral problems is situational assessment. This practice consists of conducting systematic observations of behaviors that occur in the environment to which students intend to go after high school (for example, the college or work environment) for the purpose of learning, practicing, and generalizing appropriate behaviors before learners enter the new environment (Sitlington et al., 2000). Each component of the transition program must be measured for optimal student success; most CLD learners with EBD probably may have had numerous negative experiences in the school context by the time they are in transition.

## Empowering Students and Parents

Maintaining an empowering, positive attitude is essential for success with CLD youth in transition (Campbell-Whatley & Gardner, 2002). Teachers and service providers must adopt the attitude that the learner's disability is just a disability and that the learner is not deliberately perpetrating social ineptitudes on them. They must believe their teaching will be successful and that students can learn to negotiate the dominant culture with social competence to the degree that they are able, given their disability. General and special education teachers and service providers must recognize that these learners can attain academic aptitude and can learn vocational skills necessary for success in the adult world (Bakken & Obiakor, 2008).

To empower learners, initial assessment and ongoing data collection must include information on their strengths; and instructional planning must include methods to reinforce and generalize appropriate behavior. Making appropriate behavior habitual and permanent requires consistency over time. General and special educators must create positive classroom and work environments and help learners by making expectations realistic. The more social skills learners lack, the more structured their environment will probably need to be (Braaten, 1998). Teachers and job coaches must cautiously appraise learners' social skills before placing them into environments where they will have frequent interpersonal contacts that may precipitate failure. An empowering, positive environment will facilitate a good esprit de corps in an environment where students are not allowed to harass each other (Obiakor, 1999; Obiakor & Beachum, 2005a; Obiakor, Harris, & Wilder, 2003). Clearly, learners with EBD must be empowered to self-evaluate their behavioral patterns and know that these behaviors can conflict with "normal" work environments.

Another solution for improving opportunities for success for CLD youth is empowering parents, guardians, or mentors in transition planning. Parental involvement may be the most important predictor of postsecondary success, because parents usually provide the most stable, consistent, and long-term support for their children (Boone, 1992; Harry, 1992). Earlier, Hasazi, Gordon, and Roe (1985) found that employment outcomes improve for learners with disabilities when interested family and friends participate in school-to-work transitions. Family support and assistance from community support groups are considered best practices in effective transitions (Kohler, 1993; Wehman, 1990); these individuals and groups help youth with EBD find jobs, teach them what they need to do to be successful in postsecondary schooling or on the job, and provide a social-emotional support system for them when times are tough. Friends and family members can give CLD learners with EBD feedback as to the appropriateness of their behavior, and supporters can offer advice on how to manage their social-emotional difficulties in a skilled manner. In addition, the advice of these mentors may help learners stay in school or on the job, as well as assist them in solving problems (Zionts, Zionts, & Simpson, 2002).

Participation can be improved by encouraging parents to select an advocate they trust to accompany them to meetings with school personnel and teaching parents about the IEP/transition process (Boone, 1992; Harry, 1992). For example, Harry acknowledged that the involvement of parents of CLD learners in the IEP process is less than that of White parents. Of course, a number of barriers (including time conflicts, language differences, inadequate information, transportation problems, and previous negative experiences) may limit this participation. Therefore, school personnel must use strategies specifically effective with parents of CLD learners.

## Engaging Students in Career Counseling and Job Exploration

It is essential that general and special education professionals offering career counseling and job exploration services to CLD learners with EBD or any other disability are well aware of their own cultural biases and values. For example, most career theories are oriented for European American males and may not adequately generalize to suit CLD youth with EBD (Isaacson & Brown, 2000). When using a theory as a foundation for counseling, counselors or teachers must assess the culture of the learner and determine how well the assumptions of the theory fit that culture. Common differences occur in career decision-making styles of different cultures. For instance, European American values may call for an independent and individual decision-making style, whereas other cultures may value collaborative and group decision-making processes (Bowman, 1993; Cartledge, 2004; Leong, 1991; Obiakor, 2001a, 2004, 2007).

CLD people in the United States seem to be concentrated in a small range of careers (Isaacson & Brown, 2000). African Americans and Hispanic Americans, for example, are over-represented in low-prestige careers and under-represented in all other careers. Though they may have the same level of career aspiration as European Americans, they may be less optimistic about being hired for those jobs. These problems may be due in part to tracking biases while they are in school. Many of those learners who could engage in more challenging careers are placed on vocational tracks, which limits opportunities for high-level careers (Obiakor & Harris-Obiakor, 1997). Consideration must therefore be taken for the acculturation of the learner during career assessment and placement processes to make sure that he or she is placed on an appropriate track. In addition, counselors and teachers ought to alert CLD learners with EBD to the wide spectrum of careers available to them; many students may ignore certain occupations that are viewed as nontraditional for their cultures. They may not know anyone working in a particular occupation and may not recognize it as an option for them. Likewise, they may not be aware of what careers are available to choose from or what academic or vocational training is required for specific careers (Bakken & Aloia, 1999; Bakken & Obiakor, 2008). Identifying role models who have gone beyond cultural traditions and having those role models integrally involved in the transition process with the student can be helpful strategies (Bowman, 1993; Campbell-Whatley, Algozzine, & Obiakor, 1997; Obiakor & Beachum, 2005a; Obiakor & Harris-Obiakor, 1997).

Transition specialists should use career interest inventories and vocational and employability assessments to help students with disabilities choose appropriate career paths (Bakken & Aloia, 1999; Venn, 2000). When learners have emotional or behavioral difficulties, school personnel should also use behavioral rating scales, observations, and other social-emotional data to determine to what degree the learners can be placed into careers in which they will interact socially with others (Zionts et al., 2002).

## Infusing Transitional Programs into the Curriculum

Vocational education and counseling have been shown to be correlated with higher graduation rates and post–high school employment rates for learners with EBD, although these services are not used as often as they might be in public schools (Rylance 1997, 1998). One reason is that transitional programs are not properly infused into the general curriculum (Bakken & Aloia, 1999; Bakken & Obiakor, 2008). Earlier, Spengler, Blustein, and Strohmer (1990) warned counselors to be aware of vocational overshadowing—that is, ignoring a learner's vocational problems in lieu of his or her personal problems, a common situation for learners with EBD. All aspects of the learner's vocational, personal, and academic life must be included in the curriculum. In other words, the transition curriculum for CLD learners with EBD must include everything they will need to achieve the goals they have set (that is, everything each person will need to maximize his or her potential).

The curriculum must reflect experiences of learners who participate in it and must help them progress toward their goals. In addition, it must have elements of social skills training adapted to individual needs. Some learners may need information on sexual relations; some may desire understanding of marriage, family, neighborhood, or workplace social relationships; others may need information on appropriate behavior in a particular postsecondary school environment. Some of those who have participated in the judicial system may need direct teaching about and experience practicing civic rights and responsibilities. Learners with EBD are likely to need a mental health curriculum daily (Zionts et al., 2002). Some may need specific training for identified career paths. Many careers require a level of competence with technology.

Although school personnel must be careful not to place CLD learners into vocational tracks that are below their ability levels, vocational education can be identified as an alternative to dropping out because it provides a curriculum that is pragmatic and prepares them directly for employment (Harvey, 2001). Learners with vocational training may have enhanced chances for postschool employment (Arum & Shavit, 1995). Some may need a curriculum that increases academic skills or language proficiency or a curriculum that teaches them to apply for postsecondary training opportunities, including college (Clark & Patton,

1997). The curriculum must be tailored according to the student's interests, aptitude, culture, and disability.

Other curricular items that are useful for CLD learners with EBD to learn and practice are peer mediation and conflict resolution strategies. In peer mediation, an adult teaches a student's peer the appropriate social skills to model, reinforce, and then prompt a student with EBD during a natural social situation. Conflict resolution is a specific set of procedures for mediating and then resolving conflicts between two parties (Jolivette et al., 2000; Obiakor, Mehring, & Schwenn, 1997). To a large measure, it helps learners deal with their respective crises.

Sitlington et al. (2000) identified self-determination as another curricular item needed for smooth transition of students. It is necessary to incorporate the skills, knowledge, and beliefs associated with self-determination and self-advocacy into the transition curriculum. Clearly, learners need to learn and practice these skills as early as elementary school and must establish competence by the time they reach adulthood. It is also important that CLD learners understand the relationship between "self" and resiliency (see Obiakor & Beachum, 2005a). Parents, teachers, and community leaders, as well as state and federal agencies, must help these learners to develop their "selves" through appropriate, nonbiased educational programming (Obiakor et al., 2002). Learners with EBD who are deemed capable of self-advocacy can participate in transition plan development, educational/vocational training, and postsecondary or job application processes. If the learner is not deemed capable, a guardian should be appointed to facilitate the transition process (Bakken & Obiakor, 2008; Wilder, 2002b, 2004; Wilder, Obiakor, & Algozzine, 2003).

## MULTICULTURAL TRANSITION MODEL

Given current issues, practices, and proposed solutions in transitioning CLD learners with EBD to their chosen postsecondary environments, we recommend as a necessity a new multicultural transition model (MTM) that contains essential elements suggested by researchers. This model includes elements of the learner's (1) career interests; (2) cognitive, academic, vocational, and social-emotional aptitude; (3) disability; and (4) culture (Figure 2.1). The model is supported by continued positive mentoring support and incorporates a consistent, strengths-based approach.

**FIGURE 2.1    Four Pillars of the Multicultural Transition Model (MTM)**

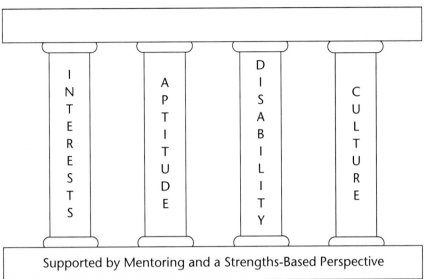

CLD learners with EBD can be better prepared by general educators, special educators, or transition specialists using what we call the four pillars of the MTM. First, transition specialists, including a career counselor and teachers, should assess the learner's personal career interests through a vocational inventory and interviews with the learner and his or her parents. This assessment will enable the learner to participate in a systematic, planned program of career exploration to further determine his or her interests.

Second, transition specialists should conduct a comprehensive assessment of the learner's cognitive abilities, academic achievement, vocational aptitude, and social-emotional developmental level, delineating specific strengths and weaknesses in each of the assessment categories. (The first and second pillars may occur in reverse order, as deemed appropriate by transition specialists.)

Third, considering a learner's individual disability is important in improving his or her chances for success in the postsecondary environment. Considering the disability is a delicate matter, and assuming that a particular learner has the same troubles as others with the same label or that he or she will behave in a stereotyped manner is dangerous!

Many professionals and service providers are familiar with ways that learners with EBD often fail and where their imperfections may lie. The nature of special education testing has traditionally been deficit-oriented or problem-based, and because the recent focus is on learners' abilities to access the general education curriculum, current strategies for remediation must include focusing on learner strengths relative to that curriculum. However, for a learner who qualifies for special services under the EBD category, behavior should be examined closely because it is the manifestation of the disability. Transition team members must decide which appropriate behavior in the postsecondary environment can be taught, practiced, and generalized, and which inappropriate behavior is likely to continue to occur. For the latter, avoidance of situations that trigger the problem behavior may be best, and planning ahead is strongly suggested.

The last pillar is unique because it allows professionals to further individualize transition services. Considering a learner's culture during the transition, a relatively new strategy, is important because culture is a pervasive influence on behavior (Obiakor, 2001b, 2004, 2007). This strategy consists of examining the learner's beliefs, values, customs, perceptions, and family expectations and then, through situational assessment, evaluating the culture of the postsecondary environment where the learner is headed. Schools and workplaces are characterized by particular cultures; some behaviors are expected and others are deemed inappropriate. Points of possible conflict should be noted between the learner's culture and the postsecondary culture, and the learner should be given an opportunity to recognize his or her current cultural behavior and to learn behavior that is appropriate in the culture he or she will soon enter. The behavior an individual displays in the postsecondary environment may influence his or her acceptance by superiors and/or peers and ultimately determine his or her success. Understanding home, school, and postsecondary cultures and adapting to expectations and guidelines are important skills for learners to master if they are to be successful within different settings (Bakken & Aloia, 1999; Bakken & Obiakor, 2008). Culturally responsive special education services can enhance the likelihood of successful postsecondary transitions. In our belief, culture influences postsecondary outcomes in multidimensional ways (see Obiakor, 2007).

## CONCLUSION

The effectiveness of many strategies suggested in this chapter has been extrapolated from the populations for which they were found to be effective (that is, for CLD youth, youth with disabilities, or youth with EBD) to CLD youth with EBD in transition. Studies related to adolescents with EBD in transition and to CLD are scarce; therefore, we urge that generalizations be made with care. Even if some of the practices are effective for some CLD learners, there may be great variation from one CLD group to another and tremendous variation in effectiveness of practices from one learner within a CLD group to the next. Likewise, there may be great variation in the behavior and aptitude for social competence of different learners within the EBD group.

We believe the relative paucity of research specific to issues that CLD learners face in schools and in their transition to other settings must be of concern to educators and service providers involved in the transition process. This paucity is of particular concern because it has been widely recognized that these learners are disproportionately represented in EBD programs. However, we are excited about different possibilities and strategies (for example, the Response to Intervention [RTI] model) recommended by IDEIA. According to Mellard and Johnson (2008), the RTI is popular today because it "provides a process through which the achievement of all students can be enhanced" (p. 2) and is "based on a public health model of intervention whereby multiple tiers of increasingly intense interventions are directed at correspondingly smaller and smaller population segments" (p. 3). As it appears, the implementation of the RTI model for students with EBD in general education must include the use of increasingly intense, evidence-based instructional strategies.

Published research often determines special education procedures, curriculum, and evidence-based instructional interventions. The question then is, How can teachers and service providers use effective, evidence-based interventions if they are not available in the literature? The reason for this lack of availability may be that the majority of special education research has been conducted by categorizing learners according to disability alone and not according to disability and culture. The logical extension is that limited data are available to help researchers and practitioners ensure that appropriate transition services are provided to CLD learners with EBD. Such limitations clearly compromise the quality of work done in the field.

In this chapter, we recognize the complexity in designing transitional programs for CLD learners with EBD. We also recognize that professional and parental collaboration and consultation are needed to make transitions smooth. Measurable efforts must be made to reduce the traditional misidentification, misassessment, miscategorization, and misinstruction of CLD learners. The number of these learners associated with the criminal justice system should alarm all of us, especially because the United States prides itself as the premier nation where ultimate freedom reigns. To address this concern, we must begin early to infuse transitional programming into our general school curriculum. We need to identify early the strengths that CLD learners bring to school, and, if possible, use their strengths to work on their weaknesses. It is important that we focus on their unique needs as learners and capitalize on the developmental nature of their growth. We can no longer afford to continue our prejudicial assumptions about learners who come from different cultural, racial, and socioeconomic backgrounds. In the end, our paradigms and powers must be shifted in all educational programming, including the transition process. In fact, absolute urgency is needed at all educational levels if we truly want our learners and programs to survive and excel in this century.

## REFERENCES

Artiles, A. J. (1998). The dilemma of difference: Enriching the disproportionality discourse with theory and context. *Journal of Special Education, 32*, 32–36.

Artiles, A. J., & Trent, S. C. (1994). Overrepresentation of minority students in special education: A continuing debate. *Journal of Special Education, 27*, 410–437.

Arum, R., & Shavit, Y. (1995). Secondary vocational education and the transition from school to work. *Sociology of Education, 68*(3), 187–204.

Baca, L. M., & Cervantes, H. T. (1998). *The bilingual special education interface* (3rd ed.). Upper Saddle River, NJ: Prentice-Hall.

Bakken, J. P., & Aloia, G. F. (1999). Transitioning multicultural learners with exceptionalities. In F. E. Obiakor, J. O. Schwenn, & A. F. Rotatori (Eds.), *Advances in special education: Multicultural education for learners with exceptionalities* (pp. 217–232). Stamford, CT: JAI Press.

Bakken, J. P., & Obiakor, F. E. (2008). *Transition planning for students with disabilities: What educators and service providers can do.* Springfield, IL: Charles C Thomas.

Boone, R. S. (1992). Involving culturally diverse parents in transition planning. *Career Development for Exceptional Individuals, 15*(2), 205–221.

Bowman, S. L. (1993). Career intervention strategies for ethnic minorities. *The Career Development Quarterly, 42,* 14–25.

Braaten, S. (1998). *Behavioral objective sequence.* Champaign, IL: Research Press.

Braaten, S. (2002, January). *The challenging kid.* Keynote address presented as a Distinguished Visiting Professor at Brigham Young University, Provo, UT.

Braaten, S. R., Kauffman, J. M., Braaten, B., Polsgrove, L., & Nelson, C. M. (1988). The regular education initiative: Patent medicine for behavioral disorders. *Exceptional Children, 55,* 21–28.

Campbell-Whatley, G. D., Algozzine, B., & Obiakor, F. E. (1997, May). Using mentoring to improve academic performing for African American male youths with mild disabilities. *The School Counselor, 44,* 362–367.

Campbell-Whatley, G. D., & Gardner, R. (2002). *Strategies and procedures for designing proactive interventions with a culturally diverse population of students with emotional or behavioral disorders and their families/caregivers.* Arlington, VA: Council for Children with Behavioral Disorders and the Council for Exceptional Children.

Cartledge, G. (2004). Another look at the impact of changing demographics on public education for culturally diverse learners with behavior problems: Implications for preparation: A response to Festus E. Obiakor. In L. M. Bullock & R. A. Gable (Eds.), *Quality personnel preparation in emotional/behavior disorders: Current perspectives and future directions* (pp. 64–69). Denton: University of North Texas, Institute for Behavioral and Learning Differences.

Cartledge, G., Tam, K. Y., Loe, S., Miranda, A. H., Lambert, M. C., Kea, C. D., & Simmons-Reed, E. (2002). *Culturally and linguistically diverse students with behavioral disorders.* Arlington, VA: Council for Children with Behavioral Disorders and the Council for Exceptional Children.

Clark, G. M., & Patton, J. R. (1997). *Transition planning inventory.* Austin: Pro-Ed.

Coker, C. C., Menz, F. E., Johnson, L. A., & McAlees, D. C. (1997). *School outcomes and community benefits for minority youth with serious emotional disturbances: A synthesis of the research literature.* Menomonie, WI: University of Wisconsin–Stout, Publications Department, Research and Training Center, Stout Vocational Rehabilitation Institute, School of Education and Human Services. (ERIC Document Reproduction Service No. ED 424 715.)

Coutinho, M. J., Oswald, D. P., & Forness, S. R. (2002). Gender and socioeconomic factors and the disproportionate identification of culturally and linguistically diverse students with emotional disturbance. *Behavioral Disorders, 27*(2), 109–125.

D'Amico, R., & Maxwell, N. L. (1995). The continuing significance of race in minority male joblessness. *Social Forces, 73,* 969–991.

Dooley, E. A., & Voltz, D. L. (1999). Educating the African American exceptional learner. In F. E. Obiakor, J. O. Schwenn, & A. F. Rotatori (Eds.), *Advances in special education: Multicultural education for learners with exceptionalities* (pp. 15–31). Stamford, CT: JAI Press.

Epstein, M. (1999). Using strength-based assessment in programs for children with emotional and behavioral disorders. *Beyond Behavior, 9*(2), 25–27.

Fabian, E. S., Lent, R. W., & Willis, S. P. (1998). Predicting work outcomes for students with disabilities: Implications for counselors. *Journal of Counseling and Development, 76,* 311–316.

Ford, B. A., Obiakor, F. E., & Patton, J. M. (1995). *Effective education of African American exceptional learners: New perspectives.* Austin: Pro-Ed.

Forness, S. R., & Knitzer, J. (1992). A new proposed definition and terminology to replace "serious emotional disturbance" in Individuals with Disabilities Act. *School Psychology Review, 21,* 12–20.

Glover, R. W., & Marshall, R. (1993). Improving the school-to-work transition of American adolescents. *Teachers College Record, 94,* 588–610.

Grossman, H. (1991). Special education in a diverse society: Improving services for minority and working class students. *Preventing School Failure, 36*(1), 19–27.

Guetzloe, E. (1997). The power of positive relationships: Mentoring programs in the school and community. *Preventing School Failure, 41*(3), 100–105.

Harry, B. (1992). *Cultural diversity, families, and the special education system.* New York: Teachers College Press.

Harvey, M. (2001). Vocational–technical education: A logical approach to dropout prevention for secondary special education. *Preventing School Failure, 45*(3), 108–113.

Hasazi, S. B., Gordon, L. R., & Roe, C. A. (1985). Factors associated with the employment status of handicapped youth exiting high school from 1979 to 1983. *Exceptional Children, 51,* 445–469.

Hilliard, A. G. (1992). The pitfalls and promises of special education practice. *Exceptional Children, 59,* 168–172.

Hsia, M., & Hamparian, D. (1998, September). *Disproportionate minority confinement: 1997 update* (OJJDP Juvenile Justice Bulletin). Washington, DC: Department of Justice, Office of Juvenile Justice and Delinquency Prevention.

Individuals with Disabilities Education Act of 1990, Pub. L. No. 101–476 (1990).

Individuals with Disabilities Education Act of 1997, Pub. L. No. 105–17 (1997).

Individuals with Disabilities Education Improvement Act of 2004, Pub. L. No. 108–446 (2004).

Isaacson, L. E., & Brown, D. (2000). *Career information, career counseling, and career development* (7th ed.). Boston: Allyn & Bacon.

Jolivette, K., Stichter, J. P., Nelson, C. M., Scott, T. M., & Liaupsin, C. J. (2000). *Improving post-school outcomes for students with emotional and behavioral disorders.*Arlington, VA: Council for Exceptional Children. (ERIC Document Reproduction Service No. ED 447 616.) Retrieved September 28, 2009, from http://www.ericdigests.org/2001–3/post.htm

Kauffman, J. M. (2001). *Characteristics of emotional and behavioral disorders of children and youth* (7th ed.). Upper Saddle River, NJ: Merrill.

Kauffman, J. M. (2002). *Education deform? Bright people sometimes say stupid things about education.* Lanham, MD: Scarecrow Education.

Kauffman, J. M. (2003a). Reflections on the field. *Behavior Disorders, 28,* 205–208.

Kauffman, J. M. (2003b). Appearances, stigma, and prevention. *Remedial and Special Education, 24,* 195–198.

Kauffman, J. M., & Hallahan, D. P. (1995). *The illusion of full inclusion: A comprehensive critique of a current special education bandwagon.* Austin: Pro-Ed.

Kauffman, J. M., Mock, D. R., & Simpson, R. L. (2007, November). Problems related to underservice of students with emotional or behavioral disorders. *Behavioral Disorders, 31,* 43–57.

Kohler, P. D. (1993). Best practices in transition: Substantiated or implied? *Career Development for Exceptional Individuals, 16,* 107–120.

Leong, F. T. L. (1991). Career development attributes and occupational values of Asian Americans and White American college students. *The Career Development Quarterly, 39,* 221–230.

Mellard, D. F., & Johnson, E. (2008). *RTI: A practitioner's guide to implementing Response to Intervention.* Thousand Oaks, CA: Corwin Press.

Obiakor, F. E. (1999). Teacher expectations of minority exceptional learners: Impact on "accuracy" of self-concept. *Exceptional Children, 66,* 39–53.

Obiakor, F. E. (2001a). Developing emotional intelligence in learners with behavioral problems: Refocusing special education. *Behavior Disorders, 26,* 321–331.

Obiakor, F. E. (2001b). *It even happens in "good" schools: Responding to cultural diversity in today's classrooms.* Thousand Oaks, CA: Corwin Press.

Obiakor, F. E. (2004). Impact of changing demographics on public education for culturally diverse learners with behavior problems: Implications for teacher preparation. In L. M. Bullock & R. A. Gable (Eds.), *Quality personnel preparation in emotional/behavior disorders: Current perspectives and future directions* (pp. 64–69). Denton: Institute for Behavioral and Learning Differences at the University of North Texas.

Obiakor, F. E. (2007). *Multicultural special education: Culturally responsive teaching.* Upper Saddle River, NJ: Pearson/Merrill Prentice Hall.

Obiakor, F. E., Algozzine, B., Thurlow, M., Gwalla-Ogisi, N., Enwefa, S., Enwefa, R., & McIntosh, A. (2002). *Addressing the issue of disproportionate representation: Identification and assessment of culturally diverse students with emotional or behavioral disorders.* Arlington, VA: Council for Children with Behavioral Disorders, Council for Exceptional Children.

Obiakor, F. E., & Beachum, F. D. (2005a). Developing self-empowerment in African American students using the Comprehensive Support Model. *The Journal of Negro Education, 74,* 18–29.

Obiakor, F. E., & Beachum, F. D. (2005b). *Urban education for the 21st century: Research, issues, and perspectives.* Springfield, IL: Charles C Thomas.

Obiakor, F. E., & Ford, B. A. (2002). *Creating successful learning environments for African American learners with exceptionalities.* Thousand Oaks, CA: Corwin Press.

Obiakor, F. E., Grant, P. A., & Dooley, E. A. (2002). *Educating all learners: Refocusing the comprehensive support model.* Springfield, IL: Charles C Thomas.

Obiakor, F. E., & Harris-Obiakor, P. (1997, Fall). Career counseling for the minority college student: The neglected reality. *Journal of Educational Opportunity, 16,* 35–47.

Obiakor, F. E., Harris, I. M., & Wilder, L. K. (2003). Responding to school and non-school violence: Beyond tradition. *Scholar and Educator, 25,* 78–92.

Obiakor, F. E., Mehring, T. A., & Schwenn, J. O. (1997). *Disruption, disaster, and death: Helping students deal with crises.* Arlington, VA: Council for Exceptional Children.

Ortiz, A. (2001). Foreword. In C. A. Utley & F. E. Obiakor (Eds.), *Special education, multicultural education, and school reform: Components of quality education for learners with mild disabilities* (pp. xi–xiii). Springfield, IL: Charles C Thomas.

Osher, D., Woodruff, D., & Sims, A. (2002). *Exploring relationships between inappropriate and ineffective special education services for African American children and youth and their overrepresentation in the juvenile justice system.* Paper presented at the Minority Issues in Special Education Conference, Civil Rights Project, Harvard University, Cambridge, MA. Retrieved June 15, 2009, from http://www.law.harvard.edu/civilrights/conferences/speced/osherpaper2.html

Rylance, B. J. (1997). Predictors of high school graduation or dropping out for youths with severe emotional disturbances. *Behavioral Disorders, 23*(1), 5–17.

Rylance, B. J. (1998). Predictors of post high-school employment for youth identified as severely emotionally disturbed. *The Journal of Special Education, 32*(3), 184–192.

Singh, N. N. (1998). Cultural diversity: A challenge for evaluating systems of care. In M. H. Epstein, K. Kutash, & A. Duchnowski (Eds.), *Outcomes for children and youth with emotional and behavioral disorders and their families: Programs and evaluation best practices* (pp. 425–454). Austin: Pro-Ed.

Sitlington, P. L., Clark, G. M., & Kolstoe, O. P. (2000). *Transition education and services for adolescents with disabilities* (3rd ed.). Needham Heights, MA: Allyn & Bacon.

Spengler, P. M., Blustein, D. L., & Strohmer, D. C. (1990). Diagnostic treatment overshadowing of vocational problems by personal problems. *Journal of Counseling Psychology, 37*(4), 372–381.

Stinnett, T. A., Bull, K. S., Koonce, D. A., & Aldridge, J. O. (1999). Effects of diagnostic label, race, gender, educational placement, and definitional information on prognostic outlook for children with behavior problems. *Psychology in the Schools, 36*(1), 51–59.

Sue, D. W., & Sue, D. (1999). *Counseling the culturally different: Theory and practice* (3rd ed.). New York: Wiley.

Thompson, B., & Vacha-Haase, T. (2000). Psychometrics is datametrics: The test is not reliable. *Educational and Psychological Measurement, 60*(2), 174–195.

U. S. Department of Education. (2001). *Twenty-second annual report to Congress on the implementation of the Individuals with Disabilities Act.* Washington, DC: Author.

Utley, C. A., & Obiakor, F. E. (2001). *Special education, multicultural education, and school reform: Components of quality education for learners with mild disabilities*. Springfield, IL: Charles C Thomas.

Valenzuela, J. S., & Cervantes, H. T. (1997). Procedures and techniques for assessing the bilingual exceptional child. In L. M. Baca & H. T. Cervantes (Eds.), *The bilingual special education interface* (3rd ed., pp. 168–187). Upper Saddle River, NJ: Merrill.

Venn, J. J. (2000). *Assessing students with special needs* (2nd ed.). Upper Saddle River, NJ: Merrill.

Wagner, M. (1991). *Youth with disabilities: How are they doing? The first comprehensive report from the National Longitudinal Transition Study of Special Education Students* (Report No. EC 300 998). Menlo Park, CA: SRI International Contract 300–87–0054. (ERIC Document Reproduction No. ED 341 228.)

Wehman, P. (1990). School-to-work: Elements of successful programs. *Teaching Exceptional Children, 23,* 40–43.

Werner, E. E., & Smith, R. S. (1992). *Overcoming the odds: High risk children from birth to adulthood.* Ithaca, NY: Cornell University Press.

Wilder, L. K. (2001). Success in college for students with disabilities. *Theories and Practices in Supervision and Curriculum, 12,* 31–34.

Wilder, L. K. (2002a). Technology: The great equalizer. In L. K. Wilder & S. Black (Eds.), *Integrating technology in program development for children/youth with E/BD* (pp. 1–3). Arlington, VA: Council for Children with Behavioral Disorders and the Council for Exceptional Children.

Wilder, L. K. (2002b). The homeless are people too: Including homeless students in educational programming. In F. E. Obiakor, P. A. Grant, & E. A. Dooley (Eds.), *Educating all learners: Refocusing the comprehensive support model* (pp. 64–84). Springfield, IL: Charles C Thomas.

Wilder, L. K. (2004). Transitioning homeless youth. *Beyond Behavior, 13,* 17–19.

Wilder, L. K., Ashbaker, B. Y., Obiakor, F., & Rotz, E. (2006). Building multicultural transitions for ethnically diverse learners with disabilities. *Multiple Voices, 9*(1), 22–33.

Wilder, L. K., Jackson, A. P., & Smith, T. B. (2001). Secondary transition of multicultural learners: Lessons from the Navajo Native American experience. *Preventing School Failure, 45*(3), 119–124.

Wilder, L. K., Obiakor, F. E., & Algozzine, B. (2003). Homeless students in special education: Beyond the myth of socioeconomic dissonance. *Journal of At-Risk Issues, 9*(2), 9–15.

Wilder, L. K., Shepherd, T. L., Murry, F., Rogers, E., Heaton, E., & Sonntag, A. W. (2007). Teacher ratings of social skills across ethnic groups for learners with mild disabilities: Implications for teacher education. *Curriculum and Teaching, 22*(1), 47–66.

Wilder, L. K., & Sudweeks, R. (2003). Reliability of ratings across studies of the BASC. *Education and Treatment of Children, 26,* 382–399.

Winzer, M. A., & Mazurek, K. (1998). *Special education in multicultural contexts.* Upper Saddle River, NJ: Prentice-Hall.

Young, K. R., Marchant, M., & Wilder, L. K. (2004). School-based interventions for children and youth with emotional/behavioral disorders: A school-based approach. In P. Allen-Meares & M. W. Fraser (Eds.), *Intervention with children & adolescents: An interdisciplinary perspective* (pp. 175–204). Boston: Allyn & Bacon.

Zionts, P., Zionts, L., & Simpson, R. L. (2002). *Emotional and behavioral problems: A handbook for understanding and handling students.* Thousand Oaks, CA: Corwin Press.

## CHAPTER 3

# Self-Determination and Transition-Age Youth with Emotional or Behavioral Disorders: Promising Practices

**Erik W. Carter**

Adolescence can be a time of considerable change, ushering in an array of new experiences, opportunities, roles, and responsibilities for high-school students with and without disabilities. As youth develop cognitively, physically, socially, and emotionally, they typically assume increasing independence and autonomy (Zimmer-Gembeck & Collins, 2003). During this time, the influence of adults on both the decisions and opinions of youth typically diminishes, and youth begin to make important decisions about their future education, careers, and lifestyles. Within high schools, teachers often expect youth to take greater responsibility for managing their own learning and behavior and to assume a more prominent role in planning for their future. Indeed, a primary charge of high schools is to better equip youth for the roles and responsibilities of adulthood. Such efforts are designed in part to foster self-determination among youth as they launch into life after high school. For youth with emotional or behavioral disorders (EBD), promoting self-determination is now firmly established as an essential component of effective transition practices.

*Author note:* Support for preparation of this chapter was provided by a grant from the Centers for Medicare and Medicaid Services, Medicaid Infrastructure Grant to the Wisconsin Department of Health Services (CFDA No. 93.768).

## SELF-DETERMINATION: WHAT IS IT AND WHY IS IT IMPORTANT?

Although self-determination has been defined and described in many different ways (compare Deci & Ryan, 2002; Field & Hoffman, 2002; Mithaug, Mithaug, Agran, Martin, & Wehmeyer, 2003; Wehmeyer, 1999; Zimmer-Gembeck & Collins, 2003), the term refers broadly to having the capacity to steer one's own life in ways and directions that improve one's quality of life. Within the context of secondary transition, self-determination often is evidenced when youth are able to effectively express their strengths, interests, preferences, and needs to others; set personal goals that reflect their future aspirations; evaluate possible options; decide for themselves how they will achieve their goals; take steps to work toward these goals; respond well to unanticipated problems and challenges; advocate for needed services and supports; and periodically adjust their actions as they evaluate their continued progress. The Division on Career Development and Transition synthesized these various elements well when defining self-determination in the following way:

> Self-determination is "a combination of skills, knowledge, and beliefs that enable a person to engage in goal-directed, self-regulated, autonomous behavior. An understanding of one's strengths and limitations together with a belief in oneself as capable and effective are essential in self-determination. When acting on the basis of these skills and attitudes, individuals have greater ability to take control of their lives and assume the role of successful adults in society." (Field, Martin, Miller, Ward, & Wehmeyer, 1998, p. 2)

In other words, self-determination can be influenced by what youth with disabilities know, their perceptions of themselves, the abilities they possess, and the experiences they have. This construct often is discussed among researchers and educators using terms such as autonomy, self-reliance, resilience, self-direction, and responsibility. Among youth, however, it often is articulated in the language of choice ("having a say"), freedom ("doing it myself"), control ("doing it my own way"), and goals ("having plans for my future"). As will be emphasized throughout this chapter, these various perspectives all highlight the importance of coupling thoughtful instruction with meaningful opportunities for youth to practice and refine newly acquired skills that can enhance their self-determination.

## AN EMERGING EMPHASIS WITHIN SECONDARY TRANSITION

Equipping youth with disabilities with the skills, supports, and experiences that contribute to self-determination has emerged as a key recommended component of secondary transition services (Field et al., 1998; Johnson, Stodden, Emmanuel, Luecking, & Mack, 2002). Although it is now a widely used "buzzword" within special education, self-determination remains a relatively new concept. The legislative emphasis on promoting student involvement did not become prominent until the Individuals with Disabilities Education Act of 1990 and its reauthorization of 1997, when the importance of considering students' strengths, interests, and preferences and increasing student involvement in transition and educational planning were first emphasized. Throughout the 1990s and 2000s, research exploring self-determination, its key elements, and effective avenues for promoting it have proliferated, leading to the availability of a wide array of curricular packages, instructional models, and intervention strategies for increasing the self-determination of youth with disabilities (Algozzine, Browder, Karvonen, Test, & Wood, 2001; Test, Karvonen, Wood, Browder, & Algozzine, 2000). In a fairly short amount of time, self-determination has come to be endorsed as a relevant, valued, and even essential educational outcome for transition-age youth with disabilities by a range of stakeholders, including researchers (Hughes et al., 1997), policy makers (President's Commission on Excellence in Special Education, 2002), special educators (Mason, Field, & Sawilowsky, 2004; Wehmeyer, Agran, & Hughes, 2000), general educators (Carter, Lane, Pierson, & Stang, 2008), parents (Grigal, Neubert, Moon, & Graham, 2003; Zhang, Wehmeyer, & Chen, 2005), and youth with disabilities themselves (Trainor, 2005; Unruh & Bullis, 2005).

What factors have contributed to the prominent role that self-determination now assumes in discussions of transition policy and practice? Certainly, the self-advocacy movement has raised expectations for the role that people with disabilities can and should play in shaping their own lives. And the normalization principle has emphasized that, like their peers without disabilities, youth with disabilities should be supported in learning how to assume greater responsibility for directing their own lives in ways that they choose (Wehmeyer, Bersani, & Gagne, 2000). But it is the emerging link between self-determination and improved in- and postschool outcomes for youth with disabilities that may be most compelling for secondary educators. Research suggests that youth who are more self-determined may perform better academically (Martin et al., 2003; Mooney, Ryan, Uhing, Reid, & Epstein, 2005), participate more actively in their own educational and transition planning (Martin et al., 2006), remain more engaged in school (Hadre & Reeve, 2003), experience greater postsecondary involvement (Field, Sarver, & Shaw, 2003), fare better early in adulthood (Wehmeyer & Palmer, 2003), and report higher quality of life (Wehmeyer & Schwartz, 1997). For youth with or at-risk for EBD, receiving instruction and opportunities related to self-determination may even be associated with a reduction in the occurrence of challenging behaviors (Carter, Trainor, Owens, Swedeen, & Sun, in press; Shogren, Faggella-Luby, Bae, & Wehmeyer, 2004).

It is not surprising, therefore, that promoting skills and opportunities that enhance self-determination is often included as a key component of model secondary and transition programs for youth with or at-risk for EBD (Cheney & Bullis, 2004). For example, self-determination represents the first of five guiding principles in Project RENEW and is evidenced through intentional involvement of youth with EBD in personal futures planning and explicit instruction in skills that could increase self-determination and personal responsibility (Malloy et al., Chapter 10 in this volume). Similarly, the Check and Connect school dropout prevention model involves identifying mentors who can help at-risk youth learn to engage in effective problem solving to identify solutions and resolve conflicts (Clark et al., Chapter 11 in this volume). In the Transition to Independence model, efforts focus on teaching youth skills that promote personal choice, social responsibility, self-sufficiency, and confidence (Clark & Davis, 2000). For youth leaving juvenile correction facilities, Project SUPPORT instituted self-directed planning and focused guidance to assist youth in transitioning back to their communities (Unruh et al., Chapter 12 in this volume). Finally, the ARIES project emphasized self-determination within the context of individualized planning supported by a transition specialist (Bullis, Moran, Todis, Benz, & Johnson, 2002). Although the unique contributions of these self-determination components cannot be isolated from the remainder of the program, all five programs show evidence of promise as effective transition intervention packages for youth with a range of emotional and behavioral challenges.

## CURRENT EFFORTS TO PROMOTE SELF-DETERMINATION SKILLS AND OPPORTUNITIES

Despite the importance placed on and progress made in promoting self-determination among youth with disabilities, the extent to which typical practices for youth with EBD have shifted to fully reflect this new emphasis has not kept pace. Too often, a considerable gap exists between the value educators and service providers report placing on self-determination and the efforts they actually make to promote it (Grigal et al., 2003; Thoma, Nathanson, Baker, & Tamura, 2002; Wehmeyer, Agran, et al., 2000). The following section contains a review of research addressing what currently is known about the self-determination skills and capacities of youth with EBD, the extent to which schools provide opportunities for youth to learn and practice these skills, and the potential influence on postschool outcomes. These research findings clearly illustrate the need for a substantial shift in secondary emphases if youth with EBD are to leave high school well equipped for adulthood.

### Skills That Enhance Self-Determination

To what extent do youth with EBD display skills, knowledge, and attitudes that reflect self-determination? The answer seems to be that it varies. Relative to youth with learning disabilities, teachers and parents rate youth with EBD as having significantly less knowledge about self-determination, diminished ability to engage in self-determined behavior, and limited confidence regarding the effectiveness of their self-determination efforts (Carter, Lane, Pierson, & Glaeser, 2006; Carter, Trainor, Owens et al., in press). Similarly, findings from the National Longitudinal Transition Study-2 indicate that youth with EBD are more likely than any other disability group to evidence difficulties in the areas of self-advocacy and persistence (Wagner et al., 2003). Other studies reveal that youth with or at-risk for EBD who are receiving educational services within juvenile justice or alternative educational settings may know less about self-determination and the behaviors it requires (Houchins, 2002; Van Gelder, Sitlington, & Pugh, 2008). Collectively, these research studies suggest that the instructional needs in the area of self-determination for youth with EBD may be even more pronounced than those of youth with other disabilities. Still, it is both appropriate and important to acknowledge that considerable variability in perceived self-determination capacity exists across different youth with EBD. Indeed, even individual students are likely to engage in some aspects of self-determination (for example, choice making, risk taking, independence) more fluently and effectively than others (for example, problem solving, self-advocacy).

## Opportunities That Enhance Self-Determination

The acquisition of knowledge and skills that enhance self-determination is clearly influenced by the opportunities students receive in school, at home, and elsewhere to practice, refine, and maintain those skills (Carter et. al., 2006; Mithaug et al., 2003). Indeed, providing youth with quality instruction and regular practice opportunities are necessarily intertwined. The impact of instructional interventions will always remain limited if opportunities to be self-determining are not provided or are actively discouraged. Similarly, the self-determination opportunities provided by schools will be missed if youth lack the skills needed to engage in self-determined behaviors and access those opportunities (Wehmeyer et al., 2000).

Yet research suggests that efforts to promote the self-determination of youth with EBD in secondary schools may be incidental, uneven, or altogether absent (Mason et al., 2004; Zhang et al., 2005). Thoma et al. (2002) found that two thirds of special educators believed that the training they had received to facilitate self-determination was inadequate, and more than 90% were unfamiliar with commercially available person-centered planning tools and curricula. Wehmeyer et, Agran, and Hughes (2000) reported that the implementation of strategies to promote self-determination was inconsistent among special educators. Moreover, the individualized education programs (IEPs) of youth with disabilities rarely include goals related to self-determination (Mason et al., 2004; Powers et al., 2005). The opportunities that youth with EBD receive to learn about self-determination also may be influenced by where they receive their education (Geenen, Powers, Hogansen, & Pittman, 2007; Van Gelder et al., 2008). For example, more restrictive educational placements may offer somewhat limited opportunities for youth to engage in choice making, make independent decisions, advocate for their needs, or assume leadership roles.

The perspectives of youth also provide valuable insight into the extent to which self-determination is encouraged or stifled during the transition years. For example, in a national study in which youth with EBD were asked how much they enjoyed high school, 31% said "a little" and 16.6% said "not at all" (Wagner et al., 2007). The high levels of dissatisfaction with and increasing disengagement from school voiced by some youth with EBD offer another indicator of their perceptions of their self-determination opportunities. Qualitative interview and focus group studies suggest that many youth with EBD have difficulty seeing how their experiences in school connect to the rest of their lives and believe they are rarely given opportunities to have a voice in their own education and transition planning (Kortering, Braziel, & Tompkins, 2002; Trainor, 2005).

## Influence on the Postschool Attainments of Youth

Limited skills and opportunities in the area of self-determination may coalesce with other factors to shape the outcomes that youth with EBD experience after leaving high school. If the postschool outcomes of youth with disabilities serve as a meaningful indicator of the effectiveness of secondary transition services, it is clear that substantial numbers of young adults with EBD are leaving school without the skills and experiences they need to navigate adulthood successfully. Too often, the years immediately following high school are characterized by high rates of unemployment or underemployment, diminished community involvement, limited postsecondary enrollment, restrictive living arrangements, and frequent encounters with the judicial system (Armstrong, Dedrick, & Greenbaum, 2003; Osgood, Foster, Flanagan, & Ruth, 2005; Wood & Cronin, 1999; Zigmond, 2006). These postschool outcomes issue a clear call challenging high schools to design and deliver learning experiences that increase the capacities and opportunities for youth with EBD to become self-determined.

## PROMISING PRACTICES FOR PROMOTING SELF-DETERMINATION AMONG YOUTH WITH EBD

Enhancing the self-determination of youth with EBD will require more concerted efforts on the part of schools, service providers, families, and others. Although recommended practices in this area are still evolving, an emerging research base is now available upon which educators and service providers can draw. This section reviews just some of what currently is known about promising approaches and avenues for equipping youth with EBD with the skills and experiences or opportunities that can enhance their self-determination. These recommended practices are illustrated with a high-school student named Anthony.

> Like most 10th graders at Whitman High School, Anthony had big ideas for life after high school. He wanted to live in a nice apartment, make lots of money, and hang out with his friends. When his father pressed him about where he would live, the type of job he would like to have, the classes and training he would need to get hired at such a job, and how he would contribute to his community, however, Anthony had very little to say. He had never really thought about such details and seemed content to wait around for someone else to make it all happen. After all, no one at school took much time to help him think through what it would really take for him to attain his goals for adulthood.

### Exploring Self-Determination Within the Transition Assessment Process

Meaningful assessment is considered central to effective transition planning. The Individuals with Disabilities Education Improvement Act (2004) explicitly mandates that the postsecondary goals of transition-age youth with disabilities be "based upon age-appropriate transition assessments" (§300.320(b)), requiring that transition planning teams more explicitly link instruction, services, and supports to students' strengths, interests, preferences, and needs across an array of relevant domains. Self-determination, therefore, represents an important domain for planning teams to consider during the assessment process (Field & Hoffman, 2007). Unless self-determination is addressed explicitly as an integral part of ongoing assessment efforts, however, it is likely to be overlooked as a focus of transition services.

As with most transition domains, self-determination is best assessed by incorporating the perspectives of multiple stakeholders who know the student well and have had varied opportunities to spend time with him or her in different environments. Research has shown that youth with EBD are likely to perceive their strengths and needs related to self-determination and other transition-related skills more favorably than their parents and teachers (Carter et al., 2006; Carter & Wehby, 2003; Carter, Trainor, Sun, & Owens, 2009). This has important implications for the assessment process and highlights the importance of inviting youth to contribute their perspectives. Moreover, many aspects of self-determination (for example, goal setting, decision making, self-awareness) take place internally and are not always readily apparent to others. Involving youth in the assessment process not only ensures that they are aware of and can articulate their strengths, interests, preferences, and needs in this area, but the assessment process can itself become an avenue for learning skills and knowledge related to self-determination.

Because parents, teachers, and other service providers all have opportunities to get to know youth in different environments characterized by diverse sets of expectations and demands, it also is important to solicit their insights and observations of the student as well as their understandings of the meaning of self-determination. They may identify different indicators of self-determination as having greater importance or relevance than others. Ensuring that multiple perspectives are gathered during the assessment process can help planning teams compile a more complete and comprehensive portrait of a student's strengths and needs in this domain.

An array of formal and informal assessment tools are available to assist planning teams in identifying students' strengths and needs related to self-determination, developing educational and transition goals, and monitoring progress toward those goals over time (see Field & Hoffman, 2007). For example, the AIR Self-Determination Scale (Wolman, Campeau, DuBois, Mithaug, & Stolarski, 1994) is a 30-item tool designed to provide information about students' capacity for (that is, their ability to perform, perceptions of the efficacy of, and knowledge about self-determination behaviors) and opportunities (at school and at home) to engage in self-determined behavior. The perspectives of teachers, parents, and youth themselves can be compiled and compared, serving as a springboard for additional discussion and transition planning. The Arc's Self-Determination Scale (Wehmeyer & Kelchner, 1995) is a 72-item tool enabling youth to assess their own strengths and needs in the area of self-determination, as well as providing information that can be used to set goals in collaboration with their teachers. Items address areas related to autonomy, self-regulation, psychological empowerment, and self-realization. The Self-Determination Assessment Battery (Field, Hoffman, & Sawilowsky, 2004) includes both written assessments and observational checklists that can be used to examine youth, teacher, and parent perspectives on knowledge, behaviors, and affect related to self-determination. In addition, interviews, observations, checklists, person-centered planning meetings, and situational assessments all represent appropriate informal avenues for assessing strengths and needs in this area.

> Ms. Moss, a transition teacher at Whitman, recognized the importance of involving Anthony more actively in making decisions about his own future and actively taking steps to move forward toward his goals. She asked Anthony and his father to each complete a brief self-determination assessment to learn how they viewed Anthony's strengths and needs related to areas such as setting goals, making choices, taking action, and evaluating progress, as well as the opportunities he had at school and elsewhere to learn about and practice being self-determined. At the next IEP meeting, they highlighted areas in which they shared similar perspectives and discussed areas of disagreement. All agreed that Anthony knew his own strengths, interests, and needs, but acknowledged that he had difficulties effectively communicating these issues to others, advocating for needed help or information, and taking steps to work toward his goals. They also realized that Anthony currently had relatively few opportunities to learn these skills in the classroom and at home.

## Emphasizing Self-Determination as an Instructional Priority

Recommended practices suggest that instructional programs should intentionally and explicitly address self-determination within the curriculum for youth with EBD (Eisenman, 2007; Kohler & Field, 2003). Instruction typically occurs at the level of component elements that contribute to self-determination, including choice making; decision making; problem solving; goal setting and attainment; self-regulation and self-management; independence, risk-taking, and safety skills; self-advocacy and leadership; self-awareness; and self-knowledge (Wehmeyer & Field, 2007). Not only is there abundant evidence that these skills can be systematically taught, but research clearly demonstrates that the impact on the outcomes of youth can be quite substantial (Algozzine et al., 2001; Mooney et al., 2005; Test, Fowler, Brewer, & Wood, 2005).

Unfortunately, less research has been focused on the most effective approaches for teaching these component self-determination skills. Meta-analytic work suggests that combining multiple elements of self-determination within comprehensive instructional packages may be more effective than teaching individual skills in isolation (Cobb, Lehman, Newman-Gonchar, & Alwell, 2008). For example, teachers might combine experiences that allow students to explore strengths and interests with explicit instruction on choice-making, goal-setting, problem-solving, and self-evaluation skills. This comprehensive emphasis is reflected in most of the published curricular packages focused on promoting student involvement and self-determination (Test et al., 2000). In addition, educators should (1) link instructional efforts directly to those areas of need identified during the transition assessment process, (2) address self-determination component skills that are highly valued and most likely to be reinforced by others, (3) align instruction so that it addresses the type of deficit (that is, acquisition, performance, fluency) evidenced by youth, and (4) deliver instruction frequently and across multiple settings (Gresham, Sugai, & Horner, 2001).

> Ms. Moss, Anthony, Anthony's father, and the other members of the IEP team all agreed that it would be beneficial to include goals related to self-determination in Anthony's IEP. This would help ensure that consistent efforts were made across the school day to enhance Anthony's skills in these areas. One goal focused on creating opportunities for Anthony to strengthen his communication and self-advocacy skills. The other focused on teaching Anthony self-management strategies so he could keep track of his progress and make needed adjustments along

the way. His teachers agreed that these were goals that Anthony could work on within each of his various classes.

## Addressing Self-Determination Alongside Social and Other Related Skills

The effectiveness of self-determination intervention efforts is likely to be less than optimal unless youths' other related instructional and support needs are addressed concurrently. Self-determination is usually evidenced within a social context, such as during transition planning meetings, during interactions with peers, while working with teachers in the classroom, or through interactions with coworkers or supervisors. Indeed, expressing one's preferences, discussing future post school plans, asking others for advice, recruiting needed assistance and support, advocating for one's needs, and leading a planning meeting all include social aspects. Therefore, the effectiveness of self-determined behaviors may be enhanced when youth also possess greater social competence. Because many youth with EBD exhibit social-related skill deficits (Lane, Carter, Pierson, & Glaeser, 2006), self-determination instruction is likely to be maximized when it is combined with social skills instruction. Research suggests that individuals who possess greater social competence may be able to perform self-determined behaviors in more effective and socially acceptable ways (Carter, Trainor, Owens et al., in press; Pierson, Carter, Lane, & Glaeser, 2008). Whether or not youth are skilled socially can also influence the extent to which their self-determination efforts are either supported or punished by others. In other words, efforts to self-determine can be interpreted by others as challenging behavior. Addressing social and self-determination skill deficits in connection with each other may even provide a more effective, comprehensive, and engaging intervention approach for youth with EBD.

> Anthony had a reputation for having somewhat of a "quick temper." He often got frustrated when he couldn't express himself clearly to others, and the result could sometimes be a clash. Ms. Moss knew that Anthony would benefit from additional opportunities to learn effective communication strategies and to practice these social skills with others. Otherwise, his attempts to advocate for himself could inadvertently be misinterpreted as confrontational or argumentative. She

worked with the school counselor to identify a research-based curriculum that Anthony and others in his class might benefit from receiving.

## Supporting Student Involvement in Transition Planning

The importance of promoting student involvement in educational planning is clearly emphasized throughout special education law and policy (Individuals with Disabilities Education Improvement Act, 2004; President's Commission on Excellence in Special Education, 2002). Youth who are more actively involved in their own transition planning are expected to be more motivated—and more likely—to work toward and ultimately accomplish their goals for life during and after high school. But students also must be equipped with the skills, knowledge, and attitudes needed to participate actively, meaningfully, and effectively.

The transition planning process offers an ideal context to teach, support, and reinforce the skills and dispositions that can enhance self-determination. For example, Snyder and colleagues taught youth with EBD to introduce members of the IEP team, review their past goals and performance, discuss their future IEP goals, and adjourn the meeting (Snyder, 2002; Snyder & Shapiro, 1997). Such meetings provide meaningful opportunities for youth to learn to set personal short- and long-term goals; become more aware of and learn to articulate their strengths, interests, preferences, and needs; reflect on their progress over the previous year; and communicate their need for specific opportunities, supports, or linkages (Test et al., 2005). Successfully leading a meeting can also increase students' confidence and promote greater sense of ownership for working toward and meeting their goals.

Yet this avenue for self-determination continues to represent a missed opportunity for many youth with disabilities. According to the National Longitudinal Transition Study 2, teachers reported that 6% of youth with EBD did not attend their planning meeting; 30.4% were present but provided little input; 52.8% were moderately active participants; and only 10.8% were reported to have taken a leadership role (Cameto, Levine, & Wagner, 2004). For most youth, playing a central role in transition planning will require advance preparation. Several programs and curricular materials have been designed to prepare youth with disabilities for their IEP meeting using a fairly structured approach.

In particular, *Self-Directed IEP* (Martin, Marshall, Maxson, & Jerman, 1993), *Whose Future Is it Anyway?* (Wehmeyer et al., 2004), *TAKE CHARGE for the Future* (Powers, Ellison, Matuszewski, & Turner, 2004), and *NEXT S.T.E.P.* (Halpern, Herr, Doren, & Wolf, 2000) have all been evaluated in studies involving youth with EBD. At the same time, youth will also need instruction in how to effectively navigate differing perspectives or disagreements with other team-planning members related to their education.

> Recognizing that planning meetings can provide a mean-ingful—and safe—context for practicing self-advocacy and leadership skills, Anthony worked with Ms. Moss throughout the semester to prepare to lead his next IEP meeting. He personally invited all of the participants, made introductions at the start of the meeting, described his strengths and future goals, discussed his progress to date, and shared what help and instruction he thought he would need to achieve his goals. Anthony even created a brief PowerPoint to help him commu-nicate important points to the team. He then invited others to share their perspectives on what they thought he might need to prepare for a successful transition. He was surprised at how different the tone of the meeting was when others were talking to him, rather than about him.

## Offering Authentic Learning Opportunities

High-school redesign efforts have emphasized the importance of coupling a rigorous curriculum with relevant learning experiences. This emphasis means that educational experiences should be engaging for youth, draw upon and expand their interests and future aspirations, and equip them with the varied life skills they will need to experience a high quality of life. For example, service learning, school-based enterprises, internships, school-sponsored work experiences, extracurricular clubs, and other career development or vocational experiences have been advocated as providing authentic contexts within which youth with EBD can learn and apply skills that enhance their self-determination (Carter & Lunsford, 2005; Eisenman, 2007). Such contexts provide students with opportunities to better understand and broaden their strengths, goals, and interests, as well as to apply self-determination skills within the environments in which they will actually need them. These contexts can also increase students' awareness of new options and possibilities related to future careers, leisure activities, and lifestyle choices, information that is essential to making meaningful, informed decisions about issues that matter. At the same time, self-determination can be shaped by the competencies youth possess in other transition areas, such as academics, career development, leisure and recreation, daily living, and community skills. Self-determination can be enhanced when youth are more skilled in these related areas, and youth are likely to become more competent when they are more self-determining. Because many youth with EBD typically have limited access to these hands-on learning experiences and career development programs (Wagner & Davis, 2006), planning teams must be very intentional about ensuring that the full range of curricular offerings are considered for these youth.

> During the IEP meeting, everyone brainstormed ways in which Anthony might experience learning opportunities that would help further his transition goals and provide him with opportunities to learn about and practice important self-determination skills. One teacher suggested that Anthony consider joining the DECA club, which would help him develop his entrepreneurial skills and explore leadership responsibilities within the club. Another teacher mentioned the newly formed business education partnership, in which local employers volunteered to mentor high-school students in various career areas. Having a willing mentor and an off-campus work experience could provide Anthony with a more meaningful context for making choices about his future and adjusting his actions when things did not go as he anticipated.

## Addressing Self-Determination Within the General Curriculum

Legislative and policy efforts to increase accountability, raise standards, and promote access to the general curriculum are affecting both the location and focus of instruction for youth with EBD. With the general education classroom emerging as the primary instructional context for increasing numbers of youth with disabilities, concerns have been raised about the feasibility of promoting self-determination instruction within the core curriculum (Sitlington & Neubert, 2004). Research suggests, however, that the dual goals of promoting inclusion and fostering self-determination are not incompatible and may, in fact, enhance each other. Carter, Lane et al. (2008) found that both general and special education high-school teachers attached considerable importance to providing instruction addressing seven skills related to self-determination (for example, problem solving, self-management, decision making) and reported teaching these skills somewhat regularly within their classrooms. Moreover, state curricular standards often address self-determination component elements, suggesting that self-determination may have an integral place in the secondary curriculum for all students (Wehmeyer & Field, 2007). Such findings bolster calls to further infuse self-determination instruction throughout the general education curriculum rather than addressing it exclusively as a curricular "add-on" or adjunct. Although opportunities for promoting self-determination clearly exist in general education classes, it is essential that teachers carefully examine whether and how the curriculum in these classrooms may need to be adapted or augmented to ensure that youth with EBD are accessing available instruction and ultimately acquiring targeted skills. Simply being enrolled in or even sitting in an inclusive classroom does not ensure that youth are accessing the curriculum delivered within that setting.

Recent advances in the areas of self-directed learning strategies are revealing new avenues for helping youth with EBD capitalize on self-determination opportunities within the classroom that also promote academic benefits. In their systematic research review, Mooney et al. (2005) found that teaching self-management strategies (that is, self-monitoring, self-evaluation, self-instruction, goal setting, strategy instruction) produced a large positive impact on the academic outcomes of students with EBD. Applying these self-management strategies within general education classrooms may offer an avenue for increasing both engagement and academic performance. For example, the Self-Determined Learning Model of Instruction has been identified as an evidence-based practice for promoting both self-determination and access to the general curriculum (Martin et al., 2003; Palmer, Wehmeyer, Gipson, & Agran, 2004). This three-phase instructional process involves teaching students to (1) set learning goals, (2) develop and implement a plan to meet those goals, and (3) evaluate progress and make adjustments toward meeting their goals. The same process also can be applied effectively to help youth work toward their career development and other transition-related goals (Benitez, Lattimore, & Wehmeyer, 2005).

It should be noted, however, that some skills related to self-determination—such as leadership skills, self-advocacy skills, and self-awareness—may require additional instructional attention outside of the classroom. For example, these skills may best be promoted within educational planning meetings, self-advocacy groups, and youth leadership activities (Pocock et al., 2002; Test et al., 2005). Moreover, youth with EBD may benefit from additional, more explicit, and systematic instruction to acquire certain self-determination skills (Carter et al., 2006; Eisenman, 2007).

> After the IEP meeting, the school counselor pointed out to Ms. Moss that skills related to goal setting, choice making, problem solving, self-evaluation, and leadership were ones that many students at Whitman struggled with. He suggested that they look more closely at the ways in which other teachers were embedding instruction related to these skills into their classrooms. At the same time, he mentioned that he could work with the other school counselors to explore ways of providing more focused instruction to students as part of a supplemental intervention strategy.

## Partnering with Parents and Caregivers in Culturally Responsive Ways

Although youth spend a substantial portion of their week at school or with friends, the critical role families can play in supporting—or hindering—self-determination should not be overlooked. Differences reported in the perspectives and priorities related to self-determination among educators and parents highlight the importance of discussing their understandings of self-determination and efforts to promote it in each context (Carter et al., 2006). Although promoting family involvement is widely acknowledged as a core and best practice in secondary transition (Cheney & Osher, 1997; Kohler & Field, 2003), such collaborative relationships continue to be elusive in many schools. Moreover, parents and caregivers may hold different values and beliefs regarding self-determination than do educators or other members of the planning team (Trainor, 2002). When educators and parents regularly communicate and work together to identify priority self-determination skills and to encourage and reinforce their use across settings, the in- and postschool outcomes youth experience are likely to be enhanced. It is essential that planning teams strive to gather a clear understanding of parents' expectations related to self-determination. Schools might also explore approaches for helping parents learn more about and support self-determination among their children (Zhang & Benz, 2006). Such efforts, however, may be particularly challenging for youth living in foster care, juvenile justice, or other out-of-home placements.

> Anthony's father was really impressed with the way that Anthony had "stepped up" and took a leadership role at the IEP meeting. It was a side to Anthony he had rarely seen before. At home, he began trying to gradually provide Anthony with more responsibilities around the house and spoke more frequently with his son about Anthony's future goals and the decisions that Anthony was making to achieve those goals. Periodically, he talked with Ms. Moss by phone to share ideas for encouraging and supporting Anthony to assume greater responsibility for his future.

## Addressing Self-Determination Early and Across the Grade Span

The development of self-determination is a lifelong endeavor—one that begins at an early age, continues throughout one's school career, and extends into adulthood (Sands & Doll, 1996). Although high school represents an opportune time to address many elements of self-determination, several factors highlight the importance of laying an early foundation for students with EBD. Early withdrawal and high dropout rates for youth with EBD continue to be alarming and call attention to the need to equip youth with skills and opportunities they need to self-determine. Disengagement in school often begins early and progresses over time rather than occurring in a discrete event in high school. Recognizing that efforts beginning in high school simply begin too late, Eisenman (2007) advised that an earlier emphasis on promoting self-determination should comprise one element of schools' dropout prevention efforts. Unfortunately, intentional efforts to promote student involvement and self-determination often do not begin until high school if at all.

Opportunities for building a foundation for self-determination are available throughout the elementary and middle-school curriculum (Stang, Carter, Lane, & Pierson, 2009), but they usually look somewhat different from efforts made in high school. Younger children differ in their capacities and expectations related to self-determination, so instruction should be adapted to reflect the interests, needs, capacities, and experiences of children (Palmer & Wehmeyer, 2003). In elementary school, this might involve teaching children to set short-term goals, evaluate their own class work, and use basic self-management strategies. In middle school, children might become more involved in making decisions about their classes, requesting needed accommodations and supports, leading their own IEP meetings, and exploring their interests and strengths through extracurricular clubs, elective courses, and after-school activities. These efforts should begin early in the elementary grades and increase in prominence throughout middle and high school. To infuse self-determination throughout the grade span, coordinated efforts across the school levels may be needed to ensure that these instructional and practice opportunities are consistently offered and appropriately accessible. Moreover, as our profession learns more about effective strategies for promoting self-determination among adolescents, efforts should be made to systematically extend these strategies downward.

> Over time, Anthony became more and more confident in his ability to take charge of his own future. But it was definitely an ongoing process. He did not always make the best choices, and he often got frustrated when things did not go as he had expected. Still, Anthony appreciated having a greater voice in his own transition and he liked having the opportunity to assume more responsibilities. He also knew he had the support of his team along the way.

## EMERGING DIRECTIONS FOR RESEARCH AND PRACTICE

Educators and administrators must be intentional about ensuring that promoting self-determination for youth with EBD is an instructional priority reflected both in the guiding values and everyday practices of the school. Faced with the multifaceted academic, social, behavioral, vocational, and other needs evidenced by youth with EBD, educators may not always consider promoting self-determination the highest educational priority. However, promoting self-determination should be considered throughout all aspects of transition education—assessment, planning, instruction, and evaluation. It should be apparent in the IEP and transition goals of youth and evidenced in the nature of the interactions that take place during informal and formal planning meetings. It should also be reflected in the culture of the school as well as in classroom- and school-level practices (Field & Hoffman, 2002). At the same time, elementary-, middle-, and high-school teachers must recognize the importance of promoting self-determination, feel prepared to teach these skills, and know how to seamlessly integrate self-determination instruction across the grade span.

All of the above, however, is predicated on the extent to which educators, paraprofessionals, school counselors, administrators, and other service providers are aware of the importance of self-determination and receive training on recommended or evidence-based practices for fostering self-determination. Unfortunately, preservice training and professional development opportunities for future and current teachers remains fairly limited (Wehmeyer, Agran, et al., 2000; Thoma et al., 2002). Although a number of curricular resources, assessment tools, research syntheses, and practitioner articles have emerged during the last decade, the extent to which teachers are accessing these resources for their work remains limited. The leadership of school administrators and program directors is essential here because they can be instrumental in both developing a vision for self-determination at their schools and ensuring that sufficient resources and professional development opportunities are available to their staff.

At the same time, additional research efforts are needed to establish a depth of evidence-based practices for promoting self-determination truly responsive to and reflective of the diversity of educational settings and contexts within which youth with EBD are served. The majority of empirical research evaluating efforts to promote self-determination has focused on youth with learning disabilities or significant intellectual disabilities. The extent to which these intervention strategies may need to be adapted or expanded to reflect the unique emotional and behavioral challenges displayed by youth with EBD has yet to be fully explored. Establishing the possibilities and boundaries of these strategies will certainly necessitate closer partnerships among researchers and schools, adult service providers, families, and others. At the same time, we know relatively little about the long-term outcomes associated with the efforts secondary schools make to promote self-determination. Longitudinal research examining the short- and long-term impact of self-determination instruction on the lives and outcomes of youth could shed important light on how the experiences youth have during secondary school shape and support their attainment of a meaningful and productive life into and throughout adulthood.

## CONCLUSION

A successful high-school experience must be defined by more than such outcomes as receiving a diploma, finding a job, or getting into college. It also includes acquiring the skills, knowledge, and attitudes that enable youth to chart their future course in meaningful ways and valued directions. Self-determination develops over time as youth accrue varied experiences, acquire new skills, and encounter new challenges. Structuring these instructional, curricular, and other learning opportunities to promote student self-determination is an essential component of effective secondary transition services. Indeed, these lifelong skills can shape the trajectories and outcomes of youth throughout high school and into adulthood. Much remains to be learned about how the skills, attitudes, and knowledge youth acquire interact with the school opportunities and emerging demands of adolescence to foster self-determination. As educators and researchers, our charge is to discover, share, and implement these effective strategies.

## REFERENCES

Algozzine, B., Browder, D., Karvonen, M., Test, D. W., & Wood, W. M. (2001). Effects of interventions to promote self-determination for individuals with disabilities. *Review of Educational Research, 71,* 219–277.

Armstrong, K. H., Dedrick, R. F., & Greenbaum, P. E. (2003). Factors associated with community adjustment of young adults with serious emotional disturbance: A longitudinal analysis. *Journal of Emotional and Behavioral Disorders, 11,* 66–76.

Benitez, D. T., Lattimore, J., & Wehmeyer, M. L. (2005). Promoting the involvement of students with emotional and behavioral disorders in career and vocational planning and decision-making: The self-determined career development model. *Behavioral Disorders, 30,* 431–447.

Bullis, M., Moran, T., Todis, B., Benz, M., & Johnson, M. (2002). Description and evaluation of the ARIES project: Achieving rehabilitation, individualized education, and employment success for adolescents with emotional disturbance. *Career Development for Exceptional Individuals, 25,* 41–58.

Cameto, R., Levine, P., & Wagner, M. (2004). *Transition planning for students with disabilities. A special topic report of findings from the National Longitudinal Transition Study-2.* Menlo Park, CA: SRI International.

Carter, E. W., Lane, K. L., Pierson, M. R., & Glaeser, B. (2006). Self-determination skills and opportunities of transition-age youth with emotional disturbance and learning disabilities. *Exceptional Children, 72,* 333–346.

Carter, E. W., Lane, K. L., Pierson, M. R., & Stang, K. K. (2008). Promoting self-determination for transition-age youth: Views of high school general and special educators. *Exceptional Children, 75,* 55–70.

Carter, E. W., & Lunsford, L. B. (2005). Meaningful work: Preparing transition-age youth with emotional and behavioral disorders for employment. *Preventing School Failure, 49*(2), 63–69.

Carter, E. W., Trainor, A. A., Owens, L., Swedeen, B., & Sun, Y. (in press). Self-determination prospects of youth with high-incidence disabilities: Divergent perspectives and related factors. *Journal of Emotional and Behavioral Disorders.*

Carter, E. W., Trainor, A. A., Sun, Y., & Owens, L. (2009). Assessing the transition-related strengths and needs of adolescents with high-incidence disabilities. *Exceptional Children, 76,* 74–94.

Carter, E. W., & Wehby, J. H. (2003). Job performance of transition-age youth with emotional and behavioral disorders. *Exceptional Children, 69,* 449–465.

Cheney, D., & Bullis, M. (2004). The school-to-community transition of adolescents with emotional and behavioral disorders. In R. B. Rutherford, M. M. Quinn, & S. R. Mathur (Eds.), *Handbook of research in emotional and behavioral disorders* (pp. 369–384). New York: Guilford Press.

Cheney, D., & Osher, T. (1997). Target number four of the National Agenda for Youth with Serious Emotional Disturbance: Enhancing collaboration with families. *Journal of Emotional and Behavioral Disorders, 5,* 36–44.

Clark, H. B., & Davis, M. (Eds.). (2000). *Transition to adulthood: A resource for assisting young people with emotional or behavioral difficulties.* Baltimore: Paul H. Brookes.

Cobb, B., Lehman, J., Newman-Gonchar, R., & Alwell, M. (2008). *Self-determination for students with disabilities: A narrative meta-synthesis.* Charlotte, NC: National Secondary Transition Technical Assistance Center.

Deci, E. L., & Ryan, R. M. (Eds.). (2002). *Handbook of self-determination research.* Rochester: University of Rochester Press.

Eisenman, L. T. (2007). Self-determination interventions: Building a foundation for school completion. *Remedial and Special Education, 28,* 2–8.

Field, S., & Hoffman, A. (2002). Preparing youth to exercise self-determination: Quality indicators of school environments that promote the acquisition of knowledge, skills, and beliefs related to self-determination. *Journal of Disability Policy Studies, 13,* 113–118.

Field, S., & Hoffman, A. (2007). Self-determination in secondary transition assessment. *Assessment for Effective Intervention, 32,* 181–190.

Field, S., Hoffman, A., & Sawilowsky, S. (2004). *Self-determination assessment battery.* Detroit: Wayne State University Press.

Field, S. S., Martin, J. E., Miller, R. J., Ward, M., & Wehmeyer, M. L. (1998). Self-determination for persons with disabilities: A position statement of the Division on Career Development and Transition. *Career Development for Exceptional Individuals, 21,* 113–128.

Field, S., Sarver, M. D., & Shaw, S. F. (2003). Self-determination: A key to success in postsecondary education for students with learning disabilities. *Remedial and Special Education, 24,* 339–349.

Geenen, S. J., Powers, L. E., Hogansen, J. M., & Pittman, J. O. E. (2007). Youth with disabilities in foster care: Developing self-determination within a context of struggle and disempowerment. *Exceptionality, 15,* 17–30.

Gresham, F. M., Sugai, G., & Horner, R. H. (2001). Interpreting outcomes of social skills training for students with high-incidence disabilities. *Exceptional Children, 67,* 331–344.

Grigal, M., Neubert, D. A., Moon, M. S., & Graham, S. (2003). Self-determination for students with disabilities: Views of parents and teachers. *Exceptional Children, 70,* 97–112.

Hadre, P., & Reeve, J. (2003). A motivational model of rural students' intentions to persist in, versus drop out of, high school. *Journal of Educational Psychology, 92,* 347–356.

Halpern, A. S., Herr, C. M., Doren, B., & Wolf, N. K. (2000). *Next S.T.E.P.: Student transition and educational planning* (2nd ed.). Austin: Pro-Ed.

Houchins, D. E. (2002). Self-determination knowledge instruction and incarcerated students. *Emotional and Behavioural Difficulties, 7,* 132–151.

Hughes, C., Hwang, B., Kim, J., Killian, D. J., Harmer, M. L., & Alcantera, P. (1997). A preliminary validation of strategies that support the transition from school to adult life. *Career Development for Exceptional Individuals, 20,* 1–14.

Individuals with Disabilities Education Act of 1990, Pub. L. No. 101–476 (1990).

Individuals with Disabilities Education Act of 1997, Pub. L. No. 105–17 (1997).

Individuals with Disabilities Education Improvement Act of 2004, Pub. L. No. 108–446 (2004).

Johnson, D. R., Stodden, R. A., Emanuel, E. J., Luecking, R., & Mack, M. (2002). Current challenges facing secondary education and transition services: What research tells us. *Exceptional Children, 68,* 519–531.

Kohler, P., & Field, S. (2003). Transition-focused education: Foundation for the future. *Journal of Special Education, 37,* 174–184.

Kortering, L. J., Braziel, P. M., & Tompkins, J. R. (2002). The challenge of school completion among youths with behavioral disorders: Another side of the story. *Behavioral Disorders, 27,* 142–154.

Lane, K. L., Carter, E. W., Pierson, M. R., & Glaeser, B. C. (2006). Academic, social, and behavioral characteristics of high school students with emotional disturbances or learning disabilities. *Journal of Emotional and Behavioral Disorders, 14,* 108–117.

Martin, J. E., Marshall, L., Maxson, L. L., & Jerman, P. (1993). *Self-directed IEP.* Longmont, CO: Sopris West.

Martin, J. E., Mithaug, D. E., Cox, P., Peterson, L. Y., Van Dycke, J. L., & Cash, M. E. (2003). Increasing self-determination: Teaching students to plan, work, evaluate, and adjust. *Exceptional Children, 69,* 431–447.

Martin, J. E., Van Dycke, J. L., Greene, B. A., Gardner, J. E., Christensen, W. R., Woods, L. L., & Lovett, D.L. (2006). Direct observation of teacher-directed IEP meetings: Establishing the need for student IEP meeting instruction. *Exceptional Children, 72,* 187–200.

Mason, C., Field, S., & Sawilowsky, S. (2004). Implementation of self-determination activities and student participation in IEPs. *Exceptional Children, 70,* 441–451.

Mithaug, D. E., Mithaug, D., Agran, M., Martin, J., & Wehmeyer, M. L. (Eds.). (2003). *Self-determined learning theory: Construction, verification, and evaluation.* Mahwah, NJ: Lawrence Erlbaum.

Mooney, P., Ryan, J. B., Uhing, B. M., Reid, R., & Epstein, M. H. (2005). A review of self-management interventions targeting academic outcomes for students with emotional and behavioral disorders. *Journal of Behavioral Education, 14,* 203–221.

Osgood, D. W., Foster, E. M., Flanagan, C., & Ruth, G. R. (Eds.). (2005). *On your own without a net: The transition to adulthood for vulnerable populations.* Chicago: University of Chicago Press.

Palmer, S. B., & Wehmeyer, M. L. (2003). Promoting self-determination in early elementary school: Teaching self-regulated problem-solving and goal-setting skills. *Remedial and Special Education, 24,* 115–126.

Palmer, S. B., Wehmeyer, M. L., Gipson, K., & Agran, M. (2004). Promoting access to the general curriculum by teaching self-determination skills. *Exceptional Children, 70,* 427–439.

Pierson, M. R., Carter, E. W., Lane, K. L., & Glaeser, B. (2008). Factors influencing the self-determination of transition-age youth with high incidence disabilities. *Career Development for Exceptional Individuals, 31,* 115–125.

Pocock, A., Lambros, S., Karvonen, M., Test, D. W., Algozzine, B., Wood, W., & Martin, J. E. (2002). Successful strategies for promoting self-advocacy among students with LD: The LEAD group. *Intervention in School and Clinic, 37,* 209–216.

Powers, K. M., Gil-Kashiwabara, E., Geenan, S. J., Powers, L., Balandran, J., & Palmer, C. (2005). Mandates and effective transition planning practices reflected in IEPs. *Career Development for Exceptional Individuals, 28,* 47–59.

Powers, L. E., Ellison, R., Matuszewski, J., & Turner, A. (2004). *TAKE CHARGE for the future.* Portland, OR: Portland State University Regional Resource Center.

President's Commission on Excellence in Special Education. (2002). *A new era: Revitalizing special education for children and their families.* Washington, DC: U. S. Department of Education, Office of Special Education and Rehabilitative Services.

Sands, D. J., & Doll, B. (1996). Fostering self-determination is a developmental task. *The Journal of Special Education, 30,* 58–76.

Shogren, K. A., Faggella-Luby, M. N., Bae, S. J., & Wehmeyer, M. L. (2004). The effect of choice-making for problem behavior: A meta-analysis. *Journal of Positive Behavioral Interventions, 6,* 228–237.

Sitlington, P. L., & Neubert, D. A. (2004). Preparing youth with emotional or behavioral disorders for transition to adult life: Can it be done within the standards-based reform movement? *Behavioral Disorders, 29,* 279–288.

Snyder, E. P. (2002). Teaching students with combined behavioral disorders and mental retardation to lead their own IEP meetings. *Behavioral Disorders, 27,* 340–357.

Snyder, E. P., & Shapiro, E. S. (1997). Teaching students with emotional/behavioral disorders the skills to participate in the development of their own IEPs. *Behavioral Disorders, 22,* 246–249.

Stang, K. K., Carter, E. W., Lane, K. L., & Pierson, M. R. (2009). Perspectives of general and special educators on fostering self-determination in elementary and middle schools. *The Journal of Special Education, 43,* 94–106.

Test, D. W., Fowler, C. H., Brewer, D. M., & Wood, W. M. (2005). A content and methodological review of self-advocacy intervention studies. *Exceptional Children, 72,* 101–125.

Test, D. W., Karvonen, M., Wood, W. M., Browder, D., & Algozzine, B. (2000). Choosing a self-determination curriculum. *Teaching Exceptional Children, 33*(2), 48–54.

Thoma, C. A., Nathanson, R., Baker, S. R., & Tamura, R. (2002). Self-determination: What do special educators know and where do they learn it? *Remedial and Special Education, 23,* 242–247.

Trainor, A. A. (2002). Self-determination for students with learning disabilities: Is it a universal value? *International Journal of Qualitative Studies in Education, 15,* 711–725.

Trainor, A. A. (2005). Self-determination perceptions and behaviors of diverse students with LD during the transition process. *Journal of Learning Disabilities, 38,* 233–249.

Unruh, D., & Bullis, M. (2005). Facility-to-community transition needs for adjudicated youth with disabilities. *Career Development for Exceptional Individuals, 28,* 67–79.

Van Gelder, N., Sitlington, P. L., & Pugh, K. M. (2008). Perceived self-determination of youth with emotional and behavior disorders: A pilot study of the effect of different educational environments. *Journal of Disability Policy Studies, 19,* 182–190.

Wagner, M., & Davis, M. (2006). How are we preparing students with emotional disturbances for the transition to young adulthood? Findings from the National Longitudinal Transition Study-2. *Journal of Emotional and Behavioral Disorders, 14,* 86–98.

Wagner, M., Marder, C., Blackorby, J., Cameto, R., Newman, L., Levine, P., & Davies-Mercier, E. (2003). *The achievements of youth with disabilities during secondary school: A report from the National Longitudinal Transition Study-2*. Menlo Park, CA: SRI International.

Wagner, M., Newman, L., Cameto, R., Levine, P., & Marder, C . (2007). *Perceptions and expectations of youth with disabilities*. Menlo Park, CA: SRI International.

Wehmeyer, M. L. (1999). A functional model of self-determination: Describing development and implementing instruction. *Focus on Autism and Other Developmental Disabilities, 14,* 53–61.

Wehmeyer, M. L., Agran, M., & Hughes, C. (2000). A national survey of teachers' promotion of self-determination and student-directed learning. *The Journal of Special Education, 34,* 58–68.

Wehmeyer, M. L., Bersani, H., & Gagne, R. (2000). Riding the third wave: Self-determination and self-advocacy in the 21st century. *Focus on Autism and Other Developmental Disabilities, 15,* 106–115.

Wehmeyer, M. L., & Field, S. (2007). *Instructional and assessment strategies to promote the self-determination of students with disabilities*. Thousand Oaks, CA: Corwin Press.

Wehmeyer, M. L., & Kelchner, K. (1995). *The Arc's Self-Determination Scale*. Arlington, TX: The Arc of the United States.

Wehmeyer, M. L., Lawrence, M., Kelchner, K., Palmer, S., Garner, N., & Soukup, J. (2004). *Whose future is it anyway? A student-directed transition planning process* (2nd ed.). Lawrence, KS: Beach Center on Disability.

Wehmeyer, M. L., & Palmer, S. B. (2003). Adult outcomes for students with cognitive disabilities three years after high school: The impact of self-determination. *Education and Training in Developmental Disabilities, 38,* 131–144.

Wehmeyer, M. L., & Schwartz, M. (1997). Self-determination and positive adult outcomes: A follow-up study of youth with mental retardation or learning disabilities. *Exceptional Children, 63,* 245–255.

Wolman, J. M., Campeau, P. L., DuBois, P. A., Mithaug, D. E., & Stolarski, V. S. (1994). *AIR self-determination scale and user guide*. Palo Alto, CA: American Institutes for Research.

Wood, S. J., & Cronin, M. E. (1999). Students with emotional/behavioral disorders and transition planning: What the follow-up studies tell us. *Psychology in Schools, 36,* 327–345.

Zhang, D., & Benz, M. R. (2006). Enhancing self-determination of culturally diverse students with disabilities: Current status and future directions. *Focus on Exceptional Children, 38*(9), 1–12.

Zhang, D., Wehmeyer, M. L., & Chen, L. (2005). Parent and teacher engagement in fostering the self-determination of students with disabilities: A comparison between the United States and the Republic of China. *Remedial and Special Education, 26,* 55–64.

Zigmond, N. (2006). Twenty-four months after high school: Paths taken by youth diagnosed with severe emotional and behavioral disorders. *Journal of Emotional and Behavioral Disorders, 14,* 99–107.

Zimmer-Gembeck, M. J., & Collins, W. A. (2003). Autonomy development during adolescence. In G. R. Adams & M. D. Berzonsky (Eds.), *Blackwell handbook of adolescence* (pp. 175–204). Malden, MA: Blackwell.

# CHAPTER 4

# *Building Transition Partnerships with Families of Youth with Emotional or Behavioral Disorders*

### Amy M. Pleet and Donna L. Wandry

Students do not come into the transition process as isolated entities but as part of family systems that are as varied as the school and community systems that serve them. Practitioners who are committed to improving the transition outcomes of these youth will enhance their own competencies in building partnerships with families. This chapter provides specific strategies that professionals can implement to enhance parent partnerships in their schools or agencies.

Partnership with families is frequently cited as one of the critical ingredients in strong transition practices or programs for students with disabilities (Bakken & Obiakor, 2008; deFur, Todd-Allen, & Getzel, 2001; Hutchins & Renzaglia, 1998; Kohler & Martin, 1998; Sitlington, Clark, & Kolstoe, 2000; Test, Aspel, & Everson, 2006). This is especially true for students with emotional and behavior disorders (EBD), whose families interact with professionals in many settings over a broader period of time (Clark et al., 2002; Duncan, Burns, & Robertson, 1996; Hatter, Williford, & Dickens, 2000).

A review of the literature reveals that outreach to families, family therapy, ongoing communication with families, and inclusion of parents in individualized education program (IEP) planning are essential components of transition programs for this population. Yet research into parent involvement indicates that parents have less involvement with transition planning than they would like (Martin, Marshall, & Sale, 2004; Powers, Hogansen, Geenen, Powers, & Gil-Kashiwabara, 2008). Contributing to this challenge is the lack of school-provided formal technical assistance for parents in understanding transition services. In spite of compelling calls for empowering parent partnerships in transition planning, transition literature provides inadequate specific information about strategies that practitioners can implement to build partnerships with parents of students with EBD. This is an especially timely issue if one considers data from the National Longitudinal Transition Study-2 (NLTS-2) that indicate a dissatisfaction with the transition planning process among a large share of parents of students with EBD (Wagner & Cameto, 2004).

NLTS-2 Wave 3 survey data revealed that parents of youth with EBD indicated relative satisfaction with their involvement in the IEP process (77.1% of parents of youth with EBD compared with 75.1% of all parents of youth with disabilities surveyed). Data subsets indicated lesser degrees of satisfaction for parents of youth with EBD than the overall mean in several critical areas. Only 83.6% of parents of youth with EBD found the IEP goals were strong and challenging for youth (compared with 89.3% of all parents surveyed), whereas only 4.2% of parents reported their youth with EBD took a leadership role in the IEP meeting (compared with 18.8% of all parents). Further, 37.0% of parents of youth with EBD reported that they never provided assistance with homework (compared with 29.2% of all parents); and only 6.3% of parents of youth with EBD reported belonging to a support group for families of youth with disabilities (compared with 7.0% of all parents) (NTLS-2, 2009). Although parents of youth with EBD indicated a consistent satisfaction with the IEP process, nearly every question pertaining to parental activities revealed that parents of youth with EBD lag behind other parents of youth with disabilities in their engagement with schools beyond the IEP process.

This chapter has five purposes: (1) to describe the changing context of family participation in the special education process, (2) to discuss the particular characteristics and issues faced by families of youth with emotional and behavior disorders, (3) to present five emergent roles of parents implied in the transition legislative mandates accompanied by strategies that successful programs have used with this population, (4) to suggest strategies that will improve parent engagement, and (5) to provide evaluative tools for measuring program effectiveness in empowering those parent roles.

Because we believe that professionals' effectiveness with parent partnerships increases with information and specific strategies as well as from awareness of parents' perspectives on the issues, we offer Parent Perspectives, which are illustrative of parent views on transition issues, throughout the chapter. Some of these illustrations provide a historic perspective, whereas others reflect current issues. Combined, they are an opportunity to "walk in a parent's shoes" for practitioners who are committed to increasing their competence in building partnerships with families of youth with EBD.

## FAMILY PARTNERSHIPS

### Definitions

First let us define two key terms as they are used in this chapter. We will work within the construct of "parent" as defined by the Individuals with Disabilities Education Improvement Act (IDEIA) of 2004, which defines a parent as

> (A) a natural, adoptive, or foster parent of a child (unless a foster parent is prohibited by State law from serving as a parent); (B) a guardian (but not the State if the child is a ward of the State); (C) an individual acting in the place of a natural or adoptive parent (including a grandparent, stepparent, or other relative) with whom the child lives, or an individual who is legally responsible for the child's welfare; or (D) except as used in sections 615(b)(2) and 639(a)(5), an individual assigned under either of those sections to be a surrogate parent. (IDEIA, 20 USC 1401 (602)(23))

Webster's definition of "partnership" is used in this discussion. According to Webster, partnership is "a relationship resembling a legal partnership and usually involving close cooperation between parties having specified and joint rights and responsibilities." Within a practitioner–family partnership, there are a number of joint responsibilities as all parties cooperate in supporting the young adult with disabilities to make a successful transition into adult life. There also are specified responsibilities—some assumed by the school or adult service agency and others assumed by families. The specifics of the partnership will vary with the individual's disability, goals, and family circumstances.

## Importance of Partnerships with Families During Transition

The report from the Twenty-sixth Institute on Rehabilitation Issues (2000) describes partnership with families as "a relationship characterized by independence, respect, trust, and tolerance. Ideally, each partner acknowledges the value of the multiple perspectives each brings to the partnership of shared responsibility and accountability for decision making. As partnership evolves, each party may assume different roles. Integral to the partnership between the family, consumer, and the rehabilitation counselor is the realization that the family can be the most important source of information about the consumer. There is not a true partnership if the expertise that the consumer and family possess is not recognized and acknowledged" (p. 9).

Families make four critical contributions to the transition planning process. First, they are a storehouse of information about the youth, his or her background and experiences, the family values, and the youth's future hopes and aspirations (Lankard, 1994). Professionals who build partnerships early with families will tap into the storehouse of information that the family holds, investigating their past experiences, values, and priorities to avoid conflicts in desired outcomes.

Second, family members provide coordination with multiple systems during the transition years. Students with EBD often receive services from mental health professionals, physicians, and psychiatrists who manage medications; probation officers and other court officials; and education professionals. In addition, parents often are aware of natural community supports, such as potential employers, that are unknown to the professionals. Progressing into the transition years, youth and their families may need to understand and access services from unfamiliar venues, such as rehabilitation and workforce agencies. Practitioners who provide information and support to empower youth and their families to coordinate all these systems will be more likely to contribute to their postschool success. Ultimately, it is critical for school professionals, agency professionals, parents, and students to work collaboratively and consultatively to determine future goals and create successful plans (Bakken & Obiakor, 2008).

Third, with support, families can empower these young adults to develop self-management and self-determination skills and to generalize the skills that are learned in school to other natural community settings. These skills are more likely to be internalized with repetition across environments, and parents are frequently instructors and reinforcers of these competencies, especially during the early adolescent years. In fact, planning for a child's transition from adolescence to adulthood is one of the most significant things a parent can do to pave the way to a successful future (PACER Center, 2005).

Fourth, families of transitioning youth can make valuable contributions to the systems that serve them (Lankard, 1994). Parents who have been supported as full partners in the transition process can mentor other parents, provide evaluative information about the quality of services they and their youths have received, and participate in advocacy or leadership activities that could impact the effectiveness of the whole system. They have the opportunity to serve on state special education advisory councils, state rehabilitation councils, steering committees, state and community transition councils, local school boards, and site-based management teams (PACER Center, 2006). Parents who emerge in these roles are invaluable to the entire systemic infrastructure.

## Changing Context of Family Participation

An examination of practitioners' perception of parents and family members reveals an evolution from viewing parents as outsiders, often considered the cause of their young person's problems (Hatter et al., 2000; Turnbull & Turnbull, 2001), to involved team players. Indeed, parents are now considered an essential component of the process of healing and growth (Duncan et al., 1996). Increasingly, family members are being viewed as equal participants as well as proactive change agents (Henderson, 2007). Although practitioners must respect parents' and other family members' right to choose their own levels of comfort as partners in educational planning and implementation, the potential for expanded roles in transition programming is being recognized and facilitated through practitioner actions.

Parent involvement is not new, but there is a new emphasis on preparing parents to become active partners with schools and agencies in meaningful ways that will influence successful outcomes for youth. Research over the last 30 years in public education has substantiated results for students, schools, families, and communities when schools assume the responsibility to invent ways to partner with parents (Epstein, 2005; Epstein & Salinas, 2004; Henderson, 2007). A report by the National Network of Partnership Schools (NNPS) (Epstein, 2005) described 5 years of their studies on the essential elements and outcomes of parent involvement practices. The report provided conclusive evidence that students improve attendance, behavior, and homework completion and increase reading and math test scores when specifically focused activities engage parents as partners. This research, which investigated strategies, challenges, and benefits of various methods for building partnerships with parents, laid the groundwork for the Epstein Types of Family Involvement and the National PTA Standards for Family–School Partnerships (2007).

Having analyzed the research underlying these two frameworks, we carefully examined the requirements for parent involvement in the Individuals with Disabilities Education Improvement Act (2004), the Rehabilitation Act Amendments (1998), and the No Child Left Behind Act (NCLB) (2001). We concluded that, although the legal, research, and moral basis for family participation is well established, the transition field literature has not evolved far beyond a thin definition of "parent participation." Interpretations of that term too often take the form of perfunctory information sharing, but rarely do they clearly define parent roles that build reciprocal partnerships in the transition process.

In response, we developed a framework for building partnerships with families during the transition years based on five roles of families (Pleet & Wandry, 2003, 2009). These five roles are (1) parents as collaborators, (2) parents as instructors in their youths' emergent independence, (3) parents as evaluators and decision makers, (4) parents as peer mentors, and (5) parents as systems change agents. These five roles have been incorporated as major themes in this chapter, and we offer guidelines for practitioners to use in building powerful partnerships with parents. Before the discussion regarding these roles begins, it is important to consider the characteristics of families of youth having EBD.

## WALKING IN THE FAMILY'S SHOES: THE ISSUES

A supportive family is essential to transition planning for all students and greatly influences the acquisition of employment and other successful adult outcomes (PACER, 2004; Parker & Finch, 2000; Schuster, Graham, & Moloney, 2000). Parents of all youth who are evolving from school into adult roles desire that their sons and daughters become happy and productive adults (Davis & Butler, 2002). However, the transition from adolescence to adulthood, from a school context to an adult service context, may be an overwhelming struggle for families of children with EBD (Davis & Butler, 2002; Hatter et al., 2000). Clark et al. (2002) summarized the issues for these youth: "Their high school experience is often marked by high absenteeism rates, frequent discipline problems, juvenile crime, social isolation, substance abuse, and failing one or more courses" (p. 299). Their school years are defined significantly by a history of social adjustment problems, with almost three fourths of them having been suspended or expelled at least once, a rate more than twice that of youth with disabilities as a whole (Wagner & Cameto, 2004). Their alarmingly high dropout rate and dismal postschool outcomes have been well documented by researchers, who report that one in five youth with EBD leaves school early and that youth with EBD have the lowest rate of school completion among all IDEA disability categories. Further, they possess the lowest degree of social skills essential for success in the community and the workplace (Wagner, Newman, Cameto, Garza, & Levine, 2005). But what are the issues for their families?

### Family Variables

---

#### Parent Perspective 1

For families like mine—families that include a child with atypical needs, anything that threatens the current routine is disruptive and unsettling to a sometimes startling degree. We are conditioned by our earlier experiences, and past hope has not always been rewarded. We have dealt with the medical establishment and educational systems and made our adjustments. We have routinized patterns, adopted beliefs, and developed expectations.

We cope with daily rearrangement that the rest of the world can only guess at. Some of us whose sons and daughters were deemed ineligible for school services a dozen years ago are now being pushed to explore integrated community employment for those same children. We focus on today; we have difficulty thinking about the future and planning ahead. And it is that planning ahead that transition forces upon us. For these reasons, school systems, holding out a brighter promise, are encountering parents who are skeptical, parents who are fearful, parents who are angry, and still others who are resistant.

Teachers and administrators may not realize that changes in the lives of our children with special needs are trauma points for parents. Life outside the boundaries that we and our school systems have created in the past terrifies us. All of our earlier feelings are reactivated. We may once again experience grief and upset, guilt and sadness, fear and despair. Those feelings need to be acknowledged by the people who work with us. We parents need to understand that we can move beyond them once again. We can allow ourselves hope. We can actively work to create a fuller and richer future for our daughters and sons. (Moore, 1988)

As Moore's timeless account of a parent's perspective reveals, these families have a history of facing critical challenges as they address daily parenting tasks while attempting to navigate the school and community service system to secure and maintain services for their adolescents with disabilities. Often these parents must decipher not only the procedures of the public and alternative educational systems, but they must also navigate systems related to individual and family mental health counseling, medication management, psychiatric hospitalization, juvenile justice, incarceration, and probation. When parents are focused on maintaining a stable home environment, they frequently are inadequately prepared to approach these overwhelming, unfamiliar, and frequently inhospitable systems as well.

Variables within the family structure that are linked to the presence of behavior disorders in the children seem likely to impact successful service access and outcomes. Much of the research analyzing the relationships between family variables and the presence of behavioral or emotional disorders tends to be used to blame parents for their children's conditions. Youth with EBD have a cluster of characteristics associated with poorer outcomes in the general population, including a higher likelihood of being African American, living in poverty, and having a head of household with no formal education past high school (Wagner & Cameto, 2004). Children reared in single-parent households are at higher risk for poor behavioral and cognitive outcomes and are more likely to have higher levels of emotional, behavioral, and psychological problems. Larger two-parent families, if the parents are less educated and work in lower-class occupations, may have a strong contributory influence in the development and display of externalizing behavior among their male children (Carlson & Corcoran, 2001; McLanahan, 1997). The development of the important adult standards of work ethics and work readiness may be compromised because of the employment situations of the parents (Sitlington et al., 2000). In addition, the stressors that may accompany parental conflict, a change in family composition, or changes in residence may cause children to become less nurtured in the home environment as their parents try to cope and adjust. Subsequently, as adolescents, these children develop internalizing or externalizing behaviors based on self-blame and desire for attention and security. In these situations, it is also likely that parents must focus on the basics of life and not attend to securing extra supports needed by their youth with EBD (Hatter et al., 2000). It has been suggested that parenting style, as influenced by the characteristics of the family environment and conflict that is experienced in families, has an indirect relationship with late adolescents' adjustment. The subjective well-being of adolescents is dependent in large part on their relationships with their parents (McKinney & Renk, 2008; Trzcinski & Holst, 2008).

The professional who is committed to building partnerships with these parents must avoid any stereotyped reaction of hopelessness triggered by these variables in order to approach each family with a willingness to identify their unique strengths and concerns. No single family fits all the stereotypes. As in the old discussion of the chicken or the egg, the professional will need to consider whether family issues or the child's emotional and behavioral issues came first. Some families develop problems as a result of trying to cope with the problems of their children. Additionally, the debate as to whether an EBD was caused by nature or nurture—by genetic predisposition or by the child's environment—will continue, but the professional who builds partnerships with parents isn't focused on blame but rather on addressing the issues and moving forward.

## Peer Involvement

All adolescents and young adults place blending in with and being admired by their peers at high priority. Dating, social acceptance, and sexual identity development are explored and valued (Davis & Butler, 2002; Sitlington et al., 2000). The stigma of maladaptive behaviors for these youth may serve to ostracize them from the very peers from whom they seek acceptance, or it may lead them to gravitate toward youth with deviant behaviors. These are real concerns of parents. They know how important it is to "belong," but they don't want their youth to belong to the wrong crowd. Individuals who have a strong support network can handle most personal crises. Compassionate teachers and adult service providers will assist the family in nurturing mutually supportive peer relations for these youth through peer support groups or organized recreational activities.

## The Diagnosis Dilemma

One of the decisions families and youth with EBD must make as the student prepares to transition from the public education system is whether the youth should be diagnosed using an adult-based assessment by a mental health practitioner (Hatter et al., 2000). Both the special education and the adult mental health systems are shaped by the medical pathology approach based on demonstrated behavioral symptoms, but there is a significant difference in the diagnostic criteria for children and for adults. Within the special education system, the IEP team (based on team-specified assessments) may have decided that the student was eligible for special education services under the disability label of emotional disturbance. The school psychologist may also have determined a specific diagnosis, but this may not have been a part of the official records because IDEIA 2004 does not require a specific diagnosis for emotional disturbance. If the youth received mental health services outside of school through a counseling center or social worker, the mental health professional probably determined a specific childhood psychiatric diagnosis.

As young people turn 18, childhood diagnoses are no longer applicable. They will need a new assessment to determine a diagnosis under the adult criteria of the *Diagnostic and Statistical Manual of Mental Disorders* (DSM-IV-TR) (American Psychiatric Association, 2000) if they plan to pursue services, symptom management, and accommodations in adult settings. This diagnosis must be determined by a qualified professional with a clinical license, according to the specific criteria in the DSM-IV-TR, not by a school team. As a student moves from the secondary special education system to the adult service systems, the student and family need to decide whether they want to pursue a new adult diagnosis. Professionals can guide their decision using the following questions:

- Is this student likely to qualify for a different diagnosis under the adult criteria of DSM-IV-TR?
- What adult settings are being considered as potential outcomes for this youth (for example, higher education, trade school, employment, or the military)?
- Are there concerns about detrimental stigma and self-fulfilling negative perceptions as a result from this new diagnosis as the youth moves into adulthood?
- How would the DSM-IV-TR diagnosis support the youth in potential adult settings through eligibility for services, symptom management, and/or reasonable accommodations? What services, symptom management, and reasonable accommodations might be available?
- Who is qualified to make the DSM-IV-TR diagnosis (for example, a school psychologist with a clinical license, a clinical social worker, a psychiatrist, or a private psychologist outside of the school system), and who will pay for the assessment?

### Parent Perspective 2

My daughter hated being labeled emotionally disturbed while in high school. After years of humiliation from her peers and the stigma of receiving special education services, she refused to go with us to meet with the rehabilitation services counselor. She said she wanted to prove she didn't need any of "that help" next year in college. My husband and I saw this refusal as a positive sign of her determination to establish her independence so we encouraged her to try it on her own. Unfortunately, her refusal also made her ineligible for support services in college, and she encountered great difficulty with managing the stressors of academic life.

My nephew had been diagnosed with a DSM-IV-TR label of bipolar disorder and attention deficit disorder as he was preparing to leave high school. When he turned 18, this re-documented diagnosis made him eligible for supports through the state public mental health administration. He was included in a demonstration project initiative that included peer group counseling, employment placement and job coaching, medication management, independent living support in a supervised apartment, and tutoring for a class at the local community college.

Families will need information about the benefits and disadvantages of obtaining an adult diagnosis when deciding whether their young adult should seek this critical determination. Under IDEIA 2004 and the Rehabilitation Act of 1998, youth and their families are entitled to "informed consent." Therefore, they should be fully informed about all the factors to be considered before they consent to this new diagnostic process. The decision about whether to obtain a new *DSM-IV-TR* diagnosis should be based on the impact of the youth's disability on his or her performance and the individual characteristics and circumstances unique to each youth and family. Practitioners should also be sensitive to the family's and youth's need for time to consider the information before giving their informed consent.

## Maturation/Separation Issues

Another critical issue emerges during the maturation and separation stage of adolescent development. Parents of youths with EBD may experience greater difficulty "letting go" as their young adult approaches adulthood. Parents of youths with significant disabilities have a stronger drive to protect their child from the real risks that the vulnerable child will face as a young adult (Hatter et al., 2000). The National Center on Secondary Education and Transition (NCSET) (2004) emphasizes the importance of self-determination and self-advocacy skills and student-centered planning, all of which promote emergence into independent roles. Involving parents early in the transition process helps them prepare themselves and their youth for the changing roles to come. Specifically, they and their son or daughter need to understand that IDEIA 2004 created one natural "letting go" mechanism, at least within the parameters of the young adult's school involvement, through the mandate of age of majority notification. This means that states may elect to transfer educational decision-making rights to students who are "competent to give informed consent in decisions" at the age of majority, giving them responsibility for their own educational programs. Although the risks are high that students with EBD may decide to use their newfound authority to drop out, this mechanism may be considered a key step in the discussion of "letting go" for some parents (NCSET, 2002).

Implied in the ability to "let go" is the ability to engage in a healthy degree of risk taking by the family and the individual. Specifically, the family of a young adult with EBD may find it difficult to move into more interactive, less directive decision making regarding activities, relationships, etc., for fear of allowing the opportunity for negative outcomes. As the young adult moves toward adult role challenges, the practitioner should assist family members in building healthier risk-taking attitudes by identifying (1) where along the continua of input and risk they function, and (2) how they can securely move into receiving higher degrees of input from their young adult and assuming higher degrees of risk taking themselves in increasingly more complex decision-making contexts. Figure 4.1 illustrates the relationship between degree of input and risk.

## Systemic Challenges

As these youth and their families try to navigate adult support services, they may feel stigmatized and labeled by that system because of its emphasis on pathology and reject the opportunity for assistance. Professionals who understand differing eligibility requirements of the systems can empower young adults and families with information

**FIGURE 4.1    Continuum of Input and Risk**

| Degree of Input | Degree of Risk |
|---|---|
| The individual has no input into decisions regarding day-to-day life. | The choice implies very little risk and no long-term harm (for example, routine events such as apparel choices). |
| Decisions are made by parent or professional, with some input from the individual. | The decision involves mild risk with minimum possibility of harm (for example, joining friends in a social event). |
| Decision making is mutual and reciprocal. | The choice presents a moderate possibility of harm (for example, experimenting with drugs or engaging in unprotected sex). |
| Parents or professionals may have some input, but the final decision is the individual's. | The choice presents a significant possibility of harmful consequences (for example, dropping out of school at age 16). |
| The individual has complete responsibility to make a choice regarding some or even all of his or her daily life. | The decision has the highest risk of personal injury or severe consequences (for example, criminal actions). |

*Left axis: Low Input → High Input. Right axis: Low Risk → High Risk.*

about the systems' strengths and limitations as well as strategies to prepare them to advocate for themselves.

As youth with EBD age, they may interact with school-based as well as community-based service providers. Transition service planning for students with EBD frequently entails the coordination of a range of school and community services (Barnes and Bullock, 1995). Services commonly used by this population include job training, health services, counseling, mentoring, and financial counseling (Jolivette, Stichter, Nelson, Scott, & Liaupsin, 2000). Services may also extend to vocational rehabilitation, day training programs, Social Security, housing, and transportation support (NCSET, 2004).

However, parents of students with EBD may find these services to be generally unhelpful in achieving their goals and dreams. According to NLTS-2 data, 25% of parents of youth with EBD reported that the transition planning process is not very useful or not useful at all (Wagner & Cameto, 2004); they also were more likely to report that obtaining services needed by their students "took a great deal of effort." Parent centers report that families of young adults with disabilities are deeply frustrated by the lack of coordinated planning and paucity of resources (NCSET, 2004). They may feel that practitioners focus on their child as a "broken soul" and fixate on the youth's deficit rather than the child's promise. Parents and families also may feel that adult services (1) are geared more toward the younger adolescents and the older adult population rather than transitioning youth, (2) do not sufficiently or appropriately include parents, and (3) do not offer sufficient information on available services or resources (Davis & Butler, 2002). As parents and family members become defeated by these perceptions, the hope of successful engagement in transition planning, decision making, educational implementation, and systemic involvement diminishes. When this feeling of hopelessness is combined with the emotional, physical, and structural impact of problem behavior on family relationships, social networks, and daily activities, it is almost overwhelming to articulate the level of support many of these families require (Fox, Vaughan, Wyatte, & Dunlap, 2002).

Malloy, Cheney, and Cormier (1998) reported an encouraging trend to establish "wraparound" services for youth with emotional and behavior disorders and their families. They described how wraparound services differ from the traditional service delivery system in that they (1) focus on the strengths of the youth, family, school, and community, (2) are driven by the needs of the youth as opposed to the needs of agencies, (3) deal with all aspects of the youth's life, (4) provide for the youth in natural settings and use social networks such as family and friends, and (5) concentrate on needs that are basic to all individuals. Project RENEW, an example of the wraparound approach, is designed to address the unique needs of youth with EBD. Guided by the principles of self-determination, community inclusion, unconditional care, strengths-based planning and services, and flexible planning, RENEW participants have experienced significant growth in postsecondary education and employment (Malloy et al., Chapter 10 in this volume). This wraparound approach addresses many of the complaints parents have voiced about having to manage separate service delivery systems.

## PARENTS IN EMERGENT ROLES

The foundation for positive partnerships with parents has been established through the efforts of model demonstration projects, strong parent centers, and individual efforts of countless professionals in schools and agencies. Parents are assuming new roles and defining their own needs for information and involvement that will help them and their youths as well as impact the larger system. This section of the chapter provides information and strategies for supporting parents in five roles related to the transition process: (1) as collaborators in the IEP process, (2) as instructors in their youth's emerging independence, (3) as decision makers and evaluators, (4) as peer mentors, and (5) as systems change agents.

Because both IDEIA 2004 and NCLB 2001 have a strong focus on accountability, we have created a set of tools that practitioners can use to measure their effectiveness and the degree of improvement they provide in facilitating parent empowerment. First, we developed a checklist that individual practitioners can use for self-assessment related to empowering parents in each of the five roles (Figure 4.2, p. 108). Second, the Degree of Involvement Scale (Pleet & Wandry, 2009) can be used when identifying an individual parent's current levels of involvement in each role (Figure 4.3, p. 110). Third, schools or programs can use the Parent Partnership Strategic Planning Guide (Pleet & Wandry, 2009) to identify current and potential activities that would build empowering partnerships with parents in the five focused roles (Figure 4.4, p. 111).

Although we will discuss the positive aspects of building partnerships with families, we must concede that at times parents can be a detrimental influence. In instances of physical, emotional, sexual, or substance abuse, parents' lack of support or actual resistance to the transition process must be taken into consideration. In addition, poor communication patterns among family members, severe economic difficulties, or unwarranted lowered expectations for the young adult are obstacles to successful postschool outcomes (Twenty-sixth Institute on Rehabilitation Issues, 2000). An important aspect of practitioners' outreach to families includes an appraisal of the family's possible negative influences as well as the strengths the family brings to the partnership. The challenge for the professional is to identify and build on the strengths each family has to offer.

## Parents as Collaborators

According to IDEIA 2004, transition planning for each student who receives special education services will begin no later than age 16 (although some states have kept age 14, which is consistent with the IDEA 1997 regulations). The IEP team must include the student's and parent's perspectives as they consider individual measurable postsecondary goals, transition services, and annual transition-related goals. Families play a critical role in the collaboration between school and community activities and services (deFur, 2003; Pleet & Wandry, 2003; Witt, 2002). Martin et al. (2004) suggested that early implementers of PL 94–142 were skeptical of family involvement, and as time has passed, participation may still be viewed, as passive at best.

In contrast to this restrictive school view, youth with disabilities reported that they have strong relationships with their parents whom they consider a first choice for support (Wagner, Newman, Cameto, Levine, & Marder, 2007). This openness of youth to recognizing parents as partners and even leaders should be universally validated by practitioners. Student-centered transition planning must also be family-centered transition planning. In fact, professional support for student-centered planning that reflects both student and family needs is not only desirable but critical to quality transition planning (deFur, 2009).

Practitioners who support parents in becoming "reliable allies" (Turnbull & Turnbull, 2001, p. 50) are aware that they must create a welcoming, caring, culturally responsive atmosphere in which families are comfortable to discuss sensitive family issues; this may be especially true of families stressed by the presence of a young adult with EBD. Responsive programs establish practices that encourage reciprocal communication and trust, beginning with a discussion of the hopefully shared, but sometimes dichotomous, family's and student's future visions (deFur, 2009).

---

### Parent Perspective 3

The IEP meeting I attended when my daughter turned 14 was a nightmare. As we were discussing the issues around her depression, anxiety disorder, and school refusal, the guidance counselor blamed me: "You're the parent! You get her to school!" Her implication that my lack of parental competence was the source of the problem was quite intimidating, affirming my internal self-doubts. With that one statement, she shut the door on any possibility of working with her on possible solutions. Thank heavens other staff members initiated contact and supported us through some tough times.

---

These programs offer helpful connections that will assist the youth and family to expand their networks of support and empower the students and family members as resources and collaborative problem solvers in the transition process. Ultimately, families will see practitioners regard them as not just a case but a family entity with viable concerns, knowledge, visions, and contributions.

Turnbull and Turnbull (2001) discussed "reframing" as a life management strategy. Reframing is "changing the way one thinks about a situation in order to emphasize positive rather than negative aspects" (p. 47). Throughout the transition process, there are times when parents and professionals support each other by reframing difficult circumstances before they can collaboratively develop a plan of action and move on. Practitioners should be aware that families of youth with EBD who have experienced earlier dissatisfactory and stigmatizing interactions with the service system may feel distanced from school-based and community-based providers associated with transition services (deFur, 2009).

To build a partnership with many families, practitioners must be sensitive not only to a family's dynamics and history, but also to their cultural values (McGinley, 2009). Most of the transition practices that have emerged in this country are shaped by the dominant culture's view of independence and self-sufficiency. Americans of European heritage have defined success as independence within the security of a larger community safety net. Yet many families today whose youth with disabilities are engaged in transition activities may not have faith in a larger community safety net. Instead they may value an adult life that emphasizes their own cultural group identity and interdependence (Hatter et al., 2000). Further, unfamiliarity with the mandates, communication barriers, and general feelings of being unprepared may pose significant obstacles for families from different cultural contexts (deFur, 2009).

---

### Parent Perspective 4

Consider the Latino family in which the father owned a small produce stand. His eldest son, Juan, was to assume the role of running the family business after completing high school. When Juan entered his junior year, school personnel began directing him to attend community college after high school. They believed that he could aspire to employment other than the family business after graduation and encouraged him to make his own decisions contrary to his father's expectations. (Hatter et al., 2000, p. 213)

---

Parents as collaborators also bring important community connections to the table. Family members provide personal networks of relatives, friends, neighbors, community businesses, and their religious community to identify job opportunities. According to NLTS-2 data, most youth reported finding their jobs on their own (57%), but many had assistance from family members (21%) or friends or acquaintances (14%). Only 8% had assistance from an agency, school, or other program in finding their job (Cameto, 2005).

In this respect, families bring resources that will assist transition practitioners in accomplishing their professional roles. In addition, families need community connections and information sources to provide ongoing supports for their young adult, social support networks for themselves, and opportunities for involvement in the transition process at the systemic level for those who desire a more global role.

Families of youth with EBD, who may have felt defeated and stigmatized through past interactions with providers, may gain a fresh perspective through external networks of support that may help move them from passivity to a more proactive role in the home–school–community partnership.

Finally, practitioners must understand and employ the basics of communication to engage families, but this communication must be reciprocal in that both sides (parents and practitioners) openly reveal their respective needs, fears, hopes, frustrations, and constraints. Parents rely on service providers to give them systemic information, and providers should rely on parents to give them crucial, delicate, and sometimes challenging information about their young adult with EBD. Conversation must be constructive, understandable, and respectful at all levels of the partnership (Blue-Banning, Summers, Frankland, Nelson, & Beegle, 2004).

## Parents as Instructors in Their Youth's Emergent Independence

Parents are the first and often the only constant guiding influence throughout a youth's life as instructors of their children's coping skills. Educational activities, if developed within a holistic context, include opportunities for parents to support school goals and students' learning and will engage parents as partners in the continuous learning that goes on in students' lives outside of school or in adult service settings (Bateman, Bright, & Brandt, 2003).

At the heart of adolescents' success in their education, employment, and adult life is their capacity to advocate for themselves (Wehmeyer, Palmer, Agran, Mithaug, & Martin, 2000). Parents are valuable allies as schools endeavor to foster each youth's ownership of his or her own success. The central role of the school or provider in facilitating the role of parents as instructors during the transition years is to empower parents to guide their adolescents as they develop skills in self-determination and autonomy. If we consider that the parent–professional partnership can be one of reciprocal recognition of expertise, and that parents are indeed experts on their own children but may need information, guidance, and support in fulfilling these expert roles, it follows that the work toward modeling and teaching authentic skills cannot be sustained without mutual effort (Wolfendale, 2002). Parents of youth with EBD may have more access to behavioral observation of their young adult across multiple settings, but teachers may need to help them sort out whether the need for intervention is warranted. For example, modeling of teacher-preferred social skills positively affects students with EBD (Lopez, 2000), but generalization of those skills to other settings is not effective without youth development of self-monitoring behaviors and parent reinforcement and replicative modeling. Given the high stakes implied in lack of intervention and the benefits of collaborative intervention based on reciprocal support, parents should be partners with schools and community agencies providing vital social skills instruction essential to ultimate success in postschool environments.

Parents and family members of children with disabilities who tend to provide fewer opportunities in choice making, risk taking, or personal goal setting (Zhang, 2005) could serve a valuable function by learning how to reinforce self-advocacy and self-determination skills in naturalistic environments. Parents can initiate discussions of postschool dreams and goals and coach their youth to be able to articulate their preferences at the IEP meeting (Wehmeyer et al., 2000). In addition, young adults can strategize with family members on how to deal with challenging workplace situations (Twenty-sixth Institute on Rehabilitation Issues, 2000).

Linked to the concept of self-determination is that of self-disclosure, which brings together the ability to understand one's disability, the resultant needs for accommodations and supports, and the legal guidelines for appropriate and essential times to self-disclose. Many students are unprepared for this role because they have not had any modeling or instruction from home or school (Zhang, 2005), and parents may be reticent to expose their youth to what they may view as another potential venue in which their child could experience failure or sustain a blow to an already fragile self-esteem.

Throughout, parents should be encouraged to honor the choices of their young adults, even when they may be making poor choices (within safe confines). Although most parents believe that learning good decision making is a process that all young people should accomplish in becoming independent adults, they may be more hesitant in allowing their young person with a disability to be involved in this process

(Ward, 2009). As Brotherson and Berdine (1993) state, "Sometimes parents do not give their sons and daughters the right to fail" (p. 48), but they also point out that often educators have not done much better in offering meaningful choices to these students. The end result, especially for students with EBD, may be an ongoing feeling of personal incompetence and a lack of confidence in their ability to succeed (Zhang, 2005). With the support of practitioners, the value of parents in the role of instructor of life's lessons should not be ignored or underestimated.

---

### Parent Perspective 5

My son complained to me about his segregated school program. He asked how he would ever learn appropriate social skills if all his classmates had emotional and behavior problems. He had a valid point, but I explained that we would have to request an IEP team to change his placement. Because this was his idea, I told him that he would have to be prepared to explain his reasons for wanting the change and that he would have to be able to address the concerns of the school staff. He thought about their concerns and was prepared to advocate for himself effectively at his team. Teams that want to establish a central role for students during the IEP meeting will want to provide parents some tips on supporting their youths' self-determination skills.

---

## Parents as Evaluators and Decision Makers

Parents who are engaged as partners begin as evaluators and decision makers in their own youth's program, but some are willing to expand their influence to the program or system levels. First, they provide information about their son's successes at the job site or their daughter's issues in developing appropriate skills in the community. Parents are valuable in the transition decision-making process for their own youth because they are able to aggregate the categorical information from each of the teachers, therapists, employment specialists, and agency personnel and present a unified picture of the whole young adult. Parent perspective is vital for evaluating the current effectiveness of the transition plan and for making decisions about balancing interventions.

Further, schools and agencies that seek parent input into decisions regarding their youth's transition-related goals and services in the IEP will broaden their scope beyond the schoolhouse walls.

---

### Parent Perspective 6

I appreciated my son's school social worker who took the time to contact me each week to just check in. She would ask how things were going at home, with his friends in the community, with the planned summer job. She was interested in family circumstances that would impact his adjustment in school and wanted to hear of any changes in his interactions from my perspective. She would use this information to evaluate the counseling she provided, but it spoke loudly to me of her commitment to maintain an open line of communication.

---

Parents, based on their comfort level, can also provide valuable feedback at the program level. Decision-making leadership activities include parents in school decisions regarding development of new programs and evaluation of program data for improvement of existing programs. Many schools and districts now recognize the value of developing parent leaders and representatives for this purpose. IDEIA 2004 requires that parent input must be sought in the special education monitoring and evaluation process (Turnbull, Turnbull, & Wehmeyer, 2007; Wandry & Pleet, 2009). In addition, IDEIA Outcome Indicator 8 charges states to report measures of parent participation; specifically, it requires data on the "percent of parents with children receiving special education services who report that schools facilitated parent involvement as a means of improving services and results for children with disabilities" (20 USC 1416 (a)(3)(A)). Effective partnerships create multiple strategies to engage parents in the development and evaluation of special education programs and services. They listen to parents other than those who will rubber-stamp the administrative proposals. Parents provide real-life examples and bring real-life concerns to decision makers as they evaluate the efficacy of new and existing programs.

There are a number of challenges to including parents as decision makers and evaluators, including the issues that parents bring and the resistance that practitioners bring. Clearly, parent decision makers and evaluators will need information about their child's disability as well as special education and adult systems and practices. Professionals will need staff development and supportive policies to empower families in decision-making roles. Professional development will need to cover benefits for empowering parents as decision makers as well as strategies to support their assimilation into that role (Schoeller & Emanuel, 2003; Takemoto & Healy, 2009). In a recent study, parents stated their desire to become more aware of resources and system changes, as well as to become more involved in providing treatment both in school and adult settings. As Davis and Butler (2002) stated, "Parents . . . have discovered the power of information and advocacy, and they want more of both for themselves and their children" (p. 29).

## Parents as Peer Mentors

If information gathering is fostered, a natural outgrowth will be the sharing of information with and mentoring of others who need that same power of knowledge (Turnbull & Turnbull, 2001). Parents seek information, skills, and supports with which to aid their adolescents with disabilities during the transition years. They benefit from support as they gather information about adult services, future employment, education, and independent living options.

After researching parents' perceptions of formal and informal supports for mothers and fathers of students with EBD, Lehman and Irvin (1996) stated that parents most frequently turn to close family and close friends for emotional support and generally turn to school personnel for informational support. The researchers found that parents only occasionally turn to parents of other children with similar disabilities for informational support. They recommended that practitioners encourage parents to view other parents (their peers) as valuable sources of information and emotional support and establish procedures for linking parents with other knowledgeable, supportive parents.

In a study of parent support programs, Layzer, Goodson, Bernstein, and Price (2001) found that effective programs involve peer mentoring components and are linked to formal service systems. Involvement in these model programs increases positive parental attitudes and knowledge more than programs without peer support. Peer mentoring practices potentially can expand social networks, increase self-esteem, and improve parenting skills and family functioning (Cohen & Canan, 2006). Experienced, willing parents, therefore, should be supported in expanding their role to include sharing gained knowledge and information with other families who may be struggling within the system and providing leadership by offering themselves as resources. "The role of a parent advocate is to provide families with information, support, and guidance as they negotiate the system so they can have successful interactions with the system" (Cohen & Canan, 2006, p. 868). Cohen and Canan (2006) discuss the importance of this role for families of youth with EBD who are supported by mental health services. "This 'I've been there' aspect of the mentoring relationship underlies family-centered, strengths-based programs such as those in children's mental health services" (p. 875).

There are several strategies to support parents as peer mentors. Formalized training to expand the skills and knowledge base of parents who want to serve in these roles has been one effective method (Guy, Goldberg, McDonald, & Flom, 1997; Kolb, 2003). Practitioners should be prepared to share information about training and workshops provided by each state's federally funded parent information and training centers and by other parent and advocacy organizations. Parents who have been mentored often go on to mentor other parents.

---

### Parent Perspective 7

When my son was a senior in high school, I was invited to speak to a group of parents about my experiences with my son and the system during the transition years. I spoke to them about the caring and supportive professionals and those who had tried to convince me that I was wrong about what my son needed. I told these parents to trust their instincts because they know their child longer and better than anyone else. I wish someone had given me that message years before. It might have saved us from the consequences of listening to the wrong advice.

---

## Parents as Systems Change Agents

Parents who have been willing to speak out have largely been responsible for many of the systems and services that currently exist for youth with disabilities (Morningstar & Torrez, 2003; Pleet & Wandry, 2003; Turnbull & Turnbull, 2001). Fortunately, there is the beginning of a national shift from the unfriendly system against which previous parents have spoken out to the emergent welcoming system that seeks their input. The changing spirit of family involvement in special education systems is exemplified by the language in IDEIA 2004, the Rehabilitation Act Amendments of 1998, and NCLB 2001, which calls for parent representation within systemic structures. IDEIA requires that state advisory boards, appointed by the governor in most states and charged with advising the state or local office of special education on the unmet needs of students with disabilities, must have as a majority of members individuals with disabilities or parents of children with disabilities (Morningstar & Torrez, 2003; Turnbull, Huerta, & Stowe, 2006). These boards comment publicly on the rules or regulations proposed by the state and advise the state on developing evaluative measures and report the data to the U. S. Office of Special Education Programs (OSEP). These IDEIA 2004 provisions ensure that parent perspectives are incorporated into program and policy decisions, thereby allowing parents to function as systems change agents (Turnbull et al., 2007). Their potential impact on a system cannot be underestimated in that parents have been identified as essential to ensuring continuity between school and adult services, and their involvement is clearly associated with positive achievement of postschool outcomes (Morningstar, 2009).

---

### Parent Perspective 8

I was appointed to the State Rehabilitation Council because of my position in the Department of Education, but I was also there as a parent. Frankly, with my son in the midst of his transition years, he was never far from my thoughts. One of the other members worked in an agency that served transitioning youth with psychiatric issues. Together we suggested some revisions to the state plan to expand services for youth with mental health needs and increase outreach to families. Our changes were ultimately adopted, and activities were planned to benefit these youths and families.

---

In addition to the influence of parents on the implementation of IDEIA, the Rehabilitation Act mandates that state rehabilitation councils must include a representative of a parent training and information center. This presence is particularly important because the council, in consultation with the workforce investment board as mandated under the Workforce Investment Act of 1998, is empowered to engage in program evaluation and systemic change. Specifically, state boards advise governors on ways to develop the statewide workforce investment and help governors monitor statewide activities. Governors designate local workforce investment areas and oversee local workforce investment boards. Youth councils are set up as a subgroup of the local boards to guide the development and operation of programs for youth (Office of Disability Employment Policy, 2009).Youth aged 14 to 21 who are eligible for youth services include individuals who are school dropouts, are deficient in basic skills, have educational attainment that is one or more grade levels below the grade level appropriate to the individual's age, and/or are pregnant or parenting (Test et al., 2006). Given the interaction between these eligibility criteria and current statistics regarding youth with EBD (NLTS-2), parents of students with EBD should be aware of and involved in systemic activities related to the law's implementation.

In addition to parent systemic involvement supported by other laws, federal funding to the states under NCLB 2001 is based on a plan for school improvement developed by the state educational agency in conjunction with a list of collaborators, including parents (Title I, Part A). This plan must demonstrate that the state has adopted challenging academic and achievement standards that will include all students, providing reasonable adaptations and accommodations as needed for students with disabilities. The annual state report card, which will provide disaggregated data comparing students with and without disabilities, holds the state accountable for results related to students with disabilities. As part of these practices, state education agencies must support the collection and dissemination of data regarding effective parental involvement practices in its local education agencies and schools. Those practices must be based on the most current research on effective parental involvement to foster high achievement for all children, with the research itself meeting the highest professional and technical standards In addition, those practices must be geared toward lowering barriers to greater participation by parents in school planning, review, and improvement experiences (NCLB Section 1111(d), ESEA)

(U. S. Department of Education, 2004). As indicated by the parental involvement provisions in NCLB Title I, Part A, the involvement of parents in their children's education and schools is critical to that process. Former Secretary of Education Rod Paige put it succinctly when he stated, "[s]chools can't improve without the help of parents" (Paige, 2002). Once again, it is important for parents of students with disabilities, including those with EBD, to avail themselves of the opportunities for systemic involvement guaranteed under these laws.

According to research by Davis and Butler (2002), parents of young adults with EBD have already expressed definite policy goals for systems serving their youth. They rated highly the need to have policies that (1) include parents as much as possible in transition services for their children, (2) minimize out-of-home placements, (3) eliminate barriers to adult service access, and (4) minimize services that do not adequately prepare youth for adult roles. Given the specificity of these perceived needs, it would seem logical for a system that is designed to provide services to allow involvement of families who will be consumers of those services in shaping the policies that guide those services. Parents speaking before legislative bodies and funding sources can put a face on an issue in a way that can be quite compelling. Practitioners find that parents who have been empowered as collaborative partners are natural spokespersons when they champion a program or policy change that would benefit their transitioning youth and others. Therefore, it is our responsibility as practitioners to help parents who wish to assume larger systemic roles to overcome the perceived risks of being labeled difficult (Geenen, Powers, Vasquez, & Bersani, 2003), unknowledgeable, and of feeling unsupported or disconnected (Morningstar, 2009). It falls on us to empower those parents by assisting them in learning advocacy skills, sponsoring family involvement in systems venues, and collaboratively engaging in ways to shape effective transition planning and programming (Morningstar, 2009).

## CONCLUSION

Practitioners in the educational, mental health, and adult service systems that are charged with improving the transitioning outcomes of students with EBD have made a promising beginning in engaging parents. We have come a long way from the time when students with serious mental health and behavioral issues were excluded from schools and programs, yet the research indicates that there is still far to go. If we are to improve student outcomes in high-school completion, access to postsecondary education and training programs, full employment, and responsible community participation, we must collaborate with all the important stakeholders. Families have shown themselves to be ready to step forward. They have indicated their desire to work with the systems for their own youths and others. They need informational and emotional support to emerge into the five roles suggested by transition-related legislation. More important, we need them, and so do the young adults in our charge. Please join us in welcoming parents as collaborators in the IEP process, as instructors in their youths' emergent independence, as decision makers and evaluators, as peer mentors, and as systems change agents on behalf of youth with emotional and behavioral disorders.

## FIGURE 4.2    Checklist for Building Partnerships

|  | Usually | Occasionally | Never |
|---|---|---|---|
| **Indicators—*Parents as Collaborators*** | | | |
| I encourage families to share their perspectives for the youth's dreams, goals, and future outcomes. | ☐ | ☐ | ☐ |
| I establish trust so that all parties can freely communicate information and perspectives in the transition process. | ☐ | ☐ | ☐ |
| I welcome the whole family network (parents, siblings, extended family, neighbors, friends, etc.). | ☐ | ☐ | ☐ |
| I validate and reframe past negative experiences as a way to move forward. | ☐ | ☐ | ☐ |
| I practice reframing when circumstances are difficult so that we can join together in the problem-solving and decision-making processes. | ☐ | ☐ | ☐ |
| I am sensitive to cultural differences and ask for information to expand my understanding of each family's cultural values. | ☐ | ☐ | ☐ |
| I acknowledge family members for their contributions to our successful partnership. | ☐ | ☐ | ☐ |
| **Indicators—*Parents as Instructors in Their Youths' Emergent Independence*** | | | |
| I engage families as instructional partners in their youth's lifelong learning, including skills for everyday living, self-management, social appropriateness, teamwork, and developing a positive work ethic. | ☐ | ☐ | ☐ |
| I acknowledge families for their expertise and instrumental role in supporting their youth's life learning. | ☐ | ☐ | ☐ |
| I support families' efforts to prepare students for self-advocacy and self-determination throughout the transition process. | ☐ | ☐ | ☐ |
| I encourage families to support their youth's learning through making all kinds of choices. | ☐ | ☐ | ☐ |

### Indicators—Parents as Peer Mentors

| | Usually | Occasionally | Never |
|---|---|---|---|
| I link families with other families for support during the transition process. | ☐ | ☐ | ☐ |
| I support methods that allow experienced families to share their experiences with "new" families through informational meetings or informal contact. | ☐ | ☐ | ☐ |
| I provide information and support to parents emerging as trainers and mentors (either through an established parent center or informally). | ☐ | ☐ | ☐ |

### Indicators—Parents as Evaluators and Decision Makers

| | Usually | Occasionally | Never |
|---|---|---|---|
| I provide families information about their youth's disability, available options, and system procedures so that they are fully informed partners in the decision-making process and program. | ☐ | ☐ | ☐ |
| I encourage families to share their perspectives on the youth's progress and functioning—both the good and the bad. | ☐ | ☐ | ☐ |
| Families do not hesitate to contact me about issues that may impact the youth's success, knowing that I will use that information to coordinate needed supports. | ☐ | ☐ | ☐ |
| I give families information to interpret program data and empower them to engage in program or system evaluative activities so that their perspective will be considered in programmatic improvement efforts. | ☐ | ☐ | ☐ |

### Indicators—Parents as Systems Change Agents

| | Usually | Occasionally | Never |
|---|---|---|---|
| I provide families information about avenues to express their concerns or recommendations for program design and improvement. | ☐ | ☐ | ☐ |
| I encourage parents to represent their point of view at public hearings, focus groups, and on advisory boards. | ☐ | ☐ | ☐ |
| I support other professionals to consider families' perspectives and recommendations as program and system decisions and policies are formulated. | ☐ | ☐ | ☐ |

**FIGURE 4.3    Degree of Involvement Scale**

Evaluate the involvement of individual parents.

### Part I: Consider what you know about what this parent brings

- Information about the child's disability?
- Family's socioeconomic, cultural situation?
- Family's level of coping with disability?
- Family's engagement with resources outside of the school or program?

### Part II: Analyze degree of involvement in each role

Parents as collaborators:

| 1 | 2 | 3 | 4 | 5 |
|---|---|---|---|---|
| Don't attend/ unaware of IEP | Passive at team meetings | Attend team/ agree with plan | Attend team/ question plan | Contribute to plan |

Parents as instructors in their youth's emergent independence:

| 1 | 2 | 3 | 4 | 5 |
|---|---|---|---|---|
| Not aware of goals on IEP | Teach youth basic household chores | Foster skills for independence | Help reinforce IEP goals at home | Foster self-determination and personal leadership |

Parents as peer role models, mentors, and trainees:

| 1 | 2 | 3 | 4 | 5 |
|---|---|---|---|---|
| No involvement with other parents | Listen to other parents | Seek other parents/join support group | Leader in parent support group | Speaker/trainer for parents |

Parents as decision makers/evaluators:

| 1 | 2 | 3 | 4 | 5 |
|---|---|---|---|---|
| Unaware of plan | Passive at team meetings | Provide feedback on IEP | Respond to requests for program feedback | Initiate program feedback |

Parents as systems change agents:

| 1 | 2 | 3 | 4 | 5 |
|---|---|---|---|---|
| Unaware of system issues | Awareness/ opinion of system issues | Sign petitions/ write letters | Advocate for change in local school | Advocate for change in system/state/ region |

Reprinted with permission from D. L. Wandry and A. M. Pleet. (2009). *Engaging and empowering families in secondary transition: A practitioner's guide*. Arlington, VA: Council for Exceptional Children. This page may be photocopied for individual, classroom, or small-group work only.

## FIGURE 4.4 Parent Partnership Strategic Planning Guide

How well does your school/program empower parents in each role?
Rate your program (1) minimal activities to (5) systemic, ongoing activities.

|  | What we are doing now | Possible actions | First step |
|---|---|---|---|
| Parents as collaborators in the IEP process<br>1  2  3  4  5 |  |  |  |
| Instructors in their youth's emergent independence<br>1  2  3  4  5 |  |  |  |
| Decision makers and evaluators<br>1  2  3  4  5 |  |  |  |
| Peer role models, mentors, and trainers<br>1  2  3  4  5 |  |  |  |
| Systems change agents<br>1  2  3  4  5 |  |  |  |

Reprinted with permission from D. L. Wandry and A. M. Pleet. (2009). *Engaging and empowering families in secondary transition: A practitioner's guide.* Arlington, VA: Council for Exceptional Children. This page may be photocopied for individual, classroom, or small-group work only.

## REFERENCES

American Psychiatric Association. (2000). *Diagnostic and statistical manual of mental disorders* (4th ed., revised). Washington, DC: Author.

Bakken, J. P., & Obiakor, F. E. (2008). *Transition planning for students with disabilities: What educators and service providers can do.* Springfield, IL: Charles C Thomas.

Barnes, K. L., & Bullock, L. M. (1995). Educators as transition facilitators: A teacher training project. *Education and Treatment of Children, 18*(3), 360–368.

Bateman, D. F., Bright, K., & Brandt, A. (2003). Parents as instructors. In D. L. Wandry & A. M. Pleet (Eds.), *A practitioner's guide to involving families in secondary transition.* Arlington, VA: Council for Exceptional Children.

Blue-Banning, M., Summers, J. A., Frankland, H. C., Nelson, L. L., & Beegle, G. (2004). Dimensions of family and professional partnerships: Constructive guidelines for collaboration. *Exceptional Children, 70*(2), 167–184.

Brotherson, M. J., & Berdine, W. R. (1993). Transition to adult services: Support for ongoing parent participation. *Remedial and Special Education, 14*(4), 44–51.

Cameto, R. (2005). *NLTS 2: Employment of youth with disabilities after high school.* Washington, DC: National Center for Special Education Research.

Carlson, M. J., & Corcoran, M. E. (2001). Family structure and children's behavioral and cognitive outcomes. *Journal of Marriage and Family, 63*(3), 779–792.

Clark, H. B., Belkin, M. T., Obradovich, L. D., Casey, R. E., Gagnon, R., Catroni, P., & Deschênes, N. (2002). Transition from school to community: Navigating rough waters. In K. L. Lane, F. M. Gresham, & T. O'Shaughnessy (Eds.), *Interventions for children with or at risk for emotional and behavioral disorders.* Boston: Allyn & Bacon/Longman.

Cohen, E., & Canan, L. (2006). Closer to home: Parent mentors in child welfare. *Child Welfare, 85*(5), 867–884.

Davis, M., & Butler, M. (2002, June). *Service systems supports during the transition from adolescence to adulthood: Parent perspectives.* Alexandria, VA: National Technical Assistance Center for State Mental Health Planning, National Association of State Mental Health Program Directors, & National Technical Assistance Center for State Mental Health Planning. Retrieved September 28, 2009, from http://www.nasmhpd.org/general_files/publications/ntac_pubs/reports/TransitionsII.pdf

deFur, S. H. (2003). Parents as collaborators: Building partnerships with school-based and community-based providers. In D. L. Wandry & A. M. Pleet (Eds.), *A practitioner's guide to involving families in secondary transition* (pp. 27–39). Arlington, VA: Council for Exceptional Children.

deFur, S. H. (2009). Parents as collaborators. In D. L. Wandry & A. Pleet, (Eds.), *Engaging and empowering families in secondary transition: A practitioner's guide* (pp. 33–52). Arlington, VA: Council for Exceptional Children.

deFur, S. H., Todd-Allen, M., & Getzel, E. E. (2001). Parent participation in the transition planning process. *Career Development for Exceptional Individuals, 23,* 19–36.

Duncan, B., Burns, S., & Robertson, M. (1996). Family-centered and family-friendly services. In B. Duncan, D. Burns, & M. Robertson (Eds.), *Providing quality services to emotionally disturbed students and their families in California* (pp. 13–18). Sacramento: California Department of Education.

Epstein, J. L. (2005). *Developing and sustaining research-based programs of school, family, and community partnerships: Summary of five years of NNPS research.* Baltimore: National Network of Partnership Schools.

Epstein, J. L., & Salinas, K. C. (2004). Partnering with families and communities. *Educational Leadership, 61,* 8:12–18.

Fox, L., Vaughn, B. J., Wyatte, M. L., & Dunlap, G. (2002). "We can't expect other people to understand": Family perspectives on problem behavior. *Exceptional Children, 68*(4), 437–450.

Geenen, S., Powers, L., Vasquez, A. L., & Bersani, H. (2003). Understanding and promoting the transition of minority adolescents. *Career Development for Exceptional Individuals, 26*(1), 27–46.

Guy, B., Goldberg, M., McDonald, S., & Flom, R. A. (1997). Parental participation in transition systems change. *Career Development for Exceptional Individuals, 20*(2), 165–177.

Hatter, R. A., Williford, M., & Dickens, K. (2000). Nurturing and working in partnership with parents during transition. In H. B. Clark & M. Davis (Eds.), *Transition to adulthood: A resource for assisting young people with emotional or behavioral difficulties* (pp. 209–228). Baltimore: Paul H. Brookes.

Henderson, A. T. (2007, March 28). NCLB reauthorization: Effective strategies for engaging parents and communities in schools. Testimony to U. S. Senate Committee on Health, Education, Labor, and Pensions.

Hutchins, M. P., & Renzaglia, A. (1998). Interviewing families for effective transition to employment. *Teaching Exceptional Children, 64,* 72–78.

Individuals with Disabilities Education Act of 1997, Pub. L. No. 105–17 (1997).

Individuals with Disabilities Education Improvement Act of 2004, Pub. L. No. 108–446 (2004).

Jolivette, K., Stichter, J. P., Nelson, C. M., Scott, T. M., & Liaupsin, C. J. (2000). *Improving post-school outcomes for students with emotional and behavioral disorders.*Arlington, VA: Council for Exceptional Children. (ERIC Document Reproduction Service No. ED 447 616.) Retrieved September 28, 2009, from http://www.ericdigests.org/2001–3/post.htm

Kohler, P., & Martin, J. (1998). *Transition from school to life: A workshop series for educators and transition service providers.* Arlington, VA: Council for Exceptional Children.

Kolb, S. M. (2003). Parents as trainers, role models, and mentors. In D. L. Wandry & A. M. Pleet (Eds.), *A practitioner's guide to involving families in secondary transition* (pp. 59–70). Arlington, VA: Council for Exceptional Children.

Lankard, B. A. (1994). Parents and the school-to-work transition of special needs youth. *ERIC Digest 142.*

Layzer, J. L., Goodson, B. D., Bernstein, L., & Price, C. (2001). *National evaluation of family support programs: Final report, volume A: The meta-analysis.* Cambridge, MA: Abt Associates.

Lehman, C. M., & Irvin, L. K. (1996). Support for families with children who have emotional or behavior disorders. *Education and Treatment of Children, 19*(3), 335–354.

Lopez, M. F. (2000). A comparison of self-modeling and peer-modeling as interventions to improve the teacher-preferred social skills of at-risk and special education students. (Doctoral dissertation, University of California, Riverside, 1999.) *Dissertation Abstracts International, Section A, 60*(12-A), 4318.

Malloy, J., Cheney, D., & Cormier, G. (1998). Interagency collaboration and the transition to adulthood for students with emotional or behavioral disabilities. *Education and Treatment of Children, 21*(3), 303–320.

Martin, J. E., Marshall, L. H., & Sale, P. (2004). A 3-year study of middle, junior high, and high school IEP meetings. *Exceptional Children, 70*(3), 285–297.

McGinley, V. (2009). Defining the family: Changing demographics. In D. L. Wandry & A. M. Pleet (Eds.), *Engaging and empowering families in secondary transition: A practitioner's guide* (pp. 21–32). Arlington, VA: Council for Exceptional Children.

McKinney, C., & Renk, K. (2008). Multivariate models of parent–late adolescent gender dyads: The importance of parenting processes in predicting adjustment. *Child Psychiatry and Human Development, 39*(2), 147–170.

McLanahan, S. S. (1997). Parent absence or poverty: Which matters more? In G. J. Duncan & J. Brooks Gunn (Eds.), *Consequences of growing up poor* (pp. 35–48). New York: Russell Sage Foundation.

Moore, C. (1988, Winter). Parents and transition "make it or break it." *The Pointer.* Publication of the Association for Retarded Citizens in Montgomery County, Maryland.

Morningstar, M. (2009). Parents as systems change agents. In D. L. Wandry & A. M. Pleet, (Eds.), *Engaging and empowering families in secondary transition: A practitioner's guide* (pp.119–139). Arlington, VA: Council for Exceptional Children.

Morningstar, M., & Torrez, J. (2003). Parents as systems change agents. In D. L. Wandry & A. M. Pleet, (Eds.), *A practitioner's guide to involving families in secondary transition* (pp. 83–96). Arlington, VA: Council for Exceptional Children.

National Center on Secondary Education and Transition. (2002). *Person-centered planning: A tool for transition.* Minneapolis: Author.

National Center on Secondary Education and Transition. (2004). *Current challenges facing the future of secondary education and transition services for youth with disabilities in the United States.* Minneapolis: Author.

National Longitudinal Transition Study–2. (2001, 2003, 2005). Retrieved September 28, 2009 from http://www.nlts2.org.

National PTA. (2007). *National standards for family–school partnerships.* Retrieved September 28, 2009 from http://www.pta.org/Documents/National_Standards.pdf

No Child Left Behind Act of 2001, Pub. L. No. 107–110 (2001).

Office of Disability Employment Policy. (2001). *Education Kit 2001—Workforce Investment Act of 1998: Its application to people with disabilities.* Retrieved September 28, 2009 from http://www.dol.gov/odep/pubs/ek01/act.htm

PACER Center. (2004). *Person-centered planning: A tool for transition.* Minneapolis: Author.

PACER Center. (2005). *Ten tips that may help ease your child's transition to adulthood.* Minneapolis: Author.

PACER Center. (2006). *Measuring transition success: Focus on youth and family participation.* Minneapolis: Author.

Paige, R. (2002, April 8). Schools can't improve without the help of parents. *USA Today,* A13.

Parker, E., & Finch, T. (2000). The family as a critical partner in the achievement of a successful employment outcome. *Institute on Rehabilitation Issues, 26,* 29–43.

Pleet, A. M., & Wandry, D. L. (2003). Introduction to the role of parents in secondary transition. In D. L. Wandry & A. M. Pleet (Eds.), *A practitioner's guide to involving families in secondary transition* (pp. 1–14). Arlington, VA: Council for Exceptional Children.

Pleet, A. M., & Wandry, D. L. (2009). Introduction to the role of families in secondary transition. In D. L. Wandry & A. M. Pleet (Eds.), *Engaging and empowering families in secondary transition: A practitioner's guide* (pp. 1–20). Arlington, VA: Council for Exceptional Children.

Powers, K., Hogansen, J., Geenen, S., Powers, L., & Gil-Kashiwabara, E. (2008). Gender matters in transition to adulthood: A survey study of adolescents with disabilities and their families. *Psychology in the Schools, 45*(4), 349–364.

Rehabilitation Act Amendments of 1998, Pub. L. No. 105–22 (1998).

Schoeller, K., & Emanuel, E. (2003). Parents as evaluators and decision-makers. In D. L. Wandry & A. M. Pleet (Eds.), *A practitioner's guide to involving families in secondary transition* (pp. 41–58). Arlington, VA: Council for Exceptional Children.

Schuster, J., Graham, S., & Moloney, M. (2000). *Building a future: Working with the post-high school expectations of students and parents.* Boston: Institute for Community Inclusion.

Sitlington, P. L., Clark, G. M., & Kolstoe, O. P. (2000). *Transition education and services for adolescents with disabilities* (3rd ed.). Needham Heights, MA: Allyn & Bacon.

Takemoto, C., & Healy, C. (2009). Parents as evaluators and decision makers. In D. L. Wandry & A. M. Pleet (Eds.), *Engaging and empowering families in secondary transition: A practitioner's guide* (pp. 81–99). Arlington, VA: Council for Exceptional Children.

Test, D. W., Aspel, N. P., & Everson, J. M. (2006). *Transition methods for youth with disabilities.* Upper Saddle River, NJ: Pearson.

Trzcinski, E., & Holst, E. (2008). Subjective well-being among young people in transition to adulthood. *Social Indicators Research, 87*(1), 83–109.

Turnbull, R., Huerta, N., & Stowe, M. (2006). *The Individuals with Disabilities Education Act as amended in 2004.* Upper Saddle River, NJ: Pearson.

Turnbull, A., & Turnbull, R. (2001). *Families, professionals, and exceptionality: Collaborating for empowerment* (4th ed.). Upper Saddle River, NJ: Prentice Hall.

Turnbull, A., Turnbull, R., & Wehmeyer, M. L. (2007). *Exceptional lives: Special education in today's schools* (5th ed.). Upper Saddle River, NJ: Pearson.

Twenty-sixth Institute on Rehabilitation Issues. (2000). *The family as critical partner in the achievement of a successful employment outcome.* Hot Springs: University of Arkansas. Retrieved February 1, 2010, from http://www.pacer.org/tatra/26IRIinside.pdf

U. S. Department of Education. (2004). *Parental involvement: Title I, Part A: Non-regulatory guidance.* Washington, DC: Author.

Wagner, M., & Cameto, R. (2004). *The characteristics, experiences, and outcomes of youth with emotional disturbance. NLTS-2 data brief: Report from the National Longitudinal Study.* Menlo Park, CA: SRI International.

Wagner, M., Newman, L., Cameto, R., Garza, N., & Levine, P. (2005). *After high school: A first look at the post-school experiences of youth with disabilities. Report from the National Longitudinal Transition Study-2 (NLTS-2).* Menlo Park, CA: SRI International.

Wagner, M., Newman, L., Cameto, R., Levine, P., & Marder, C . (2007). *Perceptions and expectations of youth with disabilities.* Menlo Park, CA: SRI International.

Wandry, D. L., & Pleet A. M. (Eds.). (2009). *Engaging and empowering families in secondary transition: A practitioner's guide.* Arlington, VA: Council for Exceptional Children.

Ward, M. (2009). Parents as instructors in their youths' emergent independence. In D. L. Wandry & A. M. Pleet (Eds.), *Engaging and empowering families in secondary transition: A practitioner's guide* (pp. 53–79). Arlington, VA: Council for Exceptional Children.

Wehmeyer, M. L. Palmer, S., Agran, M., Mithaug, D., & Martin, J. (2000). Promoting causal agency: The self-determined learning model of instruction. *Exceptional Children, 66,* 439–453.

Witt, R. (2002). Best practices in transition to post-secondary work. In A. Thomas & J. Grimes (Eds.), *Best practices in school psychology IV.* Bethesda, MD: National Association of School Psychologists.

Wolfendale, S. (2002). *Standard-bearing: Assuring quality in parent partnership services.* Paper presented at the National Network of Parent Partnership Services Conference, Birmingham, England.

Workforce Investment Act of 1998, Pub. L. No. 105–220 (1998).

Zhang, D. (2005). Parent practices in facilitating self-determination skills: The influences of culture, socioeconomic status, and children's special education status. *Research and Practice for Persons with Severe Disabilities, 30*(3), 154–162.

## CHAPTER 5

# Four Strategies to Create Positive Transition Outcomes for Students with Emotional or Behavioral Disorders

**Francie R. Murry and Michael Todd Allen**

Students with emotional or behavioral disorders (EBD) have higher dropout rates than any other disability group. They are also less likely to attend postsecondary schooling than other disability groups (Nelson, Benner, Lane, & Smith, 2004). Fifty percent of students with EBD have dropped out of school before or by the 10th grade, and school completion is no longer a target on their radar. Once they leave school, they are in the job market without adequate academic or social skills. Unless someone, such as a family member, intervenes, they will move from job to job reinforcing their negative beliefs about the world and themselves. The challenge to young adults with EBD is not limited to struggles within an academic domain. They face daily difficulties exacerbated by inappropriate emotional and behavioral responses due to a lack of self-regulation. Students with EBD often find the high-school environment less personal and the expectations for self-control greater than in earlier grades. By the time they have finished their 9th grade year, their misbehaviors have usually guaranteed that there will be few if any champions left to advocate for their success.

The dismal outcomes faced by students with EBD as they leave or graduate from high school create an insistence that special educators focus attention on the transition needs of these youth. It is the most feasible position we can take to reverse the stubborn statistics that plague this group of youth with disabilities. Walker and Gresham (2003) state that there has not been adequate recognition of the educational needs and demands of these students. They argue that educators and society at large must become involved in futures planning for these youth in order for them to make successful transitions to adulthood.

This chapter will provide school personnel with strategies that will form the foundation for positive transitions into early adulthood for students with EBD. The strategies provided in this chapter were developed through the integration of current research in best practices for the educational retention of students with EBD. The four strategies discussed are (1) to promote students' engagement with school to achieve retention, (2) to promote youth self-advocacy and self-regulation skills during social skill use, (3) to provide student support through collaboration between school personnel and community service providers, and (4) to integrate community-based mentorship programs with students' educational and transitional processes. The implementation of these strategies will benefit the federally mandated secondary transition planning process (IDEIA, 2004).

Successful transition from adolescence to young adulthood can be difficult for even the most academically successful, emotionally stable, and socially adept youth. Navigating the course from home and school to adult environments requires a well-developed portfolio of cognitive, academic, social, and affective skills. These skills are necessary in order to discern and respond to the expectations and requirements of post-secondary education (when it is appropriate), employment, independent living, adult interpersonal relationships, and membership in one's community. To be successful in adulthood, the student must have and use self-regulation skills that take into account the consequence of automatic negative emotional reactions. Gaining cognitive control over emotional and behavioral reactions during social skill use will improve transitions and retention within the workforce.

Wagner, Newman, Cameto, Garza, and Levine (2005) found that students with EBD who achieved high social skill ratings have a significantly higher likelihood of being employed compared with any youth with low ratings. Wagner, Newman, Cameto, Levine, and Marder (2007) reported that when youth with EBD were asked how they characterized their personal relationships in school, they said they had conflict in relationships, had difficulty getting along with others at school, and were less likely to say that they were cared about by other adults than youth in other disability categories. If youth act on these perceptions, they will not fare well in future environments. Thus, these issues must be addressed before students leave high school.

Wagner et al. (2005) also identified a positive correlation between increasing age (20 to 23 years) and the likelihood that youth with disabilities have acquired long-term employment. Although this correlation is very hopeful, it does not mean that youth with EBD grow out of their disability nor can they wait to age so employability is an option. The type of disability the youth has and the number of functional domains that are affected will influence the youth's chances for employment. This correlation supports the need for individualized education program (IEP) team members to promote the students' continuing active school engagement, pursuit of self-advocacy skills, and interagency collaboration and mentorship throughout high school and into early adulthood. Ensuring that a foundation of best practices in transition and educational retention planning (that is, use of the four strategies of school engagement, self-advocacy and self-regulation skills during social skill use, student support through the collaboration between school personnel and community service providers, and integration of community-based mentorship programs with students' educational and transitional processes) for students with EBD is carefully implemented throughout the students' education, creating a better chance of a student's successful transition to adulthood.

## THE FOUR STRATEGIES

### Strategy 1: Promote Students' Engagement with School to Achieve Retention

Risk factors for school disengagement vary among students and co-occur in the personal, family, and school-related domains. The co-morbidity of these risk factors for students with EBD makes it difficult to determine which factors may contribute the most to increasing the probability that students will drop out of school before graduation. Fortin, Marcotte, Potvin, Royer, and Joly (2006) and Newcomb et al. (2002) identified externalized behavior problems (that is, aggression and/or delinquency) that increase the risk of a student's dropping out of school. Marcotte, Fortin, Royer, Potvin, and Leclerc (2001) identified internalized behaviors of depression and/or anxiety as similar risk factors. In the family domain, the risk factor most often cited is low socioeconomic status (Battin-Pearson et al., 2000; Goldschmidt & Wang, 1999), followed closely by family dysfunction. Family lack of affective support, lack of communication between youth and parents and between home and school, and broken homes add to the risk of dropping out (Fortin et al. 2006; Potvin et al., 1999; and Rumberger, 1995). Research in the school domain showed significant numbers of youth dropping out of school when they were held back in grades and perceived student/teacher relationships as negative (Jimerson, Anderson, & Whipple, 2002; Lessard et al., 2008).

School disengagement leads to students with EBD dropping out of school; however, educators can improve student engagement. Entwisle, Alexander, and Olson (2004) found that when dropping out of school was viewed by educators more as a process than an event, the chances of involving and retaining students in school was far greater. Researchers have identified the importance of active school engagement to the process of retaining students in school in order to positively transition them into adulthood (Christenson, Sinclair, Lehr, & Hurley, 2000; Finn, 1993; Grannis, 1994; Hess & Copeland, 2001; Lehr, Hansen, Sinclair, & Christenson, 2003). Primarily, school engagement includes student participation, identification with school or social bonding, academic performance, and personal investment in learning (Finn, 1993; Maehr & Midgely, 1996; Wehlage, Rutter, Smith, Lesko, & Fernandez, 1989). Christenson et al. (2000) advocate that when dealing with student engagement teachers must provide support for meeting academic, social, and behavioral standards rather than simply helping the student stay in school. Ingels, Curtin, Kaufman, Alt, and Chen (2002) found that student involvement in these activities was important for keeping both females and males in school.

Participation in after-school programs has been shown to provide additional opportunities for social and affective growth. Such participation has been linked to decreased negative behaviors within school and frequently motivates students to proactively pursue social interaction in the classroom once they have experienced social success elsewhere (Kahne et al., 2001). Unfortunately, only about half of students with EBD report being involved in school or community extracurricular activities (Wagner & Cameto, 2004). Special educators can promote student identification and participation in activities that fit their unique skills and personal interests. After-school programs can provide youth with a safe and supportive adult-supervised environment and offer them various growth-enhancing opportunities, including activities and experiences that promote academic, personal, social, and recreational development. Students at risk of school failure who participate in after-school programs have shown increases in academic achievement as well (Lauer et al., 2006).

The following statements are from two students who were interested in theater but who had never had participated in it. Their special education teacher encouraged the drama teacher to have them learn stage-crew lighting techniques for the spring musical.

> Terry and Belia, age 14: We both like acting; we really can act. We don't want to do it in front of anyone, but Mrs. Ward got us to try running the lighting for the play, and it was cool. She even let us try some of our own ideas on how the lights should come on and for how long they should stay or fade out. We are a team, and we were surprised when they invited us to the cast party. (Murry, 2009)

Watson and Keith (2002) found that students with EBD scored significantly lower than nondisabled students on three quality of life factors (that is, satisfaction, well-being, and social belonging). Social belonging and disengagement at school are indicated by the lack of involvement in extracurricular activities at school, in community clubs, or after-school activities. Special education teachers can promote student feelings of satisfaction with and social belonging in school by encouraging students with disabilities to engage in these activities (Wagner, Blackorby, & Hebbeler, 1993). The comments provided by Terry and Belia as they discuss belonging and working together show the power of encouraging youth to be socially engaged.

The impact of a teacher's active promotion of a student's social engagement is also illustrated in the following statement by Chaz.

> Chaz, age 17: I knew I didn't fit in at high school. My special education teacher hooked me up with an art student at the university to help me do a project for my history class. I learned a lot about art; other high-school students paid attention to my work and started talking to me as if I belonged

> somehow. I also found out that there are a lot of people just like me, and when I leave high school I can find a place to do what I love and fit in. I plan to graduate. (Murry, 2009)

Because this teacher promoted social engagement with other people, the student was helped to maintain a positive outlook in what could be described as a chaotic transition to young adulthood.

Jimerson et al. (2002) found that students who have trouble getting along with peers at school or have problems using social skills were in jeopardy of school disengagement. Cairns, Cairns, and Neckerman (1989) found that one of the most influential factors in determining whether socially disengaged students would drop out of school was if their friends were also socially disengaged. When students are not members of a group that is socially engaged in school activities, they cannot practice the social skills that are being taught or develop positive reactions to school social situations.

It is axiomatic that students with EBD cannot receive the full benefit of transition programming unless they remain in school. Students with EBD are placed in more restrictive settings, including segregated classes and/or facilities, than students in other disability categories (Reid, Gonzalez, Nordness, Trout, & Epstein, 2004). Many supporters of inclusive settings for students with EBD attest that the reasons students disengage and express dislike for school include the isolation and separation from other students, teachers, and school functions that they experience. By the time students with EBD reach high school, their parents report that almost half of them do not like school (Newman, Davies-Mercier, & Marder, 2004). These reports are in contrast to similar surveys at the elementary level where fewer than 10% of students with EBD are reported to be disengaged (Newman & Davies, 2005). Therefore, some negative emotional reactions toward school are reinforced between elementary and high school. The EBD diagnosis and its associated negative characteristics exacerbate the inclination to place students in restrictive settings (Jolivette, Stichter, Nelson, Scott, & Liaupsin, 2000). Restrictive settings remove students from the academic opportunities of their peers and allow them to fall farther behind academically as they age (Coutinho, 1986). In order to keep students with EBD in settings where they can best benefit academically and socially, special educators must provide general educators and students with EBD strategies that allow them to overcome the negative characteristics associated with the disability.

Causal relationships have not been established; however, several factors appear to influence school disengagement. These factors include questionable retentions at grade level, noninvolvement in extracurricular activities, and lack of social supports such as parents and other family members (Lessard, Fortin, Joly, Royer, & Blaya, 2004). In addition, the relationships established with other youth and school personnel create social skill practice opportunities and attachment to the academic environment.

Of the students who dropped out of school, the decision to leave school was a process of disengagement that began as early as 3rd grade (Lehr, Sinclair, & Christenson, 2004). Many students who drop out are expressing an extreme form of disengagement from school that has been foreshadowed by indicators of withdrawal (for example, poor attendance) and unsuccessful school experiences (for example, academic or behavioral difficulties) (Rumberger, 1995).

> Michael, age 18: I knew by the time I started 4th grade that I would never finish school. The teachers hated me; I couldn't find anything comfortable about doing schoolwork and saw no reason to try. No one ever told me I had a chance of getting a job beyond the kind my dad did, and I saw no reason to think I should. (Murry, 2009)

Students who do not see schooling as a vehicle to promote future aspirations or who may not even have future aspirations need educators who will develop the vision that graduation from high school is an open door to future opportunity. Educators have the ability to promote positive social behavior by cultivating healthy social-emotional relations, which in turn will promote engagement in school and personal satisfaction. The student's reaction of withdrawal or avoidance is an example of a conditioned emotional response. For youth with EBD, school completion is an important milestone for entry into adulthood.

As early as infancy, conditioned emotional responses are learned. Conditioning involves pairing a previously neutral (that is, nonemotional) cue with an emotion-eliciting cue. The classic example of a conditioned emotional reaction is the case of "Little Albert," in which fear of a white rat (that is, a nonemotional cue) was learned by pairing the rat with a loud, startling noise (that is, an emotion-eliciting cue) (Watson & Rayner, 1920). Emotional conditioning can supply an explanation for disengagement from school. If students experience a high enough level of math, school, or test anxiety and react to it as a conditioned behavior, they will find ways to escape or avoid the discomfort.

Overt indicators of disengagement are generally accompanied by feelings of alienation, a poor sense of belonging, and general dislike for school (Ekstrom, Goertz, Pollack, & Rock, 1986). The path leading toward school withdrawal begins early. Retrospective studies show that dropouts can be identified with reasonable accuracy based on review of school performance (for example, behavior, attendance, academics) during the elementary years (Barrington & Hendricks, 1989). Faced early with repeated academic or social failures, the students acquire a pattern of negative emotions. In an attempt to avoid another failed interaction, they misbehave and achieve the desired consequence of removing themselves from an academic situation associated with negative emotions. Thus, they alienate themselves from support systems that would help them acquire the skills to overcome and control the negative emotional reactions.

Two effective ways to overcome negative emotions are through extinction (Rothbaum & Davis, 2003) and counterconditioning (Jones, 1924). Extinction involves the presentation of the learned emotional cue without the expected negative outcome. Leroy gave the following great example of extinction. He described being reprimanded by the teacher for not raising his hand in math class to answer a question; however, when he got to the next grade-level math class, the teacher expected him to join in the discussion without raising his hand. Leroy began having general anxiety about being criticized and constantly reminded in his first general education classroom to behave in a specific way, only to find he was not criticized for that behavior the next year. Thus, his anxious feelings faded away. This situation without the expected negative outcome resulted in a reduction and eventual loss of the learned emotional response.

> Leroy, age 15: Not only did I feel comfortable in class, but I started to like doing math. (Murry, 2009)

In counterconditioning, a student learns to have a positive emotional response in a situation that previously produced a learned negative emotional response. An example of counterconditioning occurs when a teacher knows that a student is faced with an anxiety-producing task and either breaks the difficult task into smaller, easier steps or provides a problem that is easier than the one the student will ultimately complete. In doing the easier task, the student learns to associate that task with a positive outcome rather than with the negative emotion of anxiety.

In the past decade, engagement of alienated youth in school and learning has emerged as a key component of prevention and intervention efforts (Grannis, 1994). Interventions supporting student engagement in the development of connections with the learning environment across a variety of domains, such as in school, after school, and in extracurricular activities, have been found effective.

## Strategy 2: Promote Self-Advocacy and Self-Regulation Skills During Social Skill Use

Service learning projects with an adult (either school or community personnel) provide development of self-regulation skills and allow for future career exploration and opportunities to practice self-advocacy skills (Nelson & Eckstein, 2008). Teacher sensitivity is required when students begin to engage in the processes of critical thinking and self-regulation as displayed by their attempts at self-determination for their future goals.

> Mickie, age 17: I know I am different from other kids. I don't view adults the same way for one thing. I don't believe most adults know any better than I do about what I should do or not do. Rarely do they listen to what I think, or when they pretend to listen, they don't act on it. Every time I can remember trying to speak in school, I was told I was inappropriate and would have a point taken from me or dropped a level. Even now, it is as if they believe I am just dreaming about my abilities and the fact that I think I can really be someone. Most of them sitting in those meetings do not believe in me. It makes me even more angry, and they wonder why I won't be more cooperative. (Murry, 2004, p. 88)

Due to the structured and teacher-directed nature of most instructional experiences, self-advocacy and self-regulation deficits frequently are not fully evident until students with EBD enter the adult world, especially the workplace. Given the social stigma of mental illness, or whatever term the student has experienced while in school, many students with EBD are reluctant to self-identify to their supervisors, even though many employers have expressed willingness to work with and accommodate individuals with disabilities (Carter & Wehby, 2003). As a result, many employees with EBD are either reprimanded or terminated without recourse for actions that are disability related. Teachers should provide students with self-advocacy instruction and practice opportunities that are both socially acceptable and sensitive to the reactions of the listeners early in the school experience.

Despite the use of social skill training in schools, many students with EBD have difficulty generalizing these skills to the workplace and to adult friendships. Frequently, they are unable to prioritize between two or more socially appropriate actions or to discriminate between audiences and environments. For example, topics appropriate for discussion with coworkers may be considered insubordinate or disrespectful when they are communicated to supervisors. Providing instruction to students beyond the *hows* in social skills and supporting students through practice to discriminate the proper *whens* and *wheres* will lay the foundation for successful interactions with coworkers and supervisors in the workplace. Combining social skill delivery with self-regulation planning gives students with EBD a chance for successful social and employment outcomes.

In addition, teachers can empower students with EBD to use techniques such as behavior mapping (Cohen-Mansfield, 1997) and self-talk strategies (Patton, Jolivette, & Ramsey, 2006) to control impulsive or angry behaviors. By gradually increasing opportunities for self-determined choices, teachers can prepare students with EBD to eventually lead their formal transition-planning process and to advocate effectively for the vocational, educational, and living options that best match their future goals (Eber & Nelson, 1997).

Special educators can promote successful outcomes for students with EBD by continuing to provide direct instruction and practice in social skills throughout the students' educational experience. General educators can increase the efficacy and generalization of the skills by emphasizing the need to discern the appropriate application of various skills across multiple environments, and they can provide a diverse set of opportunities to practice self-regulation. In order to reinforce these skills, special educators need to share techniques that general educators can integrate into their teaching routines. Students with EBD can be taught to create "environmental scans" by using one of the many techniques that are available, such as MAPS (O'Brien, Forest, Snow, & Hasbury, 1987), to construct a web of the different contexts and environments in which they function (for example, home, school, after-school programs and clubs, church, etc.). Teachers, with student input, can list all the possible interactions that might occur for students in those environments rather than restricting instruction to the scenarios provided in the social skills curriculum. During behavior planning and disciplinary actions, special educators can advocate for consequences that do not automatically remove the student with EBD from the general education classroom. Keeping the student in the general education environment provides more varied opportunities for social interactions than those that occur only in a special education classroom. The interactions also provide an opportunity to replace negative patterns of behavior with new positive responses.

Youth with EBD are the most likely to be reported as having low social skills (Wagner & Cameto, 2004). The more often students with EBD are included in general education environments with positive behavioral support, the more opportunities will exist for them to refine their social and self-regulation skills. When these opportunities are paired with guidance for skill implementation, students will experience fewer incidents of misconstrued communication with teachers and peers. Having clear expectations for academic performance behavior will reduce frustrations that lead to inappropriate behavior. Including students with EBD in general education settings will provide opportunities for them to practice skills and receive the reinforcement necessary for their continued use. Social opportunities for youth happen at school and during after-school and community activities. Social interactions occur daily with friends in the hallway, between classes, and during extracurricular activities. These interactions impact and influence the pattern of emotional and social behaviors that eventually become the students' behavioral norm. Students must be at school in the general education environment in order to engage in these practices with guidance from school personnel. The needed general education interaction makes it necessary for special educators to inform school personnel who interact with these students which skills should be reinforced.

As students are taught these skills and attempt use them, they need guidance to assert themselves more clearly and directly. Because these assertions may appear to adults as disrespectful, hostile, rebellious, or even noncompliant, school personnel need to know what social skills students are trying to use. Doc's attempts at self-advocacy may be regarded as disrespectful to the teacher as well as other students; however, a knowledgeable special education teacher could mediate interactions and guide reactions toward positive outcomes.

> Doc, age 15: In 9th grade, I was put in with a bunch of kids who everyone called retards. I couldn't read very well at all so the teacher thought she could help me in that room. . . . I couldn't read, and so I couldn't go to the general education vocational classes, so I was in the special education vocational program with the same class. . . . I wanted to learn about computer repair, and these students were learning to do janitorial work. I wasn't going to work with guys like that or a job like that when I got out of high school. (Murry, 2004, p. 90)

Special educators could help in this situation by teaching Doc how to communicate his concerns to the adults in the meeting so that it would be more palatable to them. In this way, he would be more likely to achieve his desired outcome.

As early as middle school, school counselors routinely begin advising students about educational and career trajectories and about the academic preparation required to pursue various options. School personnel will have the most lasting impact on improving the social and academic experiences of students with EBD if they can identify the students who need early goal-planning support. Such identification would have helped students like Doc plan for a future career and obtain the vocational training they desire.

Special educators can use a wide range of teacher-created or commercially available products to conduct interest exploration activities and then assist students with EBD in completing the processes for identifying vocational interests and potential careers. For students with EBD to experience these activities positively, special education teachers must consult with the program directors (for example, the directors of business programs and student clubs) who can provide advice and assistance in successfully including these students in exploratory vocational programs. This advice and assistance is analogous to the accommodations, modifications, and behavioral interventions that special education teachers provide to general educators so their students can achieve academic success. The premise that youth with EBD as a group and as individuals deserve to have a potential future of both successes and failures must be founded on the belief that they are capable of learning from educational programs that allow options. Special education teachers who are willing to promote community engagement must invest time, hard work, patience, and a team effort in supporting youth in exploring their interests and goals. Through learning the successful use of social skills, advocacy, and self-regulation, students with EBD become more self-reliant, independent, and integrated as part of a sustained workforce. The use of these skills creates the foundation for positive transitions into early adulthood.

Teachers of students with EBD can assess students' needs for social support through discussions with parents, guardians, and the students themselves. Using the information from this assessment, the IEP team can determine the type of social support most beneficial to the individual student. This support can include a peer, a formal mentoring relationship with a trusted adult, a tutor, a teacher with whom the student feels comfortable, or a volunteer who spends time at the school. These efforts require substantial planning, communication, and support if they are to be sustained. In the long run, the investment can have a significant payoff in terms of a sustainable workforce in the community, youth and parents with a future perspective that includes hope and goals, better prepared youth for higher education, and individuals with less dependence on others who are able to self-advocate for their needs. Last, it may be an important value to consider that a diploma may not be the only option through which students can access a postsecondary setting. Certainly, teachers do not want to be seen as advocating that a student drop out of school; however, if the student has already made headway toward dropping out of school or has earned very few credits late in high school, special educators have an obligation to discuss alternatives and available options.

## Strategy 3: Provide Increased Student Support Through Collaboration Between Teachers and Community Service Providers

In light of their low school completion and unemployment rates, and high rates of arrest, it is of paramount importance that students with EBD get beyond the problems created by their emotional and behavioral difficulties during high school. If they do, they can be prepared to attend college, keep a job, maintain friendships and engage in social situations, plan ahead, and attend to multiple tasks. So much of the time, students and their families have already spent a great deal of time and energy coping with the symptoms and the stressors that accompany the emotional and behavioral difficulties. There is little energy left to continue when students graduate from high school and are ready to enter the adult system. The last two U.S. censuses indicate the status of youth ages 20 through 24 who are still residing with their parents (U.S. Census Bureau, 2008).

Although parents have been the emotional, financial, and informational support system for their youths for years, they may be viewed as a challenge to the youth's movement into adulthood. There is a possibility that this perception is not held as much by youth as by the adults in social service agencies, higher education sectors (Seiffe-Krenke, 2006), and state age of majority and federal lawmakers (IDEIA, 2004).

If students can be aligned with services that they may qualify for before leaving high school, the family can better prepare for their transition; however, students who may qualify for mental health services under 21 years of age in the school system may not qualify for services upon leaving school. Connecting students and their families with social service personnel can be an asset for future planning and support.

> A parent: I appreciated my son's school social worker, who took the time to contact me each week to just "check in." She would ask how things were going at home, with his friends in the community, with the planned summer job. She was interested in family circumstances that would impact his adjustment in school. . . . She would use this information to evaluate the treatment that she provided, but it spoke loudly to me of her commitment to maintain an open line of communication. (Pleet, Wandry, & Gunsch, 2004, p. 72)

Special educators have a responsibility to facilitate communication between students with EBD and teachers or peers when students have difficult interactions or unresolved issues. The same level of responsibility is necessary to increase communication pathways for parents by becoming proactive connection makers. Based on the needs of individual students and their families, special educators can create an environment that facilitates interactions with community agencies. Many social service programs are difficult to navigate due to the use of agency-specific jargon and high amounts of required paperwork. Special educators should become familiar with the procedures and required paperwork and could even redraft bureaucratic documents into parent-friendly language and provide support for accessing resources.

Perhaps most important, special educators should establish communication channels with community agencies by initiating youth- and/or parent-requested contacts rather than simply providing lists of phone numbers for vocational, medical, mental health, and other services. It is typical that someone in the school has established working relationships with community agency personnel (and if this is not the case, someone should develop such informal partnerships). A call from the special education teacher can ensure that parents are directed to the appropriate office or individual without endless false starts.

This aspect of connection making may be critical for parents for whom English is a second language and whose own social skills are not well developed. Special educators should involve the student with EBD in making connections with the desired community services whenever it is age and situation appropriate. These interactions provide an opportunity for students with EBD to observe teacher modeling of appropriate social skills. An enhanced relationship experience between the student and parents may develop as a result of the parents' observing the empowered behavior of the student in important situations. Because parents of students with EBD more often hear about their children's inappropriate or disempowering behaviors, the importance of observing socially adept behaviors cannot be underestimated. The collaboration between the community service agency and school personnel provides a bridge for the youth to leave high school and successfully transition to services needed in adulthood.

## Strategy 4: Mentoring

The positive impact of mentoring has been documented in many areas. Mentoring has a positive influence on grades and other academic indicators by improving the relationship between the youth and the parent and by boosting the youth's perception of his or her academic abilities (Rhodes, Grossman, & Resch, 2000). Several mentoring studies have concluded that mentoring has a positive impact on the number of unexcused absences (Aseltine, Dupre, & Lamlein, 2000; Tierney, Grossman, & Resch, 1995) and students' overall positive attitude toward school (LoSciuto, Rajala, Townsend, & Taylor, 1996). In addition to tests and attendance data, teachers in one study indicated that mentored youth were less likely to be disruptive and more likely to be engaged in what was going on in the classroom (Blakely, Menon, & Jones, 1995). In the landmark Big Brothers Big Sisters impact study, some groups of mentored youth were shown to have a slight improvement in grades (Howard, 2008). Results increased exponentially for students the longer they were mentored (Tierney et al., 1995).

Karcher, Kuperminc, Portwood, Sipe, and Taylor (2006) proposed that psychosocial and academic outcomes are likely interrelated, with positive changes in one facilitating improvements in the other. Promoting either connectedness or grades through mentoring could prevent underachievement, dropping out, and problem behaviors (Herrera et al., 2007; Karcher, 2005). Effective mentoring programs have been identified as occurring in in-school, after-school, or community-based settings (Rhodes, 2008).

Evaluations by many current researchers of one-to-one mentoring programs have indicated that they are successful in promoting students' use of social, academic, and behavioral skills (DeWit et al., 2006; DuBois, Holloway, Valentine, & Cooper, 2002; Herrera et al., 2007; Karcher, 2005; Keating, Tomashina, Foster, & Allesandri, 2002). Family and other natural supports remain the strongest and the most consistent factors correlated with successful school and adult outcomes (Pleet et al., 2004). However, many students with EBD often lack these out-of-school support systems due in part to unique characteristics of their families and households. For some students with EBD, a meaningful relationship with a mentor from the community may represent their most consistent and sustainable support system.

---

## Mavis and Amy: A Mentor and a Mentee

Mavis was late in joining the summer research group and therefore was assigned Amy, the only student left with whom she could work. Amy's first mentor left after working only two days with her. Amy was withdrawn and sullen most of the time, identified as EBD, and reportedly had suicidal ideations. She had barely scraped through her 6th and 7th grade classes with the exception of mathematics, which she failed repeatedly. Mavis was described as "alternative," with gauges in both ears and multiple nose and tongue piercings. Amy told Mavis the first day that she hated having to do mathematics. Mavis stayed late to talk with both of the professors who were running the study. The students in the study came from Mentors and Friends, a mentoring program that served at-risk youth in collaboration with the school district.

"It is research, Mavis, and Amy's mom wants her to be part of the math tutoring and the metacognition study," said her professor.

The professor told Mavis to talk with the coordinator of the mentoring program to see how she could reinforce the additional social skills and guidance that were being given. After 6 weeks and 18 hours of metacognitive work in mathematics, Mavis and Amy appeared to have called a truce. Mavis still had an atypical appearance; however, often Amy was bright-eyed and smiling. Amy still declared that she hated math. When the study ended, Mavis and Amy asked if they could continue to work together in the Mentors and Friends program.

Two years later, Amy is looking into colleges she might attend, and Mavis has solidified her decision to become a middle-school teacher. They spend 3 hours per week in tutoring and other activities that involve sports events, ballet, opera, basketball, and just hanging. They have found a common bond and connected at a life-changing level. . Amy has plans to finish high school and continue her education; however, her affect still appears downcast at times. This Amy differs from her mother's anxious initial description of her as "on her way to a downhill slide." Amy had an opportunity to mature in a safe environment with Mavis, who championed her and provided a promise of support. Today, Amy uses social skills that had been taught to her earlier in her life and reinforced by Mavis through the mentoring program. It is noticeable that Amy displays conflict resolution and self-regulation skills, especially around the younger kids in the program, whom she finds irritating. She had the foundation but needed the intensive personal engagement of a mentor to support the outward display of those social skills.

One-to-one mentoring is one option to support youth when they are at crucial points in development (DuBois & Karcher, 2005). In this case, Amy had been taught the social skills that were necessary for her to succeed through her special education classes; however, she had not had the opportunities to practice them with the intensive guidance she needed to overcome the negative dispositions she had acquired. Mavis supported and guided Amy as she sorted through various social skill uses, conflict resolution techniques, and academic study skills. Mentoring provided the intensive personal attention that was needed to use the skills while Amy was transitioning to young adulthood.

## CONCLUSION

The strategies suggested in this chapter are based in the literature on school engagement, self-advocacy, agency connection, and mentoring. These strategies provide the necessary support to school personnel overwhelmed by the emotional and behavioral characteristics and needs of students with EBD. Given the poor school and community outcomes for students with EBD, the viability of a plan special educators make for students' successful transition to adulthood will depend on the plan's ability to integrate and link positive emotional and social supports. Students with EBD will need these support systems in place when they finish high school and enter the next phase of their transition to the adult world. The sustainability of these systems must be part of the transition plan. The investment of time and effort for creating this culture of support will not only facilitate positive long-term results but will also help students with EBD to develop successful future transition plans.

When all is said and done, we must look at the idea of creating a transition-planning model for youth with EBD in a more systematic manner. Transition plans created today should meet the unique emotional and cognitive needs of students as well as lay the foundation for future successes in academic and vocational endeavors. Special educators need to view their students as a uniquely different population of individuals whose potential must be nurtured and developed through careful planning. This can be done by exploring careers, living styles, and educational experiences that fit into society without causing students to lose their unique identities. This certainly will involve envisioning job opportunities that do not presently exist. We know that each student's transition must be addressed individually. This includes envisioning the student as an individual maturing into the next 10 years and beyond, rather than focusing on the student's current capacity. Should we need to color outside the lines for planning individual transitions to adulthood, we may heed the words of comedian Gilda Radner (1946–1989): "I wanted a perfect ending. Now I've learned, the hard way, that some poems don't rhyme and some stories don't have a clear beginning, middle, and end."

## REFERENCES

Aseltine, R. H., Dupre, M., & Lamlein, P. (2000). Mentoring as a drug prevention strategy: An evaluation of Across Ages. *Adolescent and Family Health, 1,* 11–20.

Battin-Pearson, S., Newcomb, M. D., Abbott, R. D., Hill, K. G., Catalano, R. F., & Hawkins, J. D. (2000). Predictors of early high school dropout: A test of five theories. *Journal of Educational Psychology, 92*(3), 568–582.

Barrington, B. L., & Hendricks, B. (1989). Differentiating characteristics of high school graduates, dropouts, and nongraduates. *The Journal of Educational Research 82*(6), 309–319.

Blakely, C. H., Menon, R., & Jones, D. C. (1995). *Project BELONG: Final report.* College Station: Texas A&M University, Public Policy Research Institute.

Cairns, R. B., Cairns, B. D., & Neckerman, H. J. (1989). Early school dropout: Configurations and determinants. *Child Development, 60,* 1437–1452.

Carter, E. W., & Wehby, J. H. (2003). Job performance of transition-age youth with emotional and behavioral disorders. *Exceptional Children, 69*(4), 449–465.

Christenson, S. L., Sinclair, M. F., Lehr, C. A., & Hurley, C. M. (2000). Promoting successful school completion. In K. M. Minke & G. C. Bear (Eds.), *Preventing school problems—Promoting school success.* Bethesda, MD: National Association of School Psychologists.

Cohen-Mansfield, J. (1997). Conceptualization of agitation: Results based on the Cohen-Mansfield Agitation Inventory and the Agitation Behavior Mapping Instrument. *International Psychogeriatrics, 8,* 309–315.

Coutinho, M. J. (1986). Reading achievement of students identified as behaviorally disordered at the secondary level. *Behavioral Disorders, 11,* 200–207.

DeWit, D. J., Lipman, E., Manzano-Munguia, M., Bisanz, J., Graham, K., Offord, D. R., O'Neill, E., Pepler, D., & Shaver, K. (2006). Feasibility of a randomized controlled trial for evaluating the effectiveness of the Big Brothers Big Sisters community match program at the national level. *Children and Youth Services Review, 29,* 383–404.

DuBois, D. L., Holloway, B. E., Valentine, J. C., & Cooper, H. (2002). Effectiveness of mentoring programs: A meta-analytical review. *American Journal of Community Psychology, 30,* 157–197.

DuBois, D. L., & Karcher, M. J. (Eds.). (2005). *Handbook of youth mentoring.* Thousand Oaks, CA: Sage Publications.

Eber, L., & Nelson, C. M. (1997). School-based wraparound planning: Integrating services for students with emotional and behavioral needs. *American Journal of Orthopsychiatry, 67*(3), 385–395.

Ekstrom, R. B., Goertz, M. E., Pollack, J. E., & Rock, D. A. (1986). Who drops out of high school and why? Findings from a national survey. *Teachers College Record, 87,* 356–373.

Entwisle, D., Alexander, K., & Olson, L. (2004). Temporary as compared to permanent high school dropout. *Social Forces, 82*(3), 1181–1205.

Finn, J. D. (1993). *School engagement and students at risk.* Buffalo: U. S. Department of Education National Center for Educational Statistics, Buffalo State College, State University of New York.

Fortin, L., Marcotte, D., Potvin, P., Royer, E., & Joly, J. (2006). Typology of students at risk of dropping out of school: Description by personal, family and school factors. *European Journal of Psychology of Education, 21*(4), 363–383.

Goldschmidt, P., & Wang, J. (1999). When can schools affect dropout behavior? A longitudinal multilevel analysis. *American Educational Research Journal, 36*(4), 715–738.

Grannis, J. C. (1994). The dropout prevention initiative in New York City: Educational reforms for at-risk students. In R. J. Rossi (Ed.), *School and students at risk: Context and framework for positive change* (pp. 182–206). New York: Teachers College, Columbia University.

Herrera, C., Grossman, J. B., Kauh, T. J., Feldman, A. F., & McMaken, J. (with Jucovy, L. Z.). (2007). *Making a difference in schools: The Big Brothers Big Sisters school-based mentoring impact study.* Philadelphia: Public/Private Ventures.

Hess, R. S., & Copeland, E. (2001). Students' stress, coping strategies, and school completion: A longitudinal perspective. *School Psychology Quarterly, 16*(4), 389–405.

Howard, A. W. (2008). Effectiveness of a youth mentorship program examined. *Chronicle of Philanthropy, 20*(8), 29.

Individuals with Disabilities Education Improvement Act of 2004, Pub. L. No. 108–446, §401 *et seq.* (2004).

Ingels, S. J., Curtin, T. R., Kaufman, P., Alt, M. N., & Chen, X. (2002). *Coming of age in the 1990s: The eighth-grade class of 1988 12 years later.* Washington, DC: National Center for Education Statistics.

Jimerson, S. R., Anderson, G. E., & Whipple, A. D. (2002). Winning the battle and losing the war: Examining the relationship between grade retention and dropping out of high school. *Psychology in the School, 39*(4), 441–458.

Jolivette, K., Stichter, J. P., Nelson, C. M., Scott, T. M., & Liaupsin, C. J. (2000). *Improving post-school outcomes for students with emotional and behavioral disorders.* Arlington, VA: Council for Exceptional Children. (ERIC Document Reproduction Service No. ED 447 616.) Retrieved September 28, 2009, from http://www.ericdigests.org/2001–3/post.htm

Jones, M. C. (1924). The elimination of children's fears. *Journal of Experimental Psychology, 7*, 382–390.

Kahne, J., Nagaoka, J., Brown, A., O'Brien, J., Quinn, T., & Thiede, K. (2001). Assessing after-school programs as contexts for youth development. *Youth & Society, 32*(4), 421–447.

Karcher, M. J. (2005). The effects of developmental mentoring and high school mentors' attendance on their younger mentees' self-esteem, social skills, and connectedness. *Psychology in the Schools, 42*, 65–77.

Karcher, M. J., Kuperminc, G., Portwood, S., Sipe, C., & Taylor, A. (2006). Mentoring programs: A framework to inform program development, research, and evaluation. *Journal of Community Psychology, 34*, 709–725.

Keating, L. M., Tomashina, M. A., Foster, S., & Allesandri, M. (2002). The effects of a mentoring program on at-risk youth. *Adolescence, 37*, 717–734.

Lauer, P. A., Akiba, M., Wilkerson, S. B., Apthorp, H. S., Snow, D., & Martin-Glenn, M. (2006). Out-of-school time programs: A meta-analysis of effects for at-risk students. *Review of Educational Research, 76*, 275–313.

Lehr, C. A., Hansen, A., Sinclair, M. F., & Christenson, S. L. (2003). Moving beyond dropout towards school completion: An integrative review of data-based interventions. *School Psychology Review, 32*(3), 342–364.

Lehr, C. A., Sinclair, M. E., & Christenson, S. L. (2004). Addressing student engagement and truancy prevention during the elementary school years: A replication study of the Check & Connect Model. *Journal of Education for Students Placed at Risk, 9*(3), 279–301.

Lessard, A. Butler-Kisber, L., Fortin, L., Marcotte, D., Potvin, P., & Royer, E. (2008). Shades of disengagement: High school dropouts speak out. *Social Psychological Education, 11*, 25–82.

Lessard, A., Fortin, L., Joly, J., Royer, É., & Blaya, C. (2004). Students at-risk for dropping out of school: Are there gender differences among personal, family and school factors? *Journal of At-Risk Issues, 10*(2), 91–127.

LoScuito, L., Rajala, A., Townsend, T. N., & Taylor, A. S. (1996). An outcome evaluation of across ages: An intergenerational mentoring approach to drug prevention. *Journal of Adolescent Research, 11*, 116–129.

Maehr, M. L., & Midgely, C. (1996). *Transforming school cultures.* Boulder, CO: Westview Press.

Marcotte, D., Fortin, L., Royer, E., Potvin, P., & Leclerc, D. (2001). L'influence du style parental, de la depression et des troubles du comportement sur le risque d'abandon scolaire. *Revue des sciences de l'education, 27*(3), 687–712.

Murry, F. R. (2004). Youths with emotional or behavioral disorders: Alternative ventures in transition. In D. Cheney (Ed.), *Transition of secondary students with emotional or behavioral disorders: Current approaches for positive outcomes* (pp. 82–101). Arlington, VA: Council for Children with Behavioral Disorders and the Division on Career Development and Transition.

Murry, F. (2009). *The relationship between intergenerational mentors and their mentees.* Unpublished manuscript.

Nelson, J. A., & Eckstein, D. (2008). A service-learning model for at-risk adolescents. *Education and Treatment of Children, 31*(2), 223–237.

Nelson, J. R., Benner, G. J., Lane, K., & Smith, B. W. (2004). Academic achievement of K–12 students with emotional and behavioral disorders. *Exceptional Children, 71*(1), 59–73.

Newcomb, M. D., Abbott, R. D., Catalano, R. F., Hawkins, J. D., Battin-Pearson, S., & Hill, K. (2002). Mediational and deviance theories of late high school failure: Process roles of structural strains, academic competence, and general versus specific problem behavior. *Journal of Counseling Psychology, 49*(2), 172–186.

Newman, L., & Davies, E. (2005). *Engagement, academics, social adjustment, and independence: The achievements of elementary and middle school students with disabilities.* Retrieved September 28, 2009, from http://www.seels.net/info_reports/engagement.htm

Newman, L., Davies-Mercier, E., & Marder, C. (2004). *Perceptions and expectations of youth with disabilities. A special topic report of findings from the National*

*Longitudinal Transition Study-2 (NLTS-2)*. Menlo Park, CA: SRI International. Retrieved September 28, 2009, from http://www.nlts2.org/reports/2007_08/index.html

O'Brien, J., Forest, M., Snow, J., & Hasbury, D. (1987). *Action for inclusion*. Toronto: Frontier College Press.

Patton, B., Jolivette, K., & Ramsey, M. (2006). Students with emotional and behavioral disorders can manage their own behavior. *Teaching Exceptional Children, 39*(2), 14–21.

Pleet, A. M., Wandry, D. L., & Gunsch, A. R. (2004) Building partnerships with families of youths with emotional or behavioral disorders. In D. Cheney (Ed.), *Transition of secondary students with emotional or behavioral disorders: Current approaches for positive outcomes* (pp. 59–81). Arlington, VA: Council for Children with Behavioral Disorders and the Division on Career Development and Transition.

Potvin, P., Deslandes, R., Beaulieu, P., Marcotte, D., Fortin, L., Royer, É., & Leclerc, D. (1999). Risque d'abandon scolaire, style parental et participation parentale au suivi scolaire. *Revue canadienne de l'éducation, 24*(4), 441–453.

Reid, R., Gonzalez, J. E., Nordness, P. D., Trout, A., & Epstein, M. H. (2004). A meta-analysis of the academic status of students with emotional/behavioral disturbance. *The Journal of Special Education, 38*(3), 130–143.

Rhodes, J. E. (2008). Improving youth mentoring interventions through research-based practice. *American Journal of Community Psychology, 41,* 35–42.

Rhodes, J. E., Grossman, J. B., & Resch, N. R. (2000). Agents of change: Pathways through which mentoring relationships influence adolescents' academic adjustment. *Child Development, 71,* 1662–1671.

Rothbaum, B., & Davis, M. (2003). Applying learning principles to the treatment of post-trauma reactions. *Annals of the New York Academy of Sciences, 1008,* 112–121.

Rumberger, R. W. (1995). Dropping out of middle school: A multilevel analysis of students and schools. *American Educational Research Journal, 32*(3), 583–625.

Seiffe-Krenke, I. (2006). Leaving home or still in the nest? Parent-child relationships and psychological health as predictors of different leaving home patterns. *Developmental Psychology, 42*(5), 864–876.

Tierney, J. P., Grossman, J. B., & Resch, N. L. (1995). *Making a difference. An impact study of Big Brothers Big Sisters*. Philadelphia: Public/Private Ventures.

U.S. Census Bureau (2008). *The 2008 statistical abstract: The national data book.* Retrieved September 28, 2009, from http://www.census.gov/compendia/statab/2008/2008edition.html

Wagner, M., Blackorby, J., & Hebbeler, K. (1993). *Beyond the report card: The multiple dimensions of secondary school performance of students with disabilities.* Menlo Park, CA: SRI International.

Wagner, M., & Cameto, R. (2004). *The characteristics, experiences, and outcomes of youth with emotional disturbance. NLTS-2 data brief: Report from the National Longitudinal Study.* Menlo Park, CA: SRI International.

Wagner, M., Newman, L., Cameto, R., Garza, N., & Levine, P. (2005). *After high school: A first look at the post-school experiences of youth with disabilities. Report from the National Longitudinal Transition Study-2 (NLTS-2).* Menlo Park, CA: SRI International.

Wagner, M., Newman, L., Cameto, R., Levine, P., & Marder, C . (2007). *Perceptions and expectations of youth with disabilities.* Menlo Park, CA: SRI International.

Walker, H. M., & Gresham, F. M. (2003). School-related behavior disorders. In W. M. Reynolds & G. E. Miller (Eds.), *Handbook of psychology: Educational psychology* (Vol. 7, pp. 511–530). New York: John Wiley & Sons.

Watson, J. B., & Rayner, R. (1920). Conditioned emotional reactions. *Journal of Experimental Psychology, 3,* 1–14.

Watson, S. M. R., & Keith, K. D. (2002). Comparing the quality of life of school-age children with and without disabilities. *Mental Retardation, 40,* 304–312.

Wehlage, G. G., Rutter, R. A., Smith, G. A., Lesko, N., & Fernandez, R. R. (1989). *Reducing the risk: Schools as communities of support.* Philadelphia: The Falmer Press.

# SECTION II

# Assessment and Planning Services
# for Students with EBD at the Secondary Level

## CHAPTER 6

# Age-Appropriate Transition Assessments: A Strategic Intervention to Help Youth with Emotional or Behavioral Disorders to Complete High School

**Larry J. Kortering, Patricia Braziel, and Patricia Sitlington**

Research shows that youth with emotional or behavioral disorders (EBD) have an alarmingly low rate of school completion, along with unfavorable postschool outcomes (see Corbett, Sanders, Clark, & Blank, 2002; Rylance, 1998; Tobin & Sugai, 1999). The Office of Special Education Program's (OSEP, 2008) Annual Report shows that during the 2002–2003 school year, 34% of youth with EBD who exited high school did so with a regular diploma, whereas 56% left as official dropouts. These data suggest a gradual improvement over the past 10 years. Specifically, for the 1993–1994 school year, only 27% of exiting youth left with a regular diploma, whereas 68% left as dropouts (OSEP, 2008). Despite the positive trend toward improvement, the overall rate of completing high school with a regular diploma remains far short of the nearly 80% of general education students who leave as high-school graduates. Furthermore, this latter rate rises to nearly 90% when accounting for the 50 to 75% of general education dropouts who obtain a high-school diploma or a General Education Development (GED) certificate within 5 years of leaving high school (Horn & Berktold, 2004).

The low rate of school or program completion among youth with EBD is of heightened concern given that the failure to attain a high-school diploma is related to difficulty becoming a productive adult. One such relationship is an increased likelihood of becoming imprisoned. High-school dropouts, while composing less than 15% of our general population, account for over 80% of the general prison population and juveniles in court (Luneberg, 1999). The prison population now accounts for over 2 million of our citizens, an increase of over 400% since 1980 (Johnson, 2007). The annual costs of simply housing, protecting, and feeding a prison inmate averages nearly $23,000 for federal and state inmates (Stephan, 2004), approaching twice the $14,600 we spend per year on educating a student with emotional disabilities (Chambers, Sckolnik, & Perez, 2003). Additional costs accrue in terms of property damage and the subsequent impact crime has on individual victims.

Another troubling outcome is that youth who drop out and manage to avoid prison still have an incredibly difficult time finding suitable employment. In part, the nature of their difficulty stems from the lack of community or adult services for school dropouts in general and for those with EBD in particular, making special education their best and often only opportunity for developing the academic and related skill sets required for suitable employment (Kortering & Braziel, 2008b). Consider, for example, that the 2004 census data show that today's dropout will earn some $8,000 less per year than a peer who graduated from high school or some $37,500 less than one who completed 4 years of college (Moretti, 2005). These annual differences, respectively, add up to from $320,000 to over $1,500,000 over a 40-year work life. Yates (2005) further highlights the challenge of securing employment without a diploma. His data show that the typical dropout takes about 3 years to start a job that will last a year and 11 years to find stable employment lasting 3 years. These figures compare to about 3 and 6 months and 1 and 3 years for peers who get a college education or high-school diploma, respectively. These figures, relative to income and finding stable employment, may be even more dramatic for youth with EBD.

The difficulty of finding stable employment reflects today's evolving labor market, which is increasingly characterized by complex knowledge, an ever-changing skill base, and foreign competition (see Friedman, 2005; Symonds, 2006). A standard high-school diploma has become a minimal requirement to access suitable postschool employment (in other words, jobs offering benefits, adequate wages, and opportunities for advancement) and postsecondary schooling or training (Kortering, deBettencourt, & Braziel, 2005; Symonds, 2006). On the near horizon, Zuckerman (2006) suggested that the evolving globalization and technology in our work world is rapidly making a college education the only way to escape the bottom of our economic ladder. Finally, the issue of wealth accumulation is a consideration. Using a national database, Gouskova and Stafford (2005) demonstrated how a household headed by someone with a terminal high-school degree accumulates 10 times more wealth than one headed by a high-school dropout.

When the Education for All Handicapped Children Act (EHA) initially passed, its boldest promise was that a "special education" would help students with disabilities to become productive members of society (United States Congressional Administration News, 1975). Like the vast majority of their nondisabled peers, students with disabilities had hope that their education would be a benefit in their future life. This benefit, anchored by a productive skill set necessary to find suitable employment or to pursue postsecondary schooling, was the basis for becoming productive taxpayers. Yet, as Edgar (1987) noted 2 decades ago, the promise of a productive adulthood remained unfulfilled for many students with disabilities. His words become even more prescient as we consider the outcomes for youth with EBD in the 21st century.

The low school completion rate among youth with EBD is unacceptable and demands interventions that work to keep them in school until they receive a regular diploma. The strategic use of age-appropriate transition assessments receives support from the following considerations. First, the ability to link one's high-school education to a career ambition is the primary motivation youth report for being in school (Kortering & Konold, 2005; Kortering, Konold, & Glutting, 1998), and such assessments make this link by identifying individual preferences and strengths and then matching them to suitable career options. Second, youth failing to complete school seldom access private or public job training services that might help offset their educational limitations (Hight, 1998). Additionally, over half of all general education dropouts eventually earn a GED certificate or their high-school diploma (Berktold, Geis, Kaufman, & Carroll, 1999), whereas few former students with EBD do so (Tobin & Sugai, 1999). Finally, the Individuals with Disabilities Education Improvement Act (IDEIA, 2004) brought renewed attention to the need to improve one's special education opportunity. Specifically, the law highlighted the importance of a results-oriented process anchored by access to transition services that facilitate one's movement from school to postschool activities. These services, which begin at 16 or even younger in some states, are to include measurable postsecondary goals along with corresponding annual goals, coordinated transition services that can be accessed after a student leaves high school, and an age-appropriate transition assessment (Shorter, 2008).

This chapter provides information to help teachers use age-appropriate transition assessments with youth identified with EBD and begins with a review of recommended areas of assessment and techniques. This section includes selected instruments that youth report they enjoy and from which they perceive benefit (Kortering & Braziel, 2008b). These instruments have adequate independent reviews (see Whitfield, Feller, & Wood, 2009) and are accessible to certified teachers with qualified experience (for example, professional credentials, course work in assessment, membership in professional organizations). We also use a pair of student examples to illustrate individual techniques and show how the results can be linked to individualized education programs (IEPs). We then provide a process for strategically deploying assessments in a local school, including an examination of features of the setting to consider and a two-level approach to assessment. The final section addresses special concerns related to youth with EBD and other emerging issues.

## AREAS OF TRANSITION ASSESSMENT

Sitlington, Neubert, Begun, Lombard, and Leconte (2007) proposed the following definition of transition assessment:

> Transition assessment is an ongoing process of collecting information on the individual's strengths, needs, preferences, and interests as they relate to the demands of current and future living, learning, and working environments. This process should begin in middle school and continue until one is graduated from or exits high school. Information from this process should drive the IEP and transition planning process and serve to develop the Summary of Performance detailing the individual's academic and functional performance and postsecondary goals. (pp. 2–3)

Transition assessment involves identifying information that helps youth better understand themselves. It further involves the use of this information to identify appropriate career options, along with resources, supports, and accommodations to facilitate students' transition from school to a productive adulthood. For practical purposes, we limit our review to assessment techniques that are appropriate for a classroom setting and practical in terms of resources (for example, costs, time, and professional requirements). The proposed process covers the areas of (1) background information, (2) interests and preferences, (3) aptitudes (or underlying abilities), (4) personal style, (5) interpersonal relationships, (6) self-determination, (7) academics and intelligence, and (8) employment-related skills. The following section briefly reviews these assessment areas and techniques. Readers are referred to other sources for more in-depth information (see Sitlington et al., 2007; Sitlington, Neubert, & Clark, 2010; Whitfield, Feller, & Wood, 2009).

We use student examples to help readers understand how they might use the transition assessments with their students. The students in these examples are a 9th and 11th grader. Tables 6.1 and 6.2 provide additional information that will be used throughout the following sections.

## Background Information

Existing records are a primary source of information about students, containing observations of teachers and others who have worked with the student. Teachers have access to previous IEPs with particular emphasis on transition-related objectives and activities. They can also ask for other formal and informal assessments that may include information on academic performance, behavior, and related learning outcomes. If other service agencies have worked with the individual, teachers may ask to review this information after receiving appropriate releases from the family.

Another technique for obtaining background information involves conducting interviews, which is by far the most commonly used assessment tool in rehabilitation (Berven, 2001). Interviews with the student, family members, teachers, employers, and friends may offer information on how the individual functions in the real world and what the person would like to do as an adult. The interview can be structured according

## TABLE 6.1   Student Description for Emma

### Background Information

Emma is a 9th grader who has been in special education since 2nd grade. She was certified as behaviorally–emotionally handicapped (BEH or BD) due to significant difficulty getting along with her peers and teachers coupled with failing grades during 6th grade. Her difficulties continued, and her reevaluations in 5th and 8th grade found that she still qualified for special education services in a program for BEH students. She has an attendance rate of 82% for the current semester. She reports enjoying making crafts and expresses an interest in jobs involving artistic skill. Her current plan is to get a diploma and attend a 2-year college. This plan is proving problematic in that she is failing key academic classes and is at risk of not getting her diploma. She does not have access to reliable transportation but has a driver's license. She has worked mowing lawns for neighbors and briefly as a nursing home aide. Her mother and stepfather work in area factories as an office assistant and production specialist, respectively. She has no contact with her birthfather. She has been referred to vocational rehabilitation (VR), and they plan to be part of her coordinated transition services.

### Previous Test Results

Emma's most recent psychological report shows a verbal (95) and performance (105) IQ in the average range, and a full-scale IQ (98) that is also average. Her achievement scores (standard scores) are as follows: broad math—84, broad reading—84, and broad written language—88. The achievement scores are all in the lower limits of the average range.

### Vocational Results

Formal test results include the Self-Directed Search—Form R, which showed scores in the high average range in the artistic category, but in the very low range in all other areas. These scores were consistent with the Career Interest Inventory—Level 1, where she scored in the average range in only arts and crafts. This score pattern suggests a rather narrow range of interests. The Student Style Questionnaire showed her personal style or preferences to include three prevailing traits: Introvert (strong), Feeling (strong), and Imaginative (moderate).

### Work Habits and Attitude

Emma has considerable difficulty in classes she deems boring or too difficult (that is, English and history this year). She fails to complete her homework and receives poor grades in her academic classes. She has good work habits and a positive attitude toward her physical education, home economics, and art classes.

## TABLE 6.2  Student Description for Josh

### Background Information

Josh is an 11th grader who has been in special education since 6th grade. He was certified as BEH due to his acting-out behavior in school and at home. His difficulties continued, although they lessened considerably as he entered high school, and his reevaluation in 9th grade found that he still qualified for special education services in a program for BEH students. He has an attendance rate of 98% for the current semester and reports enjoying physical education classes and hanging out with friends. His current plan is to get a diploma and become a truck driver or bartender. He has access to reliable transportation and has a driver's license. He has worked as a groundskeeper for a neighboring middle school and as a dishwasher at an institution. His mother works as a weaver at an area factory, but his father is unemployed. He has an older brother who works in construction and an uncle who is a truck driver. He was not interested in VR.

### Previous Test Results

Josh's most recent psychological report shows a verbal (85) and performance (91) IQ in the low average range, and a full-scale IQ also in the low average range (88). His achievement scores (standard scores) are as follows: broad math—94, broad reading—82, and broad written language—78. The math score is in the average range, whereas the reading and written language scores are in the borderline to low average range.

### Vocational Results

On the Self-Directed Search–Form R, Josh scored in the high range in realistic jobs and in the average range for social jobs. These scores were consistent with the Career Interest Inventory–Level 2, where he scored in the high average range for Machine Operation, Building Trades, Transportation, and Customer Service. The Student Style Questionnaire showed four prevailing traits: Extrovert (strong), Feeling (strong), Practical (strong), and Flexible (moderate). He also took the Differential Aptitude Test–Mechanical Reasoning Subtest, given his interests and reported ambitions. Here he scored at the 55th percentile for male age peers. He scored at the 58th percentile on the Wiesen Test of Mechanical Aptitude. On the Work Adjustment Inventory, he scored well above average on the Activity, Sociability, and Assertiveness subscales and well below average on the Empathy, Adaptability, and Emotionality subtests. Finally, on the Career Thoughts Inventory, he scored high on the External Conflict subtest and average on the Decision Making Confusion and Commitment Anxiety subtests.

### Work Habits and Attitude

Josh displays very good work habits and is responsive to direction from authority figures. He prefers working with peers rather than on his own and responds well to leadership opportunities. His most recent employer reports that Josh had perfect attendance and that he was a hard worker.

to one's objectives. We recommend a semistructured format with two major objectives. First, the interview is a way to establish rapport while providing students with an opportunity to talk about their future plans and related information. The format includes questions about the family and youth work history, career ambitions, special interests and hobbies, future living plans, and educational goals (Table 6.3). Second, as shown in Table 6.3, questions solicit information that affects the youth's ambitions. For instance, the family work history promotes understanding of how possible role models may influence a student's career development, whereas the appropriateness of the student's ambitions is an indicator of his or her overall level of career maturity. Youth with unrealistic ambitions are at risk of making inappropriate career choices.

The interviews with Emma and Josh accomplished the objectives of providing rapport and yielding information on factors affecting their career ambitions. Both students were comfortable with discussing their family and school situations and seemed almost eager to have someone listen to their thoughts about life after high school. We also learned about possible family influences, with both having parental role models who worked, albeit in careers that did not interest the students. Josh did have an uncle who might be a resource in that his job is of interest to Josh. Both students also have a work history and report tentative interests in at least one general career.

In each case, appropriate IEP goals would target summer or weekend jobs that match their interests while expanding their general world of work knowledge and helping them to learn more about their work-related skills and preferences. In addition, Emma expressed an interest in working with vocational rehabilitation (VR) to help her obtain post-secondary training or education related to the arts. VR could become part of her IEP team in a coordinated transition service. Josh, on the other hand, had no interest in self-disclosing his disability status, which would be required to access some forms of adult service.

## Interests and Preferences

Interest inventories provide considerable information for vocational assessment purposes. They offer insight into a youth's work orientation, overall career maturity, and ambitions (Fouad & Tang, 2001). The major objectives of an interest assessment are to help youth understand them-

**TABLE 6.3  Sample Questions for a Semistructured Interview**

*Family Background*

What do your parents do? Did they finish high school?

What is the level of education for your parents and older brothers and sisters?

Do you have any older brothers or sisters who have jobs? If so, please describe their jobs.

Do you have any relatives or family friends who have what you think would be a neat job?

*Student Background*

What are your favorite and least favorite classes in school (and why)?

What classes would you like to take in high school?

What do you plan to do when you get done with high school? Do you plan to go to college (if so, where and to study what)?

Where do you plan to live after you finish high school?

What are three jobs you are thinking you might like to do after finishing high school?

What are your hobbies, special interests, or things you like to do during your free time?

Have you ever had a paying job? If so, describe your previous or current jobs.

Do you have a driver's license? If no, when do you plan to get one?

Do you have access to reliable transportation? Please describe.

What are three things you would like to learn in school this year?

What are three things that would help you be more successful in school?

---

selves and their role in the career decision-making process, establish insight into tentative or stable areas of interest and lack of interest, and gauge the readiness of youth to make appropriate career choices.

We have used a number of instruments to assess students' interests or preferences. The Self-Directed Search (SDS) has proven to be a most versatile instrument (Holland, 1994). The SDS offers a variety of formats that are appropriate for college-bound youth (SDS-R), youth with limited reading (Form E), those who speak a foreign language (for example,

Spanish or French as it is spoken in Canada), and middle-school youth (Explorer Form). We have enhanced the college-bound version with a software program that provides a 14- to 22-page summary report for each respondent. We also use the Vocational Preference Inventory (Holland, 1985) as a second measure for older youth with a work history and world of work knowledge, and the Career Interest Inventory—Enhanced Version (Johansson, 2002a) for youth with limited experience. We also have had success using the Career Decision-Making System—Revised (Harrington & O'Shea, 2000) for younger youth with limited reading skills and the Career Interest Inventory—Vocational Version (Johansson, 2002b) for students with limited work experience. Other interest assessments include various nonreading pictorial inventories such as the Wide Range Interest and Occupation Test—2nd Edition (Glutting & Wilkinson, 2003) and online surveys such as the Career Key (www.careerkey.org). A special concern with the former involves whether youth understand the actual jobs portrayed in the respective pictures, whereas online tools often lack access to a manual describing key aspects of the test's development.

The interest tests indicated that Emma and Josh have tentative career interests. Emma showed a slight preference for jobs that involve artistic and creative talents, whereas Josh had a more distinct profile that showed established interests in manual trades (Realistic) and customer service (Social). Both profiles had very low scores for several occupational areas. These low scores provide insight into various jobs and courses for which the students would have little or no motivation. For instance, the students expressed no interest in jobs (and therefore probably classes) involving math and science (Investigative area on the SDS), whereas Emma showed no interest in the three other areas of the SDS (Enterprising, Conventional, and Realistic). Emma's pattern of having an interest in one area indicates that she has a narrow range of interests at this point. Appropriate IEP goals for Emma would be to expand her range of interests and knowledge by exposing her to various careers and to help her learn more about them. Josh's IEP should be tailored around his established interests to pursue a job in a manual trade, perhaps one that also entails some contact with customers. Specific goals also should include enrolling in appropriate career and technical education (CTE) classes, learning about local jobs that match his interests, and identifying relevant postsecondary training or educational options.

## Aptitudes and Underlying Abilities

Aptitude testing involves the use of instruments that establish student strengths and limitations in various aptitudes. These aptitudes, or underlying abilities, are then matched with skills required by various jobs. For instance, a welder must have mechanical and spatial aptitudes, just as a teacher must have a talent for working with and helping others. Aptitudes, although often confused with achievement skills, are relatively stable traits that are innate or developed over time (Parker, 2001). Anastasi and Urbina (1997) draw an important distinction between aptitude and achievement tests in that the latter are affected to a greater degree by one's experiential background (for example, completion of a specific training program or course of study). Aptitude testing, as a measure of one's potential to be successful at certain jobs, dates back to the ancient Greeks and Chinese and became based in empirical research with the early work of Galton (see Parker, 2001).

Today, the employment and military sectors make wide use of various aptitude test batteries, many of which are inaccessible to school-teachers. For instance, the Armed Services Aptitude Test Battery (ASVAB) is offered through local military recruiters. One notable exception is the Differential Aptitude Test (DAT) Battery—5th Edition (Psychological Corporation, 1992). The DAT was first published in 1947 and was most recently revised in 1992. The instrument provides subtests in Verbal Reasoning, Numerical Reasoning, Abstract Reasoning, Perceptual Speed and Accuracy, Mechanical Reasoning, Space Relations, Spelling, and Language Usage. These subtests range in administration time from 2 (Perceptual Speed) to 30 minutes (Spatial Relations) with a total administration time of nearly 3 hours. A more recently developed test is the Occupational Aptitude Survey and Interest Schedule—3rd Edition (Parker, 2002). This test covers six aptitudes, including Vocabulary, Computation, Spatial Relations, Word Comparison, Making Marks, and General Ability, along with an Interest Inventory. We recommend the use of subtests that match a youth's interests or represent areas of potential strength.

For instance, the mechanical reasoning subtest of the DAT (or Wiesen Test of Mechanical Aptitude) would be appropriate for youth like Josh who have an interest in mechanical occupations or mechanical skills, but it is of little use for a student with no such interests. Similarly, the Spatial Relations subtest of the DAT would only be useful for youth like Emma who demonstrate an interest or show a talent in such areas as artistic endeavors or creative design. Ultimately, an aptitude test should identify student strengths that may have gone unnoticed, and this information should help formulate more appropriate interventions (for example, specific course work) and postsecondary goals (for example, training or further school options).

Josh's interest in manual jobs suggested we use the Mechanical Subtest of the Differential Aptitude Test (DAT) or the Wiesen Test of Mechanical Aptitude (WTMA) (Wiesen, 1999). This decision reflected the fact that we already had considerable information on his academic skills. Josh wanted to take both mechanical tests, thus allowing us to collect a second set of test scores for comparison. He scored in the high average range on both tests, indicating mechanical skills were an area of relative strength for him. Of interest is that the WTMA showed him to be in the high average range among male industrial workers and college students in technical programs, whereas the DAT provided a reference group of high-school–age peers. In terms of his IEP, his program should consider gaining access to appropriate CTE courses in construction or manual trades, locating suitable 2-year college or technical programs in mechanical fields, finding a mentor who is employed in a related job, developing course work that prepares him for advanced training or a local job, and identifying area employers who have jobs that involve mechanical skills.

## Personal Style and Preferences

Assessing one's personal style or preferences involves generating information to help explain or predict a person's behavior in selected situations, including learning situations and employment sites. The key is to establish information that helps youth make more appropriate career choices given a better understanding of their personal styles and preferences while avoiding work settings that are likely to prove problematic. Interestingly, these assessments also help youth understand the problems they may have in certain settings (for example, a disorganized student trying to succeed in a rigid class setting or an independent student trying to conform to authoritative adults in school or at work).

We have used a number of instruments to help us understand the personal styles of youth with EBD. Many of these tests have proved impractical because students complained about their overall length or number of questions or were unable to understand the results. In response, we turned to the Student Style Questionnaire (SSQ) (Oakland, Glutting, & Horton, 1996). This test places an emphasis on helping students understand their personal styles and preferences rather than on trying to assess underlying psychological traits. The students take the test in about 20 minutes, and their profiles can be mapped in conjunction with a classroom applications booklet (Horton & Oakland, 1999) detailing the types of classroom structures and activities that match a student's preferences. As a measure of face validity, we have found that students instinctively share this information with friends and family and routinely say that they are impressed with the report's accuracy.

We had Emma and Josh take the SSQ. The results showed that Emma is a strong introvert and very sensitive, and is also somewhat creative. These scores suggested that she is inclined to keep her feelings to herself and is sensitive to criticism and rejection. This personal style has implications for her work and class settings. Specifically, she should have access to an adult at school with whom she can share her feelings and avoid situations in which peers might be mean to her. In addition, her creative talents and imagination suggested that it would be worth exploring what classes she might enjoy. Her IEP should take these factors into account and perhaps include more specific goals that target helping her to handle her sensitivity and introverted nature.

Josh scored as a strong extrovert, very sensitive, strongly practical, and moderately flexible. His IEP should focus on helping him to understand how best to deal with his sensitive nature while taking advantage of his preference for socializing (for example, getting him into leadership situations, group learning activities, or school sports). His practical nature implied that he would have considerable difficulty with abstract concepts such as those found in algebra or history, but would enjoy classes that are practical and hands-on in nature. For example, he might enjoy a CTE class in which he learned skills that he could apply on his own (for example, learning how to repair his car).

## Interpersonal Relationships

Interpersonal relationship skills include positive social behaviors, such as sharing, cooperating, collaborating, and exhibiting social behavior expectations in specific environments. Interpersonal relationships on the job also depend on such communication skills as expressive and listening skills. These skills are essential for nearly all work environments.

One of the best ways to gather information on interpersonal relationships is by observing the student. To be useful, behavior observation should be systematic and should take place in a variety of settings. It is also helpful for different team members to observe an individual in various situations to make sure the information gathered is valid and reliable. There are a number of different techniques that practitioners can use to observe and record behavior, including narrative recording, time sampling, event recording, and rating scales. For further information on these techniques, see Kerr and Nelson (2006).

Josh's and Emma's school histories indicated that they had experienced difficulty conforming to the demands of their teachers in middle and elementary school. This pattern was much less prominent in high school. In addition, the SSQ showed us that Josh would work best in group situations that allowed him to be an extrovert, whereas Emma would work best on her own. Both students also appeared to be quite sensitive and would have difficulty working with insensitive adults. Observations of both students in their general education classes confirmed these findings. Josh's teachers noted that he performed much better when he was working in a group, and in this situation he would often take on a leadership role. Emma's teachers indicated that she worked best on her own. Although she did openly confront other students, she tended to keep to herself when she was placed in small-group activities and responded only if she was asked a specific question.

## Self-Determination

As Field, Martin, Miller, Ward, and Wehmeyer (1998) stated, self-determination is "a combination of skills, knowledge, and beliefs that enable a person to engage in goal-directed, self-regulated, autonomous behavior" (p. 2). Self-determination skills relate to being aware of and valuing one's self, followed by setting personal goals, planning to meet those goals, and anticipating specific results. In the context of transition assessment, these skills are key to helping youth with EBD make appropriate career decisions. Although there is limited, if any, research on interventions to foster self-determination in students with EBD, it is a critical skill for everyone. One method of assessing self-determination is to observe the student in a number of different situations—inside and outside the classroom. Information can also be gained from interviewing family members and staff from other agencies who may be involved with the student.

In addition, the Transition Planning Inventory–Updated Version (TPI–UV) is a useful tool at this stage. The TPI provides student, family, and teacher input as to the student's readiness to transition from school to all areas of adult life (Clark & Patton, 2006). The comparison of multiple viewpoints on the student's perceived transition-related needs is a valuable aspect of this instrument, especially when it helps to point out youth who have an unrealistic image of their needs. Clark, Patton, and Moulton (2000) offer more detail on how to best use TPI and a number of other helpful activities.

A number of self-determination curricula include assessment measures. An advantage of these curricula is their prescribed instructional units for teaching important behaviors identified by an initial assessment. A good example is the Steps to Self-Determination Curriculum by Hoffman and Field (2005). The corresponding Self-Determination Assessment Battery (Hoffman, Field, & Sawilowsky, 2004) offers a convenient pre-test and post-test tied to the curriculum and perception scales to be independently completed by the student, parent, and teacher. Results from the scales can then be compared for similarities and differences. Although the perception scales and checklist are built around the curriculum model, they can be used independently of the curriculum. Halpern, Herr, Doren, and Wolf (2000) developed the Next S.T.E.P. curriculum program. This program has a skills inventory that allows students to evaluate themselves in each curriculum area, as well as a profile report that compares student, teacher, and family perceptions. A third option is the Choice-Maker Curriculum (see Martin et al., 1997), which offers pre-test and post-test measures that evaluate the student's level of self-determination.

Two additional assessments that evaluate self-determination independent of a formal curriculum are the AIR Self-Determination Scale (Wolman, Campeau, DuBois, Mithaug, & Stolarski, 1994) and the ARC's Self-Determination Scale (Wehmeyer, 2000). The former allows one to use up to four different forms tailored to educator, student, parent, and researcher perspectives, whereas the latter provides a four-dimensional model of self-determination.

In terms of self-determination, Josh and Emma are learning about themselves and the world of work. Josh, who is older and more experienced, appears to have established fairly stable interests. He is beginning to consider what he wants to do after school. To help understand his ability so that we could direct his educational program, we had him take the TPI. On this test, he indicated a need to identify local jobs that might interest him, understand his work-related skills, identify appropriate postsecondary training options, and set personal goals. This information was in line with what his teachers had to say and provided appropriate goals for his IEP. Emma, on the other hand, was considerably less knowledgeable and experienced. As a result, she was unable to direct her IEP at this point. She would be an ideal candidate for individual units or a semester class using one of the self-determination curricula.

## Academic and Intelligence Measures

The student's initial evaluation or reevaluation for special education services offers information on intelligence and academic achievement levels. Estimates of a student's intelligence provide insight into postsecondary educational goals, including whether a 2- or 4-year college is appropriate. Academic achievement levels are predictive of likely success in select settings. For example, students with low achievement levels in reading would have difficulty in workplace environments calling for higher-order reading skills, unless the student has access to suitable accommodations. Traditionally, we have gained this information from standardized achievement tests that youth generally take for their initial evaluation or reevaluation for special education services. Yet many youth, especially those with EBD, are turned off by these traditional tests and fail to see their relevance. These traditional methods can be augmented with alternative approaches that often offer youth a more realistic setting that helps them see the relevance of the effort. To place students with EBD in more challenging jobs, it is important to determine their academic skills and interests and match them to occupations that utilize their skills. Curriculum-based assessment instruments can focus specifically on the content being taught. Examples of curriculum-based assessment techniques include criterion-referenced testing, portfolio assessment, and performance-based assessment.

The criterion-referenced testing approach compares the individual's performance to a pre-established level of performance (for example, 80%), rather than to the performance of others or a set of norms. In this approach, the emphasis is on the knowledge or skills needed for a specific content area and whether the individual has demonstrated mastery of this knowledge. The criterion-referenced testing approach can be used in any content area in which skills can be broken down into specific subareas.

Portfolio assessment has been in use in CTE programs such as architecture, drafting, and graphic arts for a number of years. As the emphasis in assessment moves toward the concept of "authentic assessment," portfolios are being developed in a number of content areas and across content areas. Portfolio development lends itself to evaluating a variety of academic and nonacademic areas (for example, performance in CTE courses or creative arts). The materials to be included in the portfolio range from the results of vocational interest inventories to essays written by students concerning their goals, to samples of projects from graphic arts class or architectural drafting. It is critical that the student have input into the types of materials to be included in the portfolio and that guidelines be established and followed for the inclusion of materials. It is also important that the student and teacher evaluate the portfolio's material on an ongoing basis. The focus of performance-based assessment may be an actual performance (for example, a speech) or product (for example, a welding project). In either case, the observed performance or product is assessed through existing rubrics or other standards of evaluation.

In the cases of Josh and Emma, the most recent reevaluations for special education services provided sufficient information on the students' academic skill levels. Both had low average to average levels of intelligence, suggesting a potential to succeed in appropriate post-secondary training or a 2-year college environment. Both students also showed academic deficits along with relative strengths. Josh's weakest academic area was written language with a moderate weakness in reading. Emma was in the low average range in each academic area. Both patterns suggested that their IEPs include specific goals to target (1) an improvement in academic skills (for example, instruction in the use of compensatory skills or learning strategies), (2) exposure to postsecondary settings that might offer learning assistance, and (3) the infusion of assistive technology that might help to offset existing deficiencies (for example, grammar and spell-checker software for Josh and talk and type software for Emma). For Emma, the portfolio assessment approach (her art project) allowed the art teacher to conclude that Emma had talent that warranted additional instruction in basic and advanced art techniques. The performance-based assessment for Josh demonstrated that he had good basic driving and customer relations skills but needed more training in making the decisions and judgments necessary when driving even small trucks.

## Employment Skills

The most obvious areas of assessment involve actual employment skills. Employment skills encompass (1) occupational awareness, including an understanding of occupations relative to key skill and knowledge requirements and employment conditions and projections, (2) employment-related knowledge and skill sets, including general and specific work skills, proper attitude, and promotion opportunities, and (3) specific knowledge and skills relating to local and related job opportunities (Sitlington et al., 2010).

One method of obtaining employment-related information is to systematically observe students while they are in actual businesses in the community—as an exploration or training activity. Although this may be impractical for most classroom teachers, staff working with students at these sites can conduct the observations. Input from the employer at each site is also excellent information, especially if the criteria they use to evaluate students is aligned with how they evaluate their employees.

A second method involves gathering information on an individual's employment-related skills in CTE courses or work settings. This approach helps determine the students' transition-related needs based on their ongoing performance related to existing course content, while collecting information on performance in realistic settings. This method also allows for a determination of the supports and accommodations that will help the student succeed in future classes or jobs.

If the individual is in CTE classes or work experiences in the community, information can be gathered on how well the individual actually performs tasks related to specific occupations. This information can then be used to help determine whether students are interested in the specific vocational area. Observational information can also establish how well students relate to others, including peers and supervisors, and ascertain how well students work independently, stay on task, and ask for assistance when needed.

Emma had not been enrolled in CTE courses due to her program of study and the need to repeat a course. Josh indicated an interest in truck driving, construction or building trades, and customer service. Because of his age, he was not yet eligible for a truck-driving training program. He was, however, enrolled in a woodworking class. His instructor conducted a series of observations on Josh during the first month of class. She found that he was very interested in working with his hands and machinery. He performed much better with hands-on tasks than in the academic components of class. He preferred working with fellow classmates rather than on his own, and he responded well to requests and instruction from the instructor. Josh has asked that the construction trades class be placed on his program of study for his senior year.

## ESTABLISHING A PROCESS FOR TRANSITION ASSESSMENT IN YOUR SCHOOL

Establishing a formal process that helps create more effective interventions while assisting youth in developing information to help them make appropriate career decisions requires attention to several process concerns. These concerns include setting features, such as the age and experiences of the individual youth (for example, access to work role models, unrealistic self-image, and likelihood of a history of negative school experiences) and the need for creating a supportive environment that encourages youth development. A second area involves obtaining input from families and adult service providers while making sure that assessment results are properly used. Finally, the most important concept is to involve the student in all stages of the assessment process—from determining the information to be gathered, to selecting the techniques to be used, to interpreting the results.

## Setting Concerns

Appropriate methods for the transition assessment process should be developed and periodically updated with students and their families. This process should be integrated into each student's IEP and be structured to respond to their unique skills, limitations, and backgrounds. The process should address the following questions (Sitlington et al., 2007):

- What do I already know about this student that would help identify appropriate postsecondary employment and education or training outcomes (for example, access to work role models, school history, and work experiences)?

- What assessment questions should be asked during the transition assessment process?

- What information do I need to know about this individual to determine appropriate career goals (for example, unique skills and limitations and special interests)?

- What methods will best provide the desired information (for example, interviews, formal assessments, or alternative assessments)?

- How will the assessment data be collected and used in the student's IEP and transition planning process (for example, establishing roles for the youth, parents, and adult service providers)?

- How will the assessment information be used to complete the summary of performance (SOP) as the student exits from high school?

Using an appropriate assessment process ensures that methods are suitable for the individual's characteristics and career development stage. An existing transition skills assessments is helpful during an initial evaluation to develop an assessment plan. Most are helpful as screening devices to determine what the IEP team can agree they know about a student in a range of transition planning areas. Areas for which there is little information, or about which there is disagreement, suggest the need for further assessment.

Rojewski (2002) offers a useful conceptual framework for the transition assessment process. He recommends a two-level framework wherein younger youth participate in more informal assessments, including measures that will establish baseline data on their functional skills, abilities, and interests. (See Tables 6.1 and 6.2 for a comparison of the two levels.) The Level 1 assessment, exemplified by Emma, would include a personal interview, a review of existing records, an initial interest test, and selective aptitude testing. Older youth, and generally those with more work experience, would participate in a Level 2 assessment. Level 2 testing, like that for Josh, would focus more on formal assessments and include an update on the information previously collected if the youth participated in a Level 1 assessment. The formal assessments would include additional interest assessment, a personality test, and specific aptitude testing. In addition, inventories such as the Work Adjustment Scale and measures of student readiness to make career decisions (for example, the Career Thoughts Inventory; Sampson, Peterson, Lenz, Reardon, & Sanders, 1996) would be useful for youth with actual work experience or those preparing to make a career decision (for example, students who are dropping out, graduating, or identifying postschool jobs or training). Finally, information on an individual's work experiences and CTE classes would make a significant contribution to the process.

## Proper Use of Assessment Results

Clark (2007) noted that transition assessment should be a means to an end, not an end in itself. This recommendation reminds us of the need to have a process that allows us to collect a variety of information while keeping a focus on the goal of helping foster self-understanding so that youth are better prepared for career decisions. The assessment process must provide information to help educators and individual students make decisions for more appropriate programming options. These options should target identification of specific high-school courses; assistance with locating appropriate nonpaid work experiences, summer jobs, or employment during the school year; and provision of more appropriate transition planning.

The assessment process also entails stimulating action on behalf of the students and expanding their learning opportunities (Krumboltz & Vidalakis, 2000). For instance, youth need access to information that helps them to better understand appropriate career options. This information should help them make appropriate choices about such matters as the decision to stay in school, pursue a standard or vocational program, prepare for college, join the military, or seek specific summer or postschool employment. This process often involves helping the youth to discard inappropriate ambitions as they gain a better understanding of their own skills and limitations, the world of work, and specific occupations.

## Ensuring Student Involvement

An appropriate transition assessment process is by nature an ongoing youth-centered endeavor, one that should help to uniquely tailor students' IEPs to their particular circumstances (Rojewski, 2002). This point reminds us that the process must retain the active involvement of youth throughout the process. At various points, the youth's role evolves from "test taker and interviewee" to "active learner" and eventually to "decision maker." The key is to develop a process that informs youth about themselves and the world of work while helping them use this information to pursue an appropriate career.

## CONCLUSION

In summary, existing research shows that youth with EBD need coordinated transition services that help them to complete high school (Maag & Katsiyannis, 1998; Rylance, 1997). Such services must also prepare them for appropriate postschool employment and community adjustment while maintaining their motivation for staying in school. The foundation for such services is the proper use of age-appropriate transition assessments. These assessments will facilitate better self-understanding, make a better connection between school and youths' ambitions, and help teachers to better provide transition services that fulfill the promise of special education. To do anything less is to put youth with EBD on track for dead-end employment outcomes or, even worse, create a scenario that will end up costing all of us.

## REFERENCES

Anastasi, A., & Urbina, S. (1997). *Psychological testing* (6th ed.). New York: Macmillan.

Berktold, J., Geis, S., Kaufman, P., & Carroll, C. D. (1999). *Subsequent educational attainment of high school dropouts.* Washington, DC: U.S. Department of Education, National Center for Education Statistics.

Berven, N. L. (2001). Assessment interviewing. In Brian Bolton (Ed.), *Handbook of measurement and assessment in rehabilitation* (3rd ed.). Gaithersburg, MD: Aspen.

Chambers, J. G., Sckolnik, J., & Perez, M. (2003). *Total expenditures for students with disabilities, 1999–2000: Spending variation by disability.* Washington, DC: Center for Special Education Finance, Special Education Expenditure Project.

Clark, G. M. (2007). *Assessment for transition planning* (2nd ed.). Austin: Pro-Ed.

Clark, G. M., & Patton, J. R. (2006). *Transition Planning Inventory–Updated Version.* Austin, TX: PRO-ED.

Clark, G. M., Patton, J. R., & Moulton, L. R. (2000). *Informal assessments for transition planning.* Austin, TX: Pro-Ed.

Corbett, W. P., Sanders, R. L., Clark, H. B., & Blank, W. (2002). Employment and social outcomes associated with vocational programming for youths with emotional or disorders. *Behavioral Disorders, 27*, 358–370.

Edgar, E. B. (1987). Secondary programs in special education. Are many of them justifiable? *Exceptional Children, 53,* 555–561.

Field, S., Martin, J., Miller, R., Ward, M., & Wehmeyer, M. (1998). *A practical guide for teaching self-determination.* Arlington, VA: Council for Exceptional Children.

Fouad, N. A., & Tang, M. (2001). Vocational inventories. In B. Bolton (Ed.), *Handbook of measurement and assessment in rehabilitation* (3rd ed.). Gaithersburg, MD: Aspen.

Friedman, T. L. (2005). *The world is flat: A brief history of the 21st century.* New York: Farrar, Strauss, and Giroux.

Glutting, J. J., & Wilkinson, G. S. (2003). *Wide-range interest and occupation test* (2nd ed.). Austin: Pro-Ed.

Gouskova, E., & Stafford, F. (2005). *Trends in household wealth dynamics, 2001–2003.* Ann Arbor: University of Michigan Institute for Social Research.

Halpern, A. S., Herr, C. M., Doren, B., & Wolf, N. K. (2000). *Next S.T.E.P.: Student transition and educational planning* (2nd ed.). Austin: Pro-Ed.

Harrington, T. F., & O'Shea, A. J. (2000). *Career decision-making system: Revised.* Circle Pines, MN: American Guidance Service.

Hight, J. (1998). Young worker participation in post-school education and training. *Monthly Labor Review, 122,* 14–21.

Hoffman, A., & Field, S. (2005). *Steps in self-determination: A curriculum to help adolescents learn to achieve their goals* (2nd ed.). Austin: Pro-Ed.

Hoffman, A., Field, S., & Sawilowsky, S. (2004). *Self-determination assessment battery and user's guide* (3rd ed.). Detroit: Wayne State University Center for Self-Determination and Transition.

Holland, J. L. (1985). *Vocational Preference Inventory.* Lutz, FL: Psychological Assessment Resources.

Holland, J. L. (1994). *Self-directed search: Forms R, E, and Explorer.* Odessa, FL: Psychological Assessment Resources.

Horn, L., & Berktold, J. (2004). *Students with disabilities in postsecondary education: A profile of preparation, participation, and outcomes.* Washington, DC: U. S. Department of Education, National Center for Education Statistics.

Horton, C. B., & Oakland, T. (1999). *Classroom applications booklet.* San Antonio: Psychological Corp.

Individuals with Disabilities Education Improvement Act of 2004, Pub. L. No. 108–446, §401 *et seq.* (2004).

Johansson, C. B. (2002a). *Career assessment inventory: The enhanced version.* Minneapolis: Pearson Education.

Johansson, C. B. (2002b). *Career assessment inventory: The vocational version.* Minneapolis: Pearson Education.

Johnson, K. (2007, September 27). Prison population soared from 1980–2006. *USA Today,* 3A.

Kerr, M. M., & Nelson, C. H. (2006). *Strategies for addressing behavior problems in the classroom* (5th ed.). Upper Saddle River, NJ: Prentice Hall.

Kortering, L., & Braziel, P. (2008a). Age-appropriate transition assessment: A look at what students say. *Journal of At-Risk Issues, 17,* 27–35.

Kortering, L., & Braziel, P. (2008b). Introduction to special issue on school completion. *Psychology in the Schools, 45,* 461–465.

Kortering, L., deBettencourt, L., & Braziel, P. (2005). Improving performance in high school algebra: What students with learning disabilities are saying. *Learning Disabilities Quarterly, 28,* 191–204.

Kortering, L., & Konold, T. (2005). Coming to school: A comparison of youth with and without LD. *Journal of At-Risk Issues, 13,* 12–22.

Kortering, L. J., Konold, T. R., & Glutting, J. (1998). Why come to school? An empirical investigation on what youths have to say. *Journal of At-Risk Issues, 5,* 1–16.

Krumboltz, J. D., & Vidalakis, N. K. (2000). Expanding learning opportunities and using career assessments. *Journal of Career Assessment, 8,* 315–327.

Luneberg, F. C. (1999). Helping dreams survive: Dropout interventions. *Contemporary Education, 71,* 9–15.

Maag, J. W., & Katsiyannis, A. (1998). Challenges facing successful transition for youths with E/BD. *Behavioral Disorders, 23*(4), 209–221.

Martin, J.E., Huber-Marshall, L., Maxson, P., Hughes, W., Miller, T., & McGill, T. (1997). *Choice-maker curriculum.* Frederick, CO: Sopris West Publishing

Moretti, E. (2005). *Does education reduce participation in criminal activities?* Berkeley: University of California at Berkeley Department of Economics.

Oakland, T., Glutting, J. J., & Horton, C. B. (1996). *Student style questionnaire.* San Antonio: Psychological Corp.

Office of Special Education Programs (OSEP). (2008). *To ensure the free appropriate public education of all handicapped children. Twenty-seventh annual report to Congress.* Washington, DC: U. S. Department of Education.

Parker, R. M. (2001). Aptitude testing. In B. Bolton (Ed.), *Handbook of measurement and assessment in rehabilitation* (3rd ed.). Gaithersburg, MD: Aspen.

Parker, R. M. (2002). *Occupational aptitude survey* (3rd ed.). Austin: Pro-Ed.

Psychological Corporation. (1992). *Differential aptitude tests, levels one and two* (5th ed.). San Antonio, TX: Harcourt Assessment.

Rojewski, J. W. (2002). Career assessment for adolescents with mild disabilities: Critical concerns for transition planning. *Career Development for Exceptional Individuals, 25,* 73–95.

Rylance, B. J. (1997). Predictors of high school graduation or dropping out for youths with severe emotional disturbances. *Behavioral Disorders, 23*(1), 5–17.

Rylance, B. J. (1998). Predictors of post high-school employment for youth identified as severely emotionally disturbed. *The Journal of Special Education, 32*(3), 184–192.

Sampson, J. P., Peterson, G. W., Lenz, J. G., Reardon, R. C., & Saunders, D. E. (1996). *Career Thoughts Inventory.* Odessa, FL: Psychological Assessment Resources.

Shorter, T. N. (2008). *From school to post-school activities: Understanding the IDEA's transition requirements*. Horsham, PA: LRP Publications.

Sitlington, P. L., Neubert, D. A., Begun, W., Lombard, R. C., & Leconte, P. (2007). *Assess for success: A practitioner's handbook on transition assessment* (2nd ed.). Thousand Oaks, CA: Corwin Press.

Sitlington, P. L., Neubert, D. A., & Clark, G. M. (2010). *Transition education and services for adolescents with disabilities* (5th ed.). Boston: Merrill.

Stephan, J. J. (2004). *Bureau of Justice statistics special report: State prison expenditures, 2001*. Washington, DC: Department of Justice.

Symonds, W. C. (2006, November 21). America the uneducated: New study warns of a slide for the U. S. as the share of low achievers grows. *U. S. News & World Report*, 120–122.

Tobin, T. J., & Sugai, G. M. (1999). Discipline problems, placements, and outcomes for students with serious emotional disturbance. *Behavioral Disorders, 24*, 109–122.

United States Congressional Administration News. (1975). *Aid to Education of the Handicapped Act approved* (pp. 651–656). St. Paul, MN: West Publishing.

Wehmeyer, M. L. (2000). *The Arc's self-determination scale: Procedural guidelines* (rev. ed.). Silver Springs, MD: The Arc of the United States.

Whitfield, E. A., Feller, R., & Wood, C. (2009). *A counselor's guide to career assessment instruments* (5th ed.). Broken Arrow, OK: National Career Development Association.

Wiesen, J. P. (1999). *Wiesen test of mechanical aptitude*. Odessa, FL: Psychological Assessment Resources.

Wolman, J. M., Campeau, P. L., DuBois, P. A., Mithaug, D. E., & Stolarski, V. S. (1994). *AIR self-determination scale and user guide*. Palo Alto, CA: American Institutes for Research.

Yates, J. A. (2005, February). The transition from school to work: Education and work experiences. *Monthly Labor Review, 128*, 21–32.

Zuckerman, M. B. (2006, June 12). Rich man, poor man. *U. S. News & World Report*, 71–72.

## CHAPTER 7

# Development of Individualized Education Programs for Students with Emotional or Behavioral Disorders: Coordination with Transition Plans

**James G. Shriner, Anthony J. Plotner, and Chad A. Rose**

Graduation from high school marks a student's passage into the community of adults and is often among the most difficult transitions for young people in our society (McPartland, 2005; Wagner, Blackorby, Cameto, & Newman 1993). Consequently, transition into the adult world presents many problems for persons with disabilities and is often most difficult for those students with emotional or behavioral disabilities (EBD) (Jones, Erfling, & Goldsby, 2004; Test, Aspel, & Everson, 2006). As a result, transition-age youth with EBD typically lag behind their peers without disabilities in a variety of areas: employment, independent living, and enrollment in postsecondary education (Blackorby & Wagner, 1996; Cameto, Levine, & Wagner, 2004; Wittenburg & Maag, 2002). Because of these issues, calls for more comprehensive and persistent transition planning to improve postschool outcomes have been numerous (Powers et al., 2005).

The individualized education program (IEP) represents the cornerstone of educational planning for a student. It serves to document the

*Author note:* Preparation of this chapter was supported in part by a grant (R324J060002) from the U.S. Department of Education, Institute of Education Sciences, awarded to the first author. Opinions expressed herein do not necessarily reflect those of the U.S. Department of Education or offices within it.

agreements made among the student, the student's family, and service providers to support successful postschool outcomes. Therefore, it is critical that transition planning serve as the focal point of the IEP meeting for many students. Unfortunately, transition planning is commonly perceived as an add-on to an already taxing IEP process and document—a view that often results in fragmented and inadequate planning and transition services for students (deFur, 2003; Oertle & Trach, 2007). The Individuals with Disabilities Education Improvement Act (IDEIA, 2004) requires that the IEP include transition services for each student 16 years of age. Despite legal mandates and much literature supporting transition planning (Sax & Thoma, 2002; Skinner & Lindstrom, 2003; Test et al., 2006), we know that many IEPs are neither properly prepared nor executed effectively to support transition outcomes (Shriner, Trach, & Yell, 2005).

Central to comprehensive transition planning is an awareness of local graduation policies and requirements. State and local options regarding graduation requirements can vary widely (Johnson, Thurlow, & Stout, 2007). Professionals are expected to have a clear understanding of these options before beginning the IEP process. The available options should help the IEP team in maximizing the educational and transition success for students.

In the previous edition of the present book, Jones, Erfling, and Goldsby (2004) discussed IEP development and a successful graduation transition model used in Boulder, Colorado. These authors detailed the Boulder Valley School District (BVSD) model, which is intended for all populations with intensive needs. The BVSD model supported the development of a school experience that led to a diploma while ensuring that the student's experiences included suitable transition activities to achieve postschool success. To assist in the organization of their IEP-driven graduation model, BVSD implemented three graduation pathways: the traditional pathway, the semitraditional pathway, and the nontraditional pathway (Figure 7.1)

Using the graduation pathway approach, IEP teams have flexibility to create high-school experiences that merge a variety of activities to meet the individual needs of students while maintaining the common threads of curriculum, transition, and learning experiences. Building on this previous work, our intention in this chapter is to provide a general overview of the process of developing transition-rich IEPs for students with EBD that follow the provisions outlined in IDEIA.

**FIGURE 7.1   Graduation Pathways for Boulder Valley School District**

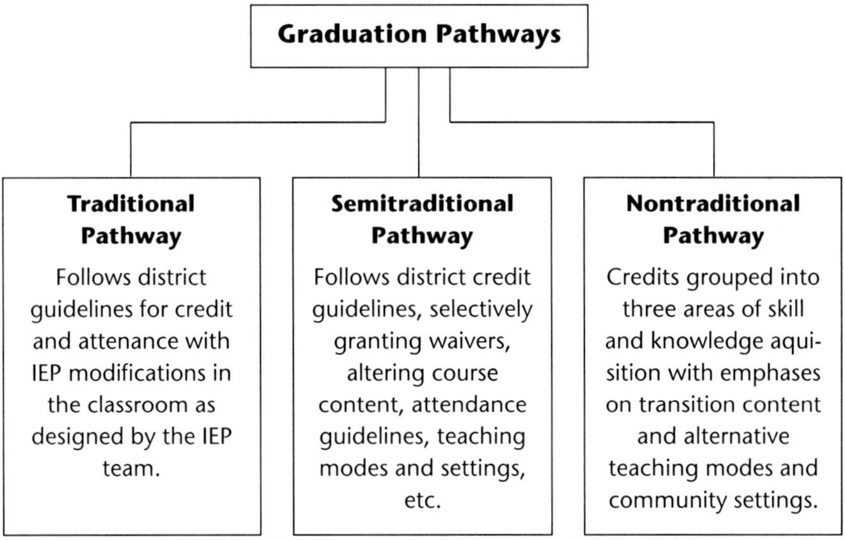

**Graduation Pathways**

| **Traditional Pathway** | **Semitraditional Pathway** | **Nontraditional Pathway** |
|---|---|---|
| Follows district guidelines for credit and attenance with IEP modifications in the classroom as designed by the IEP team. | Follows district credit guidelines, selectively granting waivers, altering course content, attendance guidelines, teaching modes and settings, etc. | Credits grouped into three areas of skill and knowledge aquisition with emphases on transition content and alternative teaching modes and community settings. |

## EARLY STUDENT-CENTERED TRANSITION PLANNING

One important discussion that occurred in the reauthorization of IDEA in 2004 concerned changing the mandatory transition planning age from 14½ years to the current 16 years under Section 614D. Our own state of Illinois has chosen to maintain the initial planning age of 14½ years, and this chapter reflects that choice of approach. We agree with other transition researchers and practitioners (for example, Kochhar-Bryant, 2007; Moses, 2008) that early inclusion of transition opportunities within IEP planning is reflective of best practice considerations, especially given the consistency of research findings that the outcomes for students with EBD are less positive than those for students with other disabilities. Almost half of students classified as EBD drop out of school permanently, and data on their postschool outcomes suggest lower employment rates than for students without disabilities (Johnson, McGrew, Bloomberg, Bruininks, & Lin, 1997). In addition, data from the National Longitudinal Transition Survey-2 (NLTS-2) indicated that about one out of five students with EBD enrolls in any type of postsecondary educational experience (SRI International, 2000). Data summarized by Sitlington and Neubert (2004) also showed less positive outcomes for students with EBD in terms of independent living and overall ratings of adult adjustment and self-efficacy. Within 2 years after leaving high school—even with a high-school diploma—fewer than 25% of students with EBD were living independently, compared to about 36% of their peers. Clearly, a coordinated effort for transition planning is a much needed service that may benefit these students; however, it is perhaps even more important to secure students' involvement in their own transition planning process (cf., Kohler, 1999; Weidenthal & Kochhar-Bryant, 2007). Early and active participation by students in IEP and transition planning is advocated by those who study concepts of self-determination and self-advocacy and their connections to school and postschool success. Students' involvement in the IEP process can help motivate them to take on the responsibility of voicing opinions about their overall transition plans, including possible diploma options. Thus, in the middle-school years, transition discussions must address many issues that may have many consequences—intended and unintended—on the student's opportunities while in school and in both postsecondary training and postsecondary employment (Kohler & Field, 2003; Sitlington & Neubert, 2004).

Assisting students with EBD to understand their own preferences, interests, strengths, and needs requires that both the academic and social behavioral areas of their education be considered. It is important that the foundation for students' postsecondary experiences and success in the rest of their lives be set during the critical K–12 years, and it is the IEP that can serve as a reference point for all decisions related to transition planning.

## REQUIREMENTS AND CONCEPTS OF IEP DEVELOPMENT

The overall requirements of IDEIA 2004, including the IEP, are discussed in Chapter 1 of this book. It is fair to say that IEP teams are faced with a seemingly expanding task with the dual purposes of meeting the group-oriented, standards-referenced requirements of the No Child Left Behind Act (NCLB, 2001) while at the same time striving to provide a free, appropriate, and individualized education for students with disabilities (Shriner et al., 2005). The essential elements of an IEP refer to the procedural and substantive requirements that schools must follow when developing IEPs. Procedural requirements refer to those aspects of IDEIA that compel schools to follow the strictures of the law when developing an IEP. However, a procedurally correct IEP is not sufficient if the student's educational program described within it does not result in that student's achieving meaningful educational benefit. Thus, the substantive requirements refer to the content of a student's special education program (including the IEP) that compels schools to provide an education that confers meaningful educational benefit to a student (IDEIA, 2004, 20 U.S.C. § 1415(f)(3)(E)(I)).

IEPs prepared for students of transition age must include four key components that entail a mixture of both procedural and substantive elements:

- An assessment process that focuses on the identification of one or more postsecondary goals for the student

- A specific listing of one or more postsecondary goals in the areas of education and training, employment, and, when appropriate, independent living

- A specific listing of IEP annual goals that are directed to assist students to meet their postsecondary goals

- A specific listing of transition services, including instructional activities and community experiences designed to help the student in transitioning from school to anticipate postschool environments and to help achieve identified postsecondary goals

It is also important to note that IDEIA now requires a useful summary of students' performance when they leave school at graduation with a diploma or have reached the maximum age of eligibility. (The details of the summary of performance [SOP] will be discussed later.) With these general guidelines in mind, we turn now to the rationale and best practice underpinnings of IEP planning that include transition considerations.

## PRIORITIZING IEP COMPONENTS

To help IEP teams conceptualize the needs of their students, it may be helpful to use a diagram to illustrate student's needs within an IEP. The outer circle of each item in Figure 7.2 represents the student's overall program, including how meeting the general curriculum and specific IEP goals will be addressed. Each inner circle represents a decision type for IEP teams, including considerations of (1) general curriculum content and skills that are most important for the student, (2) plans for access skills that will help the student be engaged meaningfully and show what the student knows and is able to do, and (3) skills related specifically to transition needs. The IEP team may craft a program that places more or less emphasis on any one of the three decision areas, with the relative importance of each reflecting the team's instructional priorities for the student.

Within this orientation, general curriculum content and skills include the academic learning standards that serve as a reference for all students' educational programs. Students are to have opportunities to address grade-level content standards, and it is within this context that the substantive requirements of the IEP call for careful consideration of how best to address the content and constructs of the standards in an individualized, meaningful way.

Access skills are skills that help students show what they know and are able to do. They may include skills and dispositions in many areas (for example, study and organizational skills, social and behavioral skills, self-regulatory skills, and self-advocacy skills). Skills specific to transition needs might include skills for daily and independent life functioning, employability, and social engagement in the community. For transition-age students with EBD, the IEP team must determine how best to plan an overall program through its emphasis on content and skills within and across these three main decision areas. Although we realize that these areas are neither mutually exclusive nor exhaustive, our approach to decision making is based on the premise that all instructional and experiential priorities for the student (in the short and long term) are consistent with the student's postsecondary options and plans.

As an example of a student with EBD whose IEP will include transition planning, we introduce a young man named Dorian. Dorian lives in Illinois, a state that has retained the provision of initial transition planning considerations for students who are 14½ years of age. The processes and decisions illustrated throughout this case example are intended to result in an IEP that includes "coordinated, measurable, annual IEP goals and transition services that will reasonably enable the child to meet the postsecondary goals" (IDEIA, 2004, 20 U.S.C. 1416 (a)(3)(B)).

**FIGURE 7.2   Prioritization of Instruction and Services as a Function of Student Need Relative to the Three Main Program Components**

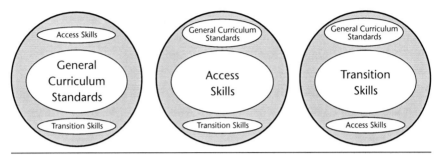

### Dorian—A Case Example of a Student with EBD

Dorian is a 14-year-old 8th grader who has two younger siblings. His parents believe he is a capable young man, and he is sometimes responsible for taking care of his younger siblings after school and on weekends. Dorian has enjoyed soccer on and off since kindergarten and has expressed interest in playing on the team at school. However, his responsibilities at home and his increasing behavior problems have prevented him from pursuing these goals.

Dorian has a history of being verbally aggressive and exhibiting disruptive behaviors directed toward his peers and teachers. These behaviors have had a negative effect on his educational development and interpersonal relationships. Thus far, his parents and pediatrician have attributed his difficulties to school and family adjustment issues. Dorian was evaluated and identified with EBD during his 4th-grade year. The comprehensive assessment procedures also led to identifications of AD/HD and anxiety disorder.

He has received special education services (250 minutes per week) for the past 3 years, including specific instruction for social skills deficits. Recently, Dorian has had difficulty regulating his emotions when he feels overwhelmed (for example, when he is in a crowded or chaotic atmosphere such as a school assembly). He has acted out both verbally and physically toward peers and was suspended recently for 3 days for pushing another student into the hallway lockers.

Dorian's mother reported that this last year has been very difficult. Although Dorian has always been her "special needs child," she is concerned that, as a teenager, he is too difficult to handle at times. These problems prompted his mother to ask the family physician to evaluate Dorian for possible use of anti-anxiety medications.

### *Future Plans*

Dorian's parents are concerned about his behavior and overall school performance. The current IEP process has prompted Dorian's family to give significant thought to his future. In preparation for the next school year and the move to high school, Dorian reports that he wants to continue to get academic and social supports so that he can "be better." Experiences that will build skills in community participation (for example, social skills and stress management) will continue to be needed. Awareness of potential career paths should be part of Dorian's overall school and community experiences.

## TRANSITION ASSESSMENT AND PRESENT LEVELS OF ACADEMIC ACHIEVEMENT AND FUNCTIONAL PERFORMANCE

Two important sections of the IEP lay the foundation for data-based decisions: transition assessment and assessment of present levels of academic achievement and functional performance. Detailed transition assessment information can lead to improved instruction and program planning by assisting students in making informed choices, taking charge of the transition process, and understanding what skills are needed for postschool environments (Test, Aspel, & Everson, 2006). Timely assessment information should identify student interests, skills, and supports necessary for successful community inclusion.

### Transition Assessment

To properly develop student goals, it is vital to collect relevant age-appropriate transition assessment information. According to the Division on Career Development and Transition (DCDT) of the Council for Exceptional Children (CEC), transition assessment is defined as an "ongoing process of collecting data on the individual's needs, preferences, and interests as they relate to the demands of current and future working, educational, living, and personal and social environments" (Sitlington, Newbert, & Leconte, 1997). Assessment data serve as the common thread in the transition process and form the basis for defining goals and services to be included in the IEP.

The initial step in developing transition-rich IEPs is to conduct age-appropriate transition assessment to determine student preferences and needs that will be added to the present levels of academic achievement and functional performance (PLAAFP) section of the IEP. There are many transition assessments from which to choose. The tools selected may include transition planning inventories, person-centered planning checklists, academic and behavioral measures, self-determination scales, and interest inventories. It is important that the overall transition assessment be student focused, inclusive of multiple perspectives and environments, and viewed as an ongoing process. Student and family interviews and other anecdotal information from teachers and others close to the student are an excellent place to start. Interviews often provide the foundation for a good transition assessment/IEP plan, but they are not adequate as a sole assessment tool. IEP teams should not rely on a single assessment. Neither is it good practice to take a "one size fits all" approach to choosing assessment tools. Teams should be informed of the assessment options available to best tailor the plan for the individual student so that the goals that eventually are written for the IEP/transition plan likely will be based on better, more focused assessment data.

## Present Levels of Academic Achievement and Functional Performance (PLAAFP)

Assessing a student's present levels of educational performance has long been a part of the IEP process. In the IDEIA 2004 reauthorization, the "present levels" section of the IEP was modified to include "statements of the student's academic achievement and functional performance . . . and descriptions of how the student's disability may affect his or her involvement and progress in the general curriculum" (§300.320). The intent of the requirement to include both assessment areas is to enhance the degree of individualization of a student's IEP. To meet this challenge, IEP teams will need to gather comprehensive assessment information to support their subsequent decisions.

Academic achievement refers generally to the student's performance in content areas (for example, English/language arts, mathematics, and science), whereas functional performance refers generally to those skills or abilities that allow the student to participate in routine activities of everyday living (for example, daily care of one's needs and social/behavioral skills) across a broad range of settings. Except for the "academic-nonacademic" differentiation, no formal definitions of academic achievement and functional performance are included in the federal regulations that enforce IDEIA.

A well-constructed PLAAFP statement provides a snapshot of the student and includes information from teacher reports, student reports, reviews of student work, standardized test scores, and informal assessments. The PLAAFP statement should be data based, but it should go beyond being a simple listing of current scores on assessments. It should include descriptions of performance that serve as the basis for identifying the student's strenths and deficit areas, priorities for the student in addressing the general curriculum, and, of course, annual goals and short-term objectives. For students with EBD of transition age, this information would include the transition assessment data that have been gathered. The PLAAFP statement should be detailed enough that if the student's name were removed from the statement, someone who knows the student well could read it and identify the student to whom the statement refers. Enough information should be provided that another local education agency could begin immediately to serve the student's needs without having to reevaluate and/or retest the student.

Table 7.1 displays Dorian's cover sheet and comprehensive PLAAFP, based on forms used in Illinois. All the features described above are incorporated into this section of his IEP.

## DEVELOPING POSTSECONDARY GOALS

The IEP for a student of transition age must include measurable postsecondary goals that articulate what the student would like to achieve after high school based on (1) the student's strengths, preferences, and interests and (2) age-appropriate transition assessment information. Postsecondary goals should be discussed, developed, and written into the IEP transition plan before developing the rest of the IEP for a transition-age student. Postsecondary goals and outcomes must be written for the following two areas: (1) education and/or training (for example, community college, university, trade, technical or vocational

TABLE 7.1 **Present Levels of Academic Achievement and Functional Performance**

## Present Level of Academic Achievement (include strengths and areas to improve)

### Strengths

Academically, Dorian performs well in a one-on-one instructional situation, especially when materials are read aloud to him. He has excellent listening comprehension skills. Dorian's skills in working with money (for example, counting money and figuring correct change and cost of items) are also very good. He is artistic, athletic, and participates in extracurricular activities. His classroom behavior has improved slightly in the last year as reported by his teachers. Based on his transition assessment, self-determination strengths are in the areas of goal setting and interest determination. He can be very creative and has shown interest in both computers and art. His personal care and daily living skills are also very good.

### Academic Achievement

Dorian is in the 8th grade and receives core instruction in general education for all subject areas. He receives accommodations and does have some modified instructional content and assignments. Current classroom averages for the quarter are math—70%, language arts—60%, social studies—55%, and science—60%. On standardized assessments Dorian performs less well than his same-aged peers. He was administered the WIAT II in 2008. He earned grade-equivalent scores of 3.2 in word reading, 4.6 in reading comprehension, 5.5 in math operations, and 5.2 in math reasoning.

### Reading and Mathematics Performance

Based on his WIAT II performance, Dorian has difficulty reading independently. His decoding problems interfere with overall comprehension. He relied heavily on word recognition for most reading tasks. On classroom reading assessments using grade-level content, he typically answers 60% or fewer comprehension and vocabulary items correctly. When he has someone read items to him, he answers approximately 80% of the items correctly. So there is a difference between his performance when he works independently as compared to when he has an accommodation.

TABLE 7.1 **(continued)**

## Present Levels of Functional Performance (include strengths and areas to improve)

Dorian was diagnosed and began receiving services under the category of emotional/behavioral disorder (EBD) at the end of 4th grade. Since Dorian's enrollment in 6th grade, he has been taking medications for a diagnosis of ADHD as well. Teacher observations and classroom reports indicate that when Dorian is properly medicated his behavior is acceptable in most situations. When his impulsive nature is reduced, he can offer sustained attention to tasks and will complete most assignments if time constraints are withdrawn. Without his appropriate medications, Dorian is easily frustrated and goes off task rather quickly. He does have the skills to seek assistance and attention appropriately but often fails to use these skills and initiates a cycle of increasing verbal and behavioral activities to gain teacher or peer attention. Dorian can become verbally and physically aggressive at times if he is not given assistance very quickly. Classroom activities that are more structured actually provide him a chance for success if teacher attention is available should he need it. However, large-group activities that are largely unstructured and with a pace that is more hectic cause Dorian to report feeling cluttered. He blames his aggressive behaviors on the environment and on his teachers and peers rather than on his own social mediation skills. Commonly, when Dorian gets in trouble, his behavior begins with modest inattentiveness, but it ends with frustration that is sometimes displayed as aggression. The functional behavior assessment that was conducted in order to create a behavior intervention plan for Dorian includes the determination that Dorian's inappropriate behaviors help him avoid or escape aversive tasks and personal interactions that are punishing to him. This pattern has become a cycle for Dorian, especially when he has a feeling of being "cluttered." Special education supports have demonstrated some positive changes in his behavior. There has been a decrease in the number of his office referrals for the behavior; however, he is still getting office referrals once a week. There have been overall increases in his social skill development and work completion. But the inconsistent implementation of the behavioral intervention plan has resulted in Dorian experiencing a continued problem with the escape and avoidance activities that he has shown over time.

A reading of his transition assessments data shows that Dorian did well on his self-determination assessment, demonstrating that he is aware of his abilities and limitations. He also demonstrated the ability to set his own goals and has the potential to change plans to achieve desired goals. According to his parents and the life skills assessment, Dorian mastered 100% of his self-care needs and scored 80% on daily living, 70% on work and study, 40% on communication, and 25% on social skills. Dorian's high scores on self-care and daily living are promising for successfully living in his own apartment. Low scores in the communication and social categories are due to his lack of social skills that lead to aggressive behaviors and suggest the need for frequent opportunities at school and in the community to practice and learn communication and socialization.

According to the results of the interest inventories, Dorian ranked high in artistic occupations. He also expressed interest in working on a computer where he can have an opportunity to be creative. Dorian completed only one third of the computerized skills assessment after getting frustrated with some of the questions. He may need to increase his understanding of how computers are used in various jobs and how to manage his social behavior (for example frustration and stress).

**Parental Educational Concerns**

Dorian's mother has ongoing concerns about his behavior both at home and at school and is worried about his declining academic performance. At home he is sometimes responsible for taking care of his younger brother and sister after school and on weekends. In the past year, his mother says he has become both verbally and physically aggressive toward his siblings. In addition, he has become somewhat more oppositional toward his parents' requests and has started to leave home without telling them where he is going. She is concerned that eventually he will engage in illegal activities. At school he has fallen farther behind in most subjects. Although he receives accommodations and modified tasks and instructions in most classes, he has become increasingly disengaged, mostly through his absences and in cutting class in the general education classrooms.

school, career field training, apprenticeship, on-the-job training, etc.) and (2) employment (for example, competitive, supported, or military). If appropriate for individual students, postsecondary goals and outcomes should be written for independent living skills.

Postsecondary goals and outcomes are not the same as the annual, measurable goals related to transition that are found in the "goals and objectives" section of the IEP. Postsecondary goals and outcomes are intended to communicate what will be achieved after high school and are therefore written as definitive statements such as "The student will enroll full time at Quality Community College in the housing industries program" or "Upon completion of high school, the student will complete a 2-year apprenticeship in carpentry with the local carpentry union's apprenticeship program." Statements that indicate possible outcomes (for example, "look for" and "wishes") are not appropriate for goals under current guidelines.

Table 7.2 presents examples of Dorian's postsecondary goals in the IEP format.

## Decisions for Annual, Measurable Goals and Short-Term Objectives

Annual goals must be prepared for all students. A student's annual goals should (1) enable the student to be involved in and make progress in the general education curriculum, and (2) meet each of the student's other educational needs that result from the student's disability (IDEIA, 2004, 34 CFR §300.320(a)(2)(i)(A)(B)). These requirements reflect both the group-oriented provisions of NCLB with respect to standards-based education, as well as the IDEIA-required responsibility of addressing students' individually determined needs based on relevant and valid assessment information.

It is important to remember, however, that the IEP represents the prioritized instructional and service targets for the student and that important learning needs that do not require the statement of an annual goal may exist. If special education or related services are needed, a goal or service statement must be presented.

For transition-age students with EBD, goals addressing academic skills, social-behavioral skills (considered functional skills in Illinois), and transition-related outcomes may be needed. All written annual goals

## TABLE 7.2 Statement of Postsecondary Outcomes

Indicate and project the desired appropriate measurable postsecondary outcomes and goals as identified by the student, parent, and IEP team. Goals are based on age-appropriate transition assessments related to employment, education, and/or training, and, where appropriate, independent living skills.

**Employment** (for example, competitive, supported, nonpaid employment as a volunteer or in training capacity, military)

> Dorian will hold a job in an area in which he has shown interest, including working with computers or other strength-related areas.

**Postsecondary Education** (for example, community college, 4-year university, or technical/vocational/trade school)

> Dorian will attend community college or vocational school, where he will major in graphic design or computer programming related to art. During his first semester, he will enroll in a computer design class to assess his interests and strengths related to the field of graphic design.

**Postsecondary Training** (for example, vocational or career field, vocational training program, independent living skills training, apprenticeship, on-the-job training, Job Corps)

> During Dorian's community college experience, he will participate in an externship (for example, in a local business, company, or organization) to assess his job-related skills and strengths related to his interests.

**Independent Living,** if applicable (for example, independent living, health/safety, self-advocacy/future planning, transportation/mobility, social relationships, recreation/leisure, financial/income needs)

> Dorian will live at home until he is financially secure enough to pay rent for an apartment and live independently.

should be logically connected to the student's postschool outcomes. However, IEP teams must write separate transition-related annual goals only if the academic and functional annual goals that are written do not directly enable the student to meet the postschool goals and outcomes listed on the transition form.

The IEP Quality Project (IEP-Q), at the University of Illinois at Urbana-Champaign, has developed and is currently testing a Web-based IEP tutorial and decision-making support system that assists educators in developing IEPs that move beyond the procedural (compliance documentation) requirements of IDEIA 2004. The IEP-Q tutorial provides direct support to IEP teams for improving the substantive (quality) components of IEPs. Specifically, we use a decision-making framework that helps IEP teams prioritize the standards and skills that are to be addressed in the form of annual goals and short-term objectives. Our approach builds on other models for writing standards-referenced annual goals (for example, Bateman & Linden, 2006; Holbrook, 2007; Lignugaris-Kraft, Marchand-Martella, & Martella, 2001; Sopko, 2003) and emphasizes that although IEPs must address the academic learning standards of the students' enrolled grade level, using the standards themselves as annual goal statements is *not* an appropriate strategy.

Our model follows several steps. First, IEP teams should ensure that the PLAAFP statements and the transition plan content (that is, postsecondary goals) have been reviewed and considered. This information is important when prioritizing skill areas to address in annual goals and provides a data-based foundation for subsequent decisions. Second, the student's specific deficit areas should be identified and matched to all areas in the learning standards that are likely to be areas of concern. Reading decoding and fluency problems, for example, would not only match to English/language arts standards, they would also be relevant to certain mathematics standards that are terminology based (for example, geometry). In conjunction with matching a student's need with the standards, the likelihood that the student can meet certain academic or functional standards with or without the use of instructional accommodations should be discussed. If the IEP team recommends accommodations (for example, oral or audio presentation of some content material or use of a spell-checker) and the student is likely to meet a standard using those accommodations within the school year, then no IEP goals are needed for that area. Next, in deciding if an identified grade-level standard is an area for which a prioritized standard or skill warrants the construction of an annual goal, the team is encouraged to consider several of its characteristics (Ainsworth, 2003). An IEP team may want to consider the following questions:

- Will the student use this standard's skills and knowledge in the long-range future?
- Will the knowledge and skills in this standard help the student in other academic or functional areas?
- Does this standard provide the skills necessary for the next level of instruction in coming years?

Transition IEP teams should, of course, think of these questions in the context of skills needed for success in both near-term (school) and far-term (postschool) environments. Consideration of these issues helps prioritize those learning standards that are worthy of specially designed instruction congruent with the student's long-range educational outcomes.

## Construction of Annual, Measurable Goals and Short-Term Objectives

Once the prioritization is completed, the task of developing annual, measurable goals that address skill areas within those learning standards is a straightforward process. The three essential components of a goal are well known to educators. These components are (1) conditions for demonstrating the behaviors(s), (2) observable, measurable descriptors of the behavior(s), and (3) criteria for demonstration of the behavior(s). By definition, annual, measurable goals are statements of expectations for achievement over 1 year's time; therefore, a stated time frame for annual goals may not be needed.

### *Annual, Measurable Goals*

Dorian's annual, measurable goals are shown in Table 7.3. The conditions statements illustrate the specific circumstances (for example, instructional environment and setting) in which students will be showing what they know and are able to do. Standards-referenced general curriculum areas may be appropriately listed as conditions. It is important to keep in mind that the conditions should be replicable (for example, 6th-grade level materials) and not overly limiting in their specifications (for example, using pages 98–120 of the "Wonderful Reading Series").

IEP teams sometimes struggle with descriptions of observable, measurable behaviors within annual, measurable goals, especially with higher-order skills. Consideration of how the student's progress toward meeting the goal will be evaluated can help describe what the performance that is of importance will look like. Observable, quantifiable terms can help the team state expectations in a positive direction, if it is at all possible. Dorian needs specially designed instruction to improve his reading skills, and the team decided that he will demonstrate his progress by "reading aloud"—an observable, measurable behavior.

Finally, the criteria for performance desired should be included to identify, how much, how frequently, or to what benchmark the student is expected to change or grow. Previously, descriptors such as "improve" or "increase" were deemed sufficient within annual, measurable goals. With the annual target for goals, a statement of reasonable growth or improvement levels is now required. Criteria listed should match the content area and method of measurement of the behavior. For example, if the behavior of interest is math computation, a percent correct criterion may be appropriate. If quality of writing is the behavior of interest, one might wish to use a rubric of some form as the basis of the criteria for performance.

### Short-Term Objectives

Not all states require the inclusion of short-term objectives in the IEP. In Illinois, however, each annual, measurable goal is to be supported by at least two objectives that use the same three-component structure (conditions, behaviors, and criteria) as the goals. Any of the three components of the goal may be modified to produce good short-term objectives that help monitor the student's progress throughout the school year. The manner in which the goal is further articulated sometimes rests on the instructional approach that is likely to be used in order to meet the goal that guides this decision. The way team members approach instruction of the skills within the goal may help them decide how to break down the goal into smaller increments.

### TABLE 7.3 Annual, Measurable Goals and Short-Term Objectives

The goals and short-term objectives or benchmarks shall meet the student's educational needs that result from the student's disability, including involvement in and progress in the general curriculum, or for preschool students, participation in appropriate activities. (The progress on annual goals is measured by the short-term objectives/benchmarks.)

#### Goal Statement

In his vocational education class, Dorian will complete 10 job applications with 100% accuracy by the end of the year.

Indicate goal area:  ☐ Academic    ☐ Functional    ☒ Transition

Short-Term Objective/Benchmark for Measuring Progress on the Annual Goal
Within the first semester of Dorian's vocational education class, Dorian will accurately complete five demographic sections and five related work experience sections of job applications with 90% accuracy.

*Short-Term Objective/Benchmark for Measuring Progress on the Annual Goal*

During the second semester of Dorian's vocational education class, Dorian will accurately complete five job-specific self-assessments of strength and weakness and develop a reference list with at least three persons listed.

#### Goal Statement

While working in group activities for career experiences, Dorian will use self-control and self-management strategies to (1) match his case manager's ratings of his behavior with 90% accuracy and (2) limit his behavioral referrals to less than one per week.

Indicate Goal Area:  ☐ Academic    ☐ Functional    ☒ Transition

*Short-Term Objective/Benchmark for Measuring Progress on the Annual Goal*

While working in group activities (with his case manager) and using a self-management prompting form, Dorian will successfully match his case manager on the self-management form for 90% of the preset behavioral criteria.

189

**TABLE 7.3** **(continued)**

*Short-Term Objective/Benchmark for Measuring Progress on the Annual Goal*

While working in group activities (with his case manager), Dorian will successfully reduce his behavioral referrals to two times or fewer per month.

### Goal Statement

Given a text passage of between 250 and 400 words at the 6th-grade reading level, Dorian will read the passage aloud with 95% accuracy in three consecutive weekly trials.

Indicate Goal Area: ☒ Academic ☐ Functional ☐ Transition

*Short-Term Objective/Benchmark for Measuring Progress on the Annual Goal*

Given a text passage of between 250 and 400 words at the 6th-grade reading level, Dorian will read aloud with 80% accuracy in three consecutive weekly trials by the end of the first semester.

*Short-Term Objective/Benchmark for Measuring Progress on the Annual Goal*

Given a text passage of between 250 and 400 words at the 6th-grade reading level, Dorian will read aloud with 90% accuracy in three consecutive weekly trials by the end of spring semester.

### Goal Statement

In a classroom setting when a teacher asks Dorian if he needs assistance or redirects him back to a task, Dorian will use appropriate language (for example, "Yes, ma'am; okay; where do you want me to start?") to respond to the teacher for 80% of any observed class period.

Indicate Goal Area: ☐ Academic ☒ Functional ☐ Transition

*Short-Term Objective/Benchmark for Measuring Progress on the Annual Goal*

By February 15, given a question or redirection from a teacher, Dorian will use a menu of possible responses (for example, "Yes, I need help; No, thank you") to respond appropriately for 80% of any observed class period.

*Short-Term Objective/Benchmark for Measuring Progress on the Annual Goal*

By May 30, given a question or redirection from a teacher, and using the STAR Strategy (Stop, Think, Act, Reward), Dorian will respond appropriately (for example, "Yes, please help me—Okay") for 80% of any observed class period.

### Goal Statement

When given a challenging academic task, Dorian will use a three-question self-monitoring tool to determine if he needs help and will request that help by raising his hand or going up to the teacher's desk without incident across all general education classes for a 2-week period.

Indicate Goal Area: ☐ Academic   ☒ Functional   ☐ Transition

*Short-Term Objective/Benchmark for Measuring Progress on the Annual Goal*

By February 15, given a three-question self-monitoring tool during instruction in the resource room setting, Dorian will use the tool to determine if he needs help and ask the teacher for help at least one time per instructional period without incident for a period of 2 weeks.

*Short-Term Objective/Benchmark for Measuring Progress on the Annual Goal*

By May 30, given academic tasks in science and math classes, Dorian will use a three-question self-monitoring tool to determine if he needs help and ask for that help by raising his hand or going up to the teacher's desk without incident for a 2-week period.

For example, if the instructional approach is to begin with less complex material that is gradually increased over time, the conditions might be adjusted within each short-term objective, while the behaviors and criterion levels remain unchanged. A second option is to require increasingly complex behaviors of the student over time. In this case, the observable, measurable behavior(s) would be adjusted throughout the year while the conditions and criteria stay the same. Finally, it may make sense to employ a changing criterion design of sorts, in which the level of achievement or performance in the objectives is adjusted over time. The conditions and behaviors remain unchanged, and improvement is noted as the student reaches new criteria for performance.

## Functional Behavioral Assessment, Behavioral Intervention Planning, and Social-Emotional Goal Development

Having addressed the overall orientation to annual, measurable goals, we now turn to another important consideration when addressing transition planning for students with EBD. By definition, these students will require support with social and behavioral concerns that will likely have a direct connection to how transition planning for their success will be approached. In this section we discuss briefly the cumulative process of functional behavioral assessment and behavioral intervention planning, and the development of social-emotional goal statements.

### *Functional Behavioral Assessment*

A functional behavioral assessment (FBA) supplies the data upon which the behavior plan and social-emotional goals will be built by detailing (1) student strengths, (2) operational definitions, (3) information, (4) antecedents and consequences, and (5) hypotheses for the behaviors (Table 7.4). We believe that the strength-based approach for all students is an important orientation. For example, Dorian is described as a student who enjoys athletics and working with computers, maintains quality relationships with adults and peers, and actively participates within his home environment. These attributes provide key information in identifying preferred reinforcers, setting functional goals, and developing a transition plan that directly relates to the student's strengths.

The FBA is grounded in the operationalization of the target behaviors. By defining a behavior in a way that is measurable and explicit, we can directly observe how the individual behaviors help to determine their overall function. Good operational definitions support better understanding of both the problem behaviors (for example, Dorian's inappropriate verbal disruptions) and the desired replacement

## TABLE 7.4   Functional Behavioral Assessment

### Student's Strengths

Dorian is an artistic student who enjoys working with computers and graphic design. His parents report that he is especially responsible at home, where he often completes his chores with no problems, willingly takes care of his siblings, and reads picture books to his younger sister. Additionally, Dorian is an athletic student who strives to participate in extracurricular activities. He especially enjoys his physical education class.

### Operational Definition of Target Behavior

When given a difficult academic task without direct access to a teacher or in unstructured time periods, especially in large groups, Dorian exhibits inappropriate verbal behaviors. These include

Behavior 1: Elevated vocal noises such as singing, humming, fake coughing—(0 to 8 per academic period)—moderate to intense—always loud enough for others/teacher to hear them

Behavior 2: Inappropriate comments generally related to the task (0 to 8 per academic period)—begin mild and may be quiet (this is dumb—why do I need to do this? this class is worthless), which can escalate quickly, especially in large groups without direct access to the teacher (within 2 to 3 minutes) to more intense statements (I hate this class—I'm not doing this! It's stupid!)

Behavior 3: Aggressive arguments with teachers/staff—generally personal in nature (0 to 2 per academic period given the other two conditions have not been addressed)—generally moderate to intense (I don't have to listen to you—shut up—I don't have to do anything you say—you aren't a good teacher! Do your job!)

### Setting

Dorian's target behaviors have been reported by teachers and observed and recorded in all classes, with the exception of physical education. However, they were usually preceded by limited access to the teacher, unstructured academic tasks, and large-group work in combination with difficult academic tasks. In classes with "hands-on" activities (for example, science) or small-group instruction (for example, resource classes), Dorian's behavior is on the lower end of the numbers given above.

**TABLE 7.4   (continued)**

His behaviors are not contingent on time of day but do relate to the structure of the class that he is in. For example, the behaviors were observed during independent work time (either group or individual), particularly when a worksheet, a large amount of text, or math word problems were involved, and during unstructured class time when he did not have clear direction regardless of the class or time of day.

### Antecedents

- Many steps or directions given at one time without immediate access to a teacher (behavior 1)
- Being given independent seatwork, particularly with large amounts of reading or directions that have not previously been orally read or explained (behaviors 1, 2, and 3)
- Large-group work that requires completing a worksheet with minimal instruction from the teacher (behaviors 1 and 2)
- Extended periods of unstructured academic time, or when others have completed the work before Dorian and the noise level in the classroom increases (behaviors 1, 2, and 3)

### Consequences (reinforcement consequences for Dorian)

During the progression, Dorian is reinforced by the following:

- Attention from peers, teachers, administrators, and parents
- Immediate escape from frustrating academic tasks or "cluttered" situations
- Long-term escape from frustrating academic tasks or "cluttered" situations
- Removal from academic environment

### Hypothesis of Behavioral Function

When given a difficult academic task without direct access to a teacher or in unstructured time periods, especially in large groups, Dorian engages in the target behaviors (described above). His behaviors appear to serve several functions in the academic classes in which they occur:

- To escape academic tasks that are above his current ability level or when he does not understand the assignment (behaviors 1, 2, and 3)

- To escape situations or unstructured periods when he feels "cluttered" due to the increased number of people in class or around him, escalated noise levels, or when his peers have finished an assignment before he has (behaviors 1, 2, and 3)
- To obtain attention from peers (behaviors 2 and 3)
- To obtain attention from teachers (behaviors 1 and 2)

---

behaviors, and help IEP teams articulate more appropriate social-emotional goals.

Following creation of the operational definitions of the target behaviors, direct documentation of the conditions and environmental settings in which the behaviors occur will be needed. This process might be accomplished through the use of an antecedent–behavior–consequence (ABC) chart or another observational tool. For example, Dorian's problem behaviors occur most often when task demands appear to be associated with (1) instruction in core academic content area classes, (2) large-group activities, and (3) unstructured work time that does not provide sufficient cues to help Dorian focus on the tasks at hand.

The observed consequences to the behaviors are important to document as well. Consequences may provide insight into the potential function of the behavior (for example, to escape a task demand) by documenting both the direct consequence (that is, the consequence delivered by the teacher) and the perceived reinforcer (that is, what the student is trying to achieve through the behavior). This information is used in hypothesis development and intervention efforts (for example, teaching replacement behaviors), as well as in writing individualized social-emotional goals.

The final portion of the FBA is the development of hypotheses or summary statements. A well-written hypothesis statement is similar to an academic goal statement in that it includes specific antecedents (that is, conditions) and a description of the target behavior and its hypothesized function (to example, to escape or attain). Based on the assessment data, it was determined that Dorian's behaviors served several functions that could not be generalized to one hypothesis statement. In this special case, the antecedents are addressed, then each function and corresponding behavior is stated individually. This method allows a case conference committee or a transition-planning team to develop specific interventions for each behavioral scenario instead of creating a blanket intervention that may not generalize to all environments.

### Behavior Intervention Plan

The behavior intervention plan (BIP) is a valuable tool for addressing deficits that may hinder progress toward postsecondary goals (Table 7.5). It contains four basic elements: (1) a summary of the FBA, (2) interventions, (3) disciplinary measures, and (4) data collection and responsibilities. A well-constructed BIP is designed with complementary goals for decreasing problem behaviors while increasing desired replacement behaviors that benefit the student's immediate and longer-term outcomes.

In addition to the replacement behaviors, the intervention section includes the environmental, instructional, support, and reinforcer modifications that will be used. Generally, the environmental and instructional interventions address both the antecedents that may be contributing to student problems and methods for developing the new behaviors. For example, Dorian's FBA revealed that his behaviors were triggered by difficult academic tasks, limited access to the teacher, and unstructured environments. Therefore, his environmental and instructional interventions address these antecedents by providing access to the instructor, breaking assignments down into distinct steps, and avoiding or limiting unstructured academic periods. Second, the positive supports intervention subsection addresses how stakeholders will foster the development of the replacement behaviors that will better serve Dorian in a variety of environments. Finally, the reinforcer subsection specifically addresses student motivators for appropriate behaviors. To be successful, the behaviors and motivators must be efficient for the student. Dorian's motivators were selected based on an informal interest inventory that revealed his interest in athletics and computers.

The disciplinary measures section of the BIP is relatively straightforward. The goal is to develop a consistent continuum of consequences for dealing with problem behaviors. Attention must be given to the initial triggers of each behavior to provide preemptive redirection and de-escalation. For example, Dorian's plan provides a continuum for

**TABLE 7.5   Behavior Intervention Plan**

### Target Behavior

Is this behavior a ⊠ skill deficit or ☐ performance deficit?

Skill Deficit: The student does not know how to perform the desired behavior.

Performance Deficit: The student knows how to perform the desired behavior but does not consistently do so.

(See the FBA for more specific information on each of these behaviors: elevated physical and vocal noises, inappropriate comments, and aggressive arguments with teachers.)

### Hypothesis of Behavioral Function

Include hypothesis developed through the FBA (attach completed form). What desired thing(s) is the student trying to get? Or what undesired thing(s) is the student trying to avoid?

When given a difficult academic task without direct access to a teacher or in unstructured time periods, especially in large groups, Dorian engages in the target behaviors (described on the FBA). His behaviors appear to serve several functions in the academic classes where they occur:

- To escape academic tasks that are above his current ability level or where he does not understand the assignment (behaviors 1, 2, and 3)
- To escape situations or unstructured periods in which he feels "cluttered" due to the increased number of people in class or around him, escalated noise levels, or when his peers have finished an assignment before he has (behaviors 1, 2, and 3)
- To obtain attention from peers (behaviors 2 and 3)
- To obtain attention from teachers (behaviors 1 and 2)

### Summary of Previous Interventions Attempted

- Dorian was given a help card to use that he would flip when he needed assistance. This system was unsuccessful because other students asked what the card was for, and Dorian immediately felt singled out and refused to continue with it. Also, teachers did not always notice the card right away, providing time for the behavior to occur.

**TABLE 7.5 (continued)**

- Dorian was moved from a general education reading class to an instructional reading class, and his problem behaviors have decreased.

- Dorian is working with his case manager on engaging in appropriate conversations, effectively dealing with frustration, and appropriately asking for help with assignments.

### *Replacement Behaviors*

Describe which new behaviors or skills will be taught to meet the identified function of the target behavior:

In his resource class, Dorian will be taught appropriate ways of asking for help and dealing with academic frustration in the classroom setting that will not result in embarrassment around peers. In addition, Dorian will join an anger management group to learn how to defuse his own anger.

- Elevated physical and vocal noises—replace with appropriate ways to ask for assistance with tasks and to relieve stress and anxiety in "cluttered" situations.

- Inappropriate comments—replace with appropriate ways to ask for assistance with academic tasks.

- Aggressive arguments with teachers and staff—replace with appropriate ways to ask for assistance with academic tasks; specific, more respectful phrases to use with adults when anger is escalating; and techniques for dealing with escalating anger and feelings of frustration that help to deescalate the anger.

### *Behavioral Intervention Strategies and Supports*

<u>Environment</u>

- Dorian should be moved closer to the teacher and away from distractions.

- Nonstructured time periods should be avoided or limited.

- Instruction should be provided in short, distinct, verbal steps.

- Extended time on a single task should be avoided.

*Positive Supports*

- The case manager must monitor Dorian's progress and attend to instruction in appropriate ways to deal with academic and social frustration and his adherence to the behavior plan.

- Dorian's counselor must work with the case manager to develop appropriate anger management training activities.

*Reinforcement*

- Participation in extracurricular activities is contingent on academic success (school policy).

- Dorian will earn points that he can apply to the following: activity time (for example, computer time), time with a trusted adult, individual work time, playing basketball in the gym before school with a chosen peer, eating lunch outside with the resource teacher.

- If Dorian's behavior remains consistent, he will be rewarded with increased administrative responsibilities (that is, passing out papers or acting as the attendance runner or the chalkboard/overhead recorder).

*Restrictive Disciplinary Measures*

The following restrictions will be documented by teachers on Dorian's daily behavior chart and given to his case manager daily. The case manager will then chart them weekly.

- The teacher will redirect and specifically identify Dorian's behavior.

- The teacher will deduct self-management points and discuss the reason for the reduction.

- Dorian may be removed from the situation or classroom as a "drain-off" period.

- If Dorian's behavior continues when he returns, the teacher will issue a detention or behavioral referral.

**Data Collection Procedures and Methods**

- *Classroom teachers* should collect anecdotal data on a daily basis. This data will be in a chart where teachers will list the number of incidences of each of Dorian's three target behaviors. A narrative section will

**TABLE 7.5    (continued)**

provide a brief account of the target behaviors observed or of the positive behaviors exhibited.

- *Dorian* will use a self-management checklist in a similar format for the three target behaviors and a reflective piece.
- *The case manager* will chart the teacher reports and Dorian's self-reports weekly and will conduct observations to collect data on Dorian's progress on the target behaviors.

---

dealing with low to moderate levels of the problem behaviors. Transition planning may be structured so that these disciplinary measures are mirrored in vocational training and structured job placements.

The final section of the BIP addresses data collection procedures. Data collection is important because the data will provide evidence of the effectiveness or ineffectiveness of the interventions. If an intervention is ineffective, a behavior plan review should be conducted to modify or develop additional interventions. In Dorian's case, data are collected anecdotally, through teacher and student reports, and direct observation.

### Social-Emotional Goal Development

The development of social-emotional goals is an important component in effective transition planning for students with EBD. Social-emotional goals are written with the same basic framework as academic and transition goals and typically are adapted directly from the FBA and BIP. For example, replacement behaviors should be clearly identified in the BIP. In addition, the conditions in which the behavior should be related to the environmental, instructional, or support intervention subsections of the BIP and the criteria for mastery of a specific goal should relate to the acquisition of reinforcers documented in the BIP.

As we mentioned earlier, some states do not require the use of short-term objectives or benchmarks for annual goals. We believe, however, that the implementation of social-emotional goals—like academic goals—is supported by well-written objectives as a guide for evaluating students' progress. Table 7.3 included examples of annual goals and short-term objectives.

Overall, the FBA, BIP, and social-emotional goals section of an IEP are created to provide students with EBD the fundamental skills and dispositions necessary to engage in a variety of settings and to support their social development. These attributes are essential for successful school and transition experiences and deserve the attention of the IEP team as they assist all students who need support in social skill development.

## DETERMINING A COURSE OF STUDY AND TRANSITION-SPECIFIC ACTIVITIES FOR STUDENTS WITH EBD

Transition goals and objectives must be linked to the student's course of study. The IEP is required to include a statement of a student's transition service needs, with a focus on the student's course of study (for example, participation in advanced-placement courses or in a vocational education program). Determining the pathway (that is, the courses) that students should take and the activities in which students should participate is central to learning and to graduation. Thus, for transition-age students, the course of study and transition-specific activities are vehicles that can provide them with opportunities to learn and practice skills needed for adult life. This coordinated set of activities is composed of the experiences and courses that students need and must take to assist them in meeting their postschool goals. As in every component of the IEP, decisions must be based on the students' needs, dreams, and strengths to increase the likelihood of students' engagement with their program of study (Kochhar-Bryant, 2007).

The course of study in the IEP makes use of the student's vision statement to plan for his or her graduation option. Classes taken by students should reflect a course of study that is determined mostly by the students' desired postschool outcomes. The sooner the student can identify these outcomes, the sooner the IEP team can help craft a course of study that seeks to accomplish those goals (Weidenthal & Kochhar-Bryant, 2007). The purpose is to create a long-range educational plan or multiyear description of the educational program that directly relates to the student's anticipated postschool goals. The IEP team should discuss the specific skills to be obtained from these course experiences. After a course of study is determined, an array of activities and services should be planned and implemented for each postschool goal. Thus, a complete picture of the classes, program options, and other opportunities for general curricular access that will lead to a successful transition is created.

As shown in Table 7.6, Dorian's course of study focuses on career exploration in one of his identified interests (computer design), understanding successful vocational behavior (vocational education), and courses that provide opportunities for building social networks and improving study skills (study hall with peer tutors and working as a member of the yearbook staff). Each of these areas was highlighted in Dorian's assessment results. Furthermore, it is important to consider that a specific course of study may change based on the student's interests and needs.

## Transition Services

To support a course of study, transition services and activities should be clearly articulated in the IEP. Activities and services may address areas such as academic instruction, related services as defined by IDEIA, community participation, career development, adult living, daily living skills, and functional vocation evaluation (McPartland, 2005). This section of the IEP may be thought of as the "action plan" or "to do" list, and it should be easily understood by the student, parents, and professionals. For example, parents should be able to read an IEP and understand their child's goals, course of study, and transition activities. Additionally, the description of transition activities should detail whether the student will complete a traditional academic or vocational course of study or whether participation in an alternative curriculum or a graduation option is necessary.

Students with EBD, such as Dorian, often have challenges with classroom behavior and need extra support in order to be engaged in the curriculum. As shown in Table 7.7, Dorian will receive instruction in smaller, co-taught classroom settings and receive one-on-one support during some group activities. Other activities that may be considered include (1) support from social service agencies; (2) assistance with medical concerns, such as learning to self-administer medications; and (3) instruction in self-advocacy skills for school, work, and community situations.

**TABLE 7.6  Course of Study for 4 Years**

Identify a course of study that is a long-range educational plan or multiyear description of the educational program that directly relates to the student's anticipated postschool goals, preferences, and interests.

| Year 1—<br>Age 14/15 | Year 2—<br>Age 15/16 | Year 3—<br>Age 16/17 | Year 4—<br>Age 17/18 |
| --- | --- | --- | --- |
| Language arts (9) | Language arts (10) | Language arts (11) | Language arts (12) |
| Algebra I | Geometry | Algebra II | Job placement |
| Earth/space science | Biology | Vocational education | Chemistry |
| World history | Vocational education | U.S. history | Government/ economy |
| Physical education/ health | Spanish I | Spanish II | Vocational education |
| Vocational education | Computer graphics | Graphic design I | Graphic design II |
| Yearbook | Yearbook | Yearbook | Yearbook |

## LINKAGES ACROSS SYSTEMS FOR THE IEP

No single agency is likely to have all the desired resources to plan and provide comprehensive transition services to students. To assist students to plan for transition, many different individuals, including educational and related services professionals, must come together. Transition planning is typically handled by members of the IEP team centered on the student and involves a variety of people who bring multiple perspectives to the planning table. The team draws on the expertise of the different members and pools their information in order to make decisions or recommendations for the student. Each planned activity in the IEP that assists students to achieve their

**TABLE 7.7  Transition Services/Activities and Linkages**

| *Instruction (if none, indicate "none")* | *Provider Position* |
|---|---|
| All of Dorian's teachers will assist in increasing the frequency that Dorian remains on task in his learning environments. This will be done by providing small-group (two or three students) instruction activities and discussion groups. | Vocational education teacher<br>Transition coordinator<br>General education teachers |
| In vocational education, Dorian will receive instruction on appropriate work habits, obtaining jobs, filling out applications, and interviewing skills 3 days a week. This course will use a peer mentor (one with similar interests) with Dorian to meet and discuss issues about working in the community and in their career exploration course. | |

| *Related Services (if none, indicate "none")* | *Provider Agency* |
|---|---|
| Dorian will access the general curriculum and participate in activities with his peers, with and without disabilities. | Guidance counselor<br>Social worker<br>General education teachers |
| Dorian will see a social worker once a week to work on any anger issues and to have conversations with peers. | |
| Dorian will meet with the counselor once a month in the school to discuss postschool plans and to get any ideas for moving forward toward a career. | |

### Community Experiences (if none, indicate "none")

The vocational education teacher will have Dorian research the Internet for local recreation and leisure activities. With assistance from the special education teacher, he will create a list of at least six clubs or groups. On the list Dorian will write the name of the activity, a contact person's name, the phone number, location, and a brief description of the activity. In one semester, he will attend at least one session for each group to determine if it interests him greatly and to assist with social skills development.

### Provider Person

Special education teacher

Vocational education teacher

### Development of Employment and Other Postschool Adult Living Objectives (if none, indicate "none")

As part of the freshman work–study program, Dorian will participate in jobs throughout the school building. The work–study coordinator will arrange for Dorian to work in the computer lab, photo lab, and performing arts studio for 12 weeks. The teacher will provide surveys and inventories to determine the level of his success and interest in these jobs. Dorian will have assignments that talk about his experience, including social behavior and work elements.

Dorian will attend a study group after school to discuss assignments and study strategies with tutors who are upperclass students.

### Provider Position

Vocational coordinator/ work–study program instructor

**TABLE 7.7  (continued)**

| Appropriate Acquisition of Daily Living Skills and/or Functional Vocational Evaluation | Provider Position |
|---|---|
| | Case manager |
| Conduct person-centered planning and schedule assignments. | |

| Linkages to After-Graduation Supports and Services | Provider Position |
|---|---|
| | Transition coordinator |
| These contacts will be made by the end of the year so they can be transitioned onto the IEP team next year (that is, Department of Mental Health, Vocational Rehabilitation, and a community rehabilitation provider). | |

postschool goals must identify an agency, or linkage, that is responsible for its implementation.

The provision of related services is an integral part of a free and appropriate public education (FAPE) for students under Part B of IDEIA 2004. As part of this requirement, linkages among related services and community service providers must be identified, and a statement of needed transition services must be included (for example, a statement of interagency responsibilities or any needed linkages) (IDEIA, 2004, 34 CFR 300.347(b)(2)). Linkages among school, family, and community service providers create the foundation for effective service provision in the school and the community (Braaten & Quinn, 2000; Kauffman, Lloyd-Baker, & Riedel, 1995). Students with EBD often have very specific needs, and to best serve their individual support needs, IEP team members must have a multidimensional approach to interagency collaboration that leads to an increased understanding of service delivery for this population.

One way to conceptualize the linkages that may benefit students' transition plans is to consider three essential features that support the transition process and service delivery. These features are (1) an awareness of the community and knowledge of available service providers, (2) relationship development and communication among professionals and agencies, and (3) active participation and collaboration of team members, school personnel, and service agencies. Each of these features helps to define the multidimensional approach to comprehensive transition planning for students with disabilities, including those with EBD.

## Community Awareness

Unfortunately, linkages among agencies and service providers are often weak and poorly coordinated (deFur & Taymans, 1995; Oertle & Trach, 2007). Special educators are required to coordinate referrals to adult service providers on a limited basis. Special educators and related service professionals often work toward the same or similar postschool outcomes independently and with no or limited awareness of the other's efforts and activities (Carlson, Brauen, Klein, Schroll, & Willig, 2002). Therefore, the IEP and transition-planning teams must be knowledgeable about all service providers in the community and their prospective roles. In Dorian's case, IEP team members should have a clear understanding of which community service agencies provide social skills training (for example, the "community youth connection social group").

## Relationship Development

Transition researchers have routinely documented the need to create frequent opportunities for professionals to communicate with each other during the planning and implementation of transition activities (Johnson et al., 1997). Exchanges of information, resources, and knowledge cannot be limited to an annual meeting. Both formal and informal communication is critical for building relationships that promote effective interagency collaboration. Communication is often difficult because terminology, procedures, and understanding are not congruent and may even conflict. In many instances, professionals do not even know each other as they are working in parallel systems. As stronger relationships are built, deeper understandings, greater expectations, and more dynamic transitions are likely to occur (Johnson et al., 1997).

## Active Participation

When various service professionals are uninvolved in transition planning, the IEP team may encounter barriers to utilizing their services, creating delays in receiving assistance for accessing employment and participating in the community (Morningstar, Kleinhammer-Tramill, & Lattin, 1999). Parallel systems in special education and adult services, such as vocational rehabilitation and community rehabilitation, often seem to operate independently rather than interdependently. As a result, youth and their families are less informed about the services and opportunities available to them. To provide students with disabilities with the appropriate support as they transition from high school into the adult world, transition professionals' active participation in inter-agency collaboration is critical. As stated previously, secondary education is a time-limited entitlement, ending at school completion. Youth leaving high school need assistance with career assessment and career guidance, and with accessing viable employment, education, and residential living (Lehmann, Cobb, & Tochterman, 2001). Various transition-related professionals can provide this assistance by linking individuals to valuable community and workplace resources (Wehman & Targett, 2002). Respectful partnerships must be developed among individuals, their families, special educators, and adult service professionals to work toward the acquisition of full community participation. Partnerships promoting interagency collaboration that include adult service professionals are a powerful means for supporting people with disabilities to become valued community members with lifelong goals (Szymanski, 1994). During transition activities and services, students encounter situations in which the transition professionals' community skills and knowledge play an important role in students' development of career paths and other needed capabilities.

## Summary of Performance

The Individuals with Disabilities Education Improvement Act (IDEIA, 2004) specifies that a complete evaluation "shall not be required before the termination of a child's eligibility under this part due to graduation from secondary school with a regular diploma, or due to exceeding the age eligibility for a free appropriate public education under State law" (§3000.305(e)(2)). Instead it calls for a summary of performance (SOP), which is completed before a student's final year of high school. The SOP includes background and demographic information, postsecondary goals, present level of performance, and needed accommodations, modifications, and assistive technology. This document should be linked directly with the IEP process by giving students the opportunity to participate in its development as they prepare for their next step as adults. Students with EBD often receive counseling, social, and therapy services through their school years. However, as students age out of secondary education, they often fall through the cracks and receive only vocational services as they transition—school professionals are not there to share educational responsibility (Kochhar-Bryant, 2007). Thus, a comprehensive SOP can assist students in attaining success as they enter higher education and employment settings.

The SOP is written to provide a description of the student's academic achievement and functional performance upon exiting school and to specify recommendations about how to assist the student in meeting postsecondary goals. The information included in the SOP that is to be provided for each student is based on the student's IEPs (current and past) and other information (such as transcripts and grade reports for the student's time in middle and high school). Transition personnel rely on the thorough information provided on the SOP as they make judgments about a student's level of performance on specific skills and his or her abilities and motivation to follow through with postsecondary recommendations. The SOP serves as a cumulative record that includes the student's academic and social-behavioral needs with a focus on transition to environments other than school throughout the time such data are kept. Because of this orientation, raising the mandatory transition planning age to 16 under IDEIA is not something that all professionals see as best practice. States and local districts can—and do—choose to require transition planning for students 14½ years of age.

## SUMMARY AND CONSIDERATIONS FOR POSTSECONDARY EDUCATION AND TRANSITION PLANNING

Crafting a comprehensive, transition-rich IEP can be demanding. There are many student-centered barriers to successful transition that can be addressed through an effective IEP process. Schools are responsible for providing individual students and their parents with information about a graduation pathway that could include academic courses, access to community agencies, supports needed for successful transition, and employment opportunities that are available to the student. To maximize the benefit for students with EBD during and after high school, a clear and comprehensive IEP is needed. For students with emotional disorders, the logical extension includes social–behavioral self-regulation and accommodation strategies beyond the academic realm for successful participation in postsecondary environments of any kind. The IEP is of particular importance here because it is clear that without attention to these issues as part of the school-based transition-planning process, students may not develop skills to compensate for their learning and behavioral problems or obtain necessary accommodations to help them effectively deal with multiple and complex tasks. In addition, students may not be able to fully develop their capabilities without proper transition planning.

In summary, the IEP process can be enhanced by constructing useful present levels of performance statements, incorporating functional behavior assessments and behavior support plans, and addressing the student's social-emotional needs during goal development. These goals must direct the student's course of study and transition activities They must also identify linkages between school and adult service agencies to best achieve a seamless transition to a satisfying adult life environment.

## REFERENCES

Ainsworth. L. (2003). *Power standards: Identifying the standards that matter most.* Englewood, CO: Advanced Learning Press.

Bateman, B. D., & Linden, M. A. (2006). *Better IEPs: How to develop legally correct and educationally useful programs* (4th ed.). Verona, WI: Attainment Co.

Blackorby, J., & Wagner, M. (1996). Longitudinal postschool outcomes of youth with disabilities: Findings from the National Longitudinal Transition Study. *Exceptional Children, 62*(5), 399–413.

Braaten, B., & Quinn, C. (2000). Successful inclusion of students with emotional and behavioral disorders: The Bryn Mawr Elementary School Program. *Preventing School Failure, 45,* 15–17.

Cameto, R., Levine, P., & Wagner, M. (2004). *Transition planning for students with disabilities. A special topic report of findings from the National Longitudinal Transition Study-2.* Menlo Park, CA: SRI International.

Carlson, E., Brauen, M., Klein, S., Schroll, K., & Willig, S. (2002). *Study of personnel needs in special education: Key findings.* Rockville, MD: WESTAT.

deFur, S. H. (2003). IEP transition planning: From compliance to quality. *Exceptionality, 11,* 115–128.

deFur, S., & Taymans, J. (1995). Competencies needed for transition specialists in vocational rehabilitation, vocational education, and special education. *Exceptional Children, 62,* 38–49.

Holbrook, M. D. (2007). *Standards-based Individualized Education Program examples.* Arlington, VA: Project FORUM, National Association of State Directors of Special Education.

Individuals with Disabilities Education Improvement Act of 2004, Pub. L. No. 108–446 (2004).

Individuals with Disabilities Education Improvement Act of 2004 Regulations, 35 CFR §300 *et seq.*

Johnson, D. R., McGrew, K., Bloomberg, L., Bruininks, R. H., & Lin, H. C. (1997). Results of a national follow-up study of young adults with severe disabilities. *Journal of Vocational Rehabilitation, 8,* 119–133.

Johnson, D., Thurlow, M., & Stout, K. (2007). *Revisiting graduation requirements and diploma optional for youth with disabilities: A national study.* (Technical Report 49.) Minneapolis: University of Minnesota, National Center on Educational Outcomes.

Jones, E. A., Erfling, J. L., & Goldsby, B. (2004). Development of individualized education programs for graduation pathways and transition plans. In D. Cheney (Ed.), *Transition of secondary students with emotional or behavioral disorders: Current approaches for positive outcomes* (pp. 123–141). Arlington, VA: Council for Exceptional Children.

Kauffman, J., Lloyd-Baker, J., & Riedel, J. (1995). Inclusion of all students with emotional or behavioral disorders? Let's think again. *Phi Delta Kappan, 76,* 542–546.

Kochhar-Bryant, C. (2007). *What every teacher should know about transition and IDEA 2004.* Boston: Allyn & Bacon.

Kohler, P.D. (1999). Implementing a transition perspective of education: A comprehensive approach to planning and delivering secondary education and transition services. In F. R. Rusch & J. G. Chadsey (Eds.), *Beyond high school: Transition from school to work* (pp. 179–205). Belmont, CA: Wadsworth.

Kohler, P., & Field, S. (2003). Transition-focused education: Foundation for the future. *Journal of Special Education, 37*(3), 174–184.

Lehmann, J., Cobb, B., & Tochterman, S. (2001). Exploring the relationships between transition and education reform initiatives. *Career Development for Exceptional Individuals, 24*(2),185–198.

Lignugaris-Kraft, B., Marchand-Martella, N., & Martella, R. (2001). Writing better goals and short-term objectives or benchmarks. *Teaching Exceptional Children, 34*(1), 52–58.

McPartland, P. (2005). *Implementing ongoing transition plans for the IEP: A student-driven approach to IDEA mandates.* Verona, WI: Attainment Co.

Morningstar, M. E., Kleinhammer-Tramill, P. J., & Lattin, D. L. (1999). Using successful models of student-centered transition planning and services for adolescents with disabilities. *Focus on Exceptional Children, 31*(9), 1–19.

Moses, J. (2008). Career search: Start charting a path for youth now. *Pacesetter, 32*(2), 6–8.

No Child Left Behind Act of 2001, Pub. L. No. 107-110 (2001).

Oertle, K. M., & Trach, J. S. (2007). Interagency collaboration: The importance of rehabilitation professional's involvement in transition. *Journal of Rehabilitation, 73*, 36–44.

Powers, K. M., Gil-Kashiwabara, E., Geenan, S. J., Powers, L., Balandran, J., & Palmer, C. (2005). Mandates and effective transition planning practices reflected in IEPs. *Career Development for Exceptional Individuals, 28*(1), 47–59.

Sax, C. L., & Thoma, C. A. (2002). *Transition assessment: Wise practices for quality lives.* Baltimore: Paul H. Brookes.

Shriner, J. G., Trach, J. S., & Yell, M. L. (2005). *The IEP Quality Improvement Project: Research and development of web-based decision support* (IES Grant No. R324J060002). Urbana: University of Illinois.

Sitlington, P. L., & Neubert, D. A. (2004). Preparing youth with emotional or behavioral disorders for transition to adult life: Can it be done within the standards-based reform movement? *Behavioral Disorders, 29*, 279–288.

Sitlington, P. L., Neubert, D. A., & Leconte, P. J. (1997). Transition assessment: The position of the Division on Career Development and Transition. *Career Development for Exceptional Individuals, 20*, 69–79.

Skinner, M. E., & Lindstrom, B. D. (2003). Bridging the gap between high school and college: Strategies for the successful transition of students with learning disabilities. *Preventing School Failure, 47*, 132–137.

Sopko, K. M. (2003). *The IEP: A synthesis of current literature since 1997.* Arlington, VA: Project FORUM, National Association of State Directors of Special Education.

SRI International. (2000). *National Longitudinal Transition Study-2 (NLTS2): Study design, timeline and data collection plan.* Menlo Park, CA: Author.

Szymanski, E. (1994). Transition: Life-span and life-space considerations for empowerment. *Exceptional Children, 60,* 402–410.

Test, D. W., Aspel, N. P., & Everson, J. M. (2006). *Transition methods for youth with disabilities.* Upper Saddle River, NJ: Pearson.

Wagner, M., Blackorby, J., Cameto, R., & Newman, L. (1993). *What makes a difference? Influences on post-school outcomes of youth with disabilities. Third comprehensive report, National Longitudinal Transition Study of Special Education Students.* Menlo Park, CA: SRI International.

Wehman, P. & Targett, P. (2002). Supported employment: The challenges of new staff recruitment, selection and retention. *Education and Training in Mental Retardation and Developmental Disabilities, 37*(4), 434–446.

Weidenthal, C., & Kochhar-Bryant, C. (2007). An investigation of transition practices for middle school youth. *Career Development for Exceptional Individuals, 47,* 147–157.

Wittenburg, D. C., & Maag, E. (2002). School to where? A literature review on economic outcomes of youth with disabilities. *Journal of Vocational Rehabilitation, 17,* 265–280.

## CHAPTER 8

# Positive Behavior Support and Transition Outcomes for Students in Secondary Settings

### Cinda Johnson and Hank Bohanon

Of the 6,033,000 students age 6 through 21 receiving services under IDEIA in 2003–2004, 483,000, or 8%, were identified as students with emotional or behavioral disorders (EBD) (U.S. Department of Education, 2006). The number of students with EBD is likely much higher, and many children and youth who could qualify for services under IDEIA may not be receiving adequate support to assist them in achieving in school settings and achieving positive outcomes after leaving high school.

The purpose of this chapter is to provide a discussion of (1) the current state of outcomes for students with EBD as they relate to transition and problematic behavior, and (2) how positive behavior support (PBS), a response to the intervention logic model, may support the creation of environments that improve postsecondary outcomes. We will begin by providing a brief review of the literature regarding transition and students with EBD, discuss three case-study applications on a continuum of positive behavior support interventions, and conclude with recommendations for implementation and future research.

*Author note:* The authors would like to thank JoAnne Malloy, University of New Hampshire; Dr. Pamela Fenning, Loyola University, Chicago; Dr. Kristyn Moroz, Illinois School District 203; and Lauren McArdle, graduate student, Loyola University, Chicago. Portions of this paper were supported by an Achievement for Dropout Prevention and Excellence II (APEX II) grant (V360A050017).

## THE CASE FOR TRANSITION AND EBD

Recent legislation emphasizes that students with disabilities have maximum access to and opportunity for success in the general education curriculum (IDEIA, 2004; NCLB, 2001). Although these students spend much of their time in the regular education classroom, the results of their participation remain poor. Students with EBD exhibit the lowest graduation rate among all students with disabilities. According to a report from the National Longitudinal Transition Study-2 (NLTS-2, 2004), 72% of youth in special education completed high school, but only 56% of students with EBD graduated. Postschool outcomes also were less positive for students with EBD. Although 79% of the youth with disabilities were engaged in either employment and/or some type of postsecondary education, 66% of young people with EBD were so engaged. Employment was the primary activity for youth with EBD (NLTS-2, 2004).

In the state of Washington, students with EBD also have rates of high-school completion comparable to the NLTS-2 study: 54% either graduated with a diploma (51%) or a General Education Development diploma (3%), whereas 46% had dropped out. For students with EBD who do graduate, their postschool status is less positive than for youth with other disabilities. For all youth with EBD, 68% were employed and/or attending some type of postsecondary education compared to 83% of youth with learning disabilities. For youth with EBD who completed high school, 75% were employed and/or attending some type of postsecondary education. In comparison, for those youth who dropped out, 54% were working and/or in school or a training program (Johnson, 2008).

Positive postschool outcomes have been associated with many features of secondary programs, including the time spent in the general education classroom (U.S. Department of Education, 2006). Access to the general education curriculum shows a notable increase for youth with EBD as represented in the NLTS and NLTS-2 studies. Students with EBD are taking more science and social studies classes (a 13% increase) and foreign language courses (an 11% increase). This represents an increase of more than 10% for youth with EBD taking general education courses in general education settings. Yet the dropout rates have not decreased significantly, nor have positive postschool outcomes increased in comparison to youth with disabilities as a whole (NLTS-2, 2004).

There are many challenges in providing appropriate transition services and supports to these youth in order to increase graduation rates and positive postschool outcomes. The typical high school is four to ten times larger than an elementary school and two to four times larger than a middle school. High schools have rigidly defined academic departments that operate independently and focus on specific content knowledge, and they have more administrators who are responsible for either departments or grade levels in the schools. Individualizing instruction and implementing various teaching strategies to meet the needs of students with disabilities is considerably more complex in the high-school setting, where teachers may teach 150 students a day compared to 30 students or fewer in the elementary building. Academic course requirements tied to higher standards, high-stakes testing, and more stringent graduation requirements, as defined by school reform legislation, make it even more difficult for teachers to meet individual student needs. Although students with disabilities may be accessing the general education curriculum, it is clearly more complicated for these students to successfully complete high school and transition into positive postschool outcomes of employment or postsecondary education or training.

Although inclusion for students with EBD provides them with opportunities to access the general education curriculum, one critical component remains constant: Both elementary and secondary general education teachers have little tolerance for disruptive, aggressive, defiant, or dangerous behaviors (Hocutt, 1996). Youth with EBD have more difficulty getting along with others (both peers and teachers) and are more likely to be involved in bullying or fighting, either as victims or perpetrators (NLTS-2, 2004). Students with EBD in high-school settings must be able to demonstrate academic achievement in mainstream classrooms and operate within a range of tolerated behavior in order to experience success in these settings.

Successful inclusive high schools actively engage students with disabilities in academic learning. Actively engaged students spend little time exhibiting inappropriate behaviors, receive focused, positive teacher attention, and benefit from having teachers who spend more than three quarters of their time focusing on and preparing students for learning and teaching them. These appear to be the important factors associated with successful inclusive high-school classrooms (Wallace, Anderson, Bartholomay, & Hupp, 2002).

Positive postschool outcomes also are associated with factors such as parental involvement, vocational education, and social integration into the school through participation in sports or other groups (NLTS-2, 2004). Two of these components, vocational education and integration into sports and clubs, are difficult to achieve for youth with EBD. As academic standards are raised, vocational technical education courses also become more challenging. Although vocational education has been shown to contribute to higher rates of both postsecondary vocational training and employment for youth with high-incidence disabilities, youth with EBD are less likely than students in the general population to take vocational education courses (NLTS-2, 2004). Although youth with EBD are taking more general education courses, the rates of young people with EBD taking vocational courses have not changed appreciably since the mid-1980s. There are fewer "hands-on" vocational courses (for example, auto and metal shop classes) available in high schools. The vocational technical courses offered are more difficult for students to access, and higher standards make it more difficult for students to achieve academic success in these classes. For example, many of these courses have prerequisite skills that must be demonstrated for class entrance. In addition to problems accessing vocational or career-technical courses, students with EBD also may have difficulty accessing high-school sports or other school activities because of low grade-point averages.

Students with EBD who have more course failures, lower grade-point averages, and far fewer credits than their nondisabled peers are more likely to drop out of the traditional high-school curriculum (NLTS-2, 2004). Inclusion for students with EBD most benefits those students who can demonstrate academic success and approximate acceptable behavior that includes following classroom rules, complying with teacher directives, and generally behaving in an orderly fashion in the secondary general education classroom. For students who do not meet these criteria, a broader continuum of services must be provided, and those services may need to be provided in settings beyond the general education classroom.

Students with EBD are not typically invested in their high school, do not feel successful in the school setting, and are often fearful of returning to the school in which they had poor attendance, poor grades, and conflicts with administrators, teachers, and peers (Bullis & Cheney, 1999). Programs for these students are typically not provided within the general education classroom but rather in classrooms with teachers trained to meet their specific social and academic needs.

Behavior-related services and supports for students with EBD are provided at reportedly higher levels than for all students with disabilities. According to the NLTS-2 (2004) report, 55% of students with EBD were receiving behavior support plans, compared to 13% of all students with disabilities. In addition, 49% of students with EBD were reportedly receiving mental health services, compared to 20% of all students with disabilities. The primary question for service providers is not whether behavior supports are being provided to students with EBD. A more relevant question regarding successful transition may be "What type of support, setting, and delivery mechanism would provide the most effective and efficient behavior support, thereby increasing postsecondary outcomes for students with EBD?" Three-tiered response to intervention (RTI) models, such as the schoolwide positive behavior support (PBS) model, may provide a way to address this dilemma (Sugai et al., 2000; Walker et al., 1996).

## POSITIVE BEHAVIOR SUPPORT, TRANSITION, AND EBD

This section of the chapter will discuss emerging work in the field of PBS, discuss how it relates to the RTI model, and provide examples of how the PBS model has been used in high schools to better meet the needs of all students, particularly those with or at risk of EBD. We begin by discussing (1) the current integration of academic and behavior supports, (2) an example of schoolwide intervention in an urban high-school setting, (3) a secondary classroom setting intervention that provided classwide support around attendance issues, and (4) an example of intensive tertiary futures planning.

Response to intervention models, such as PBS, are defined as "a process of instruction, assessment and intervention that allows schools to identify struggling students early, provide appropriate instructional interventions, and increase the likelihood that all students will be successful" (Mellard & Johnson, 2008). The logic behind this model includes (1) providing the most effective academic and behavioral instruction for all students, (2) early intervention on a continuum of support levels, (3) modifying and specializing for students who do not respond to initial interventions, (4) universal screening on academic and behavioral indicators, and (5) using students' actual behavior as an indicator for progress in the environment (Goodman & Bohanon, 2008). Positive behavior support is an RTI model in that it relies on a continuum in which the intensity of behavioral support increases relative to the needs and challenges of the student. Further, PBS highlights the key components of the RTI approach for all students by increasing response intensity based on data. This continuum is divided into a three-tiered model that includes primary, secondary, and intensive interventions (Bohanon et al., 2006; Carr et al., 2002; Sugai & Horner, 2002; Walker et al., 1996).

The PBS model fosters teaching and acknowledging positive social behaviors, maximizing academic success, and removing factors that promote or sustain problem behavior with a goal of enhancing healthy social, cognitive, and emotional growth of youth. The PBS process is characterized by a team-based approach that includes functional behavioral assessment and behavior intervention planning, a person-centered approach to comprehensive interventions, and an emphasis on targeted social skills and self-management instruction (Bohanon, Eber, Flannery, & Fenning, 2007; Carr et al., 2002). These critical features link with schoolwide academic and behavioral expectations to maximize student outcomes (Sugai & Horner, 2002). The improved outcomes for students may be supported by the increase in the number of group and individualized interventions in settings with more effective schoolwide climates (Eber, Lewandowski, Hyde, & Bohanon, 2005).

A field-based analysis of high-school PBS was developed as an outcome of a national forum on high-school PBS. The subsequent volume (Bohanon-Edmonson, Flannery, Eber, & Sugai, 2005) from this meeting was developed to identify the components of intervention, ranging from schoolwide to intensive supports, including transition. In one of the chapters, Sugai, Flannery, and Bohanon-Edmonson (2005) identified the nine components of PBS based on the literature (Colvin, Kame'enui, & Sugai, 1993; Lewis & Sugai, 1999; Safran & Oswald, 2003):

1. At least 80% of the students within a setting can identify the expected behaviors for their setting.
2. There is an increase in instructional time.
3. There is an increase in the ratio of positive to negative interactions.

4. Only evidence-based interventions are included within the continuum.

5. Decisions are made by a team and are driven by the ongoing use of data.

6. Administrators actively participate in the process.

7. Policies for differentiating classroom-managed versus office-managed behaviors are defined and implemented with consistency.

8. Discipline data are reviewed on a regular basis.

9. A range of supports is available to all students.

Sugai et al. (2005) provided a list of components that should be considered when implementing PBS in high-school settings:

1. Establish and/or consolidate a schoolwide leadership team that enables efficient communication and decision making with a large number of staff members.

2. Work within existing administrative structures.

3. Start small and prioritize time.

4. Identify naturally occurring and useful data sources and systems.

5. Increase focus on teaching and encouraging positive expectations.

6. Maximize administrator involvement.

7. Involve students and staff in decision making, development, and evaluation activities.

8. Increase opportunities for feedback to students and staff.

9. Specify and focus on measurable outcome indicators.

10. Increase opportunities for academic success and competence of *all* students.

11. Create student communities that are small in size, maximize adult interactions, and enable active supervision.

12. Prioritize, model, prompt, and acknowledge factors that contribute to a positive sense of community.

13. Move the school toward three organizational goals: (1) a common vision (that is, purpose or goal), (2) a common language (for example, communications, terminology, and information), and

(3) a common experience (for example, routines, actions, activities, and operational structures).

Scott, Eber, Malloy, and Cormier (2005) identified components of intensive support (not solely related to high-school support) that may lead to more effective person-centered transitions for students whose behavior impedes their learning. These components included (1) providing a voice and choice for youth who are the focus of the process, (2) identifying the strengths of the student, (3) focusing on supports that occur naturally in the life of the youth, (4) offering comprehensive supports that are based on the needs and preferences of the youth, and (5) continued planning for additional intensive supports (for example, behavioral support). Providing such person-centered supports may be increasingly effective in secondary climates where direct defining, teaching, and acknowledgment of expected behaviors occurs (Edmonson & Turnbull, 2002; Turnbull et al., 2002).

These practices have been used to promote PBS at the building, classroom, and student levels for students with EBD. We contend that improving schoolwide and classroom practices for all students will lead to better academic, social, vocational, and community outcomes for students with EBD.

This chapter presents three examples of applying PBS in secondary settings. We begin with an example used by high-school staff to improve discipline practices and to teach positive social skills to all students in the high school. We follow this with examples at the classroom and student levels that have improved the educational programs of students, including those with disabilities. Finally, we conclude with recommendations for implementing PBS in high schools.

## Schoolwide Positive Behavioral Support

Soto High School (student population 1,800) is a 4-year high school in the heart of a large, urban Illinois city. The total enrollment for the district at the time of this study was 438,500 students in 602 buildings. Soto High School's student population represented at least 75 countries with the following student demographics: 36% African American, 36% Hispanic, 16% Asian American, 8% Caucasian, 2% Native American, and 2% other. At least 89% of the students qualified for free and reduced lunch, and 21% had limited English proficiency. The school had an average daily attendance of 86%, a 19% dropout rate, and a 30% mobility rate; 20% of the students qualified for special education services (Bohanon et al., 2006).

In a study conducted from 2001 to 2004 (Bohanon et al., 2006), the high-school staff and external researchers identified three priorities regarding discipline in their building. These priorities were (1) the need for clear and consistent expectations for students, (2) the need for improved response time from the discipline office, and (3) the desire to focus on positive behaviors rather than constantly correcting inappropriate behaviors.

These priorities were presented to the staff along with aggregated discipline data from archival school records. At the end of these presentations, the research team provided a basic overview of PBS for the staff and administration. They briefly identified how PBS could systematically address both the quantitative and qualitative concerns of the building. Further, there was a discussion regarding how these interventions could be embedded within the school's ongoing school improvement-planning process.

The next step involved the administration and staff's forming a representative team who would meet regularly (at least once per month). To facilitate the action-planning process for the team, the staff were asked to complete the Effective Behavior Support Survey (EBS) (Safran, 2006; Sugai, Horner, & Todd, 2000). Further office discipline referral data were organized into a database to monitor ongoing progress according to number per day, per month (Phillips & Bohanon, 2006). The staff and representative leadership team were presented with the results of the EBS survey and the discipline referral data; they subsequently developed a schoolwide action plan.

The representative team, which included four students, one parent/community agency member, one administrator, two special education teachers, two general education teachers, three university graduate students, and one additional staff member, met for a day of training and developing an action plan. The content of the training included the following:

- Principles of behavior support (for example, types of reinforcement, issues regarding punishment, student-setting events such as deprivation in nutrition or attention

- Planning with data (for example, office discipline referral data and School-wide Evaluation Tool [SET] (Horner et al., 2004)
- Developing policies around discipline (for example, office- versus classroom-managed behaviors)
- Developing schoolwide expectations
- Teaching methods for making expectations explicit
- Developing a schoolwide acknowledgment system
- Reviewing other initiatives that were in place

Teams were taught to identify three to five behavioral expectations; to develop behavioral definitions for each location for the desired behaviors and provide posters for each setting; to develop lesson plans for directly teaching expectations across settings; to identify high-frequency, intermediate, and large whole-school acknowledgments; to identify specific interventions based on trends in office disciplinary referral data; and to formulate specific policies for addressing problem behavior.

The team identified four behavioral expectations:

- Be caring
- Be appropriate
- Be respectful
- Be responsible

The team also conducted a brief pilot with approximately 100 students for the schoolwide process (for example, teaching system, systematic acknowledgment). During the fall of the following year, the expectations, a brief overview of the PBS approach, results of the pilot, and the subsequent action plan were presented to staff. Four initial sessions were provided (one for each grade level) to introduce the students to the teaching, acknowledgment, and procedural expectations for the school. Students were directly taught the expectations, had opportunities to practice basic expectations, and were acknowledged for appropriate behavior.

A school store was opened (initially in the cafeteria) where students could redeem tickets for items (for example, pencils or snacks), although the store was not open as consistently as would be recommended. The school provided weekly drawings in which students' names were drawn from the redeemed tickets for prizes and public acknowledgment. Finally, the staff provided two schoolwide celebrations to acknowledge the reduction in office discipline referrals (ODRs) for the building. These included hosting a schoolwide dance in the gymnasium and providing movie tickets donated by a local movie theater for all students and staff in the building. The results of both the ongoing progress monitoring of process and outcomes (ODRs and school climate) were provided to the staff quarterly within small group meetings.

The overall level of implementation reached a total level of fidelity of approximately 80% according to the SET. Additionally, the postcomparison of staff ratings for schoolwide implementation of PBS on the EBS increased when compared with preassessment data. There was a 20% overall reduction in ODRs between years 2 and 3. Other reductions in discipline referrals included a 70% reduction in dress code violations and a 97% reduction in serious disobedience of authority. Further, there were reductions in ODRs 7 of the 10 months of the academic school year. The greatest difference per month was a 66% drop in ODRs for the month of September between years 2 and 3.

Another way to demonstrate an impact on student behavior is to examine the changes in the proportion of students receiving ODRs at three intervals. A typical expectation in the PBS model is that 80% of the students in a setting would have zero to one ODRs, 15% of the students would have between two and five ODRs, and 5% would have six or more ODRs. There has been some discussion that these proportions are different for urban settings (Turnbull et al., 2002). The trend in the ODR data, however, did seem to progress toward these more standard proportions. For example, 46% of the students had zero to one ODRs in year 1, compared to 59% in year 2. This increase indicated that there was an improvement in the number of students who were not referred for disciplinary problems at all or more than once. Further, 32% of the students in year 2 had two to five ODRs, compared to 25% in year 3. Finally, 21% of the students had six or more ODRs, compared to 16% in year 3.

According to Horner et al. (2004), the criterion for full implementation on the SET is to have the total score at least 80%, with the teaching subscore at 80%. Although this school had not reached full implementation (the teaching subscore was less than 80%), implementation did reach an overall rating of 80%. There appeared to be several positive outcomes associated with this study.

First, as the level of fidelity of implementation increased, there were significant reductions in problematic behavior. Second, the proportion of students who were referred for discipline problems decreased. These outcomes could potentially lead to fewer students being referred for more intensive supports, thereby increasing the resources available for supporting students who were truly in need. Finally, this process of creating environments that support all students may be related to improved outcomes for students with the most intense needs (Turnbull et al., 2002), including students with EBD.

## PBS at the Classroom Level

Moroz (2006) discussed the implementation of PBS at the classroom level. This study was completed at Soto High School. Within this setting, two classrooms were experiencing problematic behavior. The staff had expressed concern regarding tardiness to school. These concerns were supported by an examination of the schoolwide tardiness data. Two classrooms with tardiness issues were selected for intervention. The two teachers from the classrooms with problems were approached and agreed to participate. Two other classrooms were selected as control classrooms. Classroom 1 had 18 students and focused on environmental science. Classroom 2 had 14 students and focused on freshman algebra. The comparison classrooms (which were not exposed to the supports) were environmental science (20 students) and freshman algebra (12 students).

The intervention focused on reducing tardies, which were defined as a student's being in the hallway without an approved pass when the bell rings, with his or her entire body outside the door (Bohanon & Moroz, 2005; Moroz, 2006; Moroz, Fenning, & Bohanon, 2009). Similar to those provided in Taylor-Green et al. (1997), interventions included directly teaching the expectation for on-time behavior and providing feedback and reinforcing on-time behavior. The lesson lasted for approximately 10 minutes and included (1) a rationale for the expected behavior, (2) describing the nonexample for on-time behavior (in other words, tardy behavior), (3) describing the example of on-time behavior, (4) behavioral rehearsal of the nonexample and example behaviors, and (5) providing feedback and specific praise for being on time.

Teaching the expectations was conducted by two external research consultants (one professor and one research assistant). The classroom teachers provided ongoing feedback and acknowledgment using components of the schoolwide acknowledgement system ("cool tickets"). Once acknowledged, the students could place tickets into a bucket for a weekly drawing for prizes and public acknowledgment. Each week, students set goals for classwide on-time behavior (for example, 75% to 95% on-time behavior). If the students met the goal, a name was drawn from the acknowledgment bucket, and the student could select from a range of items (for example, gift cards). When weekly on-time goals were not met, the students were given a review of the expected behavior and a new goal was set for the following week. The punctuality goals and actual performance data were posted in each classroom, and the interventions lasted for 4 weeks. The students in the comparison classrooms received only the ongoing schoolwide supports (for example, basic teaching and acknowledging of behaviors). Additionally, the researchers completed a treatment integrity checklist each week of the study.

The on-time percentage for Classroom 1 increased from 82% to 87%. In Classroom 1, four of the five goals set by the students for the intervention were met. The comparison group actually decreased from 73% to 69% on-time behavior. On-time behavior for Classroom 2 at baseline was 76% on-time compared to 84% postintervention. The students in Classroom 2 met their goal four out of four times. On-time behavior in the second comparison class declined from 82% to 78%.

Interestingly, although the study was directly related to schoolwide PBS, it also addressed components of self-determination such as goal setting and attainment (Bohanon et al., 2007; Malloy, Cheney, Hagner, Cormier, & Bernstein, 1998). Further, in our experience, this intervention was relevant in that one of the most predominantly referred behaviors for high school is tardy-related behavior.

Instruction related to goal setting may involve teaching skills that would increase the ability for students with EBD to actively participate in their own transition planning. Goal setting is a direct component of self-determination (Wehmeyer, Baker, Blumberg, & Harrison, 2004). As previously mentioned, students with a higher level of self-determination skills may have a greater chance of demonstrating improved postsecondary outcomes (Wehmeyer & Schwartz, 1997). These classrooms may have provided an example-rich environment in which students with EBD could develop goal-setting skills through direct teaching, modeling, guided practice, and systematic feedback. The increased predictability provided by direct instruction of expectations may have led to the success of students with EBD in engaging in classroom activities from the beginning of classroom instruction until the end of the class.

## PBS at the Student Level

New Hampshire received a grant addressing dropout prevention. The project, Achievement for Dropout Prevention and Excellence II (APEX II), uses positive behavior support as a framework for implementation. The APEX II project focuses on providing tertiary supports through developing futures plans using an adapted version of the McGill Action Planning System (MAPS) (Vandercook, York, & Forest, 1989) as a framework. The components of the MAPS process include

- Stating previous personal experiences
- Defining who the student is today
- Identifying people in the student's life
- Identifying future plans
- Identifying potential barriers and roadblocks
- Clarifying goals
- Specifying next steps

Consultants from both the University of New Hampshire and the state network provide consultation for futures planning in the APEX II project.

Bohanon, Flannery, Malloy, and Fenning (2009) provided an example of a student support case occurring in a schoolwide environment within the APEX II model. Although the school team had not reached full implementation, they had begun the process of providing supports for individual students. The student mentioned in the case example was 18 and had earned 20% of his credits toward graduation. This student had a diagnosed disability until the 10th grade. Although his disability was primarily in the area of learning, his problem behavior was impeding his learning (therefore, he may have been underidentified for having EBD). The staff reported that the student was sleeping during class and was not motivated. They conducted a functional behavioral assessment that indicated that the student was acting out to escape and avoid academic instruction and that the behavior was not related to a skill deficit. A futures plan was conducted and developed by an assistant school counselor and a member of the APEX II staff over three meetings. The counselor was identified as the potential mentor for the student and provided an overview and examples of the futures planning process during their initial meeting, which included demonstrating how the student's responses would be captured on flip charts. Table 8.1 provides an example of how this case study connects with the overall schoolwide PBS and RTI models for intervention.

During the initial stages of the meeting, the student shared that he was close to being homeless and that he was rotating from one location to the next. He stated that he had not experienced academic or social problems in school before 9th grade. He stated that he received most of his support from his father and two friends. His mother, sister, and one teacher also were included on the list of people from whom he obtained support. The student further reported that he enjoyed working with his hands, including working as a roofer. His futures plans included owning a home and a car. He stated that barriers to achieving these goals included where he lived, school problems, and a lack of financial resources. The facilitator also discussed the role of depression as another barrier.

The primary areas of his futures plan included (1) obtaining a driver's license with the support of his father, (2) searching possible job opportunities with Job Corps, (3) determining alternative course completion options for credit recovery with the school counselor, and (4) determining which of his parents would be the best resource to turn to for support when needed. As a result of the plan, the student's mentor and the external consultant identified courses in which success would be most likely for the student. Also, the school counselor established a relationship with the student's father, who told the counselor that his son had contacted Job Corps regarding possible employment opportunities. The secondary planning team at the school was given the results of the student's futures plan (with the student's permission).

Over the subsequent winter break, the student was caught with drug paraphernalia. Upon returning to school, the student began a new course structure and an informal check-in and check-out system that focused on attendance and academic performance. During the spring

**TABLE 8.1   Problem Solving at the Tertiary Level: Combining Behavior Support and Person-Centered Planning**

| Problem-Solving Step | Positive Behavior Support and Person-Centered Planning Components |
| --- | --- |
| Problem identification: What is the problem? | Report from staff, interview with student during futures planning meeting |
| Analyze: Why is the problem occurring? | Functional behavioral assessment, futures planning meeting |
| Implementation: What are we (including the student) going to do about the problem? | Behavior intervention plan, action plan from futures plan |
| Evaluation: Is the plan working? | Review office discipline referrals, credit hours earned, grades, completed action steps from futures plan |

*Note:* Although curriculum-based measurement (CBM) was not used for the case study provided in this chapter, it should be considered as a part of the problem-solving process when academic deficits are addressed.

semester, the student began to earn passing grades and complete assignments. The staff also reported that the student was more active during the school day. Ultimately, he found employment and was working toward completing his GED. Although the student eventually left the school, the success and skills that he acquired through this process are relevant and transferable to both employment and postsecondary education and training settings.

## RECOMMENDATIONS FOR IMPLEMENTING SCHOOLWIDE PBS IN HIGH-SCHOOL SETTINGS

We have several recommendations for special educators, transition specialists, and administrators for implementing PBS at the secondary level for students with EBD. First, a leadership team of concerned staff must be developed and supported by the administration. This team develops a set of positive behavioral expectations for the school, including students with EBD. The expectations must be concise and taught in the classroom in such a way as to ensure that links to post-secondary environments are clearly made. These prosocial skills should be taught at the beginning of each semester as students enter new classes and should be reinforced throughout the semester during student recognition programs. This process increases the predictability of the environment, which may benefit students with EBD. Staff and students should jointly decide on (1) the topography of the expected behaviors for each classroom and (2) the types of recognition programs that are helpful for the students. Staff also should be prepared to teach, acknowledge, and redirect students through systematic professional development before program implementation (McArdle et al., 2009). If students with EBD know what is expected, are acknowledged when they exhibit appropriate behavior, and are redirected privately, we believe they are more likely to connect with their school setting. Further, if students with EBD engage in environments where these variables are present, they may be more likely to generalize socially appropriate skills across all settings of the school and beyond.

These PBS expectations are used to create a sense of normalization for all students, including those with EBD. If a behavioral support plan for a student with EBD includes teaching of appropriate skills and acknowledgment, the PBS program can be used as a foundation. Less energy will be required to teach general education staff how to incorporate this student's plan into their daily routines if they are already engaging in teaching and acknowledging behaviors. Additionally, secondary-level interventions that include goal setting may increase the level of self-determination for students with EBD, which may improve their chances for improved secondary outcomes. Also, as Eber et al. (2005) stated, schools that implement schoolwide PBS with fidelity may be more likely to support additional intensive-level supports than schools with lower levels of schoolwide PBS implementation.

Second, although the PBS program will directly address the school culture and social behavior of most students, individualized programs should be developed for students with intensive needs. Program components identified by Bullis and Cheney (1999) provide a structure for providing exemplary services to these youth. These components include gathering intake information, assessing functional skills, and conducting personal futures planning (see Table 8.1). This approach provides the information necessary to develop the individualized education program (IEP) based on the individual student's needs, preferences, and interests, and it provides the information necessary to develop a relevant and rigorous transition plan. Community-based wraparound social services link the school to appropriate adult service agencies, providing teachers with additional support while students are still in the school system. Such services develop linkages that can provide services and treatment after the student leaves school, ultimately providing support that many youth will need for success in work or postsecondary education or training.

We believe that schoolwide PBS may be related to the staff's willingness to implement secondary and tertiary supports, including transition planning. In an environment where the goal is to have at least 80% of the staff collectively address problem behavior, more effective and efficient intensive supports may result (Eber et al., 2005). The repetition of the critical features of secondary and tertiary support can be established at the initial stages of PBS. For example, PBS teams (1) develop an understanding of the importance of systems factors (such as a leadership team and regular meeting schedules), (2) implement practices that have evidence of success based on a treatment protocol (such as teaching and acknowledgment of expected behaviors), and (3) learn to link supports and subsequent adjustments in interventions to data (such as identifying specific locations to teach expected behaviors based on ODR data). Although the unit of data and intensity of support change, the basic premise of problem solving does not (Goodman & Bohanon, 2008). This final statement may provide critical links between PBS, person-centered transition planning, and RTI logic models.

Third, personal futures planning (Vandercook et al., 1989) is a vital component in addressing the needs of students in the secondary and tertiary levels of support (Bohanon et al., 2007). In the case study in this chapter, the school counselor adapted the student's course of study based on the elements of the futures plan (the student's desire for success) and the functional behavioral assessment (escaping and avoiding work). This information provides the necessary data for a robust age-appropriate transition assessment. The course of study, agency linkages, necessary transition services, and annual and postsecondary goals were identified through personal futures planning, functional behavioral assessment, age-appropriate transition assessment, and the student's present level of educational performance. In their focus on dreams and strengths and assisting students in identifying their personal networks, personal futures planning and behavioral supports are a powerful way to engage students who are disconnected from their high schools.

It was the hope of the researchers that the formalized futures planning process would guide the student described in the case study toward a successful transition. The student's problem behavior and lack of progress toward graduation may have been impeding his successful transition toward postsecondary goals. The positive behavior support intervention (that is, checking in with an interested adult), when combined with futures planning, may have led to the decrease in problem behavior and an increase in credit attainment for this student. Addressing both areas would be necessary for transitioning into any postsecondary environment for this student. Collectively working to ensure that all three levels of support are present is difficult for high-school educators, yet our case studies offer promising results in increasing successful access to general education classes and have the potential to improve postschool outcomes for youth with EBD.

## REFERENCES

Bohanon, H., Eber, L., Flannery, B., & Fenning, B. (2007). Identifying a roadmap of support for secondary students in school-wide positive behavior support applications. *International Journal of Special Education, 22*(1), 39–60.

Bohanon, H., Fenning, P., Carney, K., Minnis, M., Anderson-Harris, S., Moroz, K., Kasper, B., Hicks, K., Culos, C., & Sailor, W. (2006). School-wide application of urban high school positive behavior support: A case study. *Journal of Positive Behavior Interventions and Supports, 8*(3), 131–145.

Bohanon, H., Flannery, B., Malloy, J., & Fenning, P. (2009). Utilizing positive behavior supports in high school settings to increase school completion rates. *Exceptionality, 17*(1), 30–44.

Bohanon, H., & Moroz, K. (2005). *Positive behavior support: An overview for school psychologists.* Paper presented at the Illinois School Psychologists Association Conference, Springfield.

Bohanon-Edmonson, H., Flannery, K.B., Eber, L., & Sugai, G. (2005). *Positive behavior support in high schools.* Monograph of the 2004 Illinois High School Forum of Positive Behavioral Interventions and Supports. OSEP Technical Assistance Center on Positive Behavioral Intervention & Supports. Retrieved September 28, 2009, from http://www.pbis.org/common/pbisresources/publications/PBSMonographComplete.pdf

Bullis, M., & Cheney, D. (1999). Vocational and transition interventions for adolescents and young adults with emotional or behavioral disorders. *Focus on Exceptional Children, 31*(7), 1–24.

Carr, E., Dunlap, G., Horner, R., Koegel, R., Turnbull, A., Sailor, W., Anderson, J., Albin, R., Koegel, L., & Fox, L. (2002). Positive behavior support: Evolution of an applied science. *Journal of Positive Behavior Interventions, 4,* 4–16.

Colvin, G., Kame'enui, E. J., & Sugai, G. (1993). School-wide and classroom management: Reconceptualizing the integration and management of students with behavior problems in general education. *Education and Treatment of Children,16*(4), 361–381.

Eber, L., Lewandowski, H., Hyde, K., & Bohanon, H. (2005). *FY05 statewide PBIS summary report (Illinois Positive Behavior Support Network).* La Grange Park: Illinois State Technical Assistance Center.

Edmonson, H., & Turnbull, A. (2002). Positive behavioral supports: Creating supportive environments at home, in schools, and in the community. In W. Cohen, L. Nadel, & M. Madnick (Eds.), *Vision for the 21st century.* New York: John Wiley & Sons.

Goodman, S., & Bohanon, H. (2008). *Social behavior strand: Linking assessment to intervention for learners with intensive needs.* Paper presented at Response to Treatment Innovations Conference, Salt Lake City, UT.

Hocutt, A. (1996). Effectiveness of special education: Is placement the critical factor? *Future of Children, 6*(1), 77–102.

Horner, R. H., Todd, A.W., Lewis-Palmer, T., Irvin, L. K., Sugai, G., & Boland, J. B. (2004). The School-wide Evaluation Tool (SET): A research instrument for assessing school-wide positive behavior support. *Journal of Positive Behavior Interventions, 6*(1), 3–12.

Individuals with Disabilities Education Improvement Act of 2004, Pub. L. No. 108–446 (2004).

Johnson, C. (2008). *Post-school status report of special education leavers.* Seattle: Center for Change in Transition Services, Seattle University.

Lewis, T. J., & Sugai, G. (1999). Effective behavior support: A systems approach to proactive school-wide management. *Focus on Exceptional Children, 31*(6), 1–24.

Malloy, J. M., Cheney, D., Hagner, D., Cormier, G. M., & Bernstein, S. (1998). Personal futures planning for youth with EBD. *Reaching Today's Youth 2*(4), 25–29.

McArdle, L., Briggs, A., Hoeper, L., Carney, K, Flamini, A., Bohanon, H. et al. (2009). *Can high schools reach 80/80 (full implementation)?* Paper presented at the International Conference for the Association for Positive Behavior Support, Jacksonville, TN

Mellard, D. F., & Johnson, E. (2008). *RTI: A practitioner's guide to implementing Response to Intervention.* Thousand Oaks, CA: Corwin Press.

Moroz, K. B. (2006). *The effects of guided practice, publicly posted feedback, and acknowledgment on classroom tardies in an urban high school implementing schoolwide positive behavioral interventions and supports.* Doctoral dissertation, Loyola University, Chicago, IL. Retrieved June 1, 2009, from Dissertations & Theses Database at Loyola University, Chicago (Publication No. AAT 3243416).

Moroz, K., Fenning, P., & Bohanon, H. (2009). *The effects of guided practice, publicly posted feedback, goal setting, and acknowledgment on classroom tardies in an urban high school implementing schoolwide positive behavior supports.* Unpublished manuscript, Loyola University, Chicago, IL.

National Longitudinal Transition Study-2. (2004, August). *NLTS-2 data brief: The characteristics, experiences, and outcomes of youth with emotional disturbances. A report from the National Longitudinal Transition Study-2.* Retrieved September 28, 2009, from http://www.ncset.org/publications/viewdesc.asp?id=1687

No Child Left Behind Act of 2001, Pub. L. No. 107–110 (2001).

Phillips, M., & Bohanon, H. (2006, October 16). *Overview of data-based decision making: Implementing science- and practice-based solutions to long-standing problems, including response to intervention and positive behavior support.* Paper presented at workshop for Illinois Districts 203 and 204, Naperville.

Safran, S. P. (2006). Using the effective behavior supports survey to guide development of schoolwide positive behavior support. *Journal of Positive Behavior Interventions, 8*(1), 3–9.

Safran, S. P., & Oswald, K. (2003). Positive behavior supports: Can schools reshape disciplinary practices? *Exceptional Children, 69,* 361–373.

Scott, N., Eber, L., Malloy, J., & Cormier, G. (2005). Intensive comprehensive level of support for high school students. In H. Bohanon-Edmonson, B. Flannery, G. Sugai, & L. Eber (Eds.), *School-wide PBS in high schools* (monograph). Retrieved January 25, 2005, from http://www.pbis.org/school/high_school_pbis.aspx

Sugai, G., Flannery, K.B., & Bohanon-Edmonson, H. (2005). Chapter 1: School-wide positive behavior support in high schools: What will it take? In *Positive Behavior Support in High Schools*. Monograph from the 2004 Illinois High School Forum of Positive Behavioral Interventions and Supports. National Center on Positive Behavior Support. Retrieved July 28, 2009, from http://www.pbis.org/school/high_school_pbis.aspx

Sugai, G., & Horner, R. H. (2002). The evolution of discipline practices: School-wide positive behavior supports. *Child and Family Behavior Therapy, 24*(1/2), 23–50.

Sugai, G., Horner, R. H., Dunlap, G., Hieneman, M., Lewis, T., Nelson, M., Scott, T., Liaupsin, C., Sailor, W., Turnbull, A. P., Turnbull, H. R., Wickham, D., Wilcox, B., & Ruef, M. (2000). Applying positive behavior support and functional behavioral assessment in schools. *Journal of Positive Behavior Interventions, 2*(3), 131–143.

Sugai, G., Horner, R. H., & Todd, A. W. (2000). *Effective behavior support: Self-assessment survey.* Eugene: University of Oregon, Positive Behavioral Interventional and Supports Technical Assistance Center.

Taylor-Greene, S., Brown, D., Nelson, L., Longton, J., Gassman, T., Cohen, J. et al. (1997). School-wide behavioral support: Starting the year off right. *Journal of Behavioral Education, 7*(1), 99–112.

Turnbull, A., Edmonson, H., Griggs, P., Wickham., D., Sailor, W., Freeman, R., Guess, D., Lassen, S., McCart, A., Park, J., Riffel, L., Turnbull, R., & Warren, J. (2002). A blueprint for schoolwide positive behavior support: Full implementation of three components. *Exceptional Children, 68*(3), 337–402.

U. S. Department of Education. (2006). *Twenty-eighth annual report to Congress on the implementation of the Individuals with Disabilities Education Act.* Washington, DC: Author.

Vandercook, T., York, J., & Forest, M. (1989). The McGill Action Planning System (MAPS). *Journal of the Association for Persons with Severe Handicaps, 14*(3), 205–215.

Walker, H. M., Horner, R. H., Sugai, G., Bullis, M., Sprague, J. R., Bricker, D., & Kaufman, M. J. (1996). Integrated approaches to preventing antisocial behavior patterns among school-age children and youth. *Journal of Emotional and Behavioral Disorders, 4,* 194–209.

Wallace, T., Anderson, A., Bartholomay, T., & Hupp, S. (2002). An ecobehavioral examination of high school classrooms that include students with disabilities. *Exceptional Children, 68,* 345–359.

Wehmeyer, M. L., Baker, D.J., Blumberg, R., & Harrison, R. (2004). Self-determination and student involvement in functional assessment: Innovative practices. *Journal of Positive Behavior Interventions, 6*(1), 29–35.

Wehmeyer, M. L., & Schwartz, M. (1997). Self-determination and positive adult outcomes: A follow-up study of youth with mental retardation or learning disabilities. *Exceptional Children, 63,* 245–255.

## SECTION III

# Settings and Services for Students with EBD in Their Transition to Adulthood

## CHAPTER 9

# Preparing for Postsecondary Life: An Alternative Program Model

**Thomas G. Valore, Claudia Lann Valore,**
**Dennis A. Koenig, James Cirigliano,**
**Patricia Cirigliano, and Steven Cirigliano**

"I'm 17 and have two credits. What are ya gonna do for me?"

"At 18, do you think I'm going to sit behind a desk for 6 hours a day for 3 more years?"

"I couldn't even get up in the morning. To make things worse, my high school no longer cared. I was nothing but a bad statistic. And so the threats came. . . . They just wanted to throw me in a juvenile detention home."

These statements from interviews of students entering our alternative education program prompt the question "How does it get to this point?" Certainly, there is neither a simple answer nor a simple solution.

Late adolescence through early adulthood is a vulnerable and fragile period in the lives of students in alternative settings. Many teens are working toward the goal of returning to their home school—to participate in and benefit from inclusion and all of its rewards, including extracurricular activities, sports, and social activities. Some teens, however, do not have this goal of reintegrating to high school. Despite a possible continued interest in their peer group or some of the related high-school activities, they have no desire or commitment to return to that setting. The reasons are many and varied. For some, past experiences

*Author note:* We thank Kevin Jackson, Sharon Novak, Vonita Burke, and William Stross for providing valuable feedback and input in the revision of this chapter.

have been so full of failure and negativity that all motivation to return has evaporated. Others see themselves as so far behind in the business of earning necessary credits that they have all but given up on the possibility of graduating. Some hide behind the facade of not caring to avoid the pain of feeling incapable of meeting the academic, social, and behavioral demands of school. A few show promise in their continued desire to graduate, work, and be independent, but they simply cannot see themselves accomplishing their goals through a traditional school route, regardless of school type. Some teens face chronic mental illness that undermines their ability or desire to reintegrate. Sadly, others have simply given up, unable even to articulate the reasons. This chapter provides an in-depth description of a comprehensive educational/mental health program for troubled and troubling adolescents. It serves as an example of how theory can be put into practice. Using links to the literature, description, and brief case studies, we attempt to offer a real-life example of a program model designed for transitioning young people to the adult world.

## POSITIVE EDUCATION PROGRAM'S MIDTOWN: AN ALTERNATIVE PROGRAM MODEL

Midtown Center for Youth in Transition is part of the Positive Education Program (PEP) in Cleveland, Ohio. PEP is a principles-based program founded on the reeducation (Re-ED) model developed by Nicholas Hobbs (1994). Since 1971, PEP, an integrated special education and community-based mental health program, has helped troubled and troubling children and their families build skills to grow and learn successfully. It started as a small consulting organization established to help schools serve their most challenging students. Today PEP operates many programs, including 10 day treatment centers (serving school-aged children), two early childhood centers (providing services to families with children 6 years old or younger), Day Care Plus (a consultative service to child care providers and families with children experiencing difficulties in child care settings), Connections and Tapestry (a multisystem coordination of care programs providing individualized wraparound supports), and PEP Assist (a consulting and training service provided to schools and agencies). PEP touches the lives of approximately 3,000 children and their families annually and has a long history of developing programs in direct response to expressed community need. In contrast, the Midtown project was initiated by our staff to better address the needs of our adolescent population.

During the early 1990s, staff at one PEP day treatment center began to focus intensively on our adolescent population. Although it is inherent in our Re-ED philosophy to create programs that are individualized and personally relevant, we were not satisfied with our transition programming. New ideas, structures, and strategies to refine our services for adolescents based on student and family input, creative ideas from our staff, input garnered through relationships with other service agencies, and information from the literature were piloted. In late 1999, we acquired a building in the heart of the city, renovated it, and established the Midtown Center for Youth in Transition.

Midtown opened its doors in September 2000 with the capacity to serve 50 to 60 students. In its 9 years of operation, Midtown has served 321 students from 24 school districts and has successfully graduated 148 students from high school. All students are referred to Midtown through local school districts, and all are identified as having emotional disorders (ED) and qualify for mental health services under the category severely mentally disabled (SMD). Of the 321 students who have participated, 72% were male, 28% female, 42% Caucasian, 56% African American, and 2% other. Of the total group, 62% were court involved, 79% received psychiatric services, and 38% received speech and language services. According to the fourth edition of the *Diagnostic and Statistical Manual of Mental Disorders* (DSM-IV-R) (American Psychiatric Association, 2000), the major diagnoses of these youth have included some form of affective disorder, oppositional defiant disorder, attention-deficit/hyperactivity disorder, conduct disorder, anxiety disorder, and psychotic disorder.

Midtown is a program for youth in transition that is intentionally designed to look, feel, and be different from any other school, center, or program. When students visit or enter an alternative program, their first impression sometimes dictates whether or not they find the courage to commit to yet another attempt at school. More of the same would provide little motivation or invitation to make that new start. At Midtown, a climate that communicates expectations for mature, responsible, safe, respectful, proactive, and productive behavior is nurtured through every aspect of the program, from building design to curriculum, discipline policies, delivery of instruction, and participatory program planning and decision making. We strive to provide a program that responds to the unique developmental needs of teens attempting to navigate the passage to adulthood. The program offers a bridge that supports both of their feet—the one still firmly planted in childhood, with all of those needs, anxieties, and insecurities, and the one that is stepping into the new, conflicting territory of young adulthood, with its desires for autonomy and independence.

## MIDTOWN'S CURRICULUM: PATHS TO SUCCESSFUL ADULT LIVING

Individualized programs are designed for every student based on careful assessment, transcript analysis, desired outcomes, and plans for the future. Student input is a variable of equal or greater importance to all other sources of information because this planning activity is regarded as the initial step toward independence and taking responsibility for self. From the onset, students are granted respect for their abilities and an expectation to participate in building their own futures. The favored approach of all transition program activities is participatory and collaborative because these processes, in and of themselves, are instructive and preparatory toward successful, independent adult living. As is the case in all day treatment centers, the staff convey through every action and activity their belief in the student's ability to achieve and make good choices. Here, too, the "invisible sign" above the door (which every student intuitively reads) says, "Together, we will learn, grow, and succeed."

Midtown's program design embraces an ecological approach that is culturally sensitive, a competence model, and a curriculum framework that focuses on three primary domains represented by Midtown's motto, "Education, Employment, and Empowerment." These three domains are consistent with effective practice described in the literature (Cheney, Malloy, & Hagner, 1998; Clark, Deschênes, & Jones, 2000). First is the educational/academic domain; second, the vocational domain; and third, the community life domain. Each domain has general outcomes that are applicable to every student in the program. The process by which outcomes are achieved within the domains is conceptualized as a path. Students travel paths that accommodate their individual needs and preferences for learning and growing. A basic tenet of the curriculum design is that "one size does not fit all." Precision programming is intense, appropriately paced, and geared for each student's immediate and sustained success and progress. Goals and objectives articulated to assist each student toward achievement of outcomes are relevant; individualized; and based on need, presenting skills and aptitudes, interests, and students' specific, desired transition plans for life after school.

## Academic Domain

Driven by the individualized education program (IEP), the stated outcome of this domain is that every student will pursue a personally appropriate and rigorous educational program that leads to a high-school diploma, General Education Development (GED) diploma, acceptance to another adult education program, or the development of functional literacy. Achievement to the fullest extent of one's capabilities is an expectation communicated to every student (Figure 9.1).

The academic content reflects the general education curriculum individualized through the IEP. Transcripts are carefully evaluated and courses of study individually planned to earn the credits needed for graduation from home school districts. In most cases, the curriculum is traditional, based on the state's academic standards for high school. This traditional curriculum is modified to accommodate any learning disabilities or difficulties that students present. Adjustments in reading level or scope of coverage, for example, are made as necessary and appropriate. In other cases, the curriculum is adaptive and remedial in nature, focusing on basic skills. Students achieving significantly below grade level are encouraged to pursue a course of study that enables them to acquire the skills needed to read, write, and cipher at a functionally literate level.

Just as one outcome and one curriculum do not fit all, neither does one form of instruction. Students seeking a diploma present personal preferences and require different programs, schedules, and instructional strategies. Self-directed, motivated, independent learners often respond best to contract learning. These students receive course packets to be completed at their own pace and sequence for credit. Other students respond best to tutoring situations. They prefer an individual approach but require more direction, guidance, or assistance. This is accomplished through adult support or technology-based instruction, including Web-based online courses. Still other students

**FIGURE 9.1  Academic Domain**

**Paths to Successful Adult Living Curriculum**

Educational outcome: To pursue a personally appropriate and rigorous academic program

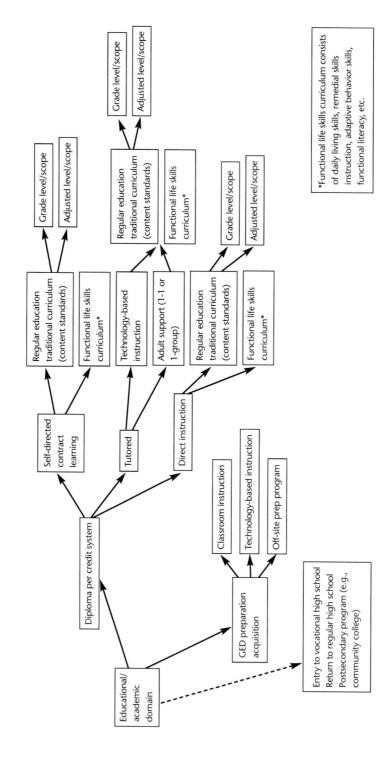

require or respond best to maximum learning support and receive that through classes led with direct teacher instruction. A fourth group consists of students who present different needs and preferences for different subject areas or disciplines. These students are scheduled accordingly.

Students who realistically choose to prepare for the GED are those whose achievement has been far below that which their ability level predicts. The GED route is not an easy one; the test is difficult. Still, for some very bright and capable students who for one reason or another have so few credits that time and age prohibit the likelihood of completing high school through the traditional credit system, the GED can be the best option. Students seeking the GED receive either direct or technology-based instruction, or attend an off-site preparation program as part of their IEP.

Most students who attend Midtown do not plan to return to a general education high school. However, if a student develops the desire to reintegrate to high school or to attend a district vocational program and is demonstrating behaviors and attitudes that predict success, reintegration is sought. Futures are not dictated, and doors are never closed. The option to return to high school is supported.

## Vocational Domain

Driven by the individual transition plan of the IEP and specific vocational plans, the stated outcome of this component is that every student will gain skills leading to employment and/or identify and pursues a career path (Figure 9.2). Because gainful employment is a condition for successful and independent adult living, it is expected that every student at Midtown work in a job setting, be involved in employability training, or participate in a vocational education program of some type. Most participate in a combination of vocational activities.

There are four levels of employment. The first is an in-house job designed to provide a simulated work experience in the highly supervised and directed setting of the center. These jobs are designed for those who are not proficient in the behaviors or skills needed to succeed in the workplace. They include work experiences in building maintenance and custodial activities, food service, office assistance, and landscaping and groundskeeping.

# FIGURE 9.2 Vocational Domain

## Paths to Successful Adult Living Curriculum

Vocational outcome(s): To gain skills leading to employment and/or to identify and begin preparation leading to a career path

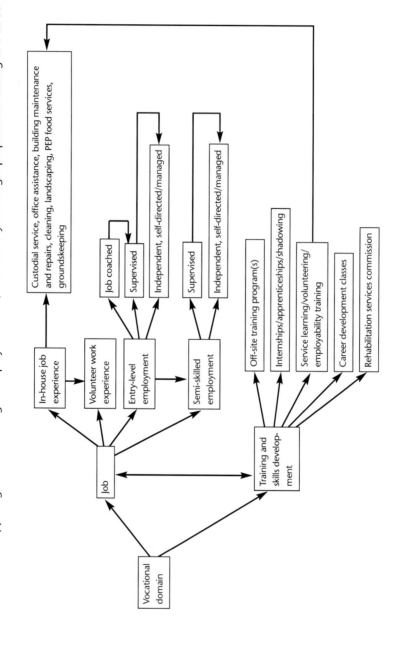

The second level is a volunteer work experience in the community that provides Midtown students with a work-based learning experience in which they have the opportunity to increase their knowledge about the world of work and establish good work habits and behaviors. At this level of job experience, students work under the supervision of Midtown staff within the local business community. This step in the vocational process helps some students build confidence and connect with the community, and it prepares them for entry-level employment.

The third level is entry-level employment, which typically pays minimum wage. With these community-based jobs, students receive the level of supervision they need to succeed. This ranges from job coaching to supervision with regular on-the-job visits to independent self-direction and self-management on the job. Some students are able to enter the semiskilled job market, which requires a higher level of competence or set of specific skills for successful performance, such as word processing in an office setting or cooking in a restaurant. Students in these jobs receive occasional on-the-job visits or provide self-reports when they demonstrate an adequate level of independence and self-management.

Vocational education and skills development in the center take several distinct forms. In addition to evaluation and assessment activities and work experiences, students are assigned to one or more instructional activities. They may participate in training off-site in a specific vocational education program or a program made available through the Rehabilitation Services Commission. They may be connected to an off-site program that involves job shadowing, apprenticing, or serving an internship of some sort.

Finally, all students participate in some vocational activities in the center. Career development classes provide a forum for debriefing problems and concerns, both real and predicted or anticipated, from students' real-life job experiences. Career development classes engage students in direct instruction of behaviors, skills, and attitudes necessary for success in the world of work and help them explore career options, opening their young eyes to opportunity.

## Community Life Domain

This third domain is the most complicated and challenging area of the curriculum (Figure 9.3). The first two domains, academic and vocational,

**FIGURE 9.3    Community Life Domain**

**Paths to Successful Adult Living Curriculum**

Community life outcome: To benefit from and contribute to a healthy, successful, and personally satisfying community life and interdependent relationships with significant others

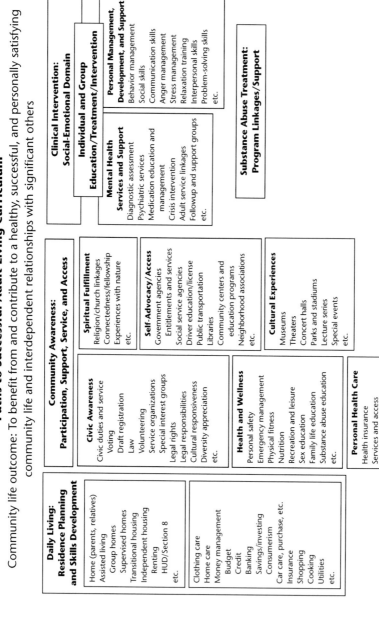

**Daily Living:**
**Residence Planning and Skills Development**

Home (parents, relatives)
Assisted living
Group homes
Supervised homes
Transitional housing
Independent housing
Renting
HUD/Section 8
etc.

Clothing care
Home care
Money management
Budget
Credit
Banking
Savings/investing
Consumerism
Car care, purchase, etc.
Insurance
Shopping
Cooking
Utilities
etc.

**Community Awareness:**
**Participation, Support, Service, and Access**

**Civic Awareness**
Civic duties and service
Voting
Draft registration
Law
Volunteering
Service organizations
Special interest groups
Legal rights
Legal responsibilities
Cultural responsiveness
Diversity appreciation
etc.

**Spiritual Fulfillment**
Religion/church linkages
Connectedness/fellowship
Experiences with nature
etc.

**Self-Advocacy/Access**
Government agencies
Entitlements and services
Social service agencies
Driver education/license
Public transportation
Libraries
Community centers and education programs
Neighborhood associations
etc.

**Health and Wellness**
Personal safety
Emergency management
Physical fitness
Nutrition
Recreation and leisure
Sex education
Family life education
Substance abuse education
etc.

**Cultural Experiences**
Museums
Theaters
Concert halls
Parks and stadiums
Lecture series
Special events
etc.

**Personal Health Care**
Health insurance
Services and access
etc.

**Clinical Intervention:**
**Social-Emotional Domain**

**Individual and Group**
**Education/Treatment/Intervention**

**Mental Health Services and Support**
Diagnostic assessment
Psychiatric services
Medication education and management
Crisis intervention
Adult service linkages
Followup and support groups
etc.

**Personal Management, Development, and Support**
Behavior management
Social skills
Communication skills
Anger management
Stress management
Relaxation training
Interpersonal skills
Problem-solving skills
etc.

**Substance Abuse Treatment:**
**Program Linkages/Support**

are relatively discrete and have obvious, traditional outcomes, resources, and strategies. This third area presents a challenging desired outcome: to effect change so that all students benefit from and contribute to a healthy, successful, and personally satisfying community life and interdependent relationships with significant others. Thus, the community life curriculum offers intervention, instruction, support, guidance, and counseling for effective, independent, and responsible living. It encompasses personal awareness, personal development, and self-management. It addresses daily living skills and a myriad of activities and skills that fall under the category of community awareness and participation. It is "Life 101." Because of its multifaceted nature, the student's program in this third curriculum domain is driven by ecological assessment and intervention as well as by the IEP process. Careful and diligent teamwork and coordination of services, activities, and opportunities are required to design, implement, and evaluate a student's program of growth in this area.

The first area of the community life domain addresses issues of daily living. Some students can rely on family support systems for continued assistance; others face independence at the age of majority either by choice or by circumstance. Independent adults need a place to live and the skills to manage a home. Options for residential living, along a continuum from home with parents to unassisted independent living, are explored, evaluated, and pursued as appropriate. Life skills are addressed in such areas as personal finances, home and car care, consumerism, and personal health care. Homemaking skills such as cleaning, cooking, shopping, and clothing care are taught as needed. An efficiency suite built in the center is used as a real-life classroom for skill development.

The second area focuses on community awareness, participation, available support, and access of services. Hobbs (1994) taught us that young people must experience the community to benefit from it. This curriculum area exposes students to their world in ways that promote an understanding of the interdependence that exists between a community and its residents. It teaches them about community and governmental services and how to access them; it also teaches personal and civic responsibility. It addresses both the private and public self, from registering to vote to seeking personal spiritual fulfillment. It promotes self-advocacy and exposes students to the many agencies, services, centers, and programs available in the community, including accessing transportation, finding information, and participating in recreational and leisure activities. Personal health, wellness, safety, and fitness are addressed through education, personal plans, practice, and knowledge regarding health care access. In short, the curriculum attempts to teach students how to meet their personal needs, wants, and desires by accessing and engaging the community.

The third area addresses social-emotional health and more intense clinical issues. Some students require psychiatric consultation and support to manage and cope. For all, good mental health, satisfying personal relationships, freedom from illicit drugs, responsible and moral self-management, and mature prosocial and communication skills are critical elements of social-emotional health and responsible, successful adult living. All staff recognize that what the earliest advocates of re-education believed still holds true today—that successful living is healing. Every day, every minute is viewed as another opportunity for staff to play their part in providing an abundance of positive experiences for the students. Healthy, helping relationships between adults and students are built through every interaction. Through both individual and group treatment, using prescribed curricula, teachable moments, everyday interaction, and various goal-driven activities, students develop knowledge, skills, and values that support interpersonal and intrapersonal growth, development, and management.

## TRANSITION IN PRACTICE: CONNECTING AND COLLABORATING

Helping adolescents make the transition to the adult world is never simple and involves overcoming numerous obstacles. Vander Stoep, Davis, and Collins (2000) discussed several issues that young adults, parents, and professionals face that hinder successful transition to agencies designed to provide supportive services:

- Institutional supports are withdrawn abruptly and are often based on the individual's age alone.

- Institution-generated transition plans are weak and ultimately are not followed.

- Continuity of care across child and adult institutions is lacking.

- Institutional supports are not designed for young adults.

- Institutions engender mistrust.

Although these factors can impede successful treatment, effective collaboration is one key to helping systems work together (Cantrell & Cantrell, 2007; Hobbs, 1994; Osher & Hanley, 2001).

## Case Study: Randy

> The following case study provides an example of how Midtown staff collaborated with a young person, his family, and other service providers to overcome certain obstacles. Originally published in the first edition of this book (Cheney, 2004), the case example includes an update on Randy's progress.

Randy, a 16-year-old youth with bipolar disorder and conduct problems, connected with Midtown personnel and did well in the structure of the school setting, but he had previous family and community problems that resulted in his placement by Juvenile Court at the Ohio Department of Youth Services. During Randy's incarceration for breaking and entering, Midtown staff and students exchanged letters and telephone calls with him, maintaining contact. Midtown staff monitored Randy's release date and maintained contact with his home school district to ensure there was a place for him at Midtown upon his discharge. He was welcomed back with open arms. Midtown staff continued to work collaboratively with Randy and his Ohio Department of Youth Services parole officer to prevent the need for future incarceration.

Academically, Randy was a bright and capable student with the exception of poor study and organizational skills and mild specific learning disabilities in mathematics calculation and reasoning. He returned to Midtown as a 17-year-old 11th grader who was slightly behind his peer group in accumulated credits for high-school graduation. Randy's transcripts were thoroughly evaluated, and course requirements and electives were subsequently identified for programming. Randy received adapted and remedial instruction in mathematics with an emphasis on functional skill acquisition and development (see Table 9.1 for examples of Randy's IEP academic goals and objectives). Randy proved to be so capable in English that Midtown staff suggested that he consider taking an entry-level course at the local community

**TABLE 9.1   Examples of Randy's IEP Academic Goals and Objectives**

## Academic Domain

| Student's Needs | Annual Goals | Objectives |
|---|---|---|
| Randy is almost on track for on-time high-school graduation. He is one credit shy of 11th grade status. Earning seven credits this year will gain Randy senior status at the start of the next school year.<br><br>In most academic areas, Randy performs close to grade level. The two major areas of concern are in math and study/organization skills, which could hinder his success at community college. Key math assessment indicates a weakness in basic concepts and operations. Randy needs to develop calculator skills. | 1. Complete academic activities to earn seven credits this school year to achieve senior status.<br><br>2. Develop functional math skills; participate in learning activities and complete assignments to earn one high-school credit for math. | 1. Complete activities in the following course areas:<br><br>  a. English (community college)   1.0<br>  b. Math   1.0<br>  c. Science   1.0<br>  d. Social Studies   1.0<br>  e. Independent Living II   .5<br>  f. Problem Solving II   .5<br>  g. Career Development I   .25<br>  h. Career Exploration II   .25<br>  i. Work Study   1.5<br><br>2a. Develop and update a budget using data from weekly pay stub.<br><br>2b. Use calculator to balance checkbook using actual or mock account.<br><br>2c. Participate in weekly grocery comparison shopping activities, using ads to develop a shopping list and a calculator to compute weekly savings. |

college. He was initially reluctant, but with staff support and encouragement he agreed to take the preliminary entrance examinations for admission through the Postsecondary Options Program, which allows high-school students the opportunity to attend and accrue college credits while completing their high-school credits for graduation. Randy did well enough on the English examination to qualify for entrance, and his home school district agreed to pay for his community college course. Midtown staff worked through the community college's Disabled Student Services Office to provide Randy with an additional support system on campus.

Like many students his age, Randy was uncertain about what he wanted to do; however, he did express an eagerness to pursue entry-level community employment and earn money. As part of his program at Midtown, he received prevocational and preoccupational skill instruction via his participation in Career Development classes. Career Development consists of small-group and individual instruction in the skills necessary to secure a job, keep a job, and pursue a better job. Randy also participated in Career Exploration classes, which included assessment of his aptitudes and interests and information regarding potential careers. Randy initially participated in the Midtown Café, an onsite food service training program that allowed for staff observation, teaching, feedback, and job coaching in a safe, comfortable environment. After 2 months with the Midtown Café, Randy was ready for community-based entry-level employment and was hired at a local supermarket 15 hours per week bagging groceries and stocking shelves. Randy continued to participate in Career Development, eventually identifying a possible interest in chef training (see Table 9.2 for examples of Randy's IEP vocational goals and objectives).

As Randy approached his 18th birthday, he faced the possibility of homelessness due to ongoing family conflict. In preparation, Midtown staff intensified their instruction in daily living skills, including residence planning and independent living skills development (see Table 9.3 for examples of Randy's IEP community life goals and objectives). Despite continued in-depth work with the family, upon turning 18 Randy was evicted from his home. Midtown personnel taught him how to access the homeless shelters while simultaneously exploring housing options. He was permitted to use Midtown's efficiency suite, which is used for the instruction of independent living skills, to shower and take care of

**TABLE 9.2  Examples of Randy's IEP Vocational Goals and Objectives**

### Vocational Domain

| Student's Needs | Annual Goals | Objectives |
|---|---|---|
| Randy has expressed a desire to work. However, he is in need of prevocational/preoccupational skill development. Randy also needs to identify and explore potential careers of interest. | 1. Randy will learn prevocational/preoccupational skills that will result in acquiring and maintaining gainful employment.<br><br>2. Randy will identify and explore potential careers of interest for the future. | 1. Randy will participate in career development focusing on development of the following:<br><br>a. Skills related to attendance, punctuality, proper grooming, hygiene, work attire, and productivity (quality and quantity)<br><br>b. Appropriate social and interpersonal skills, including anger management, problem solving, and conflict resolution<br><br>c. Knowledge of the world of work and the work culture<br><br>d. Appropriate interviewing skills<br><br>e. Creating a résumé<br><br>f. Completing applications for entry-level employment<br><br>g. Obtaining entry-level employment<br><br>2a. Randy will complete select interest inventories (Self-Directed Search, Transition Planning Inventory, Ohio Career Information System).<br><br>2b. Randy will participate in career counseling to identify two potential careers of interest for future exploration. |

**TABLE 9.3 Examples of Randy's IEP Community Life Goals and Objectives**

## Community Life

| Student's Needs | Annual Goals | Objectives |
|---|---|---|
| Randy is currently homeless and residing in shelters. He is in need of intensified training in daily and community living skills, including development of residence planning and independent living skills. | 1. Randy will learn independent living skills so that he can prepare for and be accepted into a housing assistance program.<br>2. Randy will participate in residence planning to acquire a safe and satisfactory place of residence. | 1. Randy will participate in both on-site and off-site independent living activities and learning opportunities focusing on development of the following skills:<br><br>a. Caring for personal needs (proper grooming, hygiene, attire, nutrition, common illnesses prevention and treatment, personal safety)<br><br>b. Managing personal finances (counting money and making correct change, making responsible expenditures, keeping basic financial records, calculating and paying taxes, using banking and credit services responsibly, budgeting)<br><br>c. Buying, preparing, and consuming food (purchasing food, cleaning preparation areas, storing food, preparing meals, demonstrating appropriate eating habits, planning and eating balanced meals)<br><br>d. Buying and caring for clothing (purchasing, washing, cleaning, ironing, mending, storing) |

**TABLE 9.3** **(continued)**

### Objectives (cont'd)

e. Navigating the community (demonstrating knowledge of traffic rules and safety, knowledge and use of various means of transportation, finding way around the community)

2a. Randy will apply for Medicaid, food stamps, and Supplemental Security Income to assist with funding and establishing a residence.

2b. Randy will explore and apply to potential housing programs.

2c. Randy will learn skills to assist in the selection and management of a household, focusing on development of the following:

1. Selecting adequate housing
2. Setting up a household
3. Using basic appliances and tools
4. Maintaining the interior and exterior of a home

his personal needs and to wash and store his clothes and valuables. Midtown staff also made sure that Randy received a hot breakfast and lunch. They assisted him in applying for Medicaid, food stamps, and Supplemental Security Income.

He was also referred to an adult mental health agency. This agency began to share case management responsibilities with Midtown staff and assumed primary responsibility for Randy's medication and somatic services. He was placed on their short waiting list for housing for homeless mentally ill young adults. With staff assistance in the application process, Randy was found eligible for Supplemental Security Income after an appeal. That, along with wages earned from his job, allowed Randy and Midtown staff to explore the possibility of an efficiency apartment until he was accepted into the adult mental health agency's transitional housing program. Continued efforts were made to reconnect Randy with his family throughout this period.

Randy and all who worked with him experienced many of the obstacles that hinder successful transition, according to Vander Stoep et al. (2000). Deliberate and tenacious efforts to connect and collaborate with service providers helped him successfully negotiate the course. Knowing that institutions often engender mistrust, Midtown personnel made every effort to maintain the connection and relationship previously established with Randy throughout his 6-month incarceration. They also worked collaboratively with both the Ohio Department of Youth Services and his home school district to provide a smooth transition from incarceration to readmission to our community-based program, thus ensuring the continuity of his care. Randy learned that he could depend on Midtown personnel not to abandon him.

Going to a new environment or service is only half of the transition equation. Leaving a safe and known place is the other. Randy's essential trust in Midtown staff gave him a sense of security and predictability, which provided a base for his subsequent transitions to the community college, employment, and mental health services. Even when difficulties arose—and they did—Randy and the Midtown staff refused to give up.

Midtown personnel assisted Randy in identifying and defining his needs and desires. These translated to his transition plans. The emphasis was placed on each plan's being generated by Randy as opposed to being generated by the institutions. This resulted in more meaningful planning and greater investment on Randy's part, as well as better reception from the receiving institutions. Randy, Midtown, and the receiving institutions also found that flexibility and willingness to change plans—often in midstream—were assets that resulted in more meaningful and successful outcomes.

Midtown personnel prepared Randy for each transition and let each receiving institution know that a period of overlap would occur, during which Midtown would continue to assume primary responsibility. Midtown personnel would gradually withdraw to become a secondary service provider only when Randy and the receiving institution were ready, willing, and able to make the full transition. The emphasis was placed on helping Randy connect to each receiving institution by collaborating free of professional "turf" or responsibility issues. Thus, Midtown shaped the transition process from primary service provider to secondary service provider without withdrawing supports abruptly and regardless of his age. All this took place as Randy embarked on his transitions to the community college, the world of work, and adult mental health services. By allowing the receiving institutions to gradually assume primary responsibility, Randy received continuous care, making Midtown's eventual withdrawal planned and therapeutic.

One obstacle that continues to plague Randy, Midtown, and receiving institutions is that supports are often not designed for young adults. The 18- to 22-year-old population continues to present dilemmas for adult service providers. Chronologically, people in this age group may be adults, but developmentally, socially, emotionally, and behaviorally, they often exhibit traits characteristic of adolescents. Therefore, these youth often require more direct supervision and support than is available in adult programs. This appears to be especially true with respect to transitional housing programs for young adults. In Randy's case, the adult mental health agency was reluctant to consider him for their transitional housing program because of the conduct issues that led to his being asked to leave his family's home and his apparent lack of prerequisite independent living skills. Collaboration prevailed; they were willing to reconsider his application with Midtown's pledge of continued services and support and Randy's demonstrable willingness to grow and learn.

Despite numerous obstacles, Randy has shown great resilience and continues to attend and actively participate in his program. Through his connection to Midtown staff and the continuity, opportunity, and dignity that they have nurtured, Randy continues to make progress toward the successful transition from adolescence to young adulthood. He is projected to complete the credits required for graduation from high school, and he continues to accrue college credits while exploring his interest in chef training. Randy continues to work at the local supermarket and is exploring job opportunities in food service. He is currently living in an apartment via the adult mental health agency's transitional housing program, and he has reconnected with his family to broaden his support system. Throughout the next school year, Randy, his family, Midtown, and receiving institutions will continue to work together cooperatively and collaboratively to complete his transition from adolescence to young adulthood.

## Randy's Current Status

Randy has continued to make progress toward his goals during the past 4 years. He completed the credits required for graduation from high school and attended Midtown's graduation ceremony. The college credits he accrued kept him interested and motivated to pursue his interest in chef training. Randy completed the Culinary/Cook Training Program at the local community college and has been accepted in the college's Professional Culinary/Cook Program, leading to certification by the American Culinary Federation. As he continues to be successful in school, his need to access the supports of the college's Disabled Student Services Office has diminished. Randy has maintained his job at the local supermarket and continues to reside in an apartment via the adult mental health agency's transitional housing program. Throughout the past 4 years, his family has increasingly become a stronger force in his support system. Along with Midtown staff, Randy and his family continue to work cooperatively and collaboratively with receiving institutions assisting with his transition from adolescence to young adulthood.

### Case Study: Steve

In writing this part of the chapter and to obtain a view of transition from the parent perspective, we encouraged one family, the

Ciriglianos, to include their experience with Midtown. We are pleased to say that they were willing and ready to tell their story. Steve's father's account of the situation follows.

Our son Steve completed 3rd grade with good grades, perfect attendance, and the cheery attitude he had displayed since birth. In our district, students are introduced to the concept of changing classes in 4th grade. It was just a month after Steve began 4th grade that he and his brother got the flu. They were out for 4 days. They both returned on the fifth day, but we received a call early in the morning from the nurse at Steve's school asking us to pick him up because he was not feeling well. His head hurt, he was nauseated, and he was dizzy. In retrospect, we see this as the first day of a downward spiral that Steve would struggle with for the rest of his life.

When the symptoms continued, we made an appointment with Steve's pediatrician, who referred us to a pediatric neurologist. Steve's headaches increased in both frequency and severity. The specialist identified Steve's condition as classical migraines and prescribed medication. Steve's migraines seemed to taper off, and when summer came, Steve was migraine free. But not long into 5th grade, the migraines reappeared. We began to see a psychologist, and Steve went through biofeedback sessions. Steve's migraines took on a distinct pattern. He was migraine free over the weekends and during holidays. He developed a migraine almost every school day. His attendance became an issue of concern. Still, Steve was able to maintain Bs and Cs and he was passed on to 6th grade (middle school).

For Steve, middle school developed into a nightmare. His migraines continued, with depression seeping in as he missed more and more school. He began to gain weight. Kids at school began to harass him about both. Steve was never a defiant kid. He was well behaved in his classes. He seemed to escape into his own world when the school experience became difficult. Most of the teachers liked Steve and worked with us to keep track of missed assignments. Unfortunately, some teachers and the principal reacted to Steve's missed days, identifying him as being lazy and defiant. When he was in their classes, they publicly singled him out with disparaging comments. Steve's migraines increased, and he became more depressed and began to hate school.

Our home life was in a state of turmoil. All of us were frustrated and concerned about Steve's continued headaches and increasing depression.

We all felt isolated and became frustrated, depressed, and angry. Eventually, we sought a second opinion from a hospital that led to the Positive Education Program (PEP) as a recommended placement.

Steve, Patty, and I entered the PEP school with mixed emotions. We sat down to talk with the staff and almost immediately began to feel some relief. The entire staff displayed sincere warmth and concern. They talked directly with Steve with an understanding he had never experienced in school. It was apparent that they were there to help Steve and us, not to judge us. We felt as though we were becoming members of a team with Steve being the star. One could not sit in the school for any length of time without picking up on the kindness, sincerity, and warmth among the staff members. We were impressed with the respect and ease with which they shared thoughts and plans. Perhaps this was the greatest difference we immediately noted in PEP—the elements of teamwork and respect. We were all treated with respect, including Steve. As we left the school that first day, Steve seemed to sum it up the best. He turned to us and said, "Finally, I feel like someone understands me!"

The staff at Midtown never let us down. From the very beginning, they went above and beyond what we ever dreamed possible. When Steve had a bad day and could not go to school, they would come to the home and talk with him—*with* him—not *at* him. They were honest and open with him but never negative or degrading. The positive support they offered Steve and our entire family was like a gift from heaven. When Steve could get to the school but not out of the car, they would come down to the car and sit with him (sometimes for more than an hour), always urging him on with positive support. And when we became frustrated, discouraged, or concerned, they gave us the same support. For more than a year, the psychologist called every morning with a pep talk to get Steve going. He continually supported Patty and me as well. The psychologist and the entire staff would always return our calls and talk over our concerns. The communication among the team was always open, honest, and focused on Steve's success.

Slowly, Steve's self confidence began to return. Steve was involved in all of the sessions in which his goals were developed and his progress was reviewed. His problem areas were addressed, but they were always approached with a statement of the area of concern paired with positive steps that Steve would be working on to reach his goals. Humor also played a big role in the success we have seen in Steve. Many a difficult moment was lightened up with the touch of appropriate humor from the staff!

The PEP staff helped Steve regain some self-confidence and have helped him get to school more regularly. They have helped him understand his problems, and they have urged him to vocalize his feelings and frustrations. They took a very unhappy child who wanted to crawl in a hole and hide from a world that made him miserable with its lack of understanding, and they guided him to a path with an optimistic future. They helped a boy who did not want to finish high school turn his life around, and they enabled him to attend and enjoy taking college classes. They have helped him learn the skills he will need to live independently some day. Again Steve says it best as he often states that the PEP staff "is the best thing that ever happened to me. They saved my life."

## Steve's Current Status

Steve has continued to make slow progress toward his goals over the past 4 years. He and his family relocated before he graduated from Midtown Center for Youth in Transition. He opted to take the GED, which he passed, instead of returning to high school. Steve subsequently enrolled in a small liberal arts college and commuted from home. He decided to take a break from college and has been looking for entry-level employment. Finding employment has been difficult with little experience and few connections, yet Steven remains optimistic. He intends to re-enroll in college in the future. He continues to appropriately access mental health services to deal with the trials and tribulations of everyday living. Steve's family continues to be a source of support as he moves at his own pace through young adulthood. He admits that life continues to be a struggle. "Needless to say, things are tough, and life is no walk in the park for me even after my experience at PEP, but without it, I doubt I'd still be here. I wouldn't be able to keep my mind together like I can today." He continues, "The fact that I'm hanging in there while doing so is a step forward for me."

## CONCLUSION

Randy, Steve, Midtown, and receiving institutions experienced each of the obstacles to transition that Vander Stoep et al. (2000) discussed.

However, by connecting and collaborating, they ensured that many of these obstacles were partially if not fully overcome. Transitioning young people to the adult world is often an exercise in problem solving and in overcoming obstacles. Recognizing those obstacles and planning a course that negotiates the predictable ones is key to the process. Randy's transition from school to the adult world and its services was successful because known obstacles were avoided and service gaps were filled through careful planning and purposeful collaboration. Surprise obstacles were tackled with that same spirit.

The secret to success? Simple. The student (and family) remain the central, primary concern; the young adult is the defining member of the plan and the team. Institutions, personalities, territories, and turf are realities to be dealt with, but they are relegated to a minor status. The student's needs must take precedence; the concerns of others, whether they are institutional or personal, are addressed in a manner that the student's plan can be implemented. Sharing responsibilities, advocating, and collaborating to provide support for all concerned and doing whatever it takes are the keys to the successful transition of young people to the world of adulthood.

Finally, the essential element that drives the entire process is the therapeutic relationship that is so carefully cultivated by staff. Staff members form trusting and caring relationships with students. A basic principle of Re-ED, "Trust is essential," resonates with the four components necessary for success that are identified in the resiliency literature (Seita, Mitchell, & Tobin, 1996). Staff work hard to build a well-connected and caring relationship (connectedness) and help the student know that they will be there every step of the way (continuity). They also make sure that each student feels very respected (dignity) and provide the student with multiple successful experiences (opportunity). It is not easy, but the hard work is rewarded when we hear something that one of Midtown's graduates stated: "I never thought I'd make it. But I did."

## REFERENCES

American Psychiatric Association. (2000). *Diagnostic and statistical manual of mental disorders* (4th ed., rev.). Washington, DC: Author.

Cantrell, M. L., & Cantrell, R. P. (2007). The ecological approach. In R. P. Cantrell & M. L. Cantrell (Eds.), *Helping troubled children and youth: Continuing evidence for the Re-ED approach.* Westerville, OH: American Re-EDucation Association.

Cheney, D. (2004). *Transition of secondary students with emotional or behavioral disorders: Current approaches for positive outcomes* (1st ed.). Arlington, VA: Council for Exceptional Children.

Cheney, D., Malloy, J., & Hagner, D. (1998). Finishing high school in many different ways: Project RENEW in Manchester, New Hampshire. *Effective School Practices, 17*(2), 43–52.

Clark, H. B., Deschênes, N., & Jones, J. (2000). A framework for the development and operation of a transition system. In H. B. Clark & M. Davis, (Eds.), *Transition to adulthood: A resource for assisting young people with emotional or behavioral difficulties* (pp. 29–51). Baltimore: Paul H. Brookes.

Hobbs, N. (1994). *The troubled and troubling child: Re-education in mental health, education, and human services programs for children and youth* (2nd ed.). Cleveland, OH: American Re-EDucation Association.

Osher, D., & Hanley, T. V. (2001). Implementing the SED National Agenda: Promising programs and policies for children and youth with emotional and behavioral problems. *Education and Treatment of Children, 24*(3), 375–403.

Seita, J., Mitchell, M., & Tobin, C. (1996). *In whose best interest?* Elizabethtown, PA: Continental Press.

Vander Stoep, A., Davis, M., & Collins, D., (2000). Transition: A time of developmental and institutional clashes. In H. B. Clark and M. Davis, (Eds.), *Transition to adulthood: A resource for assisting young people with emotional or behavioral difficulties* (pp. 3–28). Baltimore: Paul H. Brookes.

## CHAPTER 10

# The RENEW Model of Futures Planning, Resource Development, and School-to-Career Experiences for Youth with Emotional or Behavioral Disorders

**JoAnne M. Malloy, Jonathan Drake,
Kathleen Abate, and Gail M. Cormier**

> Resiliency does not come from some rare or special qualities, but from everyday magic of ordinary . . . human resources in . . . children, in their families and relationships, and in their communities.
>
> —*Masten (2001, p. 235)*

Young people with emotional or behavioral disorders (EBD) often lack access to the personal, social, family, and community resources that are available to typical youth. In addition, the needs and characteristics of adolescents with emotional and behavioral disorders are complex, multidimensional, and often resistant to change. These complex and individualized needs make it difficult for communities, systems, organizations, and individuals to respond effectively and assist youth with EBD to be successful. Effective interventions for youth with EBD must be flexible and focused on engagement of the youth "where they are at" and should include self-determination skill building, resource building, and relationship development. The RENEW (Rehabilitation, Empowerment, Natural Supports, Education, and Work) model was developed in New Hampshire in 1996 and is designed to address the unique needs of youth with EBD. Youth who received RENEW services have experienced positive outcomes when compared to the outcomes documented in the research on youth with EBD. This chapter describes the magnitude of the problem of poor secondary transition outcomes for youth with EBD, the logic and features of the RENEW model, the contexts in which RENEW has been implemented, and the evidence to suggest the efficacy of the RENEW approach.

## POOR TRANSITION OUTCOMES FOR YOUTH WITH EBD

Certain individual characteristics common among youth with EBD impede their engagement and success in school, including academic challenges and social and behavioral skill difficulties (Cullinan & Sabornie, 2004; Lane, Carter, Pierson, & Glaeser, 2006; Nelson, Benner, Lane, & Smith, 2004; Sabornie, Cullinan, Osborne, & Brock, 2005). To complicate matters, youth with EBD also tend to be poorer and to have family stressors at far greater rates than do typical students or students in other disability subgroups (Wagner, Kutash, Duchnowski, Epstein, & Sumi, 2005). Students with EBD show patterns of school disengagement, high rates of academic failure, high dropout rates, high criminal justice involvement, and somewhat lower employment rates (Bullis & Cheney, 1999; Kortering, Hess, & Braziel, 1996; Reschly & Christenson, 2006; Wagner, 1991; Wagner, Kutash, Duchnowski, & Epstein, 2005; Wehman, 1996; Zigmond, 2006). Studies have also shown that youth with EBD have high rates of mental health utilization, are more likely to be poor, and are incarcerated at significantly higher rates than the general population (Alexander, Entwisle, & Horsey, 1997; Kortering & Braziel, 1998; Lee & Burkam, 2001; Wagner, 1991; Wagner et al., 2003; Wagner, Kutash, Duchnowski, & Epstein, 2005). Despite efforts to address the educational needs of youth with EBD in regular education settings, youth with emotional disturbance typically receive their education services outside of the typical classroom at far greater rates than other students with disabilities, and they are placed in segregated educational settings at four times the rate of other students with disabilities (U.S. Department of Education, 2006; Wagner & Davis, 2006).

Schools or the special education system alone cannot address the needs of all young people with EBD. The typical large public high school is not geared to provide service coordination and linkage to other community resources, and the support needs of young people with emotional or behavioral disabilities are not typically limited to the challenges posed by their disability (Bullis & Paris, 1996). Many of these young people face instability in their residential life, poverty, drug and alcohol abuse at home, and learning disabilities that contribute to the difficulty of "blending in" and becoming a member of the high-school environment.

Given that many young people with EBD tend to be disengaged from family, school, and community support systems, it is logical to conclude that they are not accessing the secondary transition services that may help them to successfully complete high school, connect with postsecondary education programs, find employment, obtain stable and safe housing, and connect to needed support services. As a result of their lack of engagement in typical educational and social service programs and supports, many youth with EBD do not develop self-determined skills and behaviors, and many do not have the academic and vocational experiences that can make learning relevant and lead to desired postschool outcomes (Lane & Carter, 2006; Wagner & Davis, 2006).

## SETTING THE STAGE: PARADIGM SHIFTS ACROSS MULTIPLE SYSTEMS

RENEW, first developed in New Hampshire as part of a research and demonstration project and continued as a program of a nonprofit corporation and university collaboration (Bullis & Cheney, 1999; Malloy & Cormier, 2004), focuses on the multiple and individualized needs of and challenges posed by youth with serious emotional and behavioral challenges that have been identified in the research.

The development and initial implementation of the RENEW model in 1996 was a reflection of the changing values and paradigms in the special education, regular education, child welfare, and mental health systems. The Individuals with Disabilities Education Act (IDEA) created a new emphasis on inclusion and access to typical education services and supports for all students with disabilities and, in 1990, the IDEA amendments required schools to develop outcome-based transition plans for students with disabilities beginning at age 14 (now age 16). The picture of inclusion was complicated by the IDEA amendments of

1997 that put forth stipulations for the removal from school and education requirements of students with disabilities who have committed
serious behavioral infractions. These rules put a spotlight on the difficulties faced by and the disengagement of many youth with EBD from
schools because of the disciplinary problems they often experience.

The special education transition rules are designed to address the
poor outcomes of all youth with disabilities and to assist students with
disabilities and their families in planning for post-high school life.
Secondary transition services are defined in the Individuals with
Disabilities Education Improvement Act (2004) as a coordinated set of
activities for students with disabilities that would facilitate postschool
participation and outcomes. Although the emphasis on secondary transition services for youth with disabilities has yielded improved academic
outcomes for certain groups, youth with emotional or behavioral disabilities have gained little from these initiatives during the past 15 years
(Wagner & Davis, 2006).

Within the education community, The School-to-Work Opportunities (STWO) Act of 1994 represented significant reform in high-school
academic and career-focused education programs. The STWO fostered
the notions of "outcome-based" career development and identified a
variety of strategies in the framework of work- and school-based learning
and activities to connect these two learning contexts. School-to-work
activities created alliances between schools and the business community and allowed school districts to think about and recognize the
value of hands-on learning in real-world settings (U.S. Department of
Labor, 1991). The innovations of the School-to-Work initiative were
somewhat blunted by the passage of the No Child Left Behind (NCLB)
Act of 2001. NCLB pointed to the persistent achievement gap between
typical students and certain subgroups, including children with disabilities, African American children, Hispanic children, and children from
low-income families. The educational emphasis has thus been on
increasing the academic achievement of all students, with a focus on
rigorous but traditional academic instruction and delivery models.

As these major education reforms took place, a conceptual shift in
the delivery of community mental health care for children and youth
was also occurring. This shift recognizes that children with emotional
and behavioral disorders and their family members need a broad array

of services in order to keep those children in their homes and home communities (Eber & Keenan, 2004; Stroul & Friedman, 1986). As a result of this shift in thinking about what works for children and families at risk, community mental health service provision is changing from a medical treatment model to a set of community-based interventions with the goal of supporting children in living in their home communities or returning home from placements. These reforms have resulted in the development and proliferation of family- and student-focused wraparound services that center on the goals and needs of the family and child and engage community-based and natural supports (Burchard, Bruns, & Burchard, 2002; Eber, 2003).

With an emphasis on inclusion, self-determination, child-centered wraparound, and individualized, natural supports, these policy and paradigm shifts have spurred the development of research and demonstration projects aimed to create pragmatic community-based options for the educational and positive social development of youth with the most significant challenges. Researchers in the field of secondary transition and employment recommend that secondary transition services for youth with EBD have a vocational focus, include "real-world" learning, be highly individualized, and be strengths-based (Benz, Yovanoff, & Doren, 1997; Bullis, Nishioka-Evans, Fredericks, & Davis, 1993; Wagner & Davis, 2006). In addition, youth with EBD need to develop their self-determination skills and experiences, which include having opportunities to set goals, make decisions, problem-solve, and seek help (Carter, Lane, Pierson, & Glaeser, 2006; Eisenman, 2007). Researchers advocate that youth with EBD receive individualized options that assist them in completing their secondary education in alternative, community-based environments (Kutash & Duchnowski, 1997). These alternative models make use of any and all learning environments, are flexible and individualized in community-based curricula, link learning to employment, and pull together multiple agencies, systems, resources, and plans so young people can use the resources effectively. These models promote self-direction and self-determination. The students in these models remain connected to and receive their diplomas from their home school districts, or they receive General Education Development (GED) diplomas. The students in these models do not receive their education in alternative schools.

## THE RENEW MODEL: CREATING OPTIONS FOR YOUTH

RENEW is one example of an individualized community-based approach that meets the multiple and complex needs of youth with EBD, including the needs for developing self-determination skills and experiences, for connectedness to the education process, for connectedness to community resources, and for experiencing personal success.

### Five Principles of RENEW

RENEW is based on the philosophy that all youth can succeed with the proper supports, treatments, and services. As such, the RENEW model is designed to meet the known needs of youth with emotional and behavioral disorders, using the following principles to guide the practice:

> **Principle 1: Self-Determination.** Self-determined behavior includes choice making, decision making, problem solving, self-management, and self-advocacy (Carter et al., 2006; Wehmeyer, 2005). The young person is given guidance and support to reach his or her stated and "socially valued" goals. The skills to state one's preferences and hopes, knowing one's limitations and support needs, and defining the best pathway toward reaching one's goals become an integral part of the RENEW process.

> **Principle 2: Community Inclusion.** Community inclusion is steeped in the belief that the best and most reliable services and supports are those that are provided naturally in one's chosen community, and that it should be a priority of RENEW to work toward building, supporting, and filling in gaps in order for those natural supports to be effective.

> **Principle 3: Unconditional Care.** Unconditional care means that no specific behavioral criteria are required of the young person in order to qualify for and receive RENEW services. Youth with EBD need to learn that people will stay connected with them regardless of their actions and behaviors, and each youth receives support from the RENEW project to take responsibility for his or her actions.

> **Principle 4: Strengths-Based Services.** Strengths-based planning and service provision allows for a focus on what the young person *can*

do, as opposed to a focus on what he or she fails to do well. The focus is on skills, preferences, likes, dislikes, and gaps, in order to build efficacy and a positive concept of self ("success breeds success").

**Principle 5: Flexible Resources.** Flexible resource planning and development means that the RENEW facilitator helps the young person to identify exactly what he or she needs for supports and how to ask for help. It requires an extensive knowledge of natural community, agency, and community resource rules and regulations. The agencies are asked to provide support in a way that suits the young person's needs, as opposed to an emphasis on the young person meeting the criteria of the agency to obtain supports.

## Four Goals of RENEW

There are four outcomes, or measurable goals, that the RENEW process is designed to accomplish with every young person:

**Goal 1: High-School Completion.** High-school completion is a critical achievement, in light of the poor high-school completion rates among youth with EBD. If the youth has not already graduated from high school, the facilitator works with him or her toward high-school completion or graduation with a credential (a regular diploma, a GED, an adult education diploma, or local options).

**Goal 2: Employment.** Employment in a typical job for competitive wages is extremely critical to the young person's transition to adulthood, and having a job is an important step to build competence, self-determination, and self-efficacy. Many social resources become accessible through a person's job (bosses, coworkers, mentors), and the workplace offers significant learning opportunities for building social, career-related, and academic skills. Finally, the value of a paycheck and having one's own money cannot be overstated.

**Goal 3: Postsecondary Education and Training.** Many of today's competitive jobs at livable wages require postsecondary education and training. Most youth with EBD indicate that they would like postsecondary training or to attend college when they finish high school, and they will typically need substantial support and planning to achieve their goals. The RENEW facilitator provides support in the process of applying, developing financial support, and making the transition for youth who have postsecondary education goals.

**Goal 4: Community Inclusion.** Community inclusion is the final planned RENEW outcome. Youth with EBD are often isolated from the people, community organizations, and agencies that can support them and help them to achieve their goals. The RENEW process seeks to identify and connect each RENEW participant to the people, places, and services in their community that will help them now and in the future to attain their goals and keep moving forward.

## Eight Strategies of RENEW

There are eight primary strategies in the RENEW "toolbox," and the strategies are chosen based on the young person's goals and needs.

### Strategy 1: Personal Futures Planning

Various models for person-centered planning exist, including the McGill Action Planning System, or MAPS (Forest & Pearpoint, 1992; Vandercook, York, & Forest, 1989), Personal Futures Planning (Mount, 2000), Planning Alternative Tomorrows with Hope (PATH) (Pearpoint, O'Brien, & Forest, 1987), and various hybrids such as those employed by Cotton in *Elements of Design* (2003). Person-centered planning has been used primarily for planning around major life transitions for individuals with developmental disabilities, but it is more recently being used with elders and with youth in transition from high school to adult life. RENEW is one of the few models we know of that uses person-centered planning for youth with emotional and behavioral challenges.

The goal of the futures planning process is to help the young person create a meaningful, personalized, individualized plan, based on a conversation that captures the vision in the young person's words. This is done by "mapping" (1) his or her current situation, (2) elements from past experiences (increasing self-knowledge and awareness), (3) experiences that have been positive and those that have not worked well, (4) the young person's social network and other resources (to identify the supports and personal resources that can be leveraged to support the person's goals), (5) goals, dreams, and wishes (just as for typical youth, the courage to dream is a rite of passage for adolescents), (6) the challenges or possible roadblocks (to account and plan for problems), and (7) a detailed strategy or action plan (planning and implementing). The process, when conducted well, builds self-determination, unlike traditional service-planning processes, which are focused on agency needs, compliance (IEPs, for example), and treatment. As noted by Eisenman (2007):

> Theory, research, and practice have suggested that to keep youth in school, educators must encourage students' perceived competence and self-determination. They can do this by teaching students the component skills of self-determination in autonomy-supportive school environments and by helping students to apply their developing self-determination skills to self-identified goals. (p. 3)

The RENEW facilitator ensures that the futures plan is often revisited and revised. These experiences with person-centered planning have yielded positive changes in self-perceptions, motivation, interest, and engagement of youth with EBD. The goals are rarely unrealistic. What is often most helpful and instructive for the facilitator and other support persons is a list of resources that are available to the young person.

### Strategy 2: Alternative Education Options

Flexible education programming is often necessary to help each youth successfully complete a high-school program. There is a continuum of options—from simple solutions such as using a computer-based credit recovery program, changing classes, or testing out of a class, to more creative options such as gaining credit for a work-based internship or enrolling in vocational classes, to more radical options such as enrolling in an alternative or adult education program or taking the GED option. The facilitator helps the youth identify the preferred option and enlists the help of others to make it work.

### Strategy 3: School-to-Career Transition Strategies

A school-to-career transition framework focuses on the needs of adolescents with EBD for connectedness to school-based and work-based experiences as part of a coherent, "results-oriented" process of transition from school to adult life. The person-centered plan is a critical focal point to drive the secondary transition planning and program. Once a young person has identified what he or she wants to do and is good at doing and has developed post–high school goals (such as college, employment, and other goals), an individualized plan for the school-to-career transition is developed.

RENEW facilitators use the school-to-career framework for career development and education, including school- and work-based learning experiences and connecting activities, to create successful transition experiences for each youth. School-based learning experiences can include, in addition to traditional academic classes, participation in vocational classes and programs, independent study, extended learning opportunities, alternative classes or programs, classes in college, adult education classes, community education classes, and enrichment classes, among others. Work-based learning opportunities can include internships, informational interviews, job-shadow experiences, paid work experiences, apprenticeships, vocational classes tied to employment, on-the-job mentoring, and volunteer opportunities. The connecting activities are critical to the success of any school-to-work plan and may include career guidance and counseling services, vocational exploration classes and activities, mentoring and tutoring programs, and life-skills classes (personal financial management, for example), among others. The RENEW facilitator plays the role of "connector" or "broker" for each youth and must know of the available career-related programs and resources in the school and the community, including the guidance, career counseling, academic, and specialized programs.

### Strategy 4: Naturally Supported Employment

Working is an important experience for any youth. Jobs help young people learn about real-world expectations and are important as youth prepare for adult independent living. In addition to work experiences that offer high-school and college credit, youth with EBD should have opportunities for jobs after school and on weekends, just like most adolescents. A job provides the opportunity to learn about obtaining and managing money, test certain skills and abilities, and develop relationships and community connections with a new set of peers and adults. The RENEW facilitator often helps the young person use the connections in his or her "resource network" (relatives, friends, teachers) to gain access to job opportunities. If necessary and appropriate, the facilitator connects the youth with the state vocational rehabilitation agency for assistance with postsecondary education and supports, job development, on-the-job supports, and other career-related services that can bridge the gap between high-school resources and adult independence. The RENEW facilitator also works with the youth to plan for and build in important workplace supports, including an on-the-job mentor or contact person, linkages to transportation to and from work, and benefits counseling (to ensure that the job does not interfere with eligibility for critical income and insurance programs such as Supplemental Security Income or Medicaid). Finally, just as most adolescents frequently changes jobs, the appropriate process of leaving one job and finding the next is explained, or if necessary, facilitated by the RENEW facilitator.

### *Strategy 5: Individualized Resource Development*

The process of identifying the needed supports and resources begins with the person-centered plan. During the planning sessions, the RENEW facilitator works to elicit from the young person—and the people who best know the young person—a profile of the resources (human, social, financial, family, community, system) currently available to him or her. Human resources include the experiences, strengths, capabilities, and talents possessed by the young person (for example, perhaps the student is a talented guitar player). Family resources include those possessed by parents, siblings, aunts, and uncles, such as what they do for work, their volunteer activities, what they do for fun, their education, and where they live, among other valuable assets. Social resources include the connections the young person has with family members, neighbors, peers, teachers, coworkers, bosses, social workers, counselors, juvenile probation officers, and others who are valued by the young person and whom he or she wants to use to provide critical connections and supports. System resources include services and supports available from the school, the mental health clinic, and the local vocational rehabilitation office, among others. The RENEW facilitator has knowledge of these community resources and knows how to make new resource connections based on the goals expressed by the young person and the list of needed support and services.

### Strategy 6: Individually Developed Teams

The development of resources for each student is deliberately and specifically geared to the needs of the young person—not of the system—and often requires a great deal of creativity, negotiation, and asking. Additionally, the development of the young person's "team" is based on need. Individuals are invited to be part of the team because they have a critical role to play in the successful completion of the young person's plan (as identified by the young person). The team for RENEW is not the individualized education program (IEP) team, but is, instead, an invited group of people who are willing and able to help.

The systems encountered by and that support youth with EBD, including special education, regular education, mental health, vocational rehabilitation, child welfare, juvenile justice, and others, are driven by eligibility requirements and service processes that may or may not be in sync with the model of self-determination and school-to-work transition. One challenge for a RENEW facilitator, then, is to find the people who will offer solutions and overcome barriers. Interagency collaboration is an oft-used phrase, but in RENEW it means that all the involved systems and supports are "on the same page" as the young person and are working toward the young person's stated goals. Part of the RENEW service is thus focused on effective team building and communication.

### Strategy 7: Mentoring

Many youth with EBD lack relationships with older youth and adults that can be critical to their development, and mentoring can be an effective strategy to build the social connections lacking in the lives of many young people with emotional or behavioral difficulties (DuBois & Silverthorn, 2005). The problem is that "mentoring for the sake of mentoring" does not focus on the development of longer-term social resources. In the RENEW model, mentors are intentionally developed to help the young person make valuable new social connections, build social and career skills, and develop a positive sense of self. Mentors are often connected to youth in RENEW based on mutual educational and career interest and are never forced. The role of the RENEW facilitator is to identify and connect individuals who naturally possess the characteristics admired by the youth with EBD. The mentor is also part of the communication loop, if not an active member of the youth's team.

### Strategy 8: Sustainable Community Connections

When they finish high school or "age out" of the children's service system, most youth with EBD lose the cocoon of supports they received while in secondary school or a placement program. The RENEW facilitator looks to develop planned experiences in natural settings to allow each youth the opportunity to develop and learn prosocial skills and make potentially valuable community-based connections while still receiving support from adults and the service system. Despite the youth's disability and how the disability is manifested (in behavior and symptoms), and within the limits of any functional impairments, the RENEW model aims to help community members to understand how ecological factors can be manipulated or changed in order to ensure success and to support the youth. Social skills are thus developed by RENEW in the context of naturally occurring interactions (on the job, in the classroom, at the gym) through education, positive recognition, and supports.

## RENEW IMPLEMENTATION

RENEW was first developed and implemented as a federally funded model demonstration project in Manchester, New Hampshire, described in the 2000 U. S. Census as a blue-collar city of approximately 100,000, primarily white, residents. Among the empowerment zone's 7,015 residents, however, 19% of the people are nonwhite, and half speak English as a second language. The RENEW project staff were employed and supported by Keene State College and the Institute on Disability at the University of New Hampshire and were initially located at the Manchester Community Technical College, a normative setting for young people who are interested in advancing their employment.

The RENEW model was designed by the project staff with input from an interagency advisory team. This interagency team included representatives from the state's National Alliance for the Mentally Ill affiliate; a vocational rehabilitation agency; the community technical college; the Manchester School District, the state Division of Behavioral Health, the state Division of Children, Youth and Families; the Manchester mental health agency; and the Child and Family Services agency. The project team developed the model by incorporating best practices and strategies from a variety of disciplines, including child welfare, community mental health (wraparound), school-to-work (innovative crediting using work-based learning strategies), and developmental disabilities (personal futures planning) in order to create a comprehensive, flexible service that was built around five principles, four goals, and eight strategies (Cheney, Hagner, Malloy, Cormier, & Bernstein, 1998; Malloy, Cheney, & Cormier, 1998).

## Settings Where RENEW Services Have Been Provided

The primary resource needed to provide RENEW is a highly trained facilitator who is knowledgeable and skilled in person-centered planning facilitation, alternative educational models and school-to-career strategies, employment supports, community-based services and supports, team building and facilitation, and best practices in counseling. The services are provided in natural settings such as in high school, in the home, at work, and in the community. The facilitator must work to engage the youth and build trust, a component within the experiences of youth with EBD that is often missing.

RENEW services have been provided in various organizational contexts and settings. The first RENEW facilitators were supported by grant funds, trained and supervised by university research staff, and operated independently of typical youth-serving organizations and systems. When the grant ended, the project staff and the advisory committee created a nonprofit corporation, the Alliance for Community Supports, and established contracts and fee-for-service agreements with the local mental health center, the vocational rehabilitation agency, and several school districts. The Alliance for Community Supports continued to expand its fee-for-service base and its relationship with the university, providing RENEW services to adjudicated youth in a "community reentry" grant-funded project (Hagner, Malloy, Mazzone, & Cormier, 2008), and as part of two schoolwide systems change dropout prevention projects. More recently, university and Alliance for Community Supports staff have developed a model for training school counselors and community mental health therapists to provide RENEW to at-risk students in several New Hampshire communities.

### Eligibility and Enrollment

The original RENEW demonstration project established three primary criteria for eligibility for services: (1) the youth is between the ages of 16 and 21, inclusive, (2) the youth has an emotional disability as defined by a psychiatrist, psychologist, or other health or mental health practitioner (either as a primary or secondary diagnosis), and (3) the youth lives in the greater Manchester area. The project team rejected behavioral "readiness," eligibility criteria, or behavioral requirements that are often required by traditional agencies in the service system. Since the first project, RENEW has been implemented in four subsequent grant-funded projects and as a service of a nonprofit, community-based service provider.

## RENEW OUTCOMES

RENEW has been provided as part of several demonstration projects, but it has yet to be subject to a rigorous research design. Most of the outcomes reported here, then, are based on pre- and postintervention data, with promising results.

### The First RENEW Demonstration Project

The outcomes for the first RENEW cohort showed promise and led to increased support for fee-for-service contracts and additional grants:

- **High-School Completion:** Between May 1996 and September 1998, 72 youth enrolled in RENEW. At enrollment, 5 of the 72 (7%) had completed high school, and after 3 years, 42 of the 67 (63%) completed high school or its equivalent while in the project. Another 12 students were still in high school and were on course to complete high school by advancing into the next high-school grade (Hagner, Cheney, & Malloy, 1999).

- **Postsecondary Education:** National data show that postsecondary education participation among youth with EBD is 29% (Blackorby & Wagner, 1996), compared to a rate of approximately 50% among typical youth. Of the 42 youth who enrolled in RENEW and who completed high school, 18 (43%) participated in postsecondary programs. Seven of the youth were in 2-year-degree programs at the community technical college, one was a registered plumber's apprentice, and one young woman enrolled in acting classes at a licensed art school while working as an actress and model. Two young people eventually graduated from the community technical college.

- **Employment:** Studies show that youth with EBD are employed at comparable rates to other groups, but the stability of their employment and their pay rates are far short of the norm (Wagner, Newman, Cameto, Garza, & Levine, 2005; Zigmond, 2006). Upon enrollment into the first RENEW project, 15 of the 72 participants were employed (20%). While in RENEW, 71 participants obtained jobs in competitive settings and for typical wages (99%). Participants obtained an average of four jobs per person while in the project. Average wages were $6.65 an hour, with a range of $5.25 to $11.00. Each job obtained lasted an average of 6 weeks. Overall, the RENEW staff helped participants obtain 186 jobs for the 72 youth. Seventy-one of those youth were able to keep at least one of those jobs for more than 3 months.

## The Youth Reentry Cohort

Of the 21 participants in the Youth Reentry project who successfully reentered the community, nine (42.9%) returned to their neighborhood high school following detention, eight (38.1%) opted to study for the GED exam, and four (19%) obtained employment without returning to the educational system. Those who returned to their community high school were assisted to design creative alternatives to regular classroom instruction. Four participants completed high school. Two of those students have begun taking college classes. One other participant is combining GED preparation with participation in a registered apprenticeship. Twenty of the project participants residing in the community (74.1%) were employed at the end of the third year (Hagner et al., 2008).

## Outcomes for the APEX I Cohort

Of the 46 youth who completed personal futures plans in the first Achievement in Prevention and Excellence (APEX I) project dropout prevention project, nine participants received their high-school diplomas, two participants completed their GED, and three participants not yet eligible to graduate remained enrolled in school but worked independently outside of the school for course credit. Nine youth graduated out of 19 who were eligible, comprising a graduation rate of 47%. Fourteen participants (31%) remained in school classes and were promoted to the next grade level, and 6 (13%) participants re-engaged in some school program, such as vocational programs, adult education, or alternative programs. Four (9%) participants completed futures plans but were in and out of engagement throughout the school year and had no academic change, and 7 (16%) participants completed futures plans but had to discontinue services because they either moved to a new school (4), were placed in youth detention (1), or left to have a baby (2). In addition, the youth who held jobs increased from 37% at intake to 47% at discharge.

APEX included an evaluation of pre- and post-RENEW intervention effects on the functional impairment of a subgroup of 20 participants who received RENEW services and were engaged for at least 1 year. The instrument used to assess functioning was the Child and Adolescent Functional Assessment Scale (CAFAS) (Hodges and Wong, 1996; Hodges, Wong, & Latessa, 1998). The CAFAS includes assessment of functioning and interviews with the youth and the parents conducted by a staff member who is trained and certified to administer the CAFAS. The results showed a statistically significant overall improvement in functioning among the 20 youth, with greatest improvement in the school/work, home, moods and emotions, and self-harm domains. There was no change in the behavior toward others, community, substance abuse, and thinking subscales. These results indicate that participation in the RENEW process may have significant positive effects on the students' self-perceptions and their behavior in school and at home (Wells, Malloy, & Cormier, 2006).

**FIGURE 10.1    Mean Total CAFAS Scores: APEX Cohort (*N* = 20)**

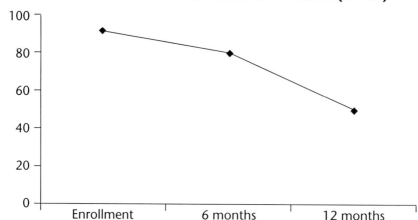

## EXPERIENCES WITH THE RENEW MODEL

### RENEW Cohorts

The youth served in the first grant-funded RENEW project were between the ages of 16 and 22 and had a label of serious mental illness or serious emotional disturbance (the state Division of Behavioral Health criteria for community mental health center eligibility for children and youth). During the period April 1996 through September 1998, 72 youth were enrolled in the project. As a group, their mean age was 18 years, 7 months; 51 participants were male, and 21 were female; all were Caucasian. At enrollment, 5 had completed high school or obtained a GED (7%), and only 15 participants (21%) were working. Five participants had concurrent diagnoses of mental retardation, severe learning disability, or cerebral palsy. Seventy-five percent of the youth carried a label of learning disabled on their IEP. Of the 72 participants, 32 received intensive, one-on-one services from the RENEW facilitators.

There were varied disabilities and environmental risk factors among the youth in the first RENEW cohort. For example, 3 enrollees were identified as having a developmental disability in addition to an emotional disturbance, and 57 were living in foster placements, were "homeless," or otherwise not living with their parents when enrolled. Twenty-seven had co-occurring substance abuse issues, and 18 had been identified as having schizophrenia.

Fifty-seven of the project's first cohort (79%) had histories of extreme externalizing behaviors such as assaults or aggression with professionals, family members, and peers; drug and alcohol abuse; and sexual offenses. Thirty-six (50%) were involved with the courts or had been involved with the state's Division of Children, Youth and Families as Children in Need of Services or as wards of the state.

Subsequent cohorts of youth for whom we have comprehensive data include the Nashua, New Hampshire, Youth Reentry Project and two high-school dropout prevention projects—APEX I, implemented in two New Hampshire high schools from 2002 to 2005, and APEX II, implemented in 10 New Hampshire high schools (2006–2009). Young people were eligible for the Nashua Youth Reentry project based on the following criteria: (1) they were between the ages of 14 and 17, (2) they were eligible for special education services or were receiving services from the mental health system, and (3) they had been removed from their school and residence for at least 2 weeks due to a charge of delinquency or adjudication as delinquent. Over a 3-year period, 1998–2001, 33 youth completed the futures planning process and engaged in individualized activities with the RENEW facilitator. Of the 33 youth in the reentry project, 66% were identified as having an emotional handicap, 30% a learning disability, and 6% had "other" disabilities.

The youth in the APEX project who received RENEW services were referred by teachers and administrators based on the criteria that they were between the ages of 16 and 22, were at high risk of dropping out of high school, and required individualized supports to move forward and complete their high-school program.

## EXAMPLES OF THE RENEW INTERVENTION PROCESS

### Engagement and the Personal Futures Planning Process

Self-determination practice with each young person begins with the personal futures planning process. The RENEW facilitators create a culture and context for the futures planning "conversation" that is based on mutual respect and trust. The personal futures plan is the lynchpin for service planning and interagency collaboration. The beauty of the process is that it is designed, directed, and overseen by the young person. Despite the difficult circumstances and discouraging experiences of these youth, all of the project's participants responded positively to the futures planning process and identified dreams and goals for themselves that were realistic and yet, given their circumstances, quite challenging.

All but a handful of RENEW participants were able to present a dream and articulate career-related goals. Several young people said to us, "No one has ever asked me if I had a dream." Similarly, nearly every young person accurately identified his or her barriers and challenges. The very first RENEW participant had a history of violent behavior against teachers, family members, and herself. The facilitator established a rapport and talked with the youth for several weeks before facilitating her futures plan. When asked what her barriers were, the youth said, "I'm afraid I might hurt my grandmother or try to kill myself"—behaviors that she had clearly exhibited and of which she was quite aware. An example of the personal futures planning process can be found in Malloy, Cheney, Hagner, Cormier, and Bernstein (1998).

The personal futures planning process, when conducted with a spirit of respect for the youth's right to self-determination, can significantly change the youth's self-perceptions and self-efficacy, and also change the way the adults view that young person's capabilities and prospects. One high-school student in the APEX project, who has a significant hearing impairment, indicated in her futures plan that she wanted to go into nursing but she was highly frustrated by her lack of progress in school and by lowered expectations of her family members, guidance counselors, and teachers. The futures plan process allowed this student to develop a realistic path toward her dream and gave her a method to communicate this path to people whom she needed to help her. She invited her family members and guidance counselor to a meeting where she presented her plan, and the meeting ended in tears as people realized the power of her dream and her resolve to be successful.

## Bringing Resources to the Table

The RENEW facilitators use the comprehensive personal futures plan as an organizing structure for gaining support for and leveraging resources from formal and informal networks. The facilitator often must "assume ownership" of each young person's situation for as long as it takes (typically 12 to 18 months) to develop the plan, organize the team, gain acceptance and support for the plan among key agencies and individuals, and assist the participants to act on their goals. Team participation is often enthusiastic and positive because the team is focused on the youth's stated goals, rather than an administrative or systems agenda.

The team composition is always individualized depending on the young person's preferences, needs, and situation. Planning does not necessarily occur in large team meetings. The RENEW staff work with each young person (and the parents, if appropriate) to prepare for the IEP, vocational rehabilitation, mental health, or wraparound meetings. This preparation includes rehearsing the presentation of the plan and self-advocacy techniques—what is known as a "pre-meeting."

With pre-preparation and the development of a strong plan, individuals and entities that are critical to the success of the plans are more likely to be supportive because the youth are well-prepared and able to express their goals and needs effectively. For example, one young woman in the first RENEW project was unable to stay in her high school. At the beginning of the day, she would enter the school by the front door, wave goodbye to her ride, and exit onto the streets by the back door. After her personal futures plan was developed, it was clear that she wanted to graduate from high school and get a job working with disabled children. The student indicated that she needed smaller classrooms, a vocational plan supporting her career dreams, and added support to help her create positive social connections to obtain her diploma. The young woman's plan called for creative thinking and creative funding for education supports not traditionally paid for by the school district. The RENEW facilitator put together a pre-meeting and coached the student and her mother about how to present her plan. The facilitator then helped the young woman and her mother invite the school district case manager, her mental health case manager, a representative from vocational rehabilitation, and her teachers to a wraparound meeting. When the meeting took place, the young woman felt confident enough to present a convincing case for the changes. The mother was able to support her daughter's goals and advocate for the changes in the IEP in an assured manner. Members of the team took responsibility to help her. The school department agreed to pay for classes at Second Start (a school with smaller classes and instruction geared for individuals with learning disabilities). Her mother agreed to pay for extra tutoring after school to increase her daughter's reading skills. The vocational specialist agreed to be available for career place-ment and additional job-related services. The RENEW facilitator agreed to coordinate the activities and to keep everyone up to date. This plan would not have been possible without prior planning and the personal futures plan. The young woman would not have known what she needed, she would not have known how to ask for help, and she would not have been motivated to take action. The parent would not have been as strong an advocate because she would have not be aware of what type of services were available to support her daughter, or her rights to request such measures be implemented. When the plan was systemat-ically drawn up, a solution to the situation became viable. In 2000, this young woman graduated from high school.

The involvement of the Bureau of Vocational Rehabilitation (VR) is critical to the successes of participants in the RENEW project. All but one of the 72 of youth served in the first RENEW cohort between April 1996 and September 1998 had obtained jobs that lasted for more than 3 months. Jobs obtained were in competitive, employer-supported environments but also include self-employment and registered appren-ticeship programs. RENEW staff developed a detailed vocational plan with each participant based on the personal futures plan, consulted with VR counselors about each plan, and developed a process with the VR counselor to identify resources needed to implement the plan.

The RENEW model takes into consideration the needs of the "whole child" as he or she transitions from childhood entitlement programs to adult life and the different systems of support for adults. This transitioning includes consideration of factors such as safe housing, financial and medical support programs, and long-term connections to the community. Two young men in the first RENEW cohort who wanted to live together received assistance from the facilitator to apply and receive approval for Housing and Urban Development Section 8 housing. One was the recip-ient of the Section 8 payment and the other served as the live-in support person. This mutually reciprocal benefit allowed the two young men to live in a two-bedroom apartment and enhanced their independent living skills. Other participants have applied for and received transitional living and housing for pregnant or single mothers. In all of these situations, RENEW staff worked closely with case managers at the community mental health center to ensure that the young adults are supported in what is, for most, their first move away from their families or guardians.

## Completing High School

It is clear that adults with high-school diplomas earn more than do high-school noncompleters, and adults with postsecondary education and training earn as much as 70% more than high-school graduates only (Day & Newburger, 2002). The youth engaged in the RENEW process seem to understand this. All but a handful of youth who worked on their futures plan identified high-school completion as a goal, but the challenge for the RENEW facilitator and student is to lay out a plan for high-school completion given where the student is today versus the diploma standards and requirements. To address this challenge, the RENEW facilitators work with students to develop a plan for graduation. This process includes (1) consideration of the best type of diploma or equivalent to pursue, (2) an assessment of the number and type of credits needed to complete those diploma or equivalent requirements, including an analysis of the school district's flexibility and feasibility of the credits being granted, and (3) the best options for completing the necessary work given the young person's learning style, abilities, and motivation to complete the requirements.

The typical requirements for obtaining a high-school diploma are a major barrier for students with challenging emotional or behavioral disabilities. In New Hampshire, guidelines for high-school completion are provided by the state's Department of Education, but local school districts are allowed to require more credits than the state standards and are also given discretion to adopt creative options, such as online courses ("virtual" high school), credit recovery options, adult education for regular credits, and extended learning opportunities, among others. Exceptions to typical diploma requirements often require approval by the school board and individualized approval by the principal. We have found that teachers, guidance counselors, and special educators are reluctant to apply creative options without assurances and supports in place. The personal futures plan, team participation, and good communication often provide the assurances that the staff and administrators need in order to "sign off" on a creative graduation plan.

Occasionally, the RENEW facilitator and student must look at how the transition from an out-of-district placement may affect the credits required and progress toward a high-school diploma. School districts may award credits through state-approved "out of district" programs, such as day and residential schools that are located through the state, but alternative programs differ greatly in their academic or vocational focus and services. A student returning to the school district from an alternative program may not receive the specific credits necessary to receive a diploma if requisite in-school requirements have not been met.

The RENEW futures planning process, with the development of various resources to contribute to the plan and the various activities that are geared to the youth's longer-range career goal, can help the school to meet the special education requirement to produce transition plans, beginning at age 16, for students who are eligible for special education services. The transition plan must include written post-high school, outcome-based transition goals and must outline activities related directly to the achievement of the transition goal. The special education rules require authentic student and parent involvement in the development of goals. The transition plans must also include a statement of what the youth will be doing after high school, such as college participation, employment, and independent living. The futures planning process can also be used as a "developmentally appropriate assessment" as required by the special education rules. In fact, we have worked with several special educators to use the personal futures plan as a primary source to construct the youth's IEP and the secondary transition portion of the IEP. For example, one young woman who has multiple health issues and an emotional disorder indicated that she wants to be a nurse or doctor in the coming years. This revelation was a complete surprise to her special education case manager, her guidance counselor, and her mother. Using that goal as a guide, we began to develop a plan for her senior year that included more science courses, college preparation, and connecting with the state vocational rehabilitation agency. We noted for her special education case manager that her futures plan can easily be translated into the school secondary transition plan. The special education case manager said, "Oh, yeah, all I have to do is copy her goals and the plan, tweak it bit, and it's done!"

Most RENEW participants are behind their age-equivalent peers for credits earned. Several students who had already been in high school for 2 or 3 years were so far behind that they would need to attend for another 2 or 3 years in order to graduate. This was not a viable option for any of them, most of whom were 17 or 18 years old. The RENEW facilitators assisted students in looking at "credit recovery" programs, extended learning opportunities (nonclassroom-based learning opportunities), and options such as the Adult Basic Education (ABE) diploma. The ABE is more flexible because it allows credit to be earned in alternative classes and learning environments. One student in the APEX II project had 12 credits of the 26 needed to graduate and had all but given up on the idea of graduating with her peers the following school year. The facilitator, with her guidance counselor and Jobs for New Hampshire Graduates (JAGs) coach, developed a plan that included utilization of the PLATO lab (a computer-based program designed for credit recovery) to gain credit for three of the classes in which she was at risk of failing, summer school for two classes for which she could not use credit recovery, online high-school accredited courses through a local community college for two more main courses she did not pass, and a credit for an internship or community service project through her JAGs course the following year. Once the student saw that it was possible for her to graduate with her peers, she became motivated to pursue the rest of her year and took immediate initiative to sign up for her online courses and PLATO.

A final option for students is the GED. The RENEW staff assist individuals who want to take the GED "pre-test" and help the students study for the final exam. Some participants with significant learning disabilities, however, cannot pass the GED test or high-school classes and are encouraged to work on diplomas through adult basic education. These students appear to profit from hands-on learning situations afforded by work-based learning.

*Community colleges* provide a "normalized" setting for students to earn credits toward high-school completion and have proved to be an ideal place for youth between the ages of 17 and 21 to finish their diploma requirements. One of RENEW's first participants was nearly 20 years old and four credits short of graduation. He initially attended the school district's summer school program and received two credits for this work. Summer school was held at the middle school, however, and he did not want to return to the regular high school to get his final two credits. Instead, RENEW staff worked with the school district and obtained approval for him to enroll in community college classes. Although the student did not complete those classes, he did earn the credits in the college's computerized learning laboratory and was able to apply them toward the diploma he received from his high school in August 1997.

One student in the APEX II project, who was far behind in credits and having tremendous difficulty staying engaged in his classes at the high school, explored the option of going to the local technical college to try a hands-on experience with a welding program there. This student began to work harder in high school because going to the technical college was contingent on his grades. After the student showed some success, the high school agreed to support additional classes at the technical school so that he could pursue his core studies as well as his technical training. This student developed a passion for studying in an environment that was more consistent his learning style.

In addition to college classes, students have attended classes at *museum schools, private institutes, and community classes.* For example, one young woman in the first RENEW cohort received help from the vocational rehabilitation agency to pay for her painting and drawing classes at a local private art school and, at the same time, she developed a process with her local high school to obtain credit toward her high-school diploma.

*Formal training and internships* are an important option for students who engage in the RENEW process. One young man, for example, entered a structured apprenticeship program for plumbers that required 144 hours of classroom instruction and 2,000 hours of on-the-job instruction annually. Another participant worked as a daycare assistant for 135 hours, keeping journals and reading books related to child development. This enabled her to receive the high-school credits she needed to obtain her diploma.

*Tutorials and independent study classes* help students who do not want to or cannot otherwise attend a class. With the RENEW facilitator's help, students develop a course of study with an instructor, work at their own pace, and meet regularly with the instructor to complete assignments and course objectives. For example, one young man in the first RENEW cohort who wanted to start his own craft business received individualized instruction in woodworking and painting as a part of his postsecondary training. Another young man in an alternative school was having difficulty staying engaged with his biology course because it did not seem relevant to his interests. The student and RENEW facilitator worked with the science teacher, the school curriculum coordinator, and the principal to develop an independent study for the core classes he needed to graduate. The student was interested in massage therapy, and he agreed to study human anatomy to count for his biology credit. To meet his math credit requirements, he learned about joint angles and other calculations that are important for a massage therapist. This strategy engaged the student and carried over to his senior year, allowing him to graduate on time with his classmates with an adult diploma through the alternative school.

*Computer-assisted instruction* is a relatively common instructional approach for students enrolled in adult basic education courses and is becoming more common in New Hampshire high schools for "credit recovery." RENEW has used these programs to help students achieve required academic outcomes and enhance literacy skills. An APEX II student was going into his senior year two credits short of graduating. In a RENEW meeting, the student's significant other suggested the option of using an accredited, online virtual high school during his last year to make up his two credits after school. The flexible classes would allow him to make up the credits and graduate on time as long as he continued to do well his senior year.

New Hampshire's community technical college system has joined forces with the Job Training Partnership Act to develop self-paced *GED training, literacy classes, and other classes geared toward the adult population.* Several RENEW participants have used this option and completed required assignments at their own pace. For example, one young man with very significant brain damage due to years of substance abuse (including inhaling butane), had a 2nd-grade reading ability and rudimentary math skills, yet his first goal was to finish high school. The team felt the first order of business was to increase his skills in the basic academic areas. The plan included using the software program of self-guided study toward completion of the GED, taking a community college class in engine repair, and receiving private tutoring for educational support. Six months after his initial enrollment, the young man raised his reading level from 2nd to 8th grade and succeeded in receiving his GED.

Finding creative solutions for high-school completion is a critical feature of the RENEW process and is clearly associated with positive outcomes for youth who would not otherwise graduate from high school. For example, a 17-year-old woman returning from residential treatment wished to complete her high-school education. Her history included several violent acts within school. Her behavior confirmed her inability to learn within the high-school classroom environment. The team felt a combination of private tutoring and competitive employment would enhance both her academic and job skills. The young woman enrolled in a college-level English course at one of the community technical colleges and was given private tutoring in United States history. She also completed an internship during the summer break. She received high-school credits for these efforts and eventually graduated with honors from her high school.

## School-to-Career Activities

Career planning and employment experiences are key predictors of vocational success for transitioning youth (Benz et al., 1997), but they are often a missing link in the educational process for youth with emotional or behavioral disorders. By using the personal futures planning process, most youth talk about future career and immediate employment goals and dreams. Only a few young people did not identify career goals or express an interest in working. In many instances, the RENEW facilitator tries to link the pursuit of a high-school diploma to the youth's employment goals. For example, one young man interested in auto body repair lacked the academic and social-emotional skills to obtain a regular education diploma. He therefore chose to pursue an Adult Basic Education diploma. During the day, he took automotive classes offered at the vocational high school and, in the afternoon, he had a cooperative education job. This decision-making process clearly has vocational implications. Youth with professional aspirations therefore are steered toward high-school degrees, while those with technical or vocational interests pursue ABE diplomas or GED completion.

*Internships* are paid or unpaid learning situations in business and organizations. Interns study with individuals in a business, usually for limited periods of time. Internships are often established for 2 to 4 weeks so that the student can have experience in a certain occupation without any commitment to the employer. It also allows employers to consider potential employees. One young man, for example, served as a plumber's intern for 6 weeks by studying a curriculum developed between the RENEW staff and the employer. The internship evolved into a registered apprenticeship when the employer accepted the long-term commitment to employ and train the intern.

*On-the-job training* (OJT) is hands-on training in a specific occupational area for a student employee. In the RENEW process, the need for additional training is typically related to the employee's disability. For example, one young man diagnosed with Attention Deficit Disorder was given OJT funds from the vocational rehabilitation agency to support the employer's time spent giving the student one-on-one training. The RENEW facilitator works closely with the Division of Vocational Rehabilitation to develop the employer OJT agreements so that employers can be paid for the hours that they spend training the students. Typically included within OJT is cooperative education.

*Cooperative education* combines academic or vocational studies with a paid or unpaid job in a related field. For example, one young man combined an office job with business education classes, and a young woman had an acting job while she took acting classes. RENEW staff worked with employers to develop curricula and learning criteria that were consistent with and complemented the student's classes.

*Registered apprenticeships* are typically multiyear programs that combine school- and work-based learning experiences in a specific occupational area or cluster that lead to the attainment of highly specialized credentials and licenses, union-paid membership, and entry into highly skilled jobs not open to people without those same credentials. The advantage of young adults entering apprenticeships is the high demand for their skills and the significant earning power of the graduates. The disadvantage of apprenticeship is the long-term commitment (often 4 years) and the stringent classroom- and work-hour requirements.

## Naturally Supported Employment

During the past several decades, sheltered employment, subminimum wage jobs, crews, and enclaves have been a major strategy to provide employment for people with significant disabilities. Crews and sheltered employment models are also used by school in an effort to prepare students for employment. During the past two decades, however, individuals with disabilities and their advocates have advocated for full social participation that includes "naturally supported employment" programs and interventions to help individuals with disabilities to obtain *real* jobs for *real* wages with *regular* employers (Bullis et al., 1993; Hagner, Rogan, & Murphy, 1992). Naturally supported employment incorporates counseling and advisement for the employer so that the employee can be properly supported at work without the stigmatizing presence of a paid support person or "job coach." The RENEW model incorporates a naturally supported employment framework so that youth with EBD will develop a strong connection to and high expectation of employment early in their work lives.

Through the futures planning process, most youth identify employment as a goal or a primary means to accomplish their goals, along with specific job or career objectives. In the context of each career-related goal identified by the youth, the RENEW facilitators work with the young person to identify how the job search will proceed. Some young people have jobs ready and waiting for them through their family network or other connections. Some individuals require job development assistance provided by the facilitator, a school-based vocational specialist. The state vocational rehabilitation (VR) agency may be the appropriate source for additional support for project participants. For example, the VR agency paid an employer to train one young man in computer repair. The agency may also pay for transportation, clothes, car repairs, and other items necessary for youth to obtain and maintain employment.

*On-the-job mentors* are sought out and developed among the employee's coworkers or bosses. These *on-the-job mentors* provide training and support to the young employee and are often asked to link the youth to other employees and watch out for them at work. Working in a real employment setting, participants have many opportunities to receive counseling from mentors and the facilitator about anger management, appropriate social skill building, and mature conflict management.

Losing one's job is considered an opportunity to learn and mature. The RENEW facilitators counsel participants who want to quit their jobs about how to do so appropriately. If a young person is fired from his or her job, the facilitator tries to help the youth analyze what happened and learn how to make the next employment experience a more positive one. The power and value of work becomes an important tool in the development and maturation of RENEW participants, and it takes place in real work settings.

## Mentoring: One-on-One Time with Each Youth

Youth with EBD have difficulty developing and maintaining reciprocal, trusting relationships with adults and peers. The value of mentoring for young people at risk has been well documented (Roth, Brooks-Gunn, Murray, & Foster, 1998), and so one of the tasks of the RENEW facilitator is to support the identification, development, and sustainability of mentoring relationships. In the first RENEW project, mentors were matched with participants based on career interests, and a mentoring plan was developed and reviewed with mentors on a regular basis. For example, one 18-year old-participant, who had a diagnosis of Asperger Syndrome and had lived his previous 3 years in a group home, had little contact with his family and few adult role models. He was extremely interested in computers and collected "shiny things." The RENEW staff matched this young man with a computer technology support staff member at a technical college who described his own adolescence as "lonely and isolated." The mentor introduced his mentee to a Saturday night "computer geek club." The young RENEW participant attended his mentor's wedding 3 years later and has become an adopted member of the family.

## Self-Determination and Personal Responsibility

For various reasons, most of the young people referred for RENEW services do not have access to choices and options open to typically developing youth. School-based meetings with teachers and administrators are often focused on what the student has done wrong and the options and choices that the student has lost as a result of his or her behavior. An important quality of the RENEW process is *how* the facilitator works with each student. There are no behavioral requirements for participation, and the RENEW staff make it clear that services will be provided unconditionally, but that inappropriate, illegal, or harmful behavior will never be condoned.

The RENEW facilitators make significant efforts to relate to youth who are difficult to engage, building trust through their actions as well and their words. It is common to work with youth who have abused drugs or alcohol or who have engaged in risky or illegal behaviors in the community while RENEW services are being offered. RENEW participants incur the natural consequences of their actions (such as arrests, loss of driver's license, suspension from work), but the facilitators discuss with them the futility of these destructive behaviors. Additional services with the local mental health center and vocational rehabilitation are often sought to provide further support for the individual youth. Thus, RENEW staff attempt to respond to individual challenges by coordination of services and bringing people to table who are reliable and who offer unconditional help and support that will build on the youth's skills, experiences, needs, and circumstances.

## CONCLUSION

In the face of unacceptably low graduation rates and during an era when parity of academic achievement is the priority, the RENEW model was developed and implemented to address the challenges posed by the most disengaged youth. The RENEW approach includes clear goals and outcomes, a strong values base, and proven strategies that allow the staff to work effectively with youth at risk of failure. The RENEW approach uses personal futures planning as an empowerment and organizing tool. Too often we are told that youth with emotional or behavioral disorders are incapable of making wise decisions in their lives. Indeed, their histories in school and the community often reinforce this perception. The RENEW staff, however, have demonstrated that by allowing these youth the opportunity to regain control of their personal futures, they are capable of charting and engaging on educational and career courses that have meaning in their lives. Self-determined and supported educational and vocational plans lead to increased, positive outcomes.

RENEW has been designed in alignment with national initiatives to develop school-to-work transition programs. Thus, career guidance and awareness, academic instruction, degree completion, and a broad range of work-based experiences are the core curriculum for RENEW participants. These curriculum components have been previously validated as strong predictors of competitive employment and productive community engagement (Benz et al., 1997). Mentoring is a key strategy to help the young person learn (or relearn) how to build a trusting, constructive one-on-one relationship with an adult who is willing to be a reliable source of support.

Finally, effective transition for these youth and young adults from school to community must emphasize access to informal and formal relationships and resources. Connecting with resources is consistent with the targets of the National Agenda to Improve Results for Children and Youth with Serious Emotional Disturbance (Osher & Hanley, 1996; U. S. Department of Education, 1994) that emphasize the importance of linking schools and agencies to support youth with EBD as they transition into the community (Kutash & Duchnowski, 1997; Smith & Coutinho, 1997). Case management, a role typically played by the mental health services system, is assumed by the RENEW facilitator in cooperation with project participants to implement the futures plan and pull together all of the necessary resources.

RENEW "graduates" often come to visit us. Many of these young people are faced with additional challenges or crises and just need a little guidance. Many come to brag about their accomplishments. True community integration happens when young people go to work at their real jobs for real employers, pay for their cars and rent on their own, take classes at the local college, and develop lasting personal relationships. Those achievements are the hallmarks of a good, typical school-to-adult-life transition model.

## REFERENCES

Alexander, K. L., Entwisle, D. R., & Horsey, C. S. (1997). From first grade forward: Early foundations of high school dropout. *Sociology and Education, 70*(2), 87–107.

Benz, M., Yovanoff, P., & Doren, B. (1997). School-to-work components that predict postschool success for children with and without disabilities. *Exceptional Children, 63*(2), 151–165.

Blackorby, J., & Wagner, M. (1996). Longitudinal postschool outcomes of youth with disabilities: Findings from the National Longitudinal Transition Study. *Exceptional Children, 62*(5), 399–413.

Bullis, M., & Cheney, D. (1999). Vocational and transition interventions for adolescents and young adults with emotional or behavioral disorders. *Focus on Exceptional Children, 31*(7), 1–24.

Bullis, M., Nishioka-Evans, V., Fredericks, H. D., & Davis, C. (1993). Identifying and assessing the job-related social skills of adolescents and young adults with emotional and behavioral disorders. *Journal of Emotional and Behavioral Disorders,1*(4), 236–250.

Bullis, M., & Paris, K. (1996). Competitive employment and service management for adolescents and young adults with emotional and behavioral disorders. *Special Services in the Schools, 10*(2), 77–96.

Burchard, J. D., Bruns, E. J., & Burchard, S. N. (2002). The wraparound approach. In B. Burns & K. Hoagwood (Eds.), *Community treatment for youth: Evidence-based interventions for severe emotional and behavioral disorders.* New York: Oxford University Press.

Carter, E. W., Lane, K. L., Pierson, M. R., & Glaeser, B. (2006). Self-determination skills and opportunities of transition-age youth with emotional disturbance and learning disabilities. *Exceptional Children, 72*(3), 333–346.

Cheney, D., Hagner, D., Malloy, J., Cormier, G., & Bernstein, S. (1998). Transition services for youth and young adults with emotional disturbance: Description and initial results of project RENEW. *Career Development for Exceptional Individuals, 21*(1), 17–32.

Cotton, P. (2003). *Elements of design: Frameworks for facilitating person-centered planning.* Durham: University of New Hampshire Institute on Disability.

Cullinan, D., & Sabornie, E. J. (2004). Characteristics of emotional disturbance in middle and high school students. *Journal of Emotional and Behavioral Disorders, 12*(3), 157–167.

Day, J. C., & Newburger, E. C. (2002). *The big payoff: Educational attainment and synthetic estimates of work-life earnings.* Washington, DC: Bureau of the Census, Economics and Statistics Administration. 14 pp.

DuBois, D. L., & Silverthorn, N. (2005). Natural mentoring relationships and adolescent health: Evidence from a national study. *American Journal of Public Health, 95*(3), 518–524.

Eber, L. (2003). *The art and science of wraparound: Completing the continuum of schoolwide behavioral support.* Bloomington: Forum on Education at Indiana University.

Eber, L., & Keenan, S. (2004). Collaboration with other agencies: Wraparound and systems of care for children and youths with emotional and behavioral disorders. In R. B. Rutherford, M. M. Quinn, & R. Sathur (Eds.), *Handbook of research in emotional and behavioral disorders* (pp. 503–516). New York: Guilford Press.

Eisenman, L. T. (2007). Self-determination interventions: Building a foundation for school completion. *Remedial and Special Education, 28*(1), 2–8.

Forest, M., & Pearpoint, J. (1992). MAPS: Action planning. In J. Pearpoint, M. Forest, & J. Snow (Eds.), *The inclusion papers: Strategies to make inclusion work* (pp. 52–56). Toronto: Inclusion Press.

Hagner, D., Cheney, D., & Malloy, J. (1999). Career-related outcomes of a model transition demonstration for young adults with emotional disturbance. *Rehabilitation Counseling Bulletin, 42*(3), 228–242.

Hagner, D., Malloy, J., Mazzone, M. W., & Cormier, G. (2008). Youth with disabilities in the criminal justice system: Considerations for transition and rehabilitation planning. *Journal of Emotional and Behavioral Disorders, 16*(4), 240–247.

Hagner, D., Rogan, P., & Murphy, S. (1992). Facilitating natural supports in the workplace: Strategies for support consultants. *Journal of Rehabilitation, 58*(1), 29–35.

Hodges, K., & Wong, M. M. (1996). Psychometric characteristics of a multidimensional measure to assess impairment: The Child and Adolescent Functional Assessment Scale. *Journal of Child and Family Studies, 5*(4), 445–467.

Hodges, K., Wong, M. M., & Latessa, M. (1998). Use of the Child and Adolescent Functional Assessment Scale (CAFAS) as an outcome measure in clinical settings. *Journal of Behavioral Health Services and Research, 25*(3), 325–336.

Individuals with Disabilities Education Act of 1990, Pub. L. No. 101–476 (1990).

Individuals with Disabilities Education Act of 1997, Pub. L. No. 105–17 (1997).

Individuals with Disabilities Education Improvement Act of 2004, Pub. L. No. 108–446 (2004).

Kortering, L., & Braziel, P. (1998). School dropout among youth with and without learning disabilities. *Career Development for Exceptional Individuals, 21*(1), 61–74.

Kortering, L. J., Hess, R. S., & Braziel, P. M. (1996). School dropouts. In G. Baer & K. Minke (Eds.), *Best practices in school psychology.* Bethesda, MD: National Association of School Psychologists.

Kutash, K., and A. Duchnowski (1997). Creating comprehensive and collaborative systems. *Journal of Emotional and Behavioral Disorders, 5*(2), 66–75.

Lane, K. L., & Carter, E. W. (2006). Supporting transition-age youth with and at risk for emotional and behavioral disorders at the secondary level: A need for further inquiry. *Journal of Emotional and Behavioral Disorders, 14*(2), 66–70.

Lane, K. L., Carter, E. W., Pierson, M. R., & Glaeser, B. C. (2006). Academic, social, and behavioral characteristics of high school students with emotional disturbances or learning disabilities. *Journal of Emotional and Behavioral Disorders, 14*(2), 108–117.

Lee, V. E., & Burkam, D. T. (2001). Dropouts in America: How severe is the problem? What do we know about intervention and prevention? In *Dropouts in America: How severe is the problem? What do we know about intervention and prevention?* Cambridge, MA: Harvard Civil Rights Project, Harvard Graduate School of Education.

Malloy, J., Cheney, D., & Cormier, G. (1998). Interagency collaboration and the transition to adulthood for students with emotional or behavioral disabilities. *Education and Treatment of Children, 21*(3), 303–320.

Malloy, J. M., Cheney, D., Hagner, D., Cormier, G. M., & Bernstein, S. (1998). Personal futures planning for youth with EBD. *Reaching Today's Youth, 2*(4), 25–29.

Malloy, J., & Cormier, G. (2004). Project RENEW: Building the community's capacity to support youths' transition from school to adult life. In D. Cheney (Ed.), *Transition of secondary students with emotional or behavioral disorders: Current approaches for positive outcomes* (pp. 180–200). Arlington, VA: Council for Children with Behavioral Disorders.

Masten, A. S. (2001). Ordinary magic. *American Psychologist, 56*(3), 227–238.

Mount, B. (2000). *Personal futures planning: Finding directions for change using personal futures planning.* St. Paul, MN: Metropolitan Council.

Nelson, J. R., Benner, G. J., Lane, K., & Smith, B. W. (2004). Academic achievement of K–12 students with emotional and behavioral disorders. *Exceptional Children, 71*(1), 59–73.

No Child Left Behind Act of 2001, Pub. L. No. 107–110 (2001).

Osher, D., & Hanley, T. (1996). Implications of the National Agenda to Improve Results for Children and Youth with or at Risk of Serious Emotional Disturbance. In R. J. Illback and C. M. Nelson (Eds.), *Emerging school-based approaches for children with emotional and behavioral problems: Research and practice in service integration* (pp. 7–36). New York: The Haworth Press.

Pearpoint, J., O'Brien, J., & Forest, M. (1987). *Planning Alternative Tomorrows with Hope (PATH): A workbook for planning positive possible futures.* Toronto: Inclusion Press.

Reschly, A. L., & Christenson, S. L. (2006). Prediction of dropout among students with mild disabilities: A case for the inclusion of student engagement variables. *Remedial and Special Education, 27*(5), 276–292.

Roth, J., Brooks-Gunn, J., Murray, L., & Foster, W. (1998). Promoting healthy adolescents: Synthesis of youth development program evaluations. *Journal of Research on Adolescents, 8*(4), 423–459.

Sabornie, E. J., Cullinan, D., Osborne, S. S., & Brock, L. B. (2005). Intellectual, academic, and behavioral functioning of students with high-incidence disabilities: A cross-categorical meta-analysis. *Exceptional Children, 72*(1), 47–63.

School-to-Work Opportunities Act of 1994, Pub. L. No. 103–239 (1994).

Smith, S. W., & Coutinho, M. J. (1997). Achieving the goals of the national agenda: Progress and prospects. *Journal of Emotional and Behavioral Disorders, 5*(1), 2–5.

Stroul, B., & Friedman, R. (1986). *A system of care for children and youth with severe emotional disturbances.* Washington, DC: Georgetown University Child Development Center, National Technical Assistance Center for Children's Mental Health.

U.S. Department of Education (1994). *Sixteenth annual report to Congress on the implementation of the Individuals with Disabilities Education Act.* Washington, DC: Author.

U.S. Department of Education, Office of Special Education Programs. (2006). Individuals with Disabilities Education Act (IDEA) database. Washington, DC: Author. Retrieved September 22, 2006, from https://www.ideadata.org/tables29th/ar_2–2.xls

U.S. Department of Labor, Secretary's Commission of Achieving Necessary Skills (SCANS). (1991). *What work requires of schools: A SCANS report for America, 2000.* Washington, DC: Author.

Vandercook, T., York, J., & Forest, M. (1989). The McGill Action Planning System (MAPS). *Journal of the Association for Persons with Severe Handicaps, 14*(3), 205–215.

Wagner, M. (1991). *Dropouts with disabilities: What do we know? What can we do? A report from the National Longitudinal Transition Study of Special Education Students.* Menlo Park, CA: SRI International.

Wagner, M., & Davis, M. (2006). How are we preparing students with emotional disturbances for the transition to young adulthood? Findings from the National Longitudinal Transition Study-2. *Journal of Emotional and Behavioral Disorders, 14*(2) 86–98.

Wagner, M., Kutash, K., Duchnowski, A., & Epstein, M. (2005). The Special Education Elementary Longitudinal Study and the National Longitudinal Transition Study: Study designs and implications for children and youth with emotional disturbance. *Journal of Emotional and Behavioral Disorders, 13*, 25–41.

Wagner, M. M., Kutash, K., Duchnowski, A. J., Epstein, M. H., & Sumi, W. C. (2005). The children and youth we serve: A national picture of the characteristics of students with emotional disturbances receiving special education. *Journal of Emotional and Behavioral Disorders, 13*(2), 79–96.

Wagner, M., Marder, C., Blackorby, J., Cameto, R., Newman, L., Levine, P. et al. (2003). *The achievements of youth with disabilities during secondary school: A report from the National Longitudinal Transition Study-2.* Menlo Park, CA: SRI International.

Wagner, M., Newman, L., Cameto, R., Garza, N., & Levine, P. (2005). *After high school: A first look at the post-school experiences of youth with disabilities. Report from the National Longitudinal Transition Study-2 (NLTS-2).* Menlo Park, CA: SRI International.

Wehman, P. (1996). *Life beyond the classroom: Transition strategies for young people with disabilities* (2nd ed.). Baltimore: Paul H. Brookes.

Wehmeyer, M. L. (2005). Self-determination and the empowerment of people with disabilities. *American Rehabilitation, 28*(1), 22–29.

Wells, R., Malloy, J. M., & Cormier, G. C. (2006). *APEX: Achievement in dropout prevention and excellence: Final report.* Concord: New Hampshire Department of Education.

Zigmond, N. (2006). Twenty-four months after high school: Paths taken by youth diagnosed with severe emotional and behavioral disorders. *Journal of Emotional and Behavioral Disorders, 14*(2), 99–107.

## CHAPTER 11

# Transition to Independence Process (TIP) Model: Understanding Youth Perspectives and Practices for Improving Their Community-Life Outcomes

**Hewitt B. "Rusty" Clark, Sarah A. Taylor, and Nicole Deschênes**

When we interviewed Pedro for a study on the successes of youth and young adults (Deschênes, Herrygers, & Clark, 2005), he came to us genuinely self-assured and proud of his accomplishments, summarizing how things were going in his life with these words: "I feel good about myself. I feel good in my heart. I feel good in my body. I feel good at school, and I feel good at work. Life is good!" (Pseudonyms are used in this chapter to protect the confidentiality of these young adults.)

Pedro's recent successes gave ample credibility to his remarks. A community college student with a rather lucrative business on the side and a beautiful girlfriend who shares his interest in education and a healthy lifestyle, Pedro has a lot to be very proud of. Looking at him today, it is hard to imagine that this young man struggled with getting passing grades in high school and staying out of jail. His experience in high school was, as he described it, "absolutely terrible." He recalled: "I had a hard time reading, I did not understand anything—it was

*Authors' note:* A portion of this chapter was included within the final research report for a grant funded by the Office of Special Education and Rehabilitative Services, Department of Education (Sarkis & Clark, 2005).

exasperating and really humiliating for me to be in class. I felt so very depressed." He added: "After a while, I just did not want to go to school anymore. . . ." Pedro finally dropped out of school to "hang out with friends who kinda liked to do drugs." One evening, when he was 16 years old, he and one of his friends were arrested by the police in connection with a robbery at a convenience store. Found guilty of robbery and of unlawful possession of firearms and illicit drugs, Pedro was sentenced to spend time in a juvenile correctional facility.

Upon his release from the correctional facility, Pedro, who was by then labeled as having an emotional or behavioral disorder (EBD) and learning difficulties, was referred to a school-based transition program located in a vocational technical training center. This program used a model referred to as the Transition to Independence Process (TIP) system and provided educational, psychosocial, and vocational training, as well as other critical transition and follow-up services for high-school students with EBD. The program applied the principles and guidelines of the TIP model in engaging students in futures planning and in the achievement of their short-term and long-term goals. The six major components of the program are as follows:

1. Person-centered planning regarding education, employment, and other transition goals

2. A community/vocational-oriented academic curriculum and employability training

3. Progressive inclusion of the students into vocational/technical educational courses based on their interests

4. Paid and unpaid practicum work experience for applying employability skills and exploring various work and career options

5. Supports and services to enable students to succeed in their school and work experiences

6. Individual and group counseling services (such as social skills development, individual and/or family therapy)

Vocational training was provided through a variety of on-campus, school-based programs and in the community. Educational classes were small, emphasizing workplace-relevant academic skills, as well as independent and community-living skills (Karpur, Clark, Caproni, & Sterner, 2005).

Pedro refused to let his encounter with the law keep him down. Rather, this experience seems to have strengthened his resolve to prove that he was a capable and talented person. In this new phase of his life, Pedro worked hard to meet the academic requirements of the program and to graduate from high school. Using his skills, and some of his charm, he found people to support and help him learn in this TIP program. At home and at school, his parents, teachers, and counselors were a constant source of support and encouragement for him. His talent for fixing appliances allowed him to focus on learning something that was of interest to him and to excel in his academic work as well. "Reading directions on how to fix appliances [was] fun," he said. Pedro won a national gold award for his work in appliance repair, which helped him develop his résumé, making him quite attractive to appliance stores such as Sears.

Pedro is now a successful young adult in every sense of the word. He seems to be happy with his personal and professional life. He is achieving many of his transition goals. He obtained his high-school diploma with remarkable grades, and he is currently working on obtaining a bachelor's degree in history. His business in appliance repair continues to be quite lucrative, supporting him financially while he completes his education. He feels much better about himself today than he did as a teenager. It is with pride that he talks about the fact that he has not had other contacts with the law "since I was young and foolish except, of course, for getting a parking ticket or two!" Upon graduation, Pedro would like to get married and have children. "I love children and would really like to have a family of my own someday," he said.

## PURPOSE OF THIS CHAPTER

How did Pedro succeed? Certainly a large part of his success is due to his hard work, perseverance, and resilience. But Pedro was also fortunate to be supported by a TIP-based program. This chapter describes the TIP model for youth and young adults with EBD, which was designed to facilitate the transition to adulthood for young people ages 14 through 29, referred to as transition-age youth and young adults (Clark, Deschênes, & Jones, 2000; Clark & Foster-Johnson, 1996). The perspectives of youth and young adults will be drawn from two exploratory studies by the authors of this chapter to illustrate the importance of features of the TIP model in effectively serving young people with EBD and their families (see pp. 333–338). Examples include youth who were able to participate in a TIP-based model and youth who were receiving "services as usual" who would have benefited from a more supportive program.

## THE TRANSITION TO INDEPENDENCE PROCESS (TIP) MODEL

Youth and young adults experience dramatic changes across all areas of development as they transition into adult roles. This period is especially challenging for youth and young adults with EBD because they experience poor secondary and postsecondary outcomes, including higher rates of secondary school dropout, arrest, homelessness, substance abuse, unemployment, and lower rates of independent living compared to their peers without disabilities (Armstrong, Dedrick, & Greenbaum, 2003; Clark & Davis, 2000; Clark & Unruh, 2009b; Vander Stoep et al., 2000; Wagner, Newman, Cameto, Garza, & Levine, 2005). Other challenges during this transition period include fragmented services, multiagency involvement, arbitrary age cutoffs, and conflicting eligibility criteria for various services (Davis, 2005; Unruh & Clark, 2009).

In response to research findings related to poor transition outcomes for youth and young adults with EBD, the TIP model was developed from the literature on best practices as well as programmatic and research efforts conducted with young people, parents, and professionals at sites across the United States over the past 15 years. The model is considered the only evidence-supported practice for effective community transition systems to improve the real-life outcomes for young people with EBD (Clark, Karpur, Deschênes, Gamache, & Haber, 2008; Clark, Pschorr, Wells, Curtis, & Tighe, 2004; Hagner, Cheney, & Malloy, 1999; Karpur et al., 2005; Koroloff, Pullmann, & Gordon, 2008).

The TIP model prepares and supports youth and young adults with EBD, ages 14 through 29, during the transition to adulthood. Some schools, agencies, and communities focus their transition programs on a subset of this broader age range (for example, 16 to 21 years old). The TIP model was developed to engage young people in their own futures planning process; provide them with developmentally appropriate services and supports; and involve them, their families, and other key players in a dialogue that facilitates movement toward greater self-sufficiency and achievement of goals related to the five transition domains: (1) employment and career, (2) educational opportunities, (3) living situation, (4) personal effectiveness and well being, and (5) community-life functioning (Clark & Hart, 2009).

## TIP SYSTEM GUIDELINES

At the heart of the TIP model are the transition facilitators, who work with these young people, their parents, and other support people. The term "transition facilitator" is used to emphasize the function of facilitating the young person's future, not directing it. Table 11.1 provides an overview of the function and role of the transition facilitator in the TIP model.

The TIP model is operationalized through seven guidelines and their associated elements that drive the practice-level activities and provide a framework for the program and community systems to engage and support young people and their families. This chapter provides a description of each of the seven TIP model guidelines. Each section in which a guideline is presented follows the same structure: the TIP system guideline and the associated practices are described briefly, then examples from the two exploratory studies are used to illustrate the application of the TIP supports, or how their absence may handicap transition-age youth (Deschênes et al., 2005; Taylor, 2007). The perspectives of youth and young adults illustrate the importance of features of the TIP model in effectively serving young people with these challenges and their families. For a more complete description of the TIP model and supporting research findings, please visit our website (http://tip.fmhi.usf.edu) or refer to *Transition of Youth and Young Adults with Emotional or Behavioral Difficulties: An Evidence-Supported Handbook* (Clark & Unruh, 2009a).

### Guideline 1: Engage Young People Through Relationship Development, Person-Centered Planning, and a Focus on Their Futures

- Use a strengths-based approach with young people, their families, and other informal and formal key players.

**TABLE 11.1   What's in a Name?—Transition Facilitator**

To ensure the continuity of planning, services, and supports, the TIP system is implemented with the assistance of *transition facilitators* who work with the young people, their parents, family members, and other informal, formal, and community supports.

The term *transition facilitator* is used to emphasize the function of *facilitating* the young person's future, not directing it.

The role is that of a proactive case manager, but no one wants to be a "case" and no one wants to be "managed."

Different sites and service systems use similar terms, such as transition specialist, resource coordinator, mentor, transition coach, TIP facilitator, service coordinator, or life coach.

*Note:* The role of transition facilitators with young people, their parents, family members, other informal and formal key players, and community representatives is illustrated more fully in this chapter and in Clark and Unruh (2009a).

- Build relationships and respect young people's relationships with family members and other informal and formal key players.
- Facilitate futures planning and goal setting.
- Include prevention planning for high-risk behaviors and situations, as necessary.
- Engage young people in positive activities of interest.
- Respect cultural and familial values and young persons' perspectives.

One of the essential functions of the transition facilitator and others who work with these youth is relationship development. Frequent compliments, smiles, and social praise for appropriate behavior, along with minimal criticism, contribute greatly to building and maintaining a relationship. It is also important for a transition facilitator to accept the uniqueness of the young person and to genuinely focus on his or her positive characteristics (for example, persistence, speaking up, or self-advocacy), which often requires reframing the young person's behavior. The transition facilitator can move the relationship development process along by being clear, consistent, and honest, yet flexible.

An equally important aspect of relationship development is recognizing that the young person probably has existing or past relationships with natural and community supports (such as a parent, an aunt, or a coach) that would benefit the young person if these relationships could be further nurtured or rekindled. Nurturing the relationship development between the young person and existing or past supports may contribute greatly to his or her future success, because this network of supports may continue when formal supports are terminated.

A person-centered planning approach provides the process and structure to assist young people in planning their goals and developing a means to achieve those goals. In a person-centered or futures planning approach, we have found that most youth do best when they have a chance to do frequent planning with one or two people who they are comfortable with (such as a transition facilitator or foster mother). Thus, the youth might have some planning partners for a given topic, then he or she and a planning partner reach out to the necessary connections who are relevant to addressing the issue or advancing the youth's goal (for example, the community college disability services coordinator or the probation officer). This ongoing futures planning process does not, however, negate the necessity of having to meet with the individualized education program (IEP) committee or attend a court hearing on foster care placement planning. The futures planning process allows the youth to guide his or her future and to build an ownership in the short-term and long-term goals. To the extent possible, these goals should be brought into play in IEP meetings and court hearings.

For the TIP facilitators to serve young people with EBD adequately, they need to be culturally competent, which means that they must demonstrate sensitivity and responsiveness to individual variations in gender, ethnicity, sexual orientation, social class, and other unique orientations and needs of each transition-age youth or young adult and his or her family. Having parents actively involved in the strengths-discovery assessment and the planning process also can be beneficial in integrating important ethnic and family cultural perspectives into a transition plan (Isaacs, Jackson, Hicks, & Wang, 2008).

Although teenagers and their parents are always a challenging mix, parents (or other family members or guardians) typically represent an essential element for the future success of transition-age youth with EBD (Ryndak, Downing, Lilly, & Morrison, 1995). Guideline 4 discusses involvement of parents and guardians in the TIP planning process.

### Youth Perspectives Regarding Relationship Development, Person-Centered Planning, and a Focus on the Future

All of the youth in Taylor's (2007) study commented on the importance of feeling that someone is making an investment in them, and they appreciated a person-centered, relational approach. Youth conceptualized this caring as listening, asking general-interest questions (for example, "How are you?" in a sincere way), and being seen as a whole person, rather than as an illness, problem, or single role (such as "patient" or "part-time worker").

In describing the differing perspectives of her mother and father, Trisha commented that her mother "understands" her, while her father sees her as just a "little girl who got mentally ill." Transition-age youth with EBD appreciate being seen as more than their diagnoses, and this appreciation was felt even when the interaction was brief. In describing her positive interactions with an intake worker at a psychiatric emergency room, Helen said, "He talked to me like I was just a person going through a hard time."

Most of the participants in the successful youth study by Deschênes et al. were future and goal oriented. Although perhaps described differently during the interviews, the significance of this theme was unmistakable. Most young people interviewed for this study seemed to have a sense of purpose, a focus, and a direction. They all had practical, realistic, attainable aspirations that were very similar to the goals and aspirations of their peers with no disability. They too, like their peers, wanted to graduate, get into college, obtain stable employment, have their own apartment, own their home, and have a family. To illustrate this point we heard comments such as "By the time I'm 25, I want to have my own apartment, be on my own. By the time I'm 40, I want to own my own house." Lucia shared with the interviewers a clear and detailed vision of her future. She, too, wanted to live alone in her own home. She said she would work as a registered nurse and may also have a child who, she acknowledges, will "slow her down" but she was "very confident" in her ability to face the future.

Madeline, another youth involved in our study, described her experience saying, "One day I woke up and I said, 'Bummer! I wanna go to college. . . .' That was like 2 years ago. I have to go to college. . . ." Madeline's mother opened a savings account for her and put in $20 to start. Madeline was saving the rest. Her goal was to save $5,000 and use the money to enroll in cosmetology school. Once Madeline identified her education and career goals, she was then motivated to achieve them. She researched the cost of cosmetology school and, like Pedro, developed a plan to go to school and succeed.

Closely related to the capacity to be goal oriented is the ability of successful youth to recognize and integrate their particular interests and abilities in everything they set out to do. For example, participants in the Deschênes et al. (2005) study expressed interest in music, auto mechanics, commercial art, childcare, nursing, carpentry, and the air force. They appreciated the help they received along the way as they were trying to find their likes and dislikes and that transition personnel focused on their strengths rather than deficits. This TIP model guideline and its associated practices are designed for transition facilitators to assist youth and young adults in exploring their interests and strengths and building on those characteristics in setting goals and achieving them.

### Guideline 2: Tailor Services and Supports to Be Accessible, Coordinated, Appealing, Nonstigmatizing, and Developmentally Appropriate, and to Build on Strengths to Enable Young People to Pursue Their Goals Across Transition Domains

- Facilitate young people's goal achievement across relevant transition domains:

  Employment and career

  Educational opportunities

  Living situation

  Personal effectiveness and well being

  Community-life functioning

- Tailor services and supports to be developmentally appropriate, addressing the needs of and building on the strengths of young people, their families, and other informal key players.
- Ensure that services and supports are accessible, nonstigmatizing, coordinated, and appealing.

- Balance the transition facilitator's role with that of the young person, his or her parents, and other informal and formal key players.

The TIP system is comprehensive in scope, encompassing the three major setting-based transition domains of employment, education, and living situation, as well as two domains that cross all aspects of life—personal effectiveness/well-being and community-life functioning (Figure 11.1). These five transition domains are useful in capturing young people's attention and a creating a focus on their futures. The domains of personal effectiveness and well-being and community-life functioning encompass several subdomains that are relevant to success in each of the other domains. (Refer to the TIP website for more detail, http://tip.fmhi.usf.edu.)

The TIP system provides and facilitates a comprehensive array of community-based service and support options within each of the five domains to accommodate the strengths, needs, and life circumstances of each young person. Transition-age youth are developmentally at an age when they want to make their own decisions, whether we believe they are ready to do so or not. To work effectively with young people with EBD, we need to design our practices and systems to recognize the realities of their developmental level and their belief in self-determination. The supports and services need to be appealing, nonstigmatizing, and developmentally appropriate (for example, a young person might find the support of a coworker mentor at a place of employment more acceptable than a vocational rehabilitation job coach who is introduced into the worksite).

Although the administrators of a transition system may think that their system and its components provide continuity for young people and their families, a system's attributes must be judged from the eyes of the beholders—that is, the young person and his or her informal supports. Continuity refers to the extent to which the relevant and timely supports and services are accessible to a young person and are provided in a coordinated fashion. All too often there is no continuity across services. Accessible, continuous services are more likely to be provided when caseloads are manageable; our program and research suggest that a transition facilitator be responsible for 15 young people at most.

**FIGURE 11.1    Transition Domains**

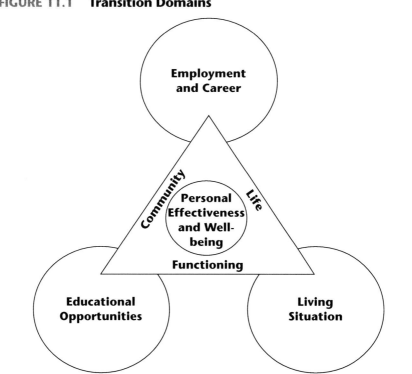

The transition facilitators and their supervisors must also operate at the system level, because linkages are required with a broad array of child- and adult-serving systems. The development of networks of individuals and organizations to assist in working with young people is also the responsibility of the TIP system. These efforts must include reaching out to ethnic communities so that culturally relevant supports are available to individuals who require them.

### *Youth Perspectives Regarding Developmentally Appropriate, Accessible, Nonstigmatizing, Coordinated, and Appealing Support Across All Transition Domains*

In Taylor's (2007) study, youth with EBD (as compared to other vulnerable youth in the sample) were much more likely to depend on formal service providers than on natural supports; therefore, helping these youth build their natural support systems is critical. Although youth reported a need for formal supports, accessing these supports was often difficult. Accessibility refers to support that is there when needed. "When needed" is difficult to specify, because youth may need support but fail to ask for it. Conversely, support that is imposed when it is not needed (or perceived as not being needed) is likely to feel intrusive. Trisha described the lack of accessibility of her mental health team:

> Another thing I wish that County [mental health] had would be a line you could call like a peer counseling line. You could call and say, "I'm having problems right now; I need to talk to somebody about it. . . ." They [county mental health staff] don't think it's a crisis. Every single time I've called, they've never had a crisis with me. . . . They still like me, but they're like, "This is my off time. I don't want to talk to you right now."

Youth also described how their support network did, or did not, help them to feel safe. The main components of safety are consistency and structure. Consistency refers to a stable, ongoing relationship with supportive people and programs. Lack of consistency caused tremendous difficulty for the youth with EBD in the sample. For example, they expressed feelings of abandonment when they were no longer able to meet with a trusted provider due to staff turnover or transition from child to adult mental health services. These types of institutional transitions, which are program initiated rather than driven by youths' developmental needs, are an extraordinary problem for youth whose primary source of support is formal service providers (Davis, 2003; Mallory, 1995).

Another important aspect of availability involves permission for the youth to leave and return to services as often as needed. Youth want to be able to leave supportive relationships to test their independence and return to them in times of difficulty. They want to know that the support would be there, even if they are not actively using it at a given time. This was an important theme for Trisha, who wanted to work and become independent of Social Security insurance but feared that she would have difficulty resuming assistance if she were unable to support herself or experienced a decomposition of her mental health.

One potential challenge experienced by young people in transition is vulnerability to chance events (Schulenberg & Maggs, 2002). Because of this special vulnerability during times of transition, availability of formal service providers is essential. Helen, one of the youth in Taylor's (2007) study, experienced a crisis during the study, and this crisis could have been avoided through increased availability of her mental health team. This crisis impacted Helen's efforts to transition into work, as illustrated in this excerpt from Taylor's study:

> About two weeks before our third meeting, Helen began experiencing negative side effects of a new medication she had been prescribed:
>
> **Helen:** It caused major mood instability as well, where I was having anger and rage. Rage like I wasn't able to hold it back like I usually do. Like when somebody irritates me, I'm [usually] like, "Okay," and I let it go.
>
> **S.T.:** Is that unusual for you?
>
> **Helen:** Yes. I'm more anxious and depressed. Yeah, I have some mood instability, but I'm usually able to kind of control it.
>
> She was feeling increasingly distressed and attempted to contact her mental health coordinator and therapist, but they were on vacation:
>
> **Helen:** He was out of town when it happened. He was down in Los Angeles and then five of the other people on the team were on vacation or out of town too.
>
> **S.T.:** So there weren't staff there that knew you?
>
> **Helen:** Not much. There was a few. And I had not seen my therapist. She was out of town in Hawaii, she's still there; I was coming to see the crisis on-call person for— because I was trying to tell her that I missed my appointment with Dr. [the psychiatrist] and that I needed some extra help and that I couldn't see my coordinator right now because he's not here and I can't see my therapist because she's not here.
>
> She went to the mental health building to speak with the on-call crisis counselor, and while there, she became angry with the receptionist. She threatened the receptionist and damaged

some property in the waiting room. The receptionist was frightened and called the police. Because Helen was in a government building during this incident, she was charged with a felony. She was held in jail for three and a half days, which she describes as "the darkest, crappiest place I've ever been in my life. It was horrible."

When Helen told her mother about the incident, her mother blamed Helen and refused to speak with her. Her father was a little more understanding; he said, "You make mistakes. You're going to learn from it I guess." Helen says her grandmother was the most supportive, and offered to encourage Helen's mother to resume contact.

Helen reported feeling supported by her mental health coordinator once he returned from vacation. She also received help from her public defender and a counselor at a nonprofit organization that assists young people with job placement. The counselor was particularly helpful because the trial was on a Friday, and Helen was concerned about taking care of herself throughout the weekend after experiencing what she imagined would be a stressful court appearance. The counselor offered to bring Helen to his office, for as long as she wanted after the trial, so that she would have a "place of refuge" in which to regain her equilibrium. Helen gratefully accepted his offer.

Our last interview was a few days before the trial, but Helen called me after the trial to report that the felony charge had been reduced to a misdemeanor. She would be on probation for a year. One of her concerns about being charged with a felony was that she was about to be offered a job as a counselor in a mental health rehabilitation facility. When the human resources staff there conducted the background check and saw the felony, they told her she would not be hired unless she "won the court case." During our telephone follow-up, she was uncertain if her misdemeanor conviction would prevent her from being offered the position.

The lack of accessibility of Helen's mental health providers contributed to decomposition in her mental health, criminal justice involvement, and possibly decreased employment opportunities. Of course, Helen's mental health team deserved a vacation from their challenging work, but Helen's story highlights the importance of planning and service coordination.

### Guideline 3: Acknowledge and Develop Personal Choice and Social Responsibility in Young People

- Encourage problem-solving methods, decision making, and evaluation of impact on self and others.
- Balance one's work with young people between two axioms:

  Maximize the likelihood of the success of young people.

  Allow young people to encounter the natural consequences of their choices.

Life comes with a continuing stream of problems—or opportunities, when reframed. Social problem-solving and decision-making methods can be particularly helpful tools for young people and for those who work with them.

Facilitators attempt to assist young people through mentoring, teaching of skills, contingency contracting, counseling, problem solving, and recognizing them for the incremental improvements they make (for example, descriptive social praise). Transition facilitators also understand that young people need to be given opportunities to make their own decisions and experience the successes and failures associated with their choices. It may be that a young man has gone through two social skills instruction groups, but it is only after being fired from his fourth job that he displays any receptivity to learning how to follow instructions and to problem solve with authority figures. Providers need to allow youth to experience setbacks, and be available when youth require support to get back on track.

To assist the transition facilitators and other personnel to be effective in working with youth and young adults, the TIP model consultants provide competency enhancement training across the following core practices: strengths discovery and needs assessment, futures planning, rationales, in vivo teaching, social-problem solving, prevention planning for high-risk behaviors, and mediation with young people and other key players. For more information about these practices, please refer to the TIP website (http://tip.fmhi.usf.edu), Clark and Hart (2009), Clark and Unruh (2009a), or Haber, Clark, and Parenteau (2009).

### Youth Perspectives Regarding Choice and Responsibility in an Atmosphere of Support

Youth in Taylor's (2007) sample described their need for interdependence (Table 11.2). Kyle articulated the problem of navigating independence as a foster youth:

> I was talking to some other foster youth a couple weeks ago about what they think "independent" means and then I talked to my older brother [Kyle's mentor] about it, and I thought, "Independent means, be[ing] able to do everything by yourself," and he's like, "Do you know anyone who does that?" And I'm like, "No." He said, "Why is that your goal?" I'm like, "I don't know." So, I talked to him about that and I talked to all these youth and they're like, "Yeah." I'm like, "What are we teaching the youth? They need to be all independent and do everything by themselves?" [. . .] I was like, "Can we change the name of ILP [Independent Living Program] because that's not realistic, not going to happen and I think you should change it to Successful Adult Living Skills."
>
> In ILP they teach us how to do job applications and stuff and you should be able to do that by yourself, you should be able to drive, but there's just things people need help with and I think that foster care, you want to get out so bad, you just want to leave and do it all by yourself, and prove to everyone, but no one does it all by themselves! That's why I was homeless. I took off when they kicked me out. I didn't call anyone, I had a cell phone, but I was like, no, they kicked me out. I'm going to do it. And I was homeless for a year. But I could have called up my ILP worker like that at that minute and it could have got me into a shelter and it could have got me out a lot faster but I didn't. I was too stubborn and I thought I would do it on my own and show them I can, but there's no one who can do it on their own. People who are rich, they don't do it on their own. They pay people to do it.

Helen expressed a similar sentiment about needing both freedom and assistance when asked what might prevent her from achieving her goals:

> Either overly helping me to where I don't have a chance to grow, or overly judging me, or dropping me completely,

**TABLE 11.2   Independence and Interdependence**

The system was originally planned to be named the Transition to *Interdependence* Process (TIP) system. However, some of the youth and young adult participants wanted the emphasis to be on independence— something they could relate to more directly. Their points were well taken, and clearly the TIP system promotes greater self-sufficiency and independence. However, the concept of interdependence is central to working effectively with young people. This concept nests the focus of independent functioning (such as budgeting money and maintaining a job) within the framework of young people learning that there is a healthy, reciprocal role of supporting others and receiving support from others (such as a social network for emotional, spiritual, and physical support). The TIP model is designed to develop understandings and competencies within young people regarding both of these concepts.

> meaning not to have any services. Or, to over help or under help.

Helen further elaborated on the mixed messages she received from mental health staff about how independent she should be:

> I don't know they just tell me, half the time, there's half the people saying, "You're too sick and mentally ill to go into school right now, or go do this and that." And I'm like, "Okay." And the other half of the county and people are going, "Yeah, I support you. You're doing great! Keep doing what you're doing." And I'm like, "Dude, make up your mind."

Trisha's mental health coordinator was aware of the difficulty in providing services to transition-age youth and discussed this when asked what might prevent Trisha from achieving her goals:

> Mental health staff that don't believe she can do it, mental health staff that tend to focus on pathology—this is an issue among the staff—[trying to determine] what she can and cannot do. Family is also an impediment—they discourage her from driving. They say, "You might hurt somebody." Those kind of things are pretty damaging because they cut right to her anxiety, and nobody knows what she is going to be like as a driver. Those kind of misstatements are going to impede her.

That's funny—her two primary support systems [mental health staff and her parents] could be her undoing—by being so close and supportive, we could damage her by not believing in her.

## Guideline 4: Ensure a Safety Net of Support by Involving a Young Person's Parents, Family Members, and Other Informal and Formal Key Players

- Involve parents, family members, and other informal and formal key players.

- Keep in mind that parents, family members, or other informal key players may need assistance in understanding this transition period or may need services and supports for themselves.

- Assist in mediating differences in the perspectives of young people, parents, and other informal and formal key players.

- Facilitate an unconditional commitment to the young person among his or her key players.

- Create an atmosphere of hopefulness and fun, along with a focus on the future.

Parents, members of the extended family, and other natural support persons are often the only source of consistent contact over time. Their involvement in identifying a youth's strengths, helping the youth plan for success, contributing to the youth's safety net, and advocating for the youth are critical. For many young people, their survival and success are related directly to a parent, aunt or uncle, peer, or spouse who has hung in there with them over time.

It is common for youth and parents to have quite different perspectives about the youths' short- and long-term goals. Transition facilitators often assist in mediating these differences to enable the young people to pursue his or her interests and maximize the level of support possible from parents and other support people.

VanDenBerg and Grealish (1996) defined unconditional commitment as never denying services because of severity of disability, changing services as the needs of the child and family change, and never rejecting the child or family from services. Although the TIP team recognizes that young people 18 years or older may legally refuse services, transition facilitators must remain creative and determined to stay with them to the extent possible, adjusting services and supports to meet their changing needs. At times, young people may "fire" us, but our program can maintain an option for them to return at a future date. Furthermore, a careful analysis of when and why youth refuse service may lead to a change in facilitation and service delivery strategies.

Unconditional commitment is a powerful expression of the TIP staff's hopefulness and positive affirmation of the young person's worth and merit (Deschênes & Clark, 1998). This feature is manifested by staff encouraging young people, speaking respectfully, involving youth and parents as partners, respecting youths' choices, and sharing a sense of humor. The strengths-discovery and person-centered planning processes also set a focus on the young person's future.

### Youth Perspectives Regarding a Safety Net of Support

All of the participants in the study of successful youth (Deschênes et al., 2005) recognized the need for support and took advantage of the help they could access along the way to overcome hurdles and cope with difficult situations. Most youth and young adults established a network of positive and supportive people, including family members, relatives, friends, community organizations, teachers, coworkers, transition facilitators, and others on whom they could rely. Support was provided in many forms, including the following:

- Emotional support from a caring and trusted person with whom the youth could share experiences
- Instrumental support providing tangible aid and services
- Informational support providing advice, suggestions, and information that youth can use to address difficulties
- Appraisal support providing information useful for self-evaluation, constructive feedback, affirmation, and social comparison

Regardless of its form, support seemed to be an important element in enabling young people to move ahead on the road to success. Common elements observed in the support provided to the participants included the following:

**Commitment:** "He was there for me," was an often-repeated phrase. "They did not give up on me. . . . They used to take me to the side, talk to me, and do special things with me. They used to do things with me without the group. That made me feel special!" "She would always be listening to me a lot when I had problems."

**Dependability:** "I can depend on him."

**Helpfulness:** "She talked to me."

**Encouragement:** "The thing that kind of made me believe in the things in life, to take things seriously, was my support system: my godmother, my family, and definitely, the Boys and Girls Club." "My godmother encouraged me to do a lot. She helped me study. She was always there for me to talk to."

**Trust:** "The teachers listened to me and made me feel special."

**Guidance:** "[They] tell me what I need to do to become what I want to be. . . . They help me become a better person." "Before, I didn't think I would be able to handle it and shop on my own. Miss [ _____ ] taught me how to relax, take everything slow, and manage my money."

**Patience:** "When I don't understand something, he explains it to me."

**Discipline:** "She saw a lot of potential in me. She didn't put up with my crap. She would call me on everything. I loved her to death. She's the only teacher I ever respected in my life."

**Confidentiality:** "'cause everything that I tell, she doesn't tell anyone else. It's confidential."

**Protection:** "When I had like one of my seizures or something, he would be right there next to me and he would wait until the nurse came and got me. He'd keep all my classmates away from me, from making fun of me or hitting me. When I was going up to the nurse's office, he'd come and check on me every once in a while."

The following story is about Lucia, a Hispanic woman, age 17. It illustrates the key role support can play for transition-age young adults. Lucia is a rather introspective and self-reliant young person, and she believes her confidence comes from her support network, her cognitive skills, and her determination to make her dreams come true. In that regard, she said, "The thing that kind of made me believe in the things in life, to take things seriously, was my support system: my godmother, my family, and definitely, the Boys and Girls Club." She added that the Boys and Girls Club enabled her to escape, do the things she liked to do, and gave her something to look forward to when she had a bad day.

Lucia was athletic and performed well academically. She would have been in a regular school if she didn't have angry outbursts. Changing schools at least four times presented challenges and increased her anger. At one point, her anger was so great that it caused her to get failing grades. Lucia felt that she was prematurely and inaccurately classified as EBD. She found the special education curriculum "boring and repetitive." Lucia recognized why she was in these special classes and what she needed to do to get back into a regular diploma course. To help her control her anger and support her in her quest to return to a regular high school, school personnel provided her with effective rewards that Lucia truly appreciated, including singling her out for activities (pizza with the principal), letting her do activities she liked (basketball), and interacting and conversing with high-level school authorities. The rewards made Lucia feel special. She appreciated the support she received in school:

> They did not give up on me. . . . They used to take me to the side, talk to me, and do special things with me. They used to do things with me without the group. That made me feel special! If I acted up, I could talk to the principal instead of talking to the behavior specialist. Going to a higher person for me is very special because sometimes you gotta deal with a lower person before you go higher and it takes a long time. The principal never was on my side. He had to take his employees' side. But I liked the principal for who he was. And I needed a talking to because it was in my best interest.

Pedro, the young man whose story we highlighted at the beginning of this chapter, also benefited from a safety net of support. Pedro said that his mother, Miss M. (his teacher), and some of the staff from the TIP program helped him the most to succeed in this program. His mother helped him with money and registration. Miss M. was "very understanding and would notice when I couldn't focus and was out of place. . . . She would always be listening to me a lot when I had problems."

Miss M. helped him become even more independent. For example, when he missed the bus and had no transportation to school, she suggested he take the metro bus. He and his mother investigated bus routes and he learned how to navigate the bus system. Miss M. also helped Pedro with his studies, even going so far as to give him her own home phone number. Pedro considers that the program staff helped him get the vocational and rehabilitation services he needed. They also helped by "giving me ideas . . . suggestions . . . 'cause they know what really is my problem." Pedro also appreciated the support he received from Dr. C., who helped him get the curriculum altered so he didn't have to do the activities that made him uncomfortable.

Lucia and Pedro were fortunate enough to have a safety net comprised of natural and formal supporters. Many transition-age young adults have difficulty connecting with their natural support network, and it is a critical task of the transition facilitator to help the young person form and strengthen these connections.

### Guideline 5: Enhance Young People's Competencies to Help Them Achieve Greater Self-Sufficiency and Confidence

- Utilize in vivo and functional assessment methods.
- Teach meaningful skills relevant to the young people across transition domains.
- Use teaching strategies in community settings.
- Develop skills related to self-management, problem solving, self-advocacy, and self-evaluation of the impact of one's choices and actions on self and others.

One of the most powerful contributions that transition facilitators can make to young people is coaching and guiding them in learning new skills relevant to what they want to achieve related to their social, school, and work arenas. In the TIP model, skill development refers to teaching skills in community settings that will equip youth and young adults with the competencies to meet the demands they will encounter in functioning in everyday life (Benz & Lindstrom, 1997; Bullis & Fredericks, 2002; Bullis, Tehan, & Clark, 2000).

Creative teachers and independent-living specialists can make their classroom instruction more community relevant to students by (1) bringing real-life stimulus materials and situations into their classrooms (for example, set up student bank accounts), (2) building on students' preferences and interests in the assignments, and (3) providing students with effective, individualized instruction to teach skills that are relevant to their daily lives. Researchers have found that youth taught with these instructional strategies tend to increase their ability to acquire the necessary skills, become more motivated to learn new skills, generalize learning to other settings, and decrease their problem behaviors (Foster-Johnson, Ferro, & Dunlap, 1992; Van Reusen & Bos, 1994).

To build competency in young people, transition facilitators and other personnel working with transition-age young people need to be comfortable in multiple roles. They must be effective teachers as well as behavior specialists, counselors, service brokers, collaborators, and mentors. As teachers, they need to be able to create and recognize opportunities to teach or, stated another way, to create and recognize "teachable moments."

### Youth Perspectives Regarding a Focus on Building Competency and Skills

Youth in Taylor's (2007) study described their need to develop life, work, and study skills (Table 11.3). It is important to note that these skills tended to "stick" better when taught in the context of ongoing, supportive relationships focused on multiple domains, not in narrowly focused one-time orientations or interactions.

Most youth in the Deschênes et al. (2005) study had exposure to school-sponsored work and volunteer projects to help them gain skills and competencies necessary for independent community living. These experiences also introduce young people to work and educational options that allowed them to explore their interests. For example, Charley's transition facilitator took him and other young people in the school's EBD program who wanted to explore working outdoors to volunteer at a landscaping nursery. In contrast, Madeline, who wanted to explore the health care arena, secured a practicum placement at a nursing home. Madeline discovered that "I didn't have much patience. . . . I couldn't handle it." Later, at a daycare center, Madeline discovered a skill and an interest in childcare: "With them, I have all the patience in the world. They help me whenever I'm like in a sad mood or something. They lift

**TABLE 11.3    Skills Young Adults Learned or Wanted to Learn
from Adults**

- Find, connect with, and self-advocate to access needed services
- Call a potential employer
- Build a network of professional colleagues
- Resolve conflicts with supervisors, peers, and others
- Navigate bureaucratic systems
- Work in a team environment
- Stay focused on long-term goals
- Manage money
- Complete the community college enrollment process
- Dress professionally
- Write college admissions essays
- Show respect for people in positions of authority

my spirit." Lucia's volunteer experience at the Boys and Girls Club turned into a part-time job. There she found an outlet for her desire to play sports and discovered an interest in working with children. She also learned to anticipate and control her behavior. "Our after-school program kept me up when I was down. If I had a bad day in school, I used to say maybe I'd have a better day tomorrow at the Boys and Girls Club."

In addition to skills that are directly applicable to employment, young people also learn important "soft" skills in volunteer and work settings. In the study of successful youth, some participants learned techniques such as reframing to deal with obstacles (impulsivity and anger, for example) that they encountered on the road to success. Consider the case of Lucia, the young woman who had lived in over 40 foster homes, who came to define success for herself as "staying out of trouble" and behaving well. During the interview, she recalled an incident that occurred at the Boys and Girls Club when, in anger, she broke one of the doors. Her foster mother was called in and she "got in trouble." Lucia said that she still gets angry now but does not "retaliate like that anymore." She developed a self-taught process where she learned to talk her anger and feelings out before "it bubbles up. I talk to family. . . . I talk to them on the phone and hang out with my friends. But anything they want to do illegal or I don't like, I won't do with them." Why? "Because it's not the right thing to do. Drug stuff is bad for you. I know drugs personally. You get addicted to drugs. Drugs can slow you down in your life from your goals that you want to reach in the future."

## Guideline 6: Maintain an Outcome Focus in the TIP System at the Individual, Program, and Community Levels

- Focus on a young person's goals and the tracking of his or her progress.
- Evaluate the responsiveness and effectiveness of the TIP system.
- Use process and outcome measures for continual TIP system improvement.

The five guidelines previously discussed involve processes that can assist youth and young adults in achieving successful outcomes across the transition domains. For each transition goal established by the young person, written, measurable objectives should be established so that progress on individualized goals and successes can be tracked over time.

The effectiveness of the system can be assessed through key outcome indicators based on the young adult's outcomes in the four transition domains. For example, aggregation of data about employment goals allows for determination of the percentage of young people who (1) are employed part time and full time, (2) are earning wages at or above a certain amount per hour, (3) have employer-paid benefits, and (4) are in jobs on career tracks that they want to pursue. These key outcome indicators, if tracked over an extended period of time, can provide stakeholders, grant writers, and policy makers with valuable information on the effectiveness of the TIP system.

Transition progress across the domains can be assessed periodically through the use of the Transition to Adulthood Program Information System (TAPIS) Progress Tracker V4.0 (Clark & Deschênes, 2009). The purpose of the TAPIS Progress Tracker is to measure a young person's progress or difficulty over time across the transition domains.

Unless the TIP guidelines and practices are incorporated adequately, individual and systemic outcomes will not be achieved. Thus, measures of process implementation for system improvement assist stakeholders by providing them with a periodic check of the state of the TIP model's responsiveness in providing high-quality services and supports. For additional information regarding instruments related to process and outcome measures, please refer to Dresser et al., 2009; the Theory and Research section of the TIP website (http://tip.fmhi.usf.edu); and the Evaluation and Resource sections of the National Network for Youth Transition website (http://nnyt.fmhi.usf.edu).

### Youth Perspectives Regarding an Outcomes Focus

An outcomes focus provides a structure and a means for youth, their families, providers, and others to measure and recognize progress. Youth in Taylor's (2007) study expressed a need for people in their support network to celebrate their accomplishments. Youth need to feel that their progress, strengths, and special talents are seen and appreciated. Clear expectations and rewards for completion of steps motivated the youth in this study.

Some participants in the Deschênes et al. (2005) study described success as making plans and succeeding in those plans. One participant said, "It doesn't matter what you do as long as you do what you set out to do. That's successful."

An illustration of how to involve young people in the quality improvement and evaluation of a transition system is provided in Clark, Deschênes et al. (2008). That chapter also describes the use of logic models, program manuals, and community resource mapping in the planning and sustainability of a transition system.

## Guideline 7: Involve Young People, Parents, and Other Community Partners in the TIP System at the Practice, Program, and Community Levels

- Maximize the involvement of young people, family members, informal and formal key players, and other community representatives.
- Tap the talents of peers and mentors:

    Hire young adults as peer mentors and peer counselors.

    Assist young people in creating peer support groups and youth leadership opportunities.

Use paid and unpaid mentors (such as coworker mentors, college mentors, or apartment roommate mentors).

- Partner with young people, parents, and others in TIP system governance and stewardship.

- Advocate for system development, expansion, and evaluation, as well as for reform of funding and policy to facilitate implementation of responsive, effective community transition systems for youth and young adults and their families.

As the previous six guidelines illustrate, transition facilitators and others working with youth and young adults should respect and encourage young people's connections with their natural and community supports. Although certain formal support personnel may wish to remain connected with a young person for extended periods, all too often funding or other eligibility criteria result in termination of this formal linkage. Whatever can be done to assist young people in maintaining and extending their positive natural and community supports will be essential to the young person's short-term and long-term success.

Peer mentors and other natural mentors can often relate to young people and share experiences with them that parents and other formal providers cannot communicate effectively. The talents of peers and other mentors can be tapped in many creative ways. For example, in college and work settings, students and employees can be trained to serve as student or coworker mentors who provide one-on-one guidance on getting oriented to the expectations of the setting, learning the relevant skills and tasks, and negotiating the social aspects of the setting. TIP systems that hire peer mentors and peer counselors to work in collaboration with transition facilitators report that this arrangement is typically beneficial for both the mentors and the young people with whom they are working.

The greater the sense of ownership that young people, parents, and others have in the TIP system, the more likely it is that the system will be valued and have an impact. The involvement of young people and parents in the governance (such as participation on management boards, decision making, advisory committee roles) of a community TIP system increases the likelihood that the system will be tailored to their needs and cultural/familial/developmental values and perspectives (West, Fetzer, Graham, & Keller, 2000). A typical side effect of this involvement is "ownership" (Hatter, Williford, & Dickens, 2000).

Parents and young people can often bring more clout to bear with policy makers than can practitioners, educators, and other professionals working in the human service and educational sectors. Some program and research professionals are coming to understand the importance of partnering with parent advocates on many fronts (such as planning community programs, designing research and evaluation, and testifying before legislative bodies). For example, at a state legislative hearing, a researcher can present research findings regarding the need for and effectiveness of a program, and the advocate can give the issue a human face and clout ("I represent a state advocacy organization of 1,100 families").

### Youth Perspectives Regarding Involvement at the Practice, Program, and System Levels

In Taylor's (2007) study, Kyle was involved in multiple statewide youth organizations related to foster youth and transgender youth. Kyle is an energetic, outspoken young man, and his involvement in these organizations not only provided an important service to his community but also gave him opportunities to build skills, foster positive relationships, and cope with challenges. Through Kyle's work, he developed public speaking, networking, and organizing skills that will serve him throughout life. As a transgender foster youth, he sometimes experienced loneliness, and his involvement with these youth organizations helped him to connect with others in similar circumstances. Finally, though he experienced many setbacks, these youth organizations provided a vehicle for him to cope with the challenges and use his personal experience to help others—a positive coping strategy. There are many articulate, energetic youth like Kyle who, with support and mentorship, can use their experiences to improve practice, programs, and systems for youth, and vigorous efforts must be made to empower them.

In our work with transition sites in communities across the country, we have seen the power of youth voice and action. For more illustrations of the voice and role of youth and young adults in community transition systems and state and national policy review and leadership, please refer to Galasso et al. (2009) and Matarese et al. (2008).

## Young Adult Perspectives: Descriptions of the Two Studies from Which Case Examples and Quotations Were Drawn

### Study 1: 'Cause I want to do something with myself: Vulnerable emerging adults navigate transitions to school and work (Taylor, 2007)

Taylor's study of transitions to school and work for vulnerable youth included five (in a sample of eleven) who were currently receiving community mental health services; their stories are highlighted in this chapter. The remaining youth in the study were considered vulnerable because they were involved in other government systems such as foster care or special education and/or were very low income (Osgood, Foster, Flanagan, & Ruth, 2005). Participants were ages 19 through 23 and engaged in a work or school transition at their time of entry to the study. Youth were tracked for an average of 3.8 months, during which time they participated in five in-person meetings (one brief screening and four in-depth interviews). Each youth was also asked to identify "a person who knows you well," and this person was interviewed by phone to provide an additional perspective on the youth's transition to work or school and the supports needed. Data were collected in the San Francisco Bay Area between March 2006 and February 2007. The case studies of youth with EBD, from Taylor (2007), listed with the youths' school/work transition status at time of entry to the study were as follows:

- David—A 19-year-old male in transition from a nonpublic school to a 2-year college and planning to begin working part-time
- Thomas—A 23-year-old male currently attending a 2-year college and engaged in a work transition
- Helen—A 22-year-old female currently attending a 2-year college and planning to begin working
- Trisha—A 23-year-old female, planning to begin working
- Kyle—A 20-year-old male currently attending a 2-year college and engaged in a work transition

One of the goals of Taylor's (2007) research was to develop a greater understanding of how youth conceptualize support—that is, the specific behaviors and communications that are helpful to them during times of transition. Though Taylor's research was not a study of the TIP model, it is notable that many of the themes that emerged overlap with TIP guidelines.

In discussing support systems for youth with EBD, it is important to remember that youth are not passive recipients of assistance, whether formal or informal. Their interactions with family, friends, counselors, employers, and others are dynamic. Young adults are capable of consenting to treatment, and, unless they are court-mandated to receive services, they are active in the process of choosing, negotiating, and using supportive relationships to help them meet their goals. Thus, it is essential that supportive services empower youth and respond to their needs.

Youth in Taylor's study described needing support in three broad categories: tangible support, teaching/mentoring, and developmentally appropriate connections with people and programs. These broad categories of need were voiced by all of the youth in the sample regardless of mental health status or other personal characteristics. Because this chapter focuses on the TIP model, not means-tested public assistance, only teaching/mentoring support and developmentally appropriate connections were described.

Needs were asked about directly and indirectly. In a follow-up question about youths' goals, they were asked, "What will help you achieve these goals?" In the last interview with participants, they were also asked, "If my dreams as a researcher were to come true, and Congress were going to read my study and spend money to help young people like you, what should it spend the money on? What kinds of programs and services do young people need?"

Needs were also discussed indirectly throughout the interviews. For example, in the course of telling a story about an attempt to obtain employment, a youth might discuss the behaviors of certain individuals, and how they helped or hindered the process, or talk about the people or things that would have been helpful had they been available. In analysis, these instances were coded as "support," "hindrance," or "wishes" and later examined to determine whether, as well as how, needs were met.

### Study 2: Transition to adulthood roles: Young adults' perspectives on factors contributing to success (Deschênes et al., 2005)

The purpose of this "success" study was to gain a better understanding of the experiences and perspectives of young adults who are considered to have achieved some indicators of success in their transitions to adulthood. The study addressed the research question, "What factors enable young people with emotional or behavioral disturbances (EBD) to successfully transition to adulthood?"

In this study, success was defined as a multidimensional concept that encompassed factors such as educational achievements, career and employment status, independent living, personal and social relationships, and social-emotional adjustment and functioning. Success was also defined as movement toward acceptable adult behavior, achievements in relation to society's norms, and developmental state (for example, improved graduation rate from regular high school, finding and keeping a job, entering a postsecondary educational program, and living on one's own). Participant recruitment was done from four Transition to Independence Process (TIP) sites in Florida, whose staff were asked to nominate young people who met all of the following qualifications: (1) had a history of EBD, (2) received some transition-to-adulthood services, (3) graduated from high school, and (4) overcame significant challenges to achieve noteworthy accomplishments.

Researchers used the Success Interview protocol, a data collection instrument containing open-ended questions, to interview seven young adult participants. In accordance with Smith's (1995) funneling technique, whereby the literature and previous analyzed data drove the directions of the questions, the open-ended interviews (Patton, 1990) encouraged the interviewees to describe their real-life experiences, to share what they view as effective transition supports and services, and to offer advice. Data from the seven interviews were analyzed using Glaser and Strauss's (1967) constant comparison method for the development of grounded theory. Reliability was addressed through inter-rater agreement regarding the interpretation of the data (Miles & Huberman, 1994).

Qualitative analysis yielded the following patterns of factors associated with successful transitions to adulthood.

**Theme 1: Goal Orientation.** Most of the participants were future and goal oriented. They had a sense of purpose, a focus, and a direction. All had practical, realistic, attainable aspirations that were very similar to the goals and aspirations of their peers with no disability. Although most young people interviewed seemed to realize it may be more difficult for them to achieve their dreams than it would be for youth who do not have EBD, they all seemed ready to do what needed to be done to accomplish what they wished to accomplish in the future.

**Theme 2: Interests and Abilities.** Youth in our sample seemed to have the ability to recognize and integrate their particular interests and abilities in everything they set out to do. Many had exposure to school-sponsored work and volunteer projects in areas of interest to them. In these projects, they learned job-related skills, refined their cognitive skills, developed support networks, and increased their self-confidence.

**Theme 3: Creative Coping Strategies.** To adapt to their often-difficult situations, the young people interviewed found strategies to cope and perform well. A variety of skills-building techniques, such as reframing or use of anger management techniques, gave the young people ways to deal with obstacles encountered on the road to success. Whether in school or on the job, most youth interviewed were willing to make sacrifices and extend extra efforts demanded by their particular situation in order to succeed. All were prepared to work hard and persist in achieving their goals.

**Theme 4: Social Support.** All of the participants recognized the need for support and took advantage of the help they could access along the way to overcome hurdles and cope with difficult situations. Most young people developed and used a network of positive and supportive people including family members, relatives, friends, community organizations, teachers, coworkers, transition facilitators, and others on whom they could rely. Support was provided to them in many forms including emotional, instrumental, and informational support. Appraisal support providing information useful for self-evaluation, constructive feedback, and affirmation was also provided.

**Theme 5: Role Models.** Finally, many of these young people had positive role models who provided encouragement and demonstrated, through their own experiences, how to succeed in the face of challenges. Many participants named role models from within the immediate family; however, some named extended family, teachers, and one celebrity. Participants had some connection with the named role model. The primary connection was a familial relationship. Other connections were a perceived shared challenge that led the young person to believe that if the role model could over-come challenge, then he or she could do the same.

The findings from this "success" study yielded a pattern of supports and services that these young adults suggested contributed to their progress and success in transitioning to adulthood roles. The implications for practitioners, educators, program administrators, and policy makers are that programs and policies should support the development of community transition systems that

- Incorporate the young person's future focus in transition planning and services
- Base transition plans on early identification of the youth's abilities and interests
- Teach creative coping techniques
- Ensure continuous and consistent social support
- Encourage young people to identify and learn from role models

These features are components of the Transition to Independence Process (TIP) model that is now considered an evidence-supported practice (Clark & Hart, 2009; Clark, Koroloff, Geller, & Sondheimer, 2008).

## CONCLUSION

This chapter describes the Transition to Independence Process (TIP) model, which is an evidence-supported practice for the provision of supports and services to youth and young adults with EBD (Clark & Hart, 2009; Clark & Unruh, 2009a). The TIP model has been developed, researched, and refined over the past 15 years with input from young people, parents, practitioners, teachers, program administrators, researchers, and policy makers. As you have read throughout this chapter, youth and young adults continue to call for developmentally appropriate, nonstigmatizing, and appealing supports and services that are tailored to their needs, interests, and goals across the transition domains that are relevant to them (Deschênes et al., 2005; Taylor, 2007).

In addition to the young adults, Taylor's (2007) study included interviews with "someone who knows you well." The following quotation, by Kyle's mentor, describes his role and the support that the mentor found most helpful in working with Kyle.

> I think what works best with Kyle—I've tried being a stern
> parental figure, being a big brother, being a distant mentor—
> the struggle with being the good buddy—I don't see how that
> changes his behavior. We have a few laughs and that's it.
> What I try to do is make him feel secure in our relationship—
> validate the feelings—acknowledge that he's come from hard-
> ship. He can achieve success—he has a myriad of skills that are
> available to him. I try to treat him with more respect. I haven't
> always treated him with respect, and I think a lot of people
> do that with youth—now I meet him where he's at.

Through a trial-and-error process, Kyle's mentor arrived naturally at a person-centered planning approach by respecting Kyle, reflecting Kyle's feelings, and seeing Kyle's strengths. The fact that Kyle's mentor ultimately succeeded in finding a role that he felt was most supportive to Kyle should be hopeful to providers working with young people with EBD.

The beauty of the TIP model is that it provides practitioners and educators with the principles and practices for engaging, coaching, teaching, and partnering with young people in ways that maximize the likelihood of them setting and achieving short-term and long-term goals. There are now six published studies demonstrating that the TIP model can improve progress and outcomes with these young people across employment, career-type schooling, personal adjustment, and community-life functioning. We hope that the TIP model practices and young people's voices and perspectives that we have shared throughout this chapter might assist you in the effectiveness of your work with young people.

For more information regarding the TIP model, the quality improvement methods, and research findings, please refer to the transition handbook (Clark & Unruh, 2009a) and visit the TIP website (http://tip.fmhi.usf.edu) and the National Network on Youth Transition (NNYT) website (http://nnyt.fmhi.usf.edu).

## REFERENCES

Armstrong, K. H., Dedrick, R. F., & Greenbaum, P. E. (2003). Factors associated with community adjustment of young adults with serious emotional disturbance: A longitudinal analysis. *Journal of Emotional and Behavioral Disorders, 11*(2), 66–76.

Benz, M. R., & Lindstrom, L. E. (1997). *Building school-to-work programs: Strategies for youth with special needs.* Austin: Pro-Ed.

Bullis, M., & Fredericks, H. D. (Eds.). (2002). *Vocational and transition services for adolescents with emotional and behavioral disorders: Strategies and best practices.* Champaign, IL: Research Press.

Bullis, M., Tehan, C. J., & Clark, H. B. (2000). Teaching and developing improved community life competencies. In H.B. Clark & M. Davis (Eds.), *Transition to adulthood: A resource for assisting young people with emotional or behavioral difficulties* (pp. 107–131). Baltimore: Paul H. Brookes.

Clark, H. B., & Davis, M. (Eds.). (2000). *Transition to adulthood: A resource for assisting young people with emotional or behavioral difficulties.* Baltimore: Paul H. Brookes.

Clark, H. B., & Deschênes, N. (2009). *Transition to Adulthood Program Information System: Progress Tracker (4.0).* Tampa: University of South Florida, National Network on Youth Transition for Behavioral Health.

Clark, H. B., Deschênes, N., & Jones, J. (2000). A framework for the development and operation of a transition system. In H. B. Clark & M. Davis (Eds.), *Transition to adulthood: A resource for assisting young people with emotional or behavioral difficulties* (pp. 29–51). Baltimore: Paul H. Brookes.

Clark, H. B., Deschênes, N., Sieler, D., Green, M., White, G., & Sondheimer, D. (2008). Services for youth in transition to adulthood in systems of care. In B. A. Stroul & G. M. Blau (Eds.), *The system of care handbook: Transforming mental health services for children, youth, and families* (pp. 491–516). Baltimore: Paul H. Brookes.

Clark, H. B., & Foster-Johnson, L. (1996). Serving youth in transition to adulthood. In B. A. Stroul (Ed.), *Children's mental health: Creating systems of care in a changing society* (pp. 533–551). Baltimore: Paul H. Brookes.

Clark, H. B., & Hart, K. (2009). Navigating the obstacle course: An evidence-supported community transition system. In H. B. Clark & D. K. Unruh (Eds.), *Transition of young people with emotional or behavioral difficulties: An evidence-supported handbook* (pp. 47–113). Baltimore: Paul H. Brookes.

Clark, H. B., Karpur, A., Deschênes, N., Gamache, P., & Haber, M. (2008). Partnerships for Youth Transition (PYT): Overview of community initiatives and preliminary findings on transition to adulthood for youth and young adults with mental health challenges. In C. Newman, C. Liberton, K. Kutash, & R. M. Friedman (Eds.), *The 20th annual research conference proceedings: A system of care for children's mental health: Expanding the research base* (pp. 329–332). Tampa: University of South Florida, Louis de la Parte Florida Mental Health Institute, Research and Training Center for Children's Mental Health.

Clark, H. B., Koroloff, N., Geller, J., & Sondheimer, D. L. (2008). Research on transition to adulthood: Building the evidence base to inform services and supports for youth and young adults with serious mental health disorders. *Journal of Behavioral Health Services and Research, 35*(4), 365–372.

Clark, H. B., Pschorr, O., Wells, P., Curtis, M., & Tighe, T. (2004). Transition into community roles for young people with emotional or behavioral difficulties: Collaborative systems and program outcomes. In D. Cheney (Ed.), *Transition of secondary approaches for positive outcomes* (pp. 201–226.). Arlington, VA: Council for Children with Behavioral Disorders and the Division of Career Development and Transition, Divisions of the Council for Exceptional Children.

Clark, H. B., & Unruh, D. (2009a). *Transition of young people with emotional or behavioral difficulties: An evidence-supported handbook.* Baltimore: Paul H. Brookes.

Clark, H. B., & Unruh, D. (2009b). Understanding and addressing the needs of transition-age youth and young adults and their families. In H. B. Clark & D. K. Unruh (Eds.), *Transition of young people with emotional or behavioral difficulties: An evidence-supported handbook* (pp. 3–22 ). Baltimore: Paul H. Brookes.

Davis, M. (2003). Addressing the needs of youth in transition to adulthood. *Administration and Policy in Mental Health, 30*(6), 495–509.

Davis, M. (2005). *Youth and young adults with serious mental health conditions in transition to adulthood.* Briefing paper for Center for Mental Health Services Transition Policy Meeting. Rockville, MD: Center for Mental Health Services and the Substance Abuse and Mental Health Services Administration.

Deschênes, N., & Clark, H. B. (1998). Seven best practices in transition programs for youth. *Reaching Today's Youth: The Community Circle of Caring Journal, 2*(4), 44–48.

Deschênes, N., Herrygers, J., & Clark, H. B. (2005). Successful pathway to adulthood: Success study. In M. Sarkis & H. B. Clark (Eds.), *Transition to Independence (TIP) study report: Preparing and facilitating transition into adulthood for students with EBD. Final report to Office of Special Education and Rehabilitation Services, U. S. Department of Education.* Tampa: University of South Florida, Louis de la Parte Florida Mental Health Institute.

Dresser, K., Zucker, P., Orlando, R., Krynski, A., White, G., Karpur, A., & Unruh, D. (2009). Quality improvement: Process, progress, outcome tools and strategies: Envisioning a collaborative system for quality improvement. In H. B. Clark & D. K. Unruh (Eds.), *Transition of young people with emotional or behavioral difficulties: An evidence-supported handbook* (pp. 291–321). Baltimore: Paul H. Brookes.

Foster-Johnson, L., Ferro, J., & Dunlap, G. (1992, November). *Does curriculum affect students' behavior?* Paper presented at the 37th Annual Conference of the Florida Educational Research Association, Winter Park, FL.

Galasso, L. Arrell, A., Webb, P., Landsman, S., Holmes, D. Ahearn, K., & Clark, H. B. (2009). More than friends: Peer supports for youth and young adults to promote discovery and recovery. In H. B. Clark & D. K. Unruh (Eds.), *Transition of young people with emotional or behavioral difficulties: An evidence-supported handbook* (pp. 209–232). Baltimore: Paul H. Brookes.

Glaser, B., & Strauss, A. (1967). *The discovery of grounded theory: Strategies for qualitative research.* Chicago: Aldine.

Haber, M., Clark, H. B., & Parenteau, R. (2009). Prevention planning: Addressing risk behaviors and situations with youth and young adults. In H. B. Clark & D. K. Unruh (Eds.), *Transition of young people with emotional or behavioral difficulties: An evidence-supported handbook* (pp. 235–262). Baltimore: Paul H. Brookes.

Hagner, D., Cheney, D., & Malloy, J. (1999). Career-related outcomes of a model transition demonstration for young adults with emotional disturbance. *Rehabilitation Counseling Bulletin, 42*(3), 228–242.

Hatter, R. A., Williford, M., & Dickens, K. (2000). Nurturing and working in partnership with parents during transition. In H. B. Clark & M. Davis (Eds.), *Transition to adulthood: A resource for assisting young people with emotional or behavioral difficulties* (pp. 209–228). Baltimore: Paul H. Brookes.

Isaacs, M. R., Jackson, V. H., Hicks, R., & Wang, E. K. S. (2008). Cultural and linguistic competence and eliminating disparities. In B. A. Stroul & G. M. Blau (Eds.), *The system of care handbook: Transforming mental health services for children, youth, and families* (pp. 201–228). Baltimore: Paul H. Brookes.

Karpur, A., Clark, H. B., Caproni, P., & Sterner, H. (2005). Transition to adult roles for students with emotional/behavioral disturbances: A follow-up study of student exiters from a transition program. *Career Development for Exceptional Individuals, 28*(1), 36–46.

Koroloff, N., Pullmann, M., & Gordon, L. (2008). Investigating the relationship between services and outcomes in a program for transition-age youth. In C. Newman, C. Liberton, K. Kutash, & R. M. Friedman (Eds.), *The 20th annual research conference proceedings: A system of care for children's mental health: Expanding the research base* (pp. 326–329). Tampa: University of South Florida, Louis de la Parte Florida Mental Health Institute, Research and Training Center for Children's Mental Health.

Mallory, B. (1995). The role of social policy in life-cycle transitions. *Exceptional Children, 62*(3), 213–224.

Matarese, M., Carpenter, M., Huffine, C., Lane, S., & Paulson, K. (2008). Partnerships with youth for youth-guided systems of care. In B. A. Stroul & G. M. Blau (Eds.), *The system of care handbook: Transforming mental health services for children, youth, and families* (pp. 275–300). Baltimore: Paul H. Brookes.

Miles, M., & Huberman, A. (1994). *Qualitative data analysis: An expanded sourcebook*. Thousand Oaks, CA: Sage Publications.

Osgood, D., Foster, E. M., Flanagan, C., & Ruth, G. (2005). Introduction: Why focus on the transition to adulthood for vulnerable populations? In D. Osgood, E. M. Foster, C. Flanagan, & G. Ruth (Eds.), *On your own without a net: The transition to adulthood for vulnerable populations* (pp. 1–26). Chicago: University of Chicago Press.

Patton, M. Q. (1990). *Qualitative evaluation and research methods* (2nd ed.). Newbury Park, CA: Sage Publications.

Ryndak, D., Downing, J., Lilly, J. R., & Morrison, A. (1995). Parents' perceptions after inclusion of their children with moderate or severe disabilities. *Journal of the Association for Persons with Severe Handicaps, 20*(2), 147–157.

Sarkis, M., & Clark, H.B. (2005). *Transition to Independence Process (TIP) study: Preparing and facilitating transition into adulthood for students with EBD. Final Report to the Office of Special Education and Rehabilitation Services, U. S. Department of Education.* Tampa: University of South Florida, Louis de la Parte Florida Mental Health Institute.

Schulenberg, J., & Maggs, J. (2002). A developmental perspective on alcohol use and heavy drinking during adolescence and the transition to young adulthood. *Journal of Studies on Alcohol, 14*(Suppl.), 54–70.

Smith, J. (1995). Semi-structured interviewing and qualitative analysis. In J. Smith, R. Harre, & L. VanLangenhove (Eds.), *Rethinking methods in psychology* (pp. 9–26). London: Sage Publications.

Taylor, S. A. (2007). 'Cause I want to do something with myself: Vulnerable emerging adults navigate transitions to school and work. Doctoral dissertation, University of California, Berkeley. Retrieved January 24, 2009, from

Dissertations & Theses Database, University of California (Publication No. AAT 3306362).

Unruh, D., & Clark, H. B. (2009). Futures focus: Practice, program, system, policy, and research. In H. B. Clark & D. K. Unruh (Eds.), *Transition of young people with emotional or behavioral difficulties: An evidence-supported handbook* (pp. 325–343). Baltimore: Paul H. Brookes.

VanDenBerg, J., & Grealish, M. (1996). Individualized services and supports through the wraparound process: Philosophy and procedures. *Journal of Child and Family Studies, 5*(1), 7–21.

Van Reusen, A. K., & Bos, C. S. (1994). Facilitating student participation in individualized education programs through motivation strategy instruction. *Exceptional Children, 60*(5), 466–475.

Vander Stoep, A., Bersford, S., Weiss, N. S., McKnight, B., Cauce, A. M., & Cohen, P. (2000). Community-based study of the transition to adulthood for adolescents with psychiatric disorder. *American Journal of Epidemiology, 152,* 353–362.

Wagner, M., Newman, L., Cameto, R., Garza, N., & Levine, P. (2005). *After high school: A first look at the post-school experiences of youth with disabilities. Report from the National Longitudinal Transition Study-2 (NLTS-2).* Menlo Park, CA: SRI International.

West, T. E., Fetzer, P. M., Graham, C., & Keller, J. (2000). Driving the system through young adult involvement and leadership. In H. B. Clark & M. Davis (Eds.), *Transition to adulthood: A resource for assisting young people with emotional or behavioral difficulties* (pp. 195–208). Baltimore: Paul H. Brookes.

# Transition Approaches for Students with EBD in Juvenile Justice

## CHAPTER 12

# Project STAY OUT: A Facility-to-Community Transition Intervention Targeting Incarcerated Adolescent Offenders

**Deanne Unruh, Miriam Waintrup, and Tim Canter**

There is little question that youth with emotional or behavioral disorders (EBD) face numerous difficulties in their developmental trajectory from adolescence to young adulthood compared with their peers from public schools. However, youth with EBD who have been incarcerated are faced with an additional obstacle along the path from the youth correctional institution to the community and on into adulthood. This unique process adds additional—and significant—challenges for these individuals to achieve positive adult outcomes.

Annually, in the United States more than 2.2 million juveniles are arrested, with more than 110,000 juveniles incarcerated in juvenile correctional facilities (Snyder & Sickmund, 2006). Not only are these adjudicated adolescents at increased risk of committing future crimes (Bullis, Yovanoff, Mueller, & Havel, 2002; McCord, 1992), they are additionally at risk of not becoming healthy, productive adults. Their continued criminality jeopardizes stable employment, career, and living options. Juvenile criminal behaviors additionally strain the resources of our legal and justice systems, burden victims and their families, and increase costs for medical and social services (Cohen, 1998). States report an average recidivism rate of nearly 55% at 12 months post-release for juvenile offenders. Costs associated with this incarceration rate are of concern (Snyder & Sickmund, 2006). Decreasing juvenile offender recidivism rates—and thereby greatly reducing the costs associated with incarcerating adolescents—can be achieved by implementing interventions that target the community adjustment process for youth with EBD leaving a correctional settting. In Washington state, the implementation of evidenced-based practices was found to reduce the need for future prison beds, thus saving money for state and local taxpayers and contributing to lower crime rates (Aos, Miller, & Drake, 2006).

Youth with EBD clearly are represented within the juvenile offending population and demonstrate poor employment rates. Transition outcomes for youth placed in the juvenile justice system are just as dismal. A 5-year longitudinal study of 531 youth, TRACS (Transition Research on Adolescents returning to Community Settings), examined their transition outcomes after leaving Oregon's juvenile correctional facilities and returning to communities on parole (Bullis et al., 2002). Within this sample, almost 60% returned to the juvenile justice system or were committed to the adult correctional system. Only a quarter enrolled in school, and fewer received a high-school completion document. Employment rates were disturbingly low—averaging less than 30%—and only a portion (about 35%) were engaged in either school or work. Few in the sample received services from community-based social agencies. When compared to participants without disabilities, those with a special education disability (58% of the total sample) were almost three times more likely than those without a disability to return to the correctional system and two times less likely to become involved in work or school. These results are especially important because participants who were engaged in work and/or school immediately after leaving juvenile custody were 2.8 times more likely to stay out of the correctional system than youth who were not so engaged.

The effect of these positive activities was especially pronounced for youth with disabilities. Those with disabilities who were working or going to school during the first 6 months after leaving custody were 3.2 times less likely to return to custody and 2.5 times more likely to remain working and/or in school 12 months after leaving the correctional facility. Clearly, youth who become engaged in work and/or school fared better in their transition than those who did not become engaged; this finding has obvious implications for service delivery.

In treatment planning, youth with EBD and other disabling conditions in the juvenile justice system often are overlooked in the implementation of and adherence to special education transition policies and regulations (Leone, Meisel, & Drakeford, 2002). As a result, the reentry outcomes for formerly incarcerated youth with a special education and/or mental health disorder are dismal compared to peers with and without disabilities (Bullis et al., 2002), and longitudinal studies suggest that many youth displaying criminal behavior will manifest continuing problems, at least to some degree, in their work, school, and family endeavors as adults (McCord, 1992). Youth with disabilities and/or mental health needs compose 40% to 70% of all incarcerated youth, compared to 10% to 12% of youth in the general population (Leone, Rutherford, & Nelson, 1991). Such a broad range of identified youth with disabilities exists as a result of systemic issues related to documenting special education and mental health disorders in the juvenile justice system. States have different mechanisms for counting and documenting individuals with disabilities. In addition, many youths' educational files may never reach a correctional facility, and those youth therefore are not accurately identified for special education services. At times, when files are found and arrive in the correctional facilities, special education assessments and plans are outdated and no longer valid, or the youth has opted out of special education services. Therefore, in this chapter we target literature that globally addresses the needs of specific transition-related services for individuals with disabilities in general. Subsequently, the fact that youth are involved in the juvenile justice system suggests that behavioral interventions would benefit these youth.

Despite the logic of providing transition services to youth in a seamless manner from the facility to the community, service coordination for adolescents with EBD is difficult. Barriers to providing a coordinated set of services is often hampered as these youth shift from child-centered social service agencies to adult-oriented agencies. This transition is complicated and difficult, which may result in diminished or ineffectual services resulting from the gaps of services among many of the agencies needed to support a youth's positive community adjustment (Vander Stoep, Davis, & Collins, 2000). Not only do these youth with EBD face individual barriers to success, but service coordination for these youth transitioning into adulthood presents a barrier.

In light of these challenges for juvenile offenders with EBD, coupled with poor service coordination to support these youth in transition, representatives of the Oregon Department of Education, Oregon Youth Authority, and the University of Oregon initiated planning in May 1998 to address these issues. The working session established the framework for a multiagency project centered on developing a collaborative process to serve incarcerated youth with disabilities (the majority with EBD) as they transitioned from a long-term correctional setting into the community. The remainder of this chapter describes the development and implementation of a multiagency state agency collaboration that has evolved into its current form: Project STAY OUT (Strategies Teaching Adolescent Young Offenders to Use Transition Skills). The preliminary project, Project SUPPORT (Service Utilization Promoting Positive Outcomes in Rehabilitation and Transition for Incarcerated Adolescents with Disabilities), was initiated as a statewide service effort managed by the Oregon Department of Education, Oregon Youth Authority, Oregon Office of Vocational Services, and the University of Oregon. In this chapter, we will use the name STAY OUT.

The project has two broad goals: (1) to develop a systemwide service delivery model resulting in lower rates of recidivism and more positive rates of employment and education outcomes for incarcerated youth with EBD returning to the community and (2) to embed the program model within existing community and state agencies to maintain sustained support for this targeted population. This chapter describes the governance and service delivery structure of the project, the ongoing process evaluation, and lessons learned from the development and implementation of the project.

## PROJECT STAY OUT SERVICE DELIVERY MODEL

The project's service delivery model was developed from existing evaluation literature on programs for youth with EBD (for example, Bullis & Cheney, 1999; Bullis & Fredericks, 2002; Bullis et al., 1994; Clark & Davis, 2000) and juvenile corrections (for example, Altschuler & Armstrong, 1991). We relied on and used recommendations from the field to overcome system barriers for transition coordination (Bridgeo, Davis, & Florida, 2000; Cheney, Hagner, Malloy, Cormier, & Bernstein, 1998; Clark, Deschênes, & Jones, 2000). As we discussed earlier, the TRACS study clearly pointed to the importance of engaging youth in work and/or school in the 12-month period immediately following exit from a correctional facility (Bullis & Yovanoff, 1997). Using this evidence, the planning team determined that project services offered to each participant must begin while the individual is in the correctional facility to ensure that services are accessed immediately upon exiting custody. The service delivery model's cornerstone is a transition specialist who works closely with facility treatment and education staff and the parole officer to ensure appropriate services are ready for the youth to access upon release from custody.

In 1999, four regions, both rural and urban, were selected from across the state as pilot sites. At the initiation of the project, these regions participated in an initial needs assessment to define existing barriers and supports present within the regions. A fifth region was added in the second year, and statewide coverage was achieved in the latter half of 2001. From 2001 through 2004, nine transition specialists provided statewide coverage of Project SUPPORT services to youth across Oregon. These transition specialists were employed by local education agencies through contracts from the Oregon Department of Education. In addition, two more transition specialists were added to population-dense regions with funding through a model demonstration grant from the Office of Special Education Programs of the U.S. Department of Education. In 2004, the Oregon Department of Education, in a change of administration, eliminated funding for the project, and only the two urban regions—Lane (Eugene/Springfield) and Multnomah (Portland) counties—maintained transition specialist positions through grant funding that ended in September 2008. The Lane County transition specialist was maintained by school district funding. The Oregon Youth Authority had maintained interest in recreating SUPPORT through developing a localized funding model; therefore, in 2008, the University of Oregon and Oregon Youth Authority collaboratively received a grant from the Office of Juvenile Justice and Delinquency Prevention through the U.S. Department of Justice to develop a localized funding model for the project. This genesis resulted in the name change of the project to STAY OUT, and, in 2009, two regions in Oregon are once again initiating project services.

## GOVERNANCE STRUCTURE

An ongoing strategic planning process at both the administrative and service levels was developed to administer the project and foster its sustainability within the existing education and correctional systems. A state management team consisting of the three state agencies (Department of Education, Office of Vocational Rehabilitation, and Youth Authority ) and the evaluation team of the University of Oregon met monthly to review project progress and to discuss new administrative or legislative changes affecting project services. The management team for STAY OUT was then expanded to include individual representation from the state's Workforce Investment Board, along with staff from the Department of Human Services in the Addiction and Mental Health Department.

Project SUPPORT was funded initially through matching funds from the three state agencies, who formed a cooperative agreement to manage disbursement of funds. With the initiation of Project STAY OUT, a localized funding model is being developed with guidance from the state agency advisory committee. To embed project services within the local communities, a sustainable funding process was defined within existing state fiscal structures through the use of state school funds. The initial start-up funds, through grant dollars, provide an opportunity for collaborative relationships across local agencies and project service and enable funding strategies to be implemented. Local memoranda of understanding provide guidance and identify responsibilities of each agency. To sustain ongoing funding to maintain the transition specialist position, Project STAY OUT uses the average daily membership (ADM) model to count the number of youth served within the project who still are eligible for state school funds. Eligibility for state school funds in Oregon includes any youth who has not received a regular high-school diploma through the age of 19 for general education students and 21 for students with a special education diagnosis. School districts also have the discretion to expand general education student access to education through the age of 21.

Because the transition specialists are school district or education service district employees who provide transition services to support a youth's educational goals and develop employability skills, the services they provide meet the criteria for project youth to qualify for state school support. This funding strategy allows the project to use the existing state school funding model to sustain the project over time. To be supported under this funding model, the transition specialist should maintain a caseload of 12 to 15 youth in the community, along with five or six youth who are receiving transition planning services while they are still in the youth correctional facility.

The state school funding model generally operates in the following manner: All Oregon public school students generate state school support through ADM monies that follow students to the district in which they are enrolled and support educational services provided to these youth. Each student enrolled in a public school is allotted 1.0 ADM, which is then forwarded to the student's district of enrollment. Oregon statutes provide higher levels of state educational support through weighted ADM amounts for populations requiring additional instructional or community services. Weighted ADM monies are allowable for the following categories of students: (1) special education, (2) English-language learners, (3) teen parents, and (4) neglected or delinquent youth status. For example, every student meeting the criteria is allotted 1.0 ADM plus monies attached to any additional category for which he or she is eligible. Youth involved in the juvenile justice system have an extremely high incidence of the characteristics that generate these higher than average levels of ADM support. These monies, as defined through the weighted ADM formulas, provide educational funds toward the additional assistance juvenile corrections students receive to remain in school or toward transition services, such as Project STAY OUT, when they leave public education.

## PROGRAM SERVICES STRUCTURE

Services are provided collaboratively with staff from the multiple agencies identified in each locality, along with community support agencies, including (1) a vocational rehabilitation (VR) counselor, (2) a treatment manager, (3) a parole officer, and (4) facility and community education staff. These staff work in collaboration with a transition specialist who provides direct services to project participants. The initial responsibility of the transition specialist is to define each youth's strengths, needs, interests, and life goals to develop a transition plan with services aligned to the unique needs and interests of each project participant. Services are not a prescriptive set of activities provided to each youth. Instead, services are chosen for each youth based on information and guidance provided to the transition specialist by the youth, parole officer, family, and other agency staff, along with culturally appropriate assessments. After a youth has been screened and referred into the project, services typically occur in three distinct phases: (1) in-facility services, (2) immediate pre-

and post-release activities, and (3) ongoing community support. Table 12.1 illustrates the phases of project services and lists typical activities during each phase.

The service model is considered a "reach-in" model in which the transition specialist spends approximately one-third of his or her time in the facility, with the remaining two-thirds spent in the community. The service model is community focused, and the transition specialists "reach in" to the facility to initiate and plan for services to support the youth's community adjustment process once he or she has exited the correctional facility. The majority of the services provided are conducted while the youth is in the community.

Referral and screening consist of a set of activities coordinated by the transition specialist to identify youth with a special education need or mental disorder who would benefit from school-to-work transition support services. Referrals can be made by any of the three agency staff—treatment manager, parole officer, and facility education staff—or youth may refer themselves to the project. Referrals are optimally made 3 to 6 months before the youth's expected exit date from the correctional facility. After the appropriate transition specialist receives a referral, he or she will have an informal meeting with the youth to assess the youth's interest in participating in the project and his or her motivation for finding employment. The transition specialist also discusses the youth's treatment and education progress with the parole officer, facility treatment managers, and education staff. Initially, project referrals were made from a list of youth residing in a youth correctional facility. Once the project became established and treatment managers, parole officers, and facility education staff became knowledgeable about the project, these staff members became the primary source for referrals.

## In-Facility Activities

Once a youth has been screened into Project STAY OUT, the transition specialist initiates the in-facility activities. The primary purpose of these activities is to develop a positive relationship with the youth and define the transition needs (educational status, pre-employment skills, ongoing treatment needs) for returning to the community. The transition specialist works with facility staff (treatment manager and facility education staff)

**TABLE 12.1   Project STAY OUT: Phases of Service Delivery**

**IN-FACILITY PHASE**
**Activities**
- Build positive relationship between transition specialist and youth.
- Define youth's interests, needs, and life and career goals.
- Develop transition plan.
- Initiate pre-employment skill building with youth.
- Ensure appropriate assessments and identification are available for immediate access to services in community.
- Liaison with parole officer and facility treatment and education staff.

**IMMEDIATE PRE-/POST-RELEASE PHASE (most intensive service phase)**
**Activities**
- Prepare and transfer IEP to community education placement.
- Develop and implement employment options for youth in community.
- Set up needed social services in community (for example, mental health, alcohol and drug treatment).
- Support youth in accessing these services once released (for example, transportation, training).
- Develop youth's independent living skills (for example, budgeting, finding appropriate housing).
- Support and follow parole plan.
- Liaison with parole officer and other needed community support staff.

**ONGOING SUPPORT PHASE**
**Activities**
- Support youth in maintaining engagement activities (such as employment, education, hobbies).
- Further develop youth's independent living skills (for example, paying taxes).
- Assess youth to ensure that former negative behaviors (such as drug use, gang activity) are not returning.
- Continue to liaison with parole officer and other community support staff.

and the youth's parole officer to gather information to develop a project transition plan. After reviewing a youth's records, the transition specialist may find that the youth has a disability that may qualify him or her for VR services. An individual's evaluation documentation (including mental health records and special education assessments) is shared with a VR counselor in the youth's region of exit, and a meeting is scheduled with this counselor to define eligibility for VR services. If a youth is not eligible for VR services, Workforce Investment Act (WIA) services are often available to youth leaving custody because they typically meet the income guidelines for such services. WIA services can support youth in their educational and employment aspirations by providing funds for postsecondary enrollment or vocational training or for employment support (such as employer-supported work experiences or assistance in purchasing work tools or clothing needed for the job).

Additionally, the transition specialist works individually with the youth to learn more about his or her career interests, aptitudes, education goals, and independent living skills. Transition specialists are trained to ensure that both the formal and informal assessments to define a youth's transition plan are culturally specific and appropriate. This phase includes assisting youth to develop skills in the following areas:

- Completing job applications accurately
- Interviewing for jobs
- Completing financial aid paperwork to enroll in school
- Completing tax forms, opening checking accounts, and handling other financial matters
- Obtaining identification documents (Social Security card, birth certificate, etc.)
- Locating appropriate community resources (for example, Narcotics Anonymous or Alcoholics Anonymous) when the youth exits custody

## Immediate Pre- and Post-Release Activities

The most critical phase of the project is immediately before and after parole from the youth correctional facility. The parole officer and transition specialist work very closely together during the immediate pre-

and post-release phase. Their responsibilities are different but both support the community reintegration of the project participant. For example, the parole officer may have specified that the youth obtain a job as part of the parole plan, but it is the transition specialist who works with the youth to accomplish this goal.

While the youth is still in the correctional facility, the transition specialist works closely with the parole officer to begin setting up services to be accessed immediately when the youth enters the community. Typically, these activities consist of assisting the youth to secure employment by connecting him or her with a VR counselor or with local one-stop centers established under the Workforce Investment Act. The transition specialist also provides employability skill development in the community in these ways:

- Coaching the youth in job-search activities, making employer contact, and completing application processes
- Reviewing appropriate attire to wear to interviews
- Job coaching to resolve problems between the employer and the youth, if needed

Other community-based services provided by the transition specialist may include assisting the youth in

- Learning to use public transportation
- Obtaining housing (for example, conducting apartment searches and completing rental applications)
- Continuing to pursue his or her education goals (for example, completing financial aid paperwork or visiting disability services office on community college campuses)
- Navigating the ever-changing health care system (such as obtaining a medical card, making appointments, or securing needed medications)
- Finding healthy leisure activities (such as sports clubs in the neighborhood)

## Ongoing Support Activities

Once a youth has stabilized in the community and is positively engaged in work, school, or a combination of work and school, the transition specialist's role is to continue collaborating with the parole officer to help maintain the youth's engagement in the community. This ongoing support phase includes maintaining contact with the youth, family, parole officer, and other community agencies. The transition specialist primarily serves as a resource and typically provides assistance in

- Continuing to develop employment or education goals (such as getting a promotion or higher-level position and receiving additional employment training)
- Developing higher levels of independent living skills (for example, completing taxes and obtaining car insurance)
- Accessing services related to parenting needs and decisions

In addition, transition specialists are trained to identify signs (such as drug use or affiliating with negative peer groups) of a youth returning to former negative habits. If these signs occur, the parole officer, transition specialist, and youth address these issues.

## ONGOING PROCESS EVALUATION

An ongoing process evaluation was completed during implementation of Project SUPPORT and was continued with the initiation of STAY OUT. In the following section, we discuss the procedures and results of this evaluation to provide a framework for how this project was developed and implemented.

At the initiation of Project SUPPORT and Project STAY OUT, a two-step needs assessment was completed in each locality to identify barriers to and support for project implementation and services. The needs assessment also identified information for the development of a memorandum of understanding. These activities provided baseline information that assisted in development of the collaborative service delivery model.

### Needs Assessment

Seven stakeholder groups were defined as critical partners for inclusion in the development of this project:

1. Incarcerated juvenile offenders with disabilities

2. VR staff

3. Parole officers

4. Facility education staff

5. Facility treatment staff

6. Business community and school-to-work partners

7. Local community service agencies

A nominal group-processing procedure was used in three regional community forums to identify both the supports and barriers present within the local communities to which the incarcerated youth would return. The information from the incarcerated youth interviews and community forums was combined and analyzed as a statewide aggregate and for each region.

Of the juvenile offender stakeholder group, two groups of three juvenile offenders from each region were interviewed. These groups included (1) individuals who had been released from the facility, reoffended or committed a parole violation, and returned to the facility and (2) individuals soon to be paroled to the community for the first time. The youth were interviewed and asked what would be helpful for—and what would create a barrier to—their success within the community upon release.

## Systems Results

Overall, broad barriers and existing supports were identified for the transition process for incarcerated youth with disabilities returning to the community from closed custody. A primary strength reported across all regions was the diverse array of community resources (such as alternative education, alcohol and other drug treatment services, and employment support services) available to maintain the transition process for these youth. Conversely, access to this array of services was judged as being extremely difficult to navigate. For example, to make certain that services were accessed immediately upon a youth leaving custody, mechanisms needed to be implemented for (1) sharing information across multiple agencies while ensuring a youth's privacy rights were not violated and (2) streamlining the diverse eligibility and intake requirements for the multiple agencies. Other supports identified by both the youth and community stakeholders included the treatment and educational services provided within the youth correctional facility.

The youth identified positive staff in the facility and "themselves" as supporting the transition process. When asked what would be a primary source of help upon exiting the youth correctional facility, a youth responded:

> Myself. Just doing what I need to do, like follow through with my goals, not get side-tracked with all the stuff that can bring me down. I know that it's going to be really hard. . . . There's a lot of opportunities and if you take it, you do or you don't. (Unruh, Povenmire-Kirk, & Yamamoto, 2009, p. 211)

In line with this point, another youth stated:

> [My biggest barriers will be] some of my old friends who are into drugs . . . some of the people I used to hang out with who are negative. There's going to be a lot of temptation to do things I shouldn't do. A lot if it's just within me. (Unruh & Bullis, 2005, p. 75)

Lack of independent living skills on the part of youth on parole was identified as a top barrier by community forum stakeholders and the youth. One youth stated that he will need help in this area once he's in the community:

> [I will need help] making my own food and like just going outside, being in public, job applications . . . just simple things. They're going to be hard like even doing my own clothes, it's going to be hard 'cause I haven't done it in a long time. (Unruh & Bullis, 2005, p. 74)

Youth and the other stakeholders also believed that youth would be faced with negative peer influences from former friends after parole to the community. A youth described this barrier, which resulted in his return to the juvenile correctional facility a second time:

> I went back to my old friends. Still seeing them. And you think, "do you want to smoke some weed?" or "do you want to do this again [be incarcerated]?" It's hard to resist when you've been friends with them ever since you were a little kid. That's one of the things you gotta stay away from day one. Can't call

them up, can't go see them, can't do things with them. (Unruh
& Bullis, 2005, p. 74)

Family support for the youth was identified as both a barrier and
support for maintaining positive engagement in the community. One
youth described his desire for a healthy family in the following way:

> I'll need support from my family [when I get out]—for them
> to be stable enough so I don't have to worry about other
> things like taking care of where I'm going to sleep, where I'm
> going to eat that night; just so I know that things are set and
> I won't have to worry about those things. (Unruh & Bullis,
> 2005, p. 72)

## Recommendations

Based on the results of the needs assessment, four recommendations
provided a foundation for the development of the systems and service
delivery models. This section describes the specific recommendations
resulting from the needs assessment process and how each was addressed
during the project's development.

### *Facilitated, Self-Directed Planning and Decision Making for Youth*

Self-directed planning and decision-making skill development was
noted as critical for supporting a youth's transition back into the
community. Transition specialists were trained in ways to facilitate
youths' decision-making processes. This focus on self-directed services
is initiated in the facility and continues once a youth is released into
the community.

### *Systems-Change Collaboration to Provide Access to Available Community Resources*

In the first project year, sharing of information across agencies was a
primary focus. Various systemic regulations had blocked the sharing of
participant information among service delivery staff from the agencies
involved in the project. Initial meetings were held with state-level staff
of each agency to define polices on information sharing. Transition
specialists were trained to obtain proper release signatures from the

youth and guardian to provide access to information for screening and referral. Local agency staff (for example, facility medical records staff, education staff, and treatment managers) were provided information about the new project and introduced to the transition specialists to ensure that policies for information sharing were accepted and embedded at the local level.

### Development of Strategies to Increase Positive Family and Peer Support

After leaving custody of the Oregon Youth Authority, youth often were not initially placed back in their families. When possible, the transition specialist now includes the family in the transition planning and implementation process. The term "family" is defined broadly to incorporate extended family, foster care, or community members who provide safe and positive networks for the youth. The transition specialists were also trained to assess youths' independent living and leisure interests. They would assist in connecting participants with community activities aligned with these interests (gym memberships, mentoring).

### Continued Development of Employment, Independent Living, and Academic Skills of Youth

Both the research literature and the needs assessment confirmed the desirability of continued development of youth in key transition areas of employment, education, and independent living. The transition specialist's initial training consisted of strategies to facilitate development of these skills in the community. This process is initiated in the facility, with specific community needs defined and organized for the youth immediately upon exiting custody.

## Participant Evaluation Results

In Project STAY OUT's evaluation plan, extensive background characteristics of project participants and participation data are collected at 2-month intervals once services have been initiated with youth. These evaluative data are collected to better understand the types of activities that participants receive, along with information about their involvement in the project goal of competitive employment or educational engagement.

### Demographic Information

A total of 508 participants were served from August 1999 through September 2007. The average age at entry into the project was 17.4 (*SD* 1.4) years, resulting in most youth being around the age of 18 when released from the correctional facility. Two-thirds of the youth were White, with the other top three ethnic groups consisting of African American, Hispanic, and Native American (in order of prevalence of involvement in the project). In Oregon, approximately 13% of the population is representative of a minority group. Over-representation of minorities in the juvenile justice systems is common throughout the United States. Slightly more than 80% of all youth involved in STAY OUT were male, which is representative of the 80:20 ratio of males to females incarcerated in Oregon.

Although only 18% of participants reported emotional disorders as a current special education diagnosis, 87% (*N* = 440) possessed a psychiatric label from the fourth edition of the *Diagnostic and Statistical Manual of Mental Disorders* (DSM-IV) of the American Psychiatric Association (1994). Surprisingly, only 46.4% had an active individualized education program (IEP) required for the receipt of special education services. This rate is under-representative of participants eligible for services, as defined in the Individual with Disabilities Act (IDEA). Many systemic issues are suspected to contribute to the under-representation of students with disabilities. For example, one explanation is that student cumulative files are not transferred to the facility to ensure that IDEA services follow the student. Another reason could be that the youth may not have been enrolled in a public school setting for several years before being incarcerated, and finding his or her cumulative file may be difficult. An additional possibility is that the student (before entering a juvenile correction facility) had been truant from school or had received drug and alcohol treatment and been declassified from special education because, at the adolescent level, it often is difficult to identify the true impediment to educational progress.

Participants also demonstrated other high-risk characteristics. A list of 22 barriers to transition was provided on the entry form. The barriers were classified into four transition domains:

- Employment (for example, unable to hold jobs)

- Education (for example, reading or math skill below the 5th- or 6th-grade level)
- Living situation (for example, foster care)
- Family and personal (for example, a history of abuse or neglect)

For the young adults served through Project STAY OUT, the top five barriers to transition were as follows:

- Excessive absenteeism from school (77.5% of participants)
- History of substance abuse (76.3% of participants)
- A reported history of running away from home or residential placements (63.6% of participants)
- Previous or current placement in foster care at the time of incarceration (61.5% of participants)
- Having attended multiple schools during their education history (almost 60% of participants)
- A reported problem with anger control (almost 60% of participants)

When examining the criminal history backgrounds of project participants, it was found that 41.5% of were adjudicated for their first crime at age of 13 or under. Of those youth, 41.6% were adjudicated for a property crime as their first offense, 40.1% for a person-to-person crime, and 13.0% for a behavioral crime.

A composite example of a typical Project STAY OUT participant appears on pages 370–372 of this chapter.

### Transition Specialist Activities

To better understand the types of activities the transition specialists were completing with each of the young adults participating in STAY OUT, the transition specialist tracked activities and reported them to the evaluators. A list of 38 activities across the transition domains of employment, education, independent living, and social/family was developed, and the transition specialist reported on each of the transition domains at each 2-month month data collection point. The list reflected only the activities for which the transition specialist interacted with the youth—and not the services from other agencies with which the youth was connected.

Figure 12.1 provides, for each domain, a summary of the top four activities that transition specialists worked on with program participants. The dark black line depicts the percentage of youth who received any one of the domain's transition activities (for example, any employment-related activity). The gray lines indicate the percentage of youth who received that type of transition specialist activity. The graph shows that

- 91% of participants received employment supports.
- 71% received some type of educational support from a transition specialist.
- 60% received training in various independent living skills.
- 66% received support from a transition specialist in relation to the family and the community.

### Initial Project Outcome

Figure 12.2 presents key outcomes on the rates of educational enrollment, employment, and engagement. A youth is defined as "engaged" if he or she has not returned to adult or juvenile custody and is employed, enrolled in school, or both. Outcomes are measured and reported on youth at 2, 4, and 6 months post-release because that period has been identified as the critical window in which youth may recidivate (Bullis & Yovanoff, 1997). Past the 6-month post-release marker, youth are less likely to participate in criminal activity. The 2-, 4-, and 6-month markers are used as a process measure to understand whether transition specialists are successful in getting youth positively engaged in transition-related activities. Currently, within 2 months after exit, more than 64% of all project participants are actively engaged in the community, 67% are engaged at 4 months, and 63% are engaged at 6 months. The overall engagement rate—approximately 60%—is promising because an earlier longitudinal study conducted in Oregon reported an engagement rate of 35% at 6 months post-release, with an overall recidivism rate of 60% (Bullis et al., 2002).

## LESSONS LEARNED

Project STAY OUT has provided strong initial outcome data, with participants who were in the project between 1999 and 2007 demonstrating

**FIGURE 12.1  Percentage of Young Adults Receiving Types of Transition Specialist Activities**

## EMPLOYMENT SERVICES

Any employment activities — 91%
Job seeking — 77%
Job application — 68%
Career exploration — 64%
Develop résumé — 44%

## EDUCATION SERVICES

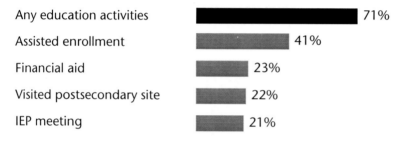

Any education activities — 71%
Assisted enrollment — 41%
Financial aid — 23%
Visited postsecondary site — 22%
IEP meeting — 21%

## INDEPENDENT LIVING SERVICES

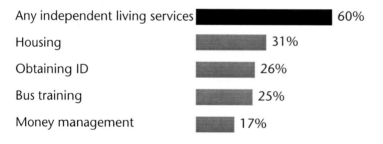

Any independent living services — 60%
Housing — 31%
Obtaining ID — 26%
Bus training — 25%
Money management — 17%

## SOCIAL/FAMILY SERVICES

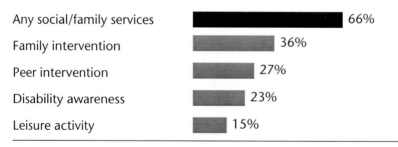

Any social/family services — 66%
Family intervention — 36%
Peer intervention — 27%
Disability awareness — 23%
Leisure activity — 15%

**FIGURE 12.2    Project STAY OUT Outcomes**

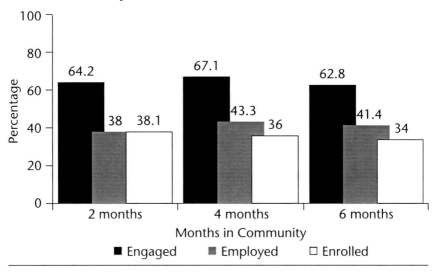

more than 63% engagement rates at 2, 4, and 6 months after leaving juvenile custody. Through the implementation of this project, numerous lessons have been learned about implementing such a project across three state agencies and about the needs of juvenile offenders with EBD as they transition into the community.

## Multiple Agency Collaboration

Time is the essential element in developing collaborative systems across multiple agencies. Specifically, time is needed to both define and build collaborative structures. Time also is needed, however, for these strategies to be practiced, refined, and embedded within the ongoing structure and culture of the state agencies. Common strategies that have been found to be effective in the development of this project include the following:

*Development and dissemination of a screening and referral process that clearly describes the targeted population for the project, eligibility criteria, and process for referral.* A screening and referral process was initiated and refined in the first year of project services. Each partner agency was involved in the initial development and dissemination process, with continuing education of eligibility criteria occurring with new agency staff.

*Education of each of the local partners (parole officers, treatment managers, education facility staff,* VR counselors, local mental health providers, and others) about the goals, target population, and pattern of services of the project. Initial education included presentations by the transition specialist at regular staff meetings of each of the partnering agencies. Other education activities are completed by the transition specialist when he or she interacts with the partnering agencies about their caseload to develop services for a specific youth, which typically lead to new referrals to the project. This type of education is a continual process in order to override the inevitable "turf" issues that arise when multiple state agencies work together in an era of tightening budgets.

*Regular planning meetings at the state management, regional, and local levels to assess program development and sustainability.* The state co-managers and University of Oregon evaluators meet monthly to share project outcomes and to plan systemic changes. Transition specialists and their supervisors (local education providers) meet quarterly with the state managers. These meetings allow for a continual review of project goals and also provide an avenue for multilevel problem-solving.

*Use of evaluation data to help review the effectiveness of project services.* The descriptive information about the types of youth guided project personnel in explaining various events. For example, examining the rate of enrollment or employment at 2, 4, and 6 months out can help determine whether project participants are being actively engaged immediately from exiting the youth correctional facility. In addition, having information about the most frequent types of transition specialist activities provided insight into what activities a new transition specialist could expect to be doing with youth.

## Providing Services for Juvenile Offenders with EBD

The greatest frustrations in providing services to youth with EBD rested in trying to prevent their return to previous criminal behaviors. The transition specialist soon learned that his or her responsibility wasn't "to get these youth jobs" but to support the youth in obtaining a job on his or her own. The concept of self-determination is critical for staff working with these high-risk youth. Incarcerated youth in the initial needs assessment asserted that it was "themselves" that would be the biggest barrier or support once they returned to the community.

Promoting self-determination has been stressed in each phase of project services. Other lessons learned through the implementation of Project STAY OUT have come about through the dedication of the transition specialists who constantly develop a new repertoire of strategies to assist project participants. These strategies include the following:

*Employment and education placement must be defined by the interests, aptitudes, and needs of the youth.* These services begin in the facility by exploring various employment and career interests with the youth. Information is provided on various employment services, educational and training opportunities, or actual jobs in alignment with the youth's interests.

*Employability skill training must go beyond the youth being employed.* The transition specialists work in conjunction with other employment services (such as VR or WIA) to develop employment and training opportunities. Youth in the program initially possessed a limited, if any, work history and needed "starter" jobs before searching for long-term, career-related employment. Once the youth is in the community, the transition specialist supports his or her job search process by working with the youth in reading want ads online and in the paper, going with the youth to the local employment office and helping him or her access these services, and practicing follow-up telephone calls to the employer after an interview. Often, the youth must suffer natural consequences for poor choices on the job and is fired from his or her position. The transition specialist assists the youth in identifying and reflecting on these poor choices while helping him or her gain further employment opportunities. This may be an ongoing process through multiple jobs while the youth is gaining basic workforce appropriate behavior.

*The involvement of the transition specialist must continue over time.* Transition specialist support does not stop once a youth gets his or her first, second, or even third job, because it is critical to help the youth maintain employment over a period of time. During the youth's employment, the transition specialist regularly checks in with the youth to assess how things are progressing on the job. Often the transition specialist will conduct problem-solving sessions with the youth about difficulties he or she may be experiencing on the job or with the supervisor and coworkers. The transition specialist may help the youth brainstorm various options to appropriately handle a situation that could escalate into the youth losing his or her job. For example, the transition specialist regularly coaches the youth about the importance of regular attendance, but if the youth "happens to be absent" from work and decides it's easier never to go back to that job, the youth must suffer the consequences for his or her absence. The transition specialist is then needed to help the youth understand strategies to maintain appropriate communication with an employer when mistakes occur.

*Additional support services are needed to assist youth in successfully reintegrating into the community.* Tertiary supports are requisite for a youth's successful transition into the community and on into adulthood. These activities are focused on the unique needs of the individual. Services often primarily include mental health or alcohol and other drug services needed by the youth. Other types of services youth have received include family counseling, independent skill development, and appropriate use of leisure time through developing new friends, activities, and interests in the community.

## Composite Example of a Typical Project STAY OUT Participant

Anthony lived with his mother and two other brothers. His mom had difficulties with stable employment and, as a family, they moved frequently based on where she could find employment. When Anthony was 10, they moved in with his mother's boyfriend, who was verbally and physically abusive to Anthony. At age 12, Anthony first became involved with law enforcement for being a minor in possession of tobacco. As he aged, he developed a pattern of running away from home, attending multiple traditional and alternative schools, and using alcohol and drugs. Anthony was eventually incarcerated at age 14 for multiple crimes including theft, stealing a car, and assault. At 16, he was released, but was returned to the correctional facility within 3 months after being adjudicated for new crimes. He said that most of the crimes were committed while under the influence of drugs. Before his incarceration, Anthony had poor grades coupled with poor school attendance. He had been identified for special education services in elementary school, but his school enrollment was so sporadic in middle and high school that he no longer had an active IEP. While incarcerated, Anthony was evaluated by the clinic and diagnosed with two mental health disorders—polysubstance abuse and conduct disorder. Medications were prescribed for him as he progressed through treatment.

Anthony's parole officer referred him to Project STAY OUT about 6 months before Anthony was scheduled to be released from the youth correctional facility. A transition specialist met with Anthony to help him define his barriers to transitioning to the community and help him outline his needs upon release. They focused on Anthony's strengths and interests. Anthony's education and career goals were unclear. He shared that he had some interest in building things and would like to play guitar in a band. Before Anthony's release, the transition specialist ensured that Anthony had proper identification cards and made sure that his health insurance would be maintained upon his release in order to continue access to his medications. It was decided that Anthony would live with his aunt when he left the facility. Various training programs and General Education Development (GED) programs were explored in the community where his aunt lived.

Anthony was released from custody just before his 18th birthday. Upon release, Anthony's transition was not smooth. The transition specialist helped him apply for food stamps and attended a youth-focused Alcoholics Anonymous group with him. The transition specialist connected Anthony with a vocational rehabilitation counselor, who identified an on-the-job training opportunity with a local construction contractor. The vocational rehabilitation counselor purchased the tools Anthony would need for this job. The transition specialist helped him apply for financial aid, and he enrolled in a GED program at a local community college.

Anthony was soon fired because of an argument with his boss. He shared that he'd stopped attending his AA meetings, had been hanging out with some of his old friends, and had been under the influence of drugs when he got into the argument with his boss. He had also sold his tools to buy drugs. The parole officer and transition specialist required Anthony to attend alcohol and drug treatment. The vocational rehabilitation counselor also referred him to another building certification program, YouthBuild, where he could learn construction as he worked on his GED. The transition specialist regularly checked in with Anthony about how this program was going and whether he was regularly attending his counseling sessions.

In the 14 months since Anthony's release from custody, he has graduated from YouthBuild and completed his GED. He is now working for a small construction company. Anthony is struggling with staying away from drugs, but he has met some new friends through work who help him stay away from his drug-involved friends. His new friends introduced him to his current girlfriend, and she has been a positive influence on him. Anthony is still living with his aunt and is now contributing to the rent. Currently, he and one of his new friends are trying to save enough money for a deposit on an apartment. Anthony still checks in with his transition specialist on occasion. She just provided information about a community program that provides housing support. He'll check into that soon.

## CONCLUSION

One of the keys to success of this project is the role of the transition specialist in working with a hard-to-serve population. This staff person provides support to the parole officer to assist in the implementation of a high-risk youth's parole plans. Equally important is the role the transition specialist plays with the juvenile offending youth with EBD. This position provides a positive, mentoring relationship with an adult who assists the youth in her or his transition to adulthood. This relationship is critical to the success of this project.

Project STAY OUT is a promising model for working with juvenile offenders with EBD. Its services are based on the collaborative efforts of three state agencies working collectively to develop a sustainable service model. Developing effective collaborative services with these youth was not easy and did not occur immediately. It is our hope that the lessons we have learned can be used by others to develop programs to promote positive outcomes for youth with EBD to become contributing members of our society.

## REFERENCES

Altschuler, D. M., & Armstrong, T. L. (1991). Intensive aftercare for the high-risk juvenile parolee: Issues and approaches in reintegration and community supervision. In T. L. Armstrong (Ed.), *Intensive interventions with high-risk youths: Promising approaches in juvenile probation and parole* (pp. 45–84). Monsey, NY: Criminal Justice Press.

American Psychiatric Association (1994). *Diagnostic and statistical manual of mental disorders* (4th ed.). Washington, DC: Author.

Aos, S., Miller, M., & Drake E. (2006). *Evidence-based public policy options to reduce future prison construction, criminal justice costs, and crime rates.* Olympia, WA: Washington State Institute for Public Policy.

Bridgeo, D., Davis, M., & Florida, Y. (2000). Helping young people to pull it all together. In H. B. Clark & M. Davis (Eds.), *Transition to adulthood: A resource for assisting young people with emotional or behavioral difficulties* (pp. 209–225). Baltimore: Paul H. Brookes.

Bullis, M., & Cheney, D. (1999). Vocational and transition interventions for adolescents and young adults with emotional or behavioral disorders. *Focus on Exceptional Children, 31*(7), 1–24.

Bullis, M., & Fredericks, H. D. (Eds.). (2002). *Vocational and transition services for adolescents with emotional and behavioral disorders: Strategies and best practices.* Champaign, IL: Research Press.

Bullis, M., Fredericks, H. D., Lehman, C., Paris, K., Corbitt, J., & Johnson, J. (1994). Description and evaluation of the Job Designs project for adolescents and young adults with emotional or behavioral disorders. *Behavioral Disorders, 19*(4), 254–268.

Bullis, M., & Yovanoff, P. (1997). *Return to close custody: Analysis of the Oregon Youth Authority's data set.* Eugene: University of Oregon, Institute on Violence and Destructive Behavior.

Bullis, M., Yovanoff, P., Mueller, G., & Havel, E. (2002). Life on the "outs"—Examination of the facility-to-community transition of incarcerated youth. *Exceptional Children, 69*(1), 7–22.

Cheney, D., Hagner, D., Malloy, J., Cormier, G., & Bernstein, S. (1998). Transition services for youth and young adults with emotional disturbance: Description and initial results of project RENEW. *Career Development for Exceptional Individuals, 21*(1), 17–32.

Clark, H. B., & Davis, M. (Eds.). (2000). *Transition to adulthood: A resource for assisting young people with emotional or behavioral difficulties.* Baltimore: Paul H. Brookes.

Clark, H. B., Deschênes, N., & Jones, J. (2000). A framework for the development and operation of a transition system. In H. B. Clark & M. Davis (Eds.), *Transition to adulthood: A resource for assisting young people with emotional or behavioral difficulties* (pp. 29–51). Baltimore: Paul H. Brookes.

Cohen, M. A. (1998). The monetary valued of saving a high-risk youth. *Journal of Quantitative Criminology, (14),* 5–32.

Leone, P. E., Meisel, S. M., & Drakeford, W. (2002). Special education programs for youth with disabilities in juvenile corrections. *Journal of Correctional Education, 53,* 46–50.

Leone, P., Rutherford, R., & Nelson, C. (1991). *Special education in juvenile corrections.* Arlington, VA: Council for Exceptional Children.

McCord, J. (1992). The Cambridge–Somerville Study: A pioneering longitudinal–experimental study of delinquency prevention. In J. McCord & R. Tremblay (Eds.), *Preventing antisocial behavior* (pp. 196–208). New York: Guilford Press.

Snyder, H. N., & Sickmund, M. (2006). *Juvenile offenders and victims: 2006 national report.* Washington, DC: U. S. Department of Justice Programs, Office of Juvenile Justice and Delinquency Prevention.

Unruh, D., & Bullis, M. (2005). Facility-to-community transition needs for adjudicated youth with disabilities. *Career Development for Exceptional Individuals, 28,* 67–79.

Unruh, D., Povenmire-Kirk, T., & Yamamoto, S. (2009). Perceived barriers and protective factors of juvenile offenders on their developmental pathway to adulthood. *Journal of Correctional Education, 60*(3), 201–224.

Vander Stoep, A., Davis, M., & Collins, D. (2000). Transition: A time of developmental and institutional clashes. In H. B. Clark and M. Davis (Eds.), *Transition to adulthood: A resource for assisting young people with emotional or behavioral difficulties* (pp. 3–28). Baltimore: Paul H. Brookes.

## CHAPTER 13

# *Practices in Transition for Youth in the Juvenile Justice System*

### Heather Griller Clark and Sarup R. Mathur

The transition from a juvenile detention or correctional facility back into the community can present major challenges to youth, especially those with disabilities. Youth who are detained or incarcerated become accustomed to a structured existence; however, upon release, very different demands are placed on them. These youth may return to communities where resources are not apparent or readily available and to school systems that do not want them. All too often, they do not have the skills to make appropriate connections in their community and to get the education and support that they need to be successful. Without the necessary skills and support, these youth fall back into the same patterns of behavior that caused their involvement in the juvenile justice system in the first place (Baltodano, Mathur, & Rutherford, 2005). This cycle of failure, of both the individual and the system, is not only disheartening to the youth, but it places a great financial burden on society. Researchers, practitioners, and policy makers have begun to look at educational programming—specifically, transition services—as a possible solution to this problem.

Despite this increased attention, few correctional education programs have proven to be successful in the transition of juvenile offenders with disabilities (Griller-Clark, 2006). In fact, transition is usually the most neglected component of correctional education programming (Griller-Clark, 2006). While detained or incarcerated, most youth do not receive adequate vocational and educational assessment and planning before release; therefore, they are less likely to successfully engage in school or work when they are released (Bullis,

Yovanoff, Mueller, & Havel, 2002; Griller-Clark, 2006). In an effort to enhance the success of youth from the juvenile justice system, many researchers and policy makers have attempted to identify effective practices that increase engagement in school and work and reduce the rate at which these youth recidivate. For example, in 2007, the National Associate of State Directors of Special Education (NASDE) and the National Disability Rights Network (NDRN) produced a document titled *Tools for Promoting Educational Success and Reducing Delinquency,* also known simply as *Tools for Success,* to address their shared interest in the disproportionate number of youth with disabilities in the juvenile justice system. This document is a compendium of best practices for promoting the educational stability of youth with disabilities and those at risk for developing disabilities. It is divided into nine sections, or steps, that track the developmental stages of children from birth through transition into adulthood. Designed for teachers and administrators, Tools for Success includes research-based, effective practices and a section, or step, exclusively on the transition and school-reenrollment of youth from the juvenile justice system (JJ/SE, 2007).

Previous research from the U.S. Department of Education (LeBlanc & Pfannenstiel, 1991) and the U.S. Department of Justice's Office of Juvenile Justice and Delinquency Prevention (Coffey & Gemignani, 1994) has also documented the need for effective practices in the education and transition of at-risk and delinquent youth. The effective practices in transition and support services outlined in the Coffey and Gemignani (1994) publication provided the first blueprint for transition services in correctional settings. These practices have since been reviewed and updated by the National Center on Education, Disability, and Juvenile Justice (Rutherford, Mathur, & Griller-Clark, 2001).

Despite the publication of these practices and the best of attempts of many researchers, policy makers, educators, transition specialists, and parents, transition remains a concern for a significant number of youth with disabilities in the juvenile justice system. In this chapter, we offer some brief explanations for the narrow success in this area. First, we provide a definition of transition and clarify the process. Then, we discuss challenges in providing transition services to youth in the juvenile justice system and highlight a number of promising practices or strategies for facilitating the transition from correctional facility to community. For clarity we have grouped these practices into the following broad categories: programming, institutional policy, coordination and collaboration, and evaluation. Finally, we present a comprehensive, six-component corrections–community transition model for youth with disabilities in the juvenile justice system.

## DEFINITION OF TRANSITION

In 1990, federal regulations first mandated the provision of transition planning for youth with disabilities beginning at age 16 with the Individuals with Disabilities Education Act (IDEA); the age was reduced to 14 with the reauthorization of the IDEA in 1997. As included in the federal definition of transition in Chapter 1 of this book, transition services are a coordinated set of activities that must be based on the student's strengths, preferences, and interests. According to the Individuals with Disabilities Education Improvement Act of 2004 (IDEIA), providing effective transition services to promote successful postschool education or employment is an important measure of success.

Correctional educators have continually struggled with the logistics of providing effective, age-appropriate, results-oriented transition services that reflect the youth's strengths, preferences, and interests while operating within the confines of the juvenile justice system. Although the federal definition of transition applies to all youth with disabilities, the concept of transition as it specifically relates to youth within the juvenile justice system has only recently been defined as

> a coordinated set of activities for a juvenile offender, designed within an outcome-oriented process, which promotes movement from the community to a correctional setting, from one correctional setting to another, or from a correctional setting to post-incarceration activities including public or alternative education, vocational training, integrated employment (including supported employment), continuing education, adult services, independent living, or community participation. (IDEIA, 2004, § 604 (34)(A))

## CHALLENGES IN PROVIDING TRANSITION SERVICES

Effectively providing transition services in a correctional setting can be a challenge. One explanation for this challenge is the dramatically different philosophies of corrections and education. The goal of corrections is to provide public safety through confinement and punishment, while the goal of education is to liberate the body and mind through knowledge. This contrast in philosophies is clearly seen in the way education is either supported or inhibited within a correctional setting (Rutherford, Griller-Clark, & Anderson, 2001).

The need for providing educational services to youth in correctional settings is evident. In fact, a proven means of successfully rehabilitating offenders and reducing recidivism is through education (Bullis & Yovanoff, 2002; Chappell, 2004; Coffey & Gemignani, 1994; Harer, 1994). A meta-analysis of research from 1990 through 1999 (Chappell, 2004) found a positive correlation between postsecondary correctional education and a reduction in recidivism. Other studies have found that inmates who receive either vocational/technical training or a General Education Development (GED) diploma while incarcerated have the highest rates of employment after release (Black et al., 1996; Brier, 1994; Haberman & Quinn, 1986). Although we know that education is a highly effective means of preventing delinquency or reoffending, the practicality of ensuring that these educational opportunities continue once the youth leaves the facility is a real challenge. For example, a study in the state of Washington found that only 21% of youth released from correctional institutions were in school 6 months after release (Webb & Maddox, 1986). In addition, a Wisconsin study found that only 1.6% of released juvenile offenders returned to school and graduated (Haberman & Quinn, 1986). Furthermore, Todis, Bullis, Waintrup, Schultz, and D'Ambrosio (2001) found that only 2 of the 15 participants in their long-term follow-up study of youth leaving the Oregon Youth Authority graduated from high school.

There are other challenges that face these youth as well, including challenges posed by schools, districts, employers, and the youths' own status as juvenile offenders. For example, youth from the juvenile justice system face substantial challenges when returning to school. In many cases, a youth may want to return to a school or district where he or she was once suspended or expelled and therefore is not welcomed. In other cases, students may be released mid-semester and told to come back at the beginning of the next term. Or, due to the highly transient nature of the population, youth may lack the documents needed to register in school (transcripts, immunization records, birth certificates). When seeking employment or returning to work, youth may lack awareness of what jobs are available, how to find a job, where to find a job, and how to keep a job. In addition, many youth have never taken a vocational interest or ability assessment and may obtain a job that is not a good match to either interest or ability. Furthermore, their status as juvenile offenders presents additional challenges to the youth, including how much information on offense history should legally and ethically be disclosed.

## PRACTICES FOR PROMOTING TRANSITION TO SCHOOL, WORK, AND THE COMMUNITY

The problems encountered by youth involved in the juvenile justice system who wish to return to school are even further exacerbated when those youth have special needs (Benz & Halpern, 1993; Edgar, Webb, & Maddox, 1987; Griller-Clark, 2006; Rutherford, Quinn, Leone, Garfinkle, & Nelson, 2002). For example, Benz and Halpern (1993) found that between 25% and 50% of the transition needs identified in the youths' individualized transition plans were not addressed during the transition planning process. Interestingly, students with learning disabilities and/or emotional disturbance were almost always the least likely to have their transition needs met.

In an effort to determine effective transition practices for youth with and without disabilities in the juvenile justice system, Edgar et al. (1987) identified six areas critical to successful transition to school (for a full description, see Edgar et al., 1987; Webb & Maddox, 1986):

1. *Awareness* of community programs and schools
2. Understanding the *eligibility criteria* for community programs and schools
3. *Exchange of information* and records between the juvenile correctional facility and the community agency
4. *Program planning before transition* to ensure that the youth has the skills and documentation needed to be successful in the post-release setting,
5. *Feedback after transition* for formative evaluation of the transition planning process
6. *Written procedures* so that everyone understands what is expected

In addition, other researchers (Coffey & Gemignani, 1994; JJ/SE Shared Agenda, 2007; Nelson, Rutherford, & Wolford, 1987; Rutherford, Mathur, & Griller-Clark, 2001) point out the importance of interagency coordination, collaborative pre-placement planning between institutions, transfer of records before a student's move from one jurisdiction to another, and specific pre-release programs (social skills, survival skills, independent living skills, pre-employment training, and law-related education) in the successful transition of these youth from the juvenile justice system back to school.

There is very little research in the area of employment preparation and transition to employment for youth in the juvenile justice system. However, because most youth in the juvenile justice system traditionally do not return to, and graduate from, high school upon release from the juvenile justice system (Todis et al., 2001), preparation for post-release employment is essential (Coffey & Gemignani, 1994). Several practices have been identified as critical to employment preparation for youth within the juvenile justice system, including a focus on the skills and competencies identified in The Secretary's Commission on Achieving Necessary Skills (SCANS) report (http://wdr.doleta.gov/SCANS): accurate vocational assessment, knowledge of the workplace, real-world application of knowledge, instruction in job search skills, employment counseling, and partnerships with employers (Coffey & Gemignani, 1994). Others have identified the following components as necessary to prepare youth for the transition to employment: occupational awareness, employment-related knowledge and skills, specific vocational knowledge and skills, and job placement and training (Sitlington, Clark, & Kolstoe, 2000). Evidence suggests that for youth with disabilities, transition planning is necessary for successful transition to employment upon release from the juvenile justice system (Sitlington et al., 2000).

The effective transition of youth with disabilities to the community involves a multidimensional service delivery system that provides personnel and support from a variety of different organizations (Halpern, 1985; Sitlington et al., 2000). However, in many places, this service delivery system is not coordinated to assist youth with disabilities to transition successfully from the juvenile justice system to the community. For example, a single youth could be receiving services from a correctional program, a state employment agency, Social Security, or a myriad of other agencies, with all of them working independently. Coordination of this system can only be accomplished through interagency collaboration and cooperation (Cook, 1990). Still, collaboration and cooperation between correctional and community agencies varies greatly (Leone, Quinn, & Osher, 2002). In addition to interagency collaboration and cooperation, successful transition to the community for youth from the juvenile justice system must include training and/or support in independent living and daily living skills, maintaining personal relationships, accessing community resources and related services, health and fitness, leisure and recreation, and substance abuse prevention.

Whether youth from the juvenile justice system are transitioning to school, work, or the community, one thing is clear: They need assistance. However, this assistance must be based on documented effective practices.

## PROMISING TRANSITION PRACTICES

Table 13.1 outlines 18 "promising practices" in the transition of youth from the juvenile justice system. These promising practices have been published as two separate documents—*EDJJ Promising Practices in Transition for Youth in the Juvenile Justice System: Long Term Correctional Facilities* and *EDJJ Promising Practices in Transition for Youth in the Juvenile Justice System: Short Term Jails and Detention Centers,* by the National Center on Education, Disability, and Juvenile Justice (Rutherford, Mathur, & Griller-Clark, 2001). These promising practices are intended to assist administrators, teachers, probation and parole officers, transition specialists, and others in designing effective transition programs, policies, collaborative relationships, and evaluation procedures for youth with and without disabilities in the juvenile justice system.

When reviewing these promising practices, it is important to keep in mind that correctional education programs are diverse. Therefore, a transition program that is effective in one system may not be as effective in another. For that reason, the research supports an array of effective programs for providing transition services to juvenile offenders.

In the following section, we present a transition model based on the promising practices outlined in Table 13.1. This model has been designed for a specific juvenile justice system; however, because it is based on effective practices, its components could be replicated and evaluated in other settings. The Arizona Detention Transition Model

**TABLE 13.1    Promising Transition Practices for Youth in the Juvenile Justice System**

To facilitate the transition of youth with disabilities from correctional facilities to the community, the following strategies are recommended:

1. A process for the immediate identification, evaluation, programming, and placement of youth with disabilities

2. An *individualized education program* obtained or developed for each student with disabilities that includes a transition plan

3. An *individual transition plan* developed with a student that includes the student's educational and vocational interests, abilities, and preferences

4. A transition planning team, formed immediately upon student entry into a detention or correctional facility, to design and implement the individual transition plan

5. Team members familiar with all county, state, local, and private programs that receive and send youth to or from short-term and long-term correctional facilities

6. Individualized pre-placement planning before the transfer of youth from jails, detention centers, or other programs to long-term correctional facilities

7. Seamless and immediate transfer of youths' educational records from public and private educational programs to short-term detention programs, long-term correctional facilities, and to the community

8. An extensive diagnostic system in detention for the educational, vocational, and social, emotional, and behavioral assessment of youth

9. Student access to a resource center that contains a variety of materials related to transition and support

10. Interagency meetings, cooperative in-service training activities, and crossover correctional and community school staff visits to ensure awareness of youth and agency transition needs

11. A variety of specific educational programs, including academics, vocational and job-related skills, social skills, independent living skills, and law-related education

382

12. A variety of support services, including work experience and placement, alcohol and drug abuse counseling, anger management, vocational counseling, health education, and training for parenthood

13. External resources such as speakers, tutors, mentors, vocational trainers, substance abuse counselors, employers, volunteers, and job counselors

14. Special funds earmarked for transition and support services

15. Coordination with probation and parole agencies to ensure a continuum of services and care in the community

16. Coordination with public and private educational program personnel to ensure that they advocate for these youth, cultivate family involvement, maintain communications with other agencies, and place students in classes with supportive teachers

17. A community-based transition system for maintaining student placement and communication after release from long-term correctional facilities

18. Periodic evaluations of the transition program and all of its components

Demonstration Project found that application of these components resulted in increased engagement and reduced recidivism for youth with disabilities released from two short-term detention facilities (Griller-Clark, Mathur, Sloane, & Helding, 2007).

## A COMPREHENSIVE CORRECTIONS–COMMUNITY TRANSITION SYSTEM

The purpose of a comprehensive corrections–community transition system is to implement evidence-based transition practices for youth with disabilities in short-term and long-term correctional facilities. These practices (see Table 13.1) have the ultimate goal of establishing a sustainable transition system for youth with disabilities entering and exiting jails and detention centers and juvenile and adult correctional facilities. To implement a comprehensive transition system, these six key components should be in place. An action guide for implementing the components can be found in Table 13.2.

## Component 1: Develop Individualized Transition Plans (ITPs)

The transition needs of youth with disabilities are recognized in IDEA's mandate to provide an individualized transition plan (ITP) as a component of the individualized education program (IEP) for all youth with disabilities aged 14 and above (see § 300.347(b) of IDEA). The ITP specifies the skills and supports required currently and in the future by the student. Transition planning and programming must be based on the youth's educational and vocational needs, abilities, interests, and preferences. The special education teacher or transition specialist, in coordination with the student, the principal, general education teachers, parents or family members, the probation or parole officer, and the school psychologist reviews and, in some cases, amends the IEPs and the ITPs of all identified special education students. However, in a study of ITPs of youth in Arizona and California juvenile correctional education programs, Hosp, Griller-Clark, and Rutherford (2001) found that most students were either unaware of their ITPs or that the ITPs provided no functional transition guidance.

## Component 2: Develop and Implement a Student Education Passport or Portfolio

Typically, detention education staff begin collecting meaningful information on students' educational and vocational needs, their strengths and competencies, and samples of work that will be transferred with students as they move along a continuum of appropriate transition services. Using portfolio assessment procedures, the special education teacher or transition specialist and the student create a student education passport or portfolio to facilitate the student's transition to school, community, and employment-related agencies or long-term correctional settings.

According to Rutherford et al. (2002), the most important function that a short-term correctional facility may perform is to facilitate a student's successful transition to the next program or placement by taking the following steps:

**TABLE 13.2    Action Guide for a Comprehensive Correction–Community Transition System**

**Component 1: Develop individualized transition plans, including the following:**

For students who are age 14 (or younger, if determined necessary):

- A statement of transition service needs
- A coordinated set of activities designed through an outcome-oriented process that includes

  Movement from school to postschool activities

  Vocational training

  Integrated employment (including supported employment)

  Continuing and adult education

  Adult services

  Independent living

  Community participation

For students who are age 16 (or younger, if determined necessary):

- A statement of the needed transition services for the student, including, if appropriate, a statement of the interagency responsibilities or any necessary linkages
- A coordinated set of activities designed through an outcome-oriented process that includes

  Movement from school to postschool activities

  Postsecondary education

  Vocational training

  Integrated employment (including supported employment)

  Continuing and adult education

  Adult services

  Independent living

  Community participation

- Identification of the student's needs, preferences, and interests (students should have access to a transition resource center to help determine preferences and interests)

**TABLE 13.2 (continued)**

In addition, the following documentation must be maintained to verify compliance with IDEA transition requirements:

- Documentation that the student was invited to attend the IEP meeting (if the student did not attend, documentation that the public agency took other steps to ensure that the student's preferences and interests were considered)

- Documentation that representatives from agencies that could be responsible for providing for or paying for transition services were invited to the IEP meeting (if an agency was invited to send a representative to a meeting and did not do so, documentation of steps taken to obtain participation of that agency in the planning of any transition services)

- Documentation that the parental notification of the IEP meeting indicated that a purpose of the meeting was the development of a statement of transition services needs (for students beginning at age 14, or younger, if appropriate), along with documentation that the student was invited to attend the meeting

- Documentation that the parental notice indicated that the purpose of the meeting was the consideration of needed transition services for the student (for students 16 or younger, if appropriate), along with documentation that the student was invited to attend the meeting and documentation identifying any other agency that was invited to send a representative

- Documentation that if a participating agency (other than the public agency) fails to provide the transition services described in the IEP, the public agency shall reconvene the IEP team to identify alternative strategies to meet the transition objectives for the student's IEP

**Component 2: Develop and implement a student education passport or portfolio that includes the following:**

- Social Security card (copy)
- Birth certificate (copy)
- Immunization records (copy)
- Documentation of disability
- Individualized education program (copy)
- Individualized transition plan (copy)

- Academic transcripts
- Strengths-based assessment information
- Curriculum-based academic assessment information
- Vocational certificates
- List of relevant community resources and contacts
- Education rights (how to advocate for services needed)
- Résumé
- Letters of recommendations
- Samples of work
- Statement of the student's needs, preferences, and interests (students should have access to a resource center to help determine these preferences and interests)

**Component 3: Establish a seamless transfer of educational records and services:**

- Examine student's records; interview the student to determine whether to proceed to check eligibility for, or past history of, special education services
- Call the school in which the student was last enrolled:

    Obtain a list of student classes and credits

    Check with the school regarding attendance status of the student. If the student is still enrolled, notify the school that the student will be receiving educational services while in the detention or correctional facility and may return with grades and benchmarks reached
- Determine whether the student was receiving or had ever received special education and related services
- Determine whether the student might be identified as having special education needs
- Determine in which institution, agency, or school the student is to be placed (if there is more than one option)
- Request records and information from previous institutions, agencies, or schools
- Follow up the telephone call with fax and regular mail requests, as appropriate

TABLE 13.2 **(continued)**

- After 10 days of the student's entry into the detention or correctional education program, notify the previous school to withdraw the student and enroll him or her in the detention or correctional education program (this step is important for funding purposes)
- Create an education file for the student
- Create a special education file for the student

**Component 4: Increase interagency linkages and communication:**

- Ensure staff awareness of programs that send and receive youth
- Conduct individualized pre-placement planning
- Arrange interagency meetings, cooperative in-services training, and crossover correctional and community school visits
- Establish coordination with public and alternative school programs and personnel
- Establish coordination with probation and parole officers

**Component 5: Establish a youth tracking system**

- A youth tracking system should

    Be coordinated with probation or parole

    Contain educational, vocational, employment, and community information

    Be maintained by more than one person

    Be easily accessible

    Be computerized

- A youth tracking system can also be used to aid in evaluation of the transition program. Evaluation should be focused on whether various elements of the transition program have been effectively implemented and whether positive student outcomes result from the process. Elements that may be evaluated include

    Number of youth with meaningful ITPs

    Number of youth with up-to-date IEPs

    Number of youth with comprehensive assessments

    Number of youth with complete education passports or portfolios

Number of quality linkages between sending and receiving agencies

Number of records requested and received

Number of youth enrolled in school

Number of youth employed

Number of youth involved in the community

Number of GEDs, diplomas, and certificates earned

Number of jobs held and hours worked

Number of youth who recidivate

**Component 6: Establish transition, special education, and related services in long-term juvenile and adult corrections, which should include:**

- A variety of educational programs such as academics, vocational courses, social skills, independent living, and law-related education

- A variety of support services including, but not limited to, work experience and placement, alcohol and drug abuse counseling, anger management, vocational counseling, health education, and training for parenthood

- A variety of external resources, including speakers, tutors, mentors, vocational trainers, substance abuse counselors, volunteers, and job coaches

- A process for the immediate identification, evaluation, placement, and programming of youth with disabilities

- Set-aside funds for transition and support services

1. Collecting prior education records, including the IEP and any previous assessment pieces

2. Conducting a comprehensive assessment of the student's current educational, vocational, social and emotional, and behavioral needs and abilities

3. Compiling a portfolio of these records, assessment data, and samples of student work

Diagnosing youth in the juvenile justice system is a complicated endeavor. The youth must not only be diagnosed in terms of his or her risk to society or risk of reoffending, but also in terms of his or her educational strengths and weaknesses, presence of a disability that affects ability to learn, vocational interests and abilities, social skills, emotional needs, and behavioral problems. The challenges come not only in completing these assessments in a specific period of time but also in the variance of the tools that are used to perform the assessments.

## Component 3: Establish a Seamless Transfer of Educational Records and Services

The seamless transfer of records and services seldom occurs as youth move from one stage of the juvenile justice system to the next. Education and treatment services can best be described as fragmented, with services at one stage bearing little relevance to services at the next stage. A student who moves among public and alternative schools, detention facilities, education, community and employment agencies, and juvenile and adult corrections systems rarely, if ever, finds educational programming and services that build on the prior placement. Similarly, a student's educational records are seldom transferred from program to program.

Detention and juvenile and adult corrections education personnel, as well as public and alternative school personnel, must expand their efforts to develop common assessment and portfolio information that will be relevant across all education programs in which students with disabilities are placed. The goal is for youth with disabilities in the juvenile justice system and their educational records to move seamlessly as they transition from one setting to the next.

## Component 4: Increase Interagency Linkages and Communication

To accomplish the first three components of a comprehensive corrections–community transition system (that is, establish ITPs, develop student education passports, and establish the seamless transfer of records and services), interagency linkages and communication must be developed and maintained with public and alternative schools, community agencies, and job and employment services, as well as with the juvenile and adult correctional agencies. These linkages and communications must be made among agencies at the administrative level and among the line staff of these schools and agencies on a student-by-student basis. Because transition programming from juvenile detention centers is initiated immediately upon entry (because of the relatively short period of time that youth are detained), predictable and reliable contacts with personnel from those facilities must be made immediately.

## Component 5: Establish a Youth Tracking System

A condition of probation or parole for many youth exiting detention centers or juvenile correctional facilities is that they be in some type of education program. In many cases, the appropriateness of those programs for youth with disabilities is questionable. In addition, because of high case loads and youth monitoring responsibilities, many probation and parole officers do not have the expertise, time, or resources to facilitate access to appropriate special education services for youth with disabilities. Thus, a number of youth with disabilities are lost within the juvenile justice system.

A corrections–community transition system, with the cooperation of probation and parole officers and public and alternative schools, community agencies, and employment services personnel, as well as with the state departments of juvenile and adult corrections, must establish a statewide youth education tracking system for students with disabilities. The purpose of this system, under the direction of the state department of education, is to enable tracking of youth with disabilities, and access to their updated IEPs and ITPs, anywhere along the continuum of special education services. Special education teachers and transition specialists in detention and correctional facilities should be able to track students and obtain short progress reports at regular intervals following release from detention or corrections. They would provide additional transition services and links if the students were not making appropriate progress. The purpose of a youth education tracking system is to ensure that no youth with disabilities is lost in the system and that all youth receive appropriate transition and special education services.

## Component 6: Establish Transition, Special Education, and Related Services in Long-Term Juvenile and Adult Corrections

Short-term detention facilities and jails are responsible for the immediate identification of students with disabilities and initiating or updating of individualized transition plans, beginning portfolio assessments and student education passports, and establishing linkages with school, community, and employment services or with juvenile and adult correctional education programs. Long-term juvenile and adult correctional education programs, within this system, are responsible for expanding and enriching the various services begun in detention centers and jails. Individual transition plans, portfolio assessments, student education passports, and establishing community linkages are dynamic activities that continue in long-term programs and constantly build toward the goal of providing viable and comprehensive educational, vocational, and transition services to youth with disabilities.

Long-term programs also provide comprehensive educational services, including literacy and functional skills instruction, special education services and supports, academic courses associated with Carnegie units or state standards, GED preparation and testing, and prevocational and vocational education (Rutherford et al., 2002). From the day a youth first enters the long-term facility, education and treatment services must be focused on his or her transition, engagement, and long-term success in the community. Providing the transition supports and helping youth with disabilities develop the skills, abilities, and strengths necessary to have productive and meaningful lives as contributing members of society must be the ultimate goal of a comprehensive corrections–community transition system.

## CONCLUSION

From the time they first enter the justice system, many youth with disabilities do not receive adequate education and treatment. These youth present unique challenges to the juvenile justice system, not the least of which is the provision of transition services. Providing transition services and support to youth in the juvenile justice system is a challenge, but if educators, policy makers, and researchers meet this challenge they will increase the likelihood of successful transitions and reduce recidivism rates. The most appropriate way to do this is by coordinating transition services across public and alternative schools, detention centers, community and employment agencies, probation and parole departments, and juvenile and adult corrections.

In this chapter, we have described the components of a comprehensive transition system that helps ensure the seamless transfer of youth with disabilities and their education records across public and alternative schools, detention centers, community and employment agencies, and corrections. Effective enactment of these components will provide students with disabilities the support they need to make the transition to school, work, and community and to prevent them from moving to or returning to long-term incarceration. These components, along with a solid educational program, help develop the resiliency that is necessary to reduce recidivism, a focal point in the juvenile justice system (Todis et al., 2001). Providing structured, sustainable transition programming among schools, detention centers, employment and community agencies, and corrections programs through a corrections–community transition system strengthens resiliency and improves the chances for success for these youth.

## REFERENCES

Baltodano, H. M., Mathur, S. R., & Rutherford, R. B. (2005). Transition of incarcerated youth with disabilities across systems and into adulthood. *Exceptionality, 13*(2), 103–124.

Benz, M. R., & Halpern, A. S. (1993). Vocational and transition services needed and received by students with disabilities during their last year of high school. *Career Development for Exceptional Individuals, 16,* 197–211.

Black, T. H., Brush, M. M., Grow, T. S., Hawes, J. H., Henry, D. S., & Hinkle, R. W. (1996). Natural Bridge transition program follow-up study. *Journal of Correctional Education, 47,* 4–11.

Brier, N. (1994). Targeted treatment of adjudicated youth with learning disabilities: Effects on recidivism. *Journal of Learning Disabilities, 27,* 215–222.

Bullis, M., & Yovanoff, P. (2002). Those who do not return: Correlates of the work and school engagement of formerly incarcerated youth who remain in the community. *Journal of Emotional and Behavioral Disorders, 10*(3), 66–78.

Bullis, M., Yovanoff, P., Mueller, G., & Havel, E. (2002). Life on the "outs"—Examination of the facility-to-community transition of incarcerated youth. *Exceptional Children, 69*(1), 7–22.

Chappell, C. A. (2004). Post-secondary correctional education and recidivism: A meta-analysis of research conducted 1990–1999. *Journal of Correctional Education, 55*(2), 148–169.

Coffey, O. D., & Gemignani, M. G. (1994). *Effective practices in juvenile correctional education: A study of the literature and research, 1980–1992.* Washington, DC: U. S. Department of Justice, National Office for Social Responsibility.

Cook, L. (1990). *Collaboration and cooperation: Key elements in bridging transition gaps for adjudicated youth.* Paper presented at the 1988 National Conference on Transitional Services for Troubled Youth. (ERIC Document Reproduction Service ED319923)

Edgar, E. B., Webb, S. L., & Maddox, M. (1987). Issues in transition: Transfer of youth from correctional facilities to public schools. In C. M. Nelson, R. B. Rutherford, & B. I. Wolford (Eds.), *Special education in the criminal justice system* (pp. 251–272). Columbus, OH: Merrill.

Griller-Clark, H. (2006). Transition services for youth with disabilities in the juvenile justice system. In S. R. Mathur (Ed.), *EDJJ professional development series*. College Park, MD: Center on Educational, Disability, and Juvenile Justice.

Griller-Clark, H., Mathur, S. R., Sloane, F. C., & Helding, B. (2007, November 16). *The results are in: The Arizona Detention Transition Project.* Paper presented at the Robert B. Rutherford Memorial TECBD Conference on Severe Behavior Disorders of Children and Youth, Tempe, AZ.

Haberman, M., & Quinn, L. (1986). The high school re-entry myth: A follow-up study of juveniles released from two correctional high schools in Wisconsin. *Journal of Correctional Education, 37,* 114–117.

Halpern, A. S. (1985). Transition: A look at the foundations. *Exceptional Children, 51,* 479–486.

Harer, M. D. (1994). *Recidivism among federal prison releasees in 1987: A preliminary report.* Federal Bureau of Prisons, Office of Research and Evaluation. Washington, DC: U. S. Government Printing Office.

Hosp, M. M., Griller-Clark, H., & Rutherford, R. B. (2001). Incarcerated youth with disabilities: Their knowledge of transition plans. *Journal of Correctional Education, 52,* 126–130.

Individuals with Disabilities Education Act of 1990, Pub. L. No. 101–476 (1990).

Individuals with Disabilities Education Act of 1997, Pub. L. No. 105–17 (1997).

Individuals with Disabilities Education Improvement Act, Pub. L. No. 108–446 (2004).

JJ/SE Shared Agenda. (2007). *Tools for promoting educational success and reducing delinquency.* Washington, DC: National Association of State Directors of Special Education and National Disability Rights Network. Retrieved September 8, 2009, from http://www.edjj.org/focus/prevention/JJ-SE/TOOLS_Complete%20(4–16–07).pdf

LeBlanc, L. A., & Pfannenstiel, J. C. (1991). *Unlocking learning: Chapter 1 in correctional facilities.* Washington, DC: U. S. Department of Education.

Leone, P. E., Quinn, M. M., & Osher, D. (2002). *Collaboration in the juvenile justice system and youth-serving agencies: Improving prevention, providing more efficient services, and reducing recidivism for youth with disabilities*. Washington, DC: Center for Effective Collaboration and the National Center on Education, Disability, and Juvenile Justice.

Nelson, C. M., Rutherford, R. B., & Wolford, B. I. (1987). *Special education in the criminal justice system*. Columbus, OH: Merrill.

Rutherford, R. B., Griller-Clark, H., & Anderson, C. W. (2001). Treating offenders with educational disabilities. In J. B. Ashford, B. D. Sales, & W. H. Reid (Eds.), *Treating adult and juvenile offenders with special needs* (pp. 221–245). Washington, DC: American Psychological Association.

Rutherford, R. B., Mathur, S. R., & Griller-Clark, H. (2001). *Promising practices in transition for short term jails and detention centers and long term correctional facilities*. National Center on Education, Disability, and Juvenile Justice. Retrieved September 28, 2009, from http://www.edjj.org/focus/TransitionAfterCare/effectivePractice.html

Rutherford, R. B., Quinn, M. M., Leone, P. E., Garfinkle, L., & Nelson, C. M. (2002). *Education, disability, and juvenile justice: Recommended practices*. Arlington, VA: Council for Children with Behavioral Disorders.

Sitlington, P. L., Clark, G. M., & Kolstoe, O. P. (2000). *Transition education and services for adolescents with disabilities* (3rd ed.). Needham Heights, MA: Allyn & Bacon.

Todis, B., Bullis, M., Waintrup, M., Schultz, R., & D'Ambrosio, R. (2001). Overcoming the odds: Qualitative examination of resilience among formerly incarcerated adolescents. *Exceptional Children, 68,* 119–139.

Webb, S. L., & Maddox, M. E. (1986). The juvenile corrections interagency transition model: Moving students from institutions into community schools. *Remedial and Special Education, 7,* 56–61.

## CHAPTER 14

# Hard Questions and Final Thoughts Regarding the School-to-Community Transition of Adolescents with Emotional or Behavioral Disorders

**Michael Bullis**

When I was a doctoral student at the University of Oregon in the early 1980s and I would read books such as this with fervent interest, I wondered what an author had to do to be invited to write the concluding—and presumably most important—chapter. Typically, the concluding chapter presents the "heavy" thoughts of the author (usually someone who has been in the field for a long period of time and written voluminous numbers of articles, chapters, and other publications on the particular topic), provides future directions for the field, and serves as the "conscience" of the product. I am honored to be asked to write such a chapter for this book—I guess I now have enough gray hair for such a job—and I am humbled by the kind things my good friend and long-time colleague Doug Cheney wrote about me in his introductory chapter. Moreover, I am more than a little stunned that I have worked with and studied adolescents with emotional or behavioral disorders (EBD) for more than 25 years.

The genesis of my interest in the transition area, and specifically the school-to-community transition of adolescents with EBD, harkens back to my undergraduate days at Purdue University. One of the few classes I attended during those years was a class on abnormal psychology, as the topic of emotional disorders fascinated me. Later, as a vocational rehabilitation counselor, my caseload consisted primarily of adolescents and young adults with mental illnesses or mental retardation. As a the son of Midwestern parents who had experienced the United States' Great Depression, I was taught to work and that if something—anything—was wrong, the best way to fix the problem was to work hard. It followed that helping the people in my caseload to find employment made—and still makes—intuitive sense to me. I was, however, more than a bit stunned when many of the jobs that the people I worked with were able to secure ended unsuccessfully, and I was mystified why they would end so. After all, wasn't hard work the elixir for whatever was wrong? When I elected to pursue a doctoral degree, I decided that I would focus my studies on employment issues for people with disabilities. One of the best choices I ever made in my life was to enroll in the interdisciplinary doctoral program in special education and rehabilitation at the University of Oregon. I was challenged daily; learned an incredible amount of arcane knowledge that I have applied almost daily in my career, along with "practical stuff" that I apply daily in my life; and was taught the everyday and research skill of thinking critically. There is no greater acumen for an academic to possess than the thinking skills necessary to define and tackle a question through the research enterprise.

At that time, however, there was no Transition Initiative, no National Longitudinal Transition Study (NLTS), and little interest in adolescents with EBD (in fact, there was no such term at that time). Most of the work in the special education field focused on students, usually elementary-age, with mental retardation or learning disabilities—students with EBD simply did not have a "high profile" in the field at that time. It wasn't until the mid 1980s that the Transition Initiative was articulated (Will, 1984) and that the national emphasis on transition and the adolescence age group began in earnest. Never having been a teacher, I thought that the Transition Initiative was a godsend because it provided me with a personalized field of study. As I anchored myself in the transition movement, I searched for a subject that would interest me and that had not been "staked out" by other academicians. Harkening back to my early interest in mental illness, I decided to begin the study of transition issues for adolescents with EBD, a choice that has led me down many paths, through volumes of literature, mountains of statistics, lengthy meetings with teachers and social service providers, and innumerable associations with the greatest teachers of all—adolescents with EBD themselves and their families.

The task I have in this chapter is daunting—how to predict the future of this field. If I *really* knew how to tell the future, I would have retired long ago, but I did commit to this narrative. I will therefore identify and discuss some key questions that were addressed in the other chapters in this book, as well as some additional issues that warrant attention. The major question I pose at the outset relates to why there are seemingly so few and scattered transition programs for adolescents with EBD. I will return to this touchstone question at the conclusion of this chapter. I trust that the discussion of the other questions I address will help frame a plausible answer to this seminal issue.

## WHO SHOULD BE SERVED?

At first blush, the issue of exactly whom we should serve through transition programs aimed at adolescents with EBD should be clear—right? My experiences and work over the past 25 years makes me believe—quite strongly—that the answer isn't so simple. This fundamental question is perhaps the most complicated, frustrating, and critical I have encountered through my career in this field, and it has been the subject of a litany of articles and publications (for example, Forness & Knitzer, 1992; Nelson, Rutherford, Center, & Walker, 1991), but surprisingly few are aimed at the transition process. Let me briefly set the context for the problem as it relates to the transition years.

For a child or adolescent to receive the special education label of "emotionally disturbed" (the current federal term) or EBD (a more inclusive and descriptive term that I prefer), he or she must have an emotional condition that adversely affects academic performance. Ideally, possession of that label would then afford the student specialized instruction paid for by school district funds. However, an individual can suffer severe depression—and I use "suffer" purposefully to emphasize the pain a young person with that insidious condition can experience—but do reasonably well in his or her studies, earning acceptable or good grades. Conversely, he or she might do relatively poorly and fly under the radar of educators in today's overcrowded schools by causing little no distress to others, but being eaten up and alone with the illness.

In either case, that young person might not come to the attention of the educational system and therefore not receive the special education designation of "emotionally disturbed" if their educational performance did not pass whatever litmus test the district imposed.

A second issue related to the special education label that must be acknowledged is that the majority of students who are identified by the public schools as having an emotional disorder are so identified by the 6th grade (Kauffman, 1988). It may be that, after this point, school personnel are reluctant to place a label on a student and instead try to serve him or her as effectively as possible, or it may be that, during middle school, students become estranged from school and begin to skip school—thus being out of the public eye. For whatever reason, adolescents tend not to be identified with the special education label of emotionally disturbed under our current educational system.

An emerging body of literature from the field of developmental psychology (Forness, 2003; Lewis & Miller, 1990) suggests, however, that during adolescence—well after the elementary grades, when the body's chemicals and hormones go awry for a period of time—serious emotional conditions may become manifest. That is, adolescents who seemed perfectly fine during the elementary grades may develop emotional disorders that can affect their lives dramatically. Moreover, during the adolescent period, young people become susceptible to peer pressure (Patterson, Reid, & Dishion, 1992). And, as is typical, many adolescents flirt with the fringes of our culture through antisocial behaviors in an effort to define themselves through such experimentation (Dryfoos, 1990). In sum, emotional disorders may become evident during adolescence, at the time when the educational system tends *not* to identify students as emotionally disturbed—a label that carries the key to receiving special education services. Further, the emergence of these conditions in adolescence may coincide with youth engaging in risky behaviors away from the monitoring and structure of their families—a potentially dangerous combination.

Complicating this whole process is that it is during the secondary grades when adolescents begin to receive the types of community-based transition services described in this book and when efforts should be made to connect these youth to social service agencies in the community. A clear problem, then, is that if the adolescent doesn't have the emotionally disturbed label, which would afford the student's access to transition services operated under the aegis of special education, then school-based transition staff may not be able to refer them to the correct agency. In other words, because the student would not qualify to receive special education transition services, he or she may not come to the attention of the school-based transition staff and program.

Conversely, social service agencies tend to place little credence in the special education label and instead rely on psychiatric labels described in the *Diagnostic and Statistical Manual of Mental Disorders* (DSM) (American Psychiatric Association, 2000) as the entry point for services. Although a fair amount has been written about the vagaries of assessing and labeling students with a special education label, to my knowledge at least, less has been written about how children and adolescents receive a DSM label. Based on my experience in the various projects I have administered over the years, I would bet that this process is at least as convoluted as that followed in the public schools. Again, the important point is that without the right label, the adolescent may not qualify for services through a community-based social service agency. (As I discuss later in this chapter, such services can be critical for individual's long-term adjustment.)

One of the stranger things I have ever encountered in my career is that it is entirely possible for an adolescent to have a special education label identifying him or her as disabled in the eyes of the special education system, but not carry a psychiatric label. On the other hand, I have also known disturbed adolescents with serious psychiatric labels who have never been identified as emotionally disturbed through the special education system. To be perfectly blunt, in most of the cases with which I am familiar, I don't think there is a dime's worth of difference between the two groups in terms of their presenting problems and transition needs.

It saddens me to admit that a fulcrum issue in the provision of transition services becomes one of assisting youth to secure those services, usually through a process of securing the right label for whatever field or agency. Twenty-five years ago, if you had told me that I would advocate labeling adolescents to receive services, I would have invited you outside for an "up-close-and-personal" talk, in which you wouldn't have had the chance to say much. But this strange situation is a reality of our educational and social service system that must be addressed either as the problem now stands—or changed in the years to come.

## WHERE DO WE SERVE THESE YOUTH?

Something that has troubled me for a long time is the issue of exactly where we should base transition programs designed to serve adolescents with EBD. The stock response, particularly from educators, is that transition programs for adolescents with EBD should be based in the schools—a position I certainly support, with some reservations.

As we know from the National Longitudinal Transition Study (see Cheney's summary in this book) and other excellent studies of the longitudinal transition adjustment of adolescents with disabilities, including those with EBD (for example, Carson, Sitlington, & Frank, 1995; Kortering & Blackorby, 1992; Neel, Meadow, Levine, & Edgar, 1988; Sitlington, Frank, & Carson, 1992), adolescents with EBD present the highest dropout rate of any disability group, approaching 60%. (The next highest dropout rate is about 35%, which is exhibited by adolescents with specific learning disabilities—nowhere near the dubious standard set by their peers with EBD). This means that *more than half* of the population identified with EBD leaves the public schools before graduation during the transition years. Moreover, I am convinced that a fair portion of those students with EBD who graduate, or who at least stay in school, are involved only peripherally in their education and so may not be served through school-based transition programs (Bullis, Moran, Todis, Benz, & Johnson, 2002).

Further complicating this issue is the fact that adolescents with EBD tend not to enroll in any sort of postsecondary or high-school completion program after leaving high school (Marder, 1992a, 1992b). Other studies suggest that adolescents with EBD who are placed in mental health or correctional settings tend not to reenroll in public school and receive transition services upon return to their home communities (Bullis, Yovanoff, & Havel, 2004; Bullis, Yovanoff, Mueller, & Havel, 2002; Bullis et al., 1994). In short, many adolescents with EBD drop out of school, not to return to any type of education, and those who enter either the mental health or correctional systems tend not to return to the public schools. *Because these youth either are not present, or are minimally involved, in high school, how then are school-based transition programs going to serve them?*

I have administered model demonstration transition programs that provide direct transition services for adolescents and young adults with EBD through higher education units (Fredericks & Bullis, 1989), mental health agencies (Bullis, 1995b), and schools (Bullis, 1995a). Something that has astonished me over that time and across projects is that many of the adolescents with whom we worked would either have formally dropped out of school or just stopped attending. However, once leaving school, they then would spend more time at school than when they were enrolled— they would come to see their friends on the street corner near the school.

The power of school as a socialization agent and "magnet," even for young people who seem disenfranchised from public education, is something that we should recognize and try to capitalize on when establishing transition programs for this population (Maughn, 1988; Mortimore, 1995). In a set of excellent and thoughtful publications, Dryfoos (1990, 1991, 1993) and Kazdin (1987, 1993) described ways in which adolescents with EBD should be served, emphasizing the central role and place of public high schools in providing such services. At the same time, each author suggested that the "traditional" type of educational services and approaches simply will not be effective in addressing the needs of this population.

Indeed, in the projects I have administered, I have found it much easier to provide community-oriented transition services to adolescents with EBD when we are based outside of the schools, because my staff were unencumbered by the expectation to be located in a classroom for most of the day. Conversely, in those same programs, we had a much harder time accessing school-based services—probably because we were not part of the educational system (Bullis & Cheney, 1999; Bullis et al., 1994; Bullis, Moran et al., 2002). Through these experiences, I have become convinced that the absolute best location for transition programs for adolescents with EBD is the public schools.

A troublesome problem that we had to address in a school-based transition project related to the community-based nature of the project. Having staff operating in the community and away from the four walls of the classroom was something that was somewhat foreign to the traditional concept of high-school education, but it was finally understood by the school administrators with whom we worked. The following comment by a special education administrator addresses this point.

> The strengths are that you have a lot of flexibility in how you
> work with kids because staff aren't tied to a classroom where

they can't spring free. They're available to work with kids so they can do a lot of innovative interventions, get out in the community, find services for kids who have left school. . . . The downside of it, though, is that they've been located off-site. But that's the strength of it. The strength of it is that they're not on-site. The down side is that it's very difficult to supervise. (Bullis, Moran et al., 2002, p. 54)

The traditional and prevailing notion of what constitutes high-school education, coupled with the recent emphasis on standards-based testing and school reform, runs at cross-purposes for the type of transition services described in this volume and elsewhere as "best practices" for adolescents with disabilities (Kohler, 1993), and specifically for adolescents with EBD (Bullis & Benz, 1998: Bullis & Cheney, 1999; Bullis & Fredericks, 2002). A looming challenge will be to figure out ways to provide community-based transition services to adolescents with EBD, who may or may not be involved in traditional schooling, through programs based in the public schools, while at the same time addressing both administrative concerns for monitoring staff who may not work for any appreciable length of time in the school building and the pressure to conform to the demands of contemporary, standards-based education.

## HOW LONG SHOULD TRANSITION SERVICES BE PROVIDED?

A question frequently asked by people who exercise, or who at least want to start an exercise program, is "What is the absolute minimum amount of exercise I need to do to achieve a positive effect on my health?" The corollary question that I am asked by transition professionals as I speak in various spots across our country is "What is the absolute minimum amount of transition services needed to positively affect the transition outcomes of adolescents with EBD?" To this query I always reply that I simply don't know. After disappointing whomever I am talking to, I then try to address the question through logic and by dividing my answer into two parts: services located in the public schools and services based in the community.

The Individuals with Disabilities Improvement Education Act is clear that transition services should begin by age 16 for students with disabilities and by age 14 if the student is likely not to complete high school (IDEIA, 2004). These two age standards always are startling to me because, in the various projects I have administered, I have seldom, if ever, seen or heard of transition services starting for adolescents with EBD by these early ages. The typical referrals we received in our work were adolescents about 17 years old who had already dropped out of school, or those who were teetering on a knife's edge between barely staying in school and leaving school to "hang out." In fact, the stock comment from the professionals who referred these adolescents to us was "We don't know what to do with them anymore; you take him (or her)."

It *is* entirely possible that the adolescents we served and studied in those projects were unique in that they were from Oregon and thus don't reflect adolescents with EBD in the rest of the United States. This possibility does not, however, obviate the fact that the majority of adolescents with EBD drop out of high school before graduation or that many have truly awful transition outcomes as young adults (see Cheney's summary of the NLTS in Chapter 1). Accordingly, it makes sense to me to begin transition services for adolescents with EBD as early as possible in their high-school careers, probably as soon as the students enter high school, and to continue those services throughout their high-school years. This position assumes, of course, that we will know which students carry an EBD label and who then should be served in such programs—but, as I wrote earlier, this topic is one in which I have little confidence.

A parallel issue relates to how long transition services should be provided. In most states, special education services (including transition services) are offered through age 21, but usually such services end far earlier (remember, about 60% of adolescents with EBD will drop out of high school). To partially answer this question, one must consider the life course of emotional disorders. Although it is possible to affect the negative, high-risk behaviors such as criminal behavior, substance abuse, serial sexual relationships, and school disengagement and failure (Donovan & Jessor, 1985; Dryfoos, 1990) that many adolescents with EBD will exhibit, controlling these behavioral "symptoms" of the emotional disorder to some degree does not mean that the individual is "cured" of his or her emotional problem. Emotional disorders are extremely resistant to various interventions and durable over time (see, for example, Kazdin, 1987, 1993; Wolf, Braukmann, & Ramp, 1987). For example, the best predictor of becoming depressed as an adult is to have been depressed as an adolescent (as found by Merikangas & Angst, 2002 and others), and the best predictor of committing a crime as an adult is having committed one as an adolescent (Patterson et al., 1992).

Are people, then, sentenced to an ironclad path to adulthood dictated by problems they experience and choices they make in adolescence? The short answer, which I believe strongly, is a resounding no. Impressive longitudinal research conducted in the United States, England, and the Scandinavian countries provides an important perspective on what happens to adolescents with EBD as they age into adulthood (for example, Cadoret, Troughton, Merchant, & Whittlers, 1990; Caspi, Elder, & Herbener, 1990; Farrington, Loeber, & Van Kammen, 1990; Magnusson, Klintberg, & Stattin, 1994; McCord, 1992; Roberts, 1990; Robins, 1978; Rutter, 1989, 1993; Rutter, Harrington, Quinton, & Pickles, 1994; Werner & Smith, 1989, 1992). Most importantly, the results of these studies have critical implications for how we may best serve these young people in adolescence and young adulthood in order to affect their life trajectories positively.

After passing through adolescence, the human body stabilizes in terms of its chemistry and hormones, physiological changes that can mark a concomitant stabilization of a person's behavior—with choices becoming more reasoned and actions more measured. This maturational effect typically means that many—I am not sure how many, but a sizeable portion—of young people with EBD will tend to act less deviant and disturbed as they enter their middle to late 20s. At this point in development, many young people who demonstrated behavioral and emotional challenges earlier in their lives will try to work to join society in some positive manner by engaging in school, work, and social relationships. The problem is, however, that these young people typically have missed the time in life (that is, adolescence through young adulthood) when most individuals learn the skills (work, career, living, social networking, and so forth) necessary to become successful adults in our contemporary society. Thus, the unfortunate fact is that many people with EBD will be relegated to working and living on the fringes of society, never really achieving at their potential. Of course, some small portion of this group, who are referred to as "resilient" in the professional literature, will overcome seemingly overwhelming challenges and obstacles to achieve at a level neither they, nor others who knew them, ever thought possible (see, for example, Garmezy, 1971; Murray, 2002; Rutter, 1985, 1987; Todis, Bullis, Waintrup, Schulz, & D'Ambrosio, 2001; Werner & Smith, 1992).

The upshot is that most adolescents with EBD will need assistance into their adult years in order to address their personal issues and to gain they type of skills they need to enter the fabric of our society with any degree of success (Wolf et al., 1987). The impact of EBD on an individual youth may diminish over time, but EBD and its varied effects do not cease simply because he or she leaves public school. Kazdin (1987) compares the treatment of EBD to the treatment of diabetes in that both treatments will vary with need, but some type of treatment, of lesser or greater dosage, will need to be in effect over the life course. So, while transition services should begin in high school, it is likely that some level of support service will need to continue for many persons with EBD into adulthood, far past the traditional ending point of public education and special education services.

Such a transition service network would then involve agencies other than education as funding sources, which requires new funding streams to be established and agencies other than special education to assume the primary responsibility for leading the continuing interventions. Frankly, securing community-based services for adolescents and young adults with EBD is one of the hardest things I have encountered in the model demonstration projects I have directed. Beyond my personal experience, the literature provides stark and sobering indications of how infrequently community-based social service agencies ever serve this population (for example, Bullis et al., 2004; Marder, 1992a, 1992b; Marder, Wechsler, & Valdes, 1993).

How long should such services be provided? I'm really not sure, but I have no doubt that many adolescents with EBD will need some type of support into their 30s, if not longer. Development just does not follow a lockstep progression of better and better adjustment—for anyone. All of us need, at least to some degree, support and assistance at different points along the development pathway to overcome life problems. It certainly seems logical that adolescents with EBD may have an even greater need for such services than those of us without such conditions. Figuring out ways to provide a consistent and uninterrupted continuum of support for adolescents with EBD into adulthood will be one of the great challenges facing the special education and transition field in the coming years.

## DOES WHAT WE DO REALLY MAKE A DIFFERENCE?

Something that grates on me in the transition field and in the behavioral disorders field is how the term "best practice" is thrown around. Throughout my career, I have seen various "facts" and "best practices" come and go, mostly in the absence of any real evidence. Although the discussion of research-based practices, or the lack thereof, in special education is far beyond the purpose of this chapter, I do want to emphasize that the way in which we provide transition services to adolescents with EBD should be based on solid theory and research (Peters & Heron, 1993). Reviews of the transition literature (for example, Kohler, 1993) and for adolescents with EBD (such as Bullis & Cheney, 1999; Bullis & Fredericks, 2002) reveal little research on what constitutes "best practice" or what the impact of the imputed "best practices" are on the transition outcomes of adolescents with EBD. In fact, there are few—if any—treatment and control studies on many of the "best practice" concepts in transition in general or for the transition of adolescents with EBD specifically that we in special education, transition, or the EBD fields embrace. Nor have many studies been conducted to document the long-term impact of such interventions on transition outcomes of adolescents with EBD. Until such work is done, we as a field would be remiss to state that we "know" that certain interventions have certain effects.

The central issue, then, is what should be studied to provide guidance to transition service providers for EBD? The following ideas are but a sampling of what needs to be studied.

## What Is the Context?

Our field is based in a larger social context that we must understand because those social forces influence our professional activities to some greater or lesser degree. Bronfenbrenner (1979) and Bandura (1986), true giants in the social sciences, write at length about the importance of understanding the context of any social exercise when considering the value or worth of that effort. Understanding the social forces of our contemporary society goes far beyond the limited field of education, special education, and transition, and the four walls of the school building—extending in the broader realm of the world in which we live. How to delineate and quantify the impact of these macro-level variables on our small field is a task that will constitute considerable effort to complete properly.

## What Constitutes the Best "Package" of Transition Services for Adolescents with EBD?

Kazdin (1987, 1993) makes a convincing case that there is a lack of evidence on what interventions, combination of interventions, and precise "dosage" of these interventions constitute the best possible intervention format for adolescents with EBD. In lieu of such knowledge, he takes the logical position that when in doubt, and given the resistance of EBD to most interventions documented in the literature, the best intervention package should be one that is composed of everything including the proverbial kitchen sink. Relative to the transition of adolescents with EBD, Kohler (1993) and I (Bullis & Cheney, 1999; Bullis & Fredericks, 2002) identified a number of intervention components that should be included in effective transition programs: Close relationship between an adult service provider and the adolescent, community-based wraparound social services, competitive employment, flexible educational programming, personal futures planning and self determination, focused social skill instruction, long-term support and follow-up services, and ongoing evaluation of the impact of transition services on program participants. In the interest of space, I will not elaborate on these components here, but other chapters in this book do an excellent job describing how such programs of services can and should be structured and implemented.

## What Works for Whom?

The "Holy Grail" of research on instructional practice is trying to figure out exactly what intervention is effective with what type of person or persons displaying common and unifying characteristics (Cronbach & Snow, 1977). Indeed, this focus on subdividing samples in research or evaluation studies into logical groups is a central tenet of research texts (for example Kerlinger, 1986; Lipsey, 1990) and has received considerable attention in clinical psychology (such as Kazdin, 1986) and the EBD fields (for example, Kavale, Forness, & Alper, 1986; Keogh & MacMillan, 1983; MacMillan & Kavale, 1986). EBD is an extraordinarily vague and inclusive term that encompasses adolescents with a number of clinically distinct conditions (unipolar depression, attention deficit disorder, conduct disorder, and others) in more young people with EBD than we would care to admit (Forness, 2003). Logically, different groups require different types of interventions, which could yield different outcomes—that is, a certain package of interventions may be effective for adolescents with certain types of disorders but not for others. Figuring out what works for whom is a major challenge this field must address (Forness, 2003).

## What Did We Do?

Something that fascinates me as a research problem relates to the nature of the service provided to participants in research and evaluation studies. Few studies with which I am familiar in this field ever address the issue of how much or what service was provided to whom to achieve what effect. At best, studies identify that participants received certain types of services, but is this enough to say with any confidence that $x$ caused $y$? I don't think so; this type of crude designation just does not provide information on the duration, nature, or intensity of services— something that the social sciences have been admonished to address in research efforts (Kazdin, 1986; Yeaton & Sechrest, 1981). The issue is how to conduct such assessment of the "dosage" of interventions and treatments. Interventions in the social sciences and education are not usually prescribed or delivered uniformly according to concise and accurate weights (such as milligrams of medication), so how might this type of information be gathered?

## How Are They Doing?

Transition services, by definition, concern themselves with preparing adolescents to enter society as contributing, well-adjusted, and reasonably successful adults. It thus stands to reason that the primary outcomes of interest relate to the adolescents' experiences in the community after leaving school. This fundamental assumption would then dictate that adolescents with EBD who are served in transition programs are queried in some regular manner after leaving the program and, typically, the public school. At one point in the history of the transition field, great debate centered on whether transition programs should focus primarily on employment outcomes or on more general life adjustment outcomes (see, for example, Halpern, 1985). This debate waned fairly quickly, with past and current versions of IDEA (1990, 1997) and IDEIA (2004) clearly stating that we should prepare students broadly in employment, independent living, and social domains. It follows that we should also gather data on our former participants' achievements and experiences in these areas if we are to truly gauge and document the impact of our programs. This type of evaluation can use quasi-experimental procedures (Cook & Campbell, 1979), assume the form of a naturally occurring experiment in which logical subgroups (for example, girls versus boys, program completers versus noncompleters) are tracked longitudinally (Robins, 1981), or use random assignment to treatment or control conditions (Campbell & Stanley, 1966). Whatever choice is made regarding the design, this type of data collection is difficult to complete in an accurate manner and is seldom understood by administrators, some funding agencies, and practitioners. The bottom line is that in this era of fiscal belt-tightening and skepticism regarding the way in which public schools spend money, this type of objective evidence is exactly what is needed to convince bureaucrats, funders, the general public, and other professionals of the value of these types of programs. Unfortunately, few transition programs with which I am familiar conduct such data collection routinely; there is a clear need to change this reality.

## CONCLUSION

One of my former professors once told me that I should develop a healthy disdain for the status quo and anything that is just "okay." What we as a field do is too important *not* to push the envelope of research and practice to improve the opportunities offered adolescents with EBD and increase the skills they learn through our various interventions. Further, the mark of a true scholar is to be grand in his or her goals and conservative in his or her claims (unfortunately, I see too many professionals doing just the opposite).

I wish you good luck and perseverance in your efforts to educate and assist this group of young people. My greatest hope is that the questions I have discussed here will resonate with readers and spark a line of work that will actually improve the lives of adolescents with EBD who are trying to find their way in our contemporary society.

## REFERENCES

American Psychiatric Association. (2000). *Diagnostic and statistical manual of mental disorders* (4th ed., revised). Washington, DC: Author.

Bandura, A. (1986). *Social foundations of thought and action: A social cognitive theory.* Englewood Cliffs, NJ: Prentice-Hall.

Bronfenbrenner, U. (1979). *The ecology of human development.* Cambridge, MA: Harvard University Press.

Bullis, M. (1995a). *Achieving rehabilitation, independent living, and employment success for adolescents and young adults with serious emotional disorders and severe mental illness.* Rehabilitation Services Administration, Directed Competition on the Community Transition of Persons with Serious Emotional Disorders. Eugene: University of Oregon.

Bullis, M. (1995b). *Examination of the effect of vocational placements and service management on the development and continuation of serious emotional disturbances with adolescents with emotional and behavioral problems.* Office of Special Education Programs, Directed Competition on the Prevention of Serious Emotional Disturbance. Eugene: University of Oregon.

Bullis, M., & Benz, M. (1998). Community-based transition programs for adolescents with antisocial behavioral disorders. *Reaching Today's Youth, 2*(4), 64–68.

Bullis, M., & Cheney, D. (1999). Vocational and transition interventions for adolescents and young adults with emotional or behavioral disorders. *Focus on Exceptional Children, 31*(7), 1–24.

Bullis, M., & Fredericks, H. D. (Eds.). (2002). *Vocational and transition services for adolescents with emotional and behavioral disorders: Strategies and best practices.* Champaign, IL: Research Press.

Bullis, M., Fredericks, H. D., Lehman, C., Paris, K., Corbitt, J., & Johnson, J. (1994). Description and evaluation of the Job Designs project for adolescents and young adults with emotional or behavioral disorders. *Behavioral Disorders, 19*(4), 254–268.

Bullis, M., Moran, T., Todis, B., Benz, M., & Johnson, M. (2002). Description and evaluation of the ARIES project: Achieving rehabilitation, individualized education, and employment success for adolescents with emotional disturbance. *Career Development for Exceptional Individuals, 25,* 41–58.

Bullis, M., Yovanoff, P., & Havel, E. (2004). The importance of getting started right: Further examination of the community engagement of formerly incarcerated youth. *The Journal of Special Education, 38,* 80–94.

Bullis, M., Yovanoff, P., Mueller, G., & Havel, E. (2002). Life on the "outs"— Examination of the facility-to-community transition of incarcerated youth. *Exceptional Children, 69*(1), 7–22.

Cadoret, R., Troughton, E., Merchant, L., & Whittlers, A. (1990). Early life psychosocial events and adult affective symptoms. In L. Robins & M. Rutter (Eds.), *Straight and devious paths from childhood to adulthood.* Cambridge, UK: Cambridge University Press.

Campbell, D., & Stanley, J. (1966). *Experimental and quasi-experimental designs for research.* Skokie, IL: Rand McNally.

Carson, R., Sitlington, P., & Frank, A. (1995). Young adulthood for individuals with behavior disorders: What does it hold? *Behavioral Disorders, 20,* 127–135.

Caspi, A., Elder, G., & Herbener, E. (1990). Childhood personality and the prediction of life-course patterns. In L. Robins & M. Rutter (Eds.), *Straight and devious paths from childhood to adulthood.* Cambridge, UK: Cambridge University Press.

Cook, T., & Campbell, D. (1979). *Quasi-experimentation.* Boston: Houghton Mifflin.

Cronbach, L., & Snow, R. (1977). *Aptitudes and instructional methods.* New York: Irvington.

Donovan, J., & Jessor, R. (1985). Structure of problem behavior in adolescence and young adulthood. *Journal of Consulting and Clinical Psychology, 53,* 890–904.

Dryfoos, J. (1990). *Adolescents at risk.* New York: Oxford University Press.

Dryfoos, J. (1991). Adolescents at risk: A summation of works in the field— Programs and policies. *Journal of Adolescent Health, 12,* 630–637.

Dryfoos, J. (1993). Schools as places for health, mental health, and social services. In R. Takanishi (Ed.), *Adolescence in the 90's: Risk and opportunity* (pp. 82–109). New York: Teachers College Press.

Farrington, D., Loeber, R., & Van Kammen, W. (1990). Long-term criminal outcomes of hyperactivity-impulsivity-attention deficit and conduct problems in childhood. In L. Robins & M. Rutter (Eds.), *Straight and devious paths from childhood to adulthood* (pp. 62–81). Cambridge, UK: Cambridge University Press.

Forness, S. (2003). Parting reflections on education of children with emotional or behavioral disorders. *Behavioral Disorders, 28,* 198–201.

Forness, S. R., & Knitzer, J. (1992). A new proposed definition and terminology to replace "serious emotional disturbance" in Individuals with Disabilities Act. *School Psychology Review, 21,* 12–20.

Fredericks, H. D., & Bullis, M. (1989). *Community-based supported work program for adolescents with emotional and behavioral disorders.* Rehabilitation Services Administration, Directed Competition on Model Development in Supported Employment. Monmouth: Teaching Research Division, Western Oregon State College.

Garmezy, N. (1971). Vulnerability research and the issue of primary prevention. *American Journal of Orthopsychiatry, 41,* 101–116.

Halpern, A. S. (1985). Transition: A look at the foundations. *Exceptional Children, 51,* 479–486.

Individuals with Disabilities Education Act of 1990, Pub. L. No. 101–476 (1990).

Individuals with Disabilities Education Act of 1997, Pub. L. No. 105–17 (1997).

Individuals with Disabilities Education Improvement Act of 2004, Pub. L. No. 108–446, §§1400 *et seq.* (2004).

Kauffman, J. (1988). *Characteristics of children's behavior disorders* (4th ed.). Columbus, OH: Charles E. Merrill.

Kavale, K., Forness, S., & Alper, A. (1986). Research in behavioral disorders/ emotional disturbance: A survey of subject identification criteria. *Behavioral Disorders, 11,* 159–167.

Kazdin, A. (1986). Comparative outcome studies of psychotherapy: Methodological issues and strategies. *Journal of Consulting and Clinical Psychology, 54,* 95–105.

Kazdin, A. (1987). Treatment of antisocial behavior in children: Current status and future directions. *Psychological Bulletin, 102,* 187–203.

Kazdin, A. (1993). Adolescent mental health: Prevention and treatment programs. *American Psychologist, 48,* 127–141.

Keogh, B., & MacMillan, D. (1983). The logic of sample selection: Who represents what? *Exceptional Education Quarterly, 4,* 84–96.

Kerlinger, F. N. (1986). *Foundations of behavioral research* (3rd ed.). New York: Holt, Rinehart and Winston.

Kohler, P. D. (1993). Best practices in transition: Substantiated or implied? *Career Development for Exceptional Individuals, 16,* 107–120.

Kortering, L., & Blackorby, J. (1992). High school dropout and students identified with behavioral disorders. *Behavioral Disorders, 18,* 24–32.

Lewis, M., & Miller, S. (Eds.). (1990). *Handbook of developmental psychopathology.* New York: Plenum Press.

Lipsey, M. (1990). *Design sensitivity: Statistical power for experimental research.* Newbury Park, CA: Sage Publications.

MacMillan, D., & Kavale, K. (1986). Educational interventions. In H. Quay & J. Werry (Eds.), *Psychopathological disorders of childhood* (3rd ed.) (pp. 583–621). New York: John Wiley & Sons.

Magnusson, D., Klintberg, B., & Stattin, H. (1994). Juvenile and persistent offenders: Behavioral and psychological characteristics. In R. Ketterlinus & M. Lamb (Eds.), *Adolescent problem behaviors: Issues and research* (pp. 81–92). Hillsdale, NJ: Lawrence Erlbaum.

Marder, C. (1992a). Education after secondary school. In M. Wagner, R. D'Amico, C. Marder, L. Newman, & J. Blackorby (Eds.), *What happens next? Trends in postschool outcomes of youth with disabilities.* Menlo Park, CA: SRI International.

Marder, C. (1992b). *Secondary students classified as seriously emotionally disturbed: How are they being served?* Menlo Park, CA: SRI International.

Marder, C., Wechsler, M., & Valdes, K. (1993). *Services for youth with disabilities after secondary school.* Menlo Park, CA: SRI International.

Maughn, B. (1988). School experiences as risk/protective factors. In M. Rutter (Ed.), *Studies of psychosocial risk* (pp. 200–220). Cambridge, UK: Cambridge University Press.

McCord, J. (1992). The Cambridge–Somerville Study: A pioneering longitudinal–experimental study of delinquency prevention. In J. McCord & R. Tremblay (Eds.), *Preventing antisocial behavior* (pp. 196–208). New York: Guilford Press.

Merikangas, K., & Angst, J. (2002). The challenge of depressive disorders in adolescence. In M. Rutter (Ed.), *Psychosocial disturbances in young people: Challenges for prevention* (pp. 131–165). Cambridge, UK: Cambridge University Press.

Mortimore, P. (1995). The positive effects of schooling. In M. Rutter (Ed.), *Psychosocial disturbances in young people: Challenges for prevention* (pp. 333–367). Cambridge, UK: Cambridge University Press.

Murray, C. (2002). Risk factors, protective factors, vulnerability, and resilience: A framework for understanding and supporting adult transitions of youth with high-incidence disabilities. *Remedial and Special Education, 24,* 16–26.

Neel, R., Meadow, N., Levine, P., & Edgar, E. (1988). What happens after special education: A statewide follow-up study of secondary students who have behavioral disorders. *Behavioral Disorders, 13,* 209–216.

Nelson, C. M., Rutherford, R. B., Center, D., & Walker, H. M. (1991). Do public schools have an obligation to serve troubled children and youth? *Exceptional Children, 57,* 406–415.

Patterson, G. R., Reid, J., & Dishion, T. (1992). *Antisocial boys.* Eugene, OR: Castalia.

Peters, M., & Heron, T. (1993). When the best is not good enough: An examination of best practice. *Journal of Special Education, 26,* 371–385.

Roberts, J. (1990). High-risk children in adolescence and young adulthood: Course of global adjustment. In L. Robins & M. Rutter (Eds.), *Straight and devious paths from childhood to adulthood.* Cambridge, UK: Cambridge University Press.

Robins, L. N. (1978). Sturdy childhood predictors of adult antisocial behavior: Replications from longitudinal studies. *Psychological Medicine, 8,* 611–622.

Robins, L. (1981). Epidemiological approaches to natural history research: Antisocial disorders in children. *Journal of the American Academy of Child Psychiatry, 20,* 556–580.

Rutter, M. (1985). Resilience in the face of adversity: Protective factors and resistance to psychiatric disorder. *British Journal of Psychiatry, 147,* 598–611.

Rutter, M. (1989). Isle of Wight revisited: Twenty-five years of child psychiatric epidemiology. *Journal of the American Academy of Child and Adolescent Psychiatry, 28,* 233–253.

Rutter, M. (1993). Cause and course of psychopathology: Some lessons from longitudinal data. *Pediatric and Perinatal Epidemiology, 7,* 105–120.

Rutter, M., Harrington, R., Quinton, D., & Pickles, A. (1994). Adult outcome of conduct disorder in childhood: Implications for concepts and definitions of patterns of psychopathology. In R. Ketterlinus & M. Lamb (Eds.), *Adolescent problem behaviors: Issues and research* (pp. 57–80). Hillsdale, NJ: Lawrence Erlbaum.

Sitlington, P., Frank, A., & Carson, R. (1992). Adult adjustment among high school graduates with mild disabilities. *Exceptional Children, 59,* 221–233.

Todis, B., Bullis, M., Waintrup, M., Schultz, R., & D'Ambrosio, R. (2001). Overcoming the odds: Qualitative examination of resilience among formerly incarcerated adolescents. *Exceptional Children, 68,* 119–139.

Werner, E., & Smith, R. (1989). *Vulnerable but invincible: A longitudinal study of resilient children and youth.* New York: Adams-Bannister-Cox.

Werner, E. E., & Smith, R. S. (1992). *Overcoming the odds: High risk children from birth to adulthood.* Ithaca, NY: Cornell University Press.

Will, M. (1984). *OSERS program for the transition of youth with disabilities: Bridges from school to working life.* Washington, DC: Office of Special Education and Rehabilitative Services.

Wolf, M., Braukmann, C., & Ramp, K. (1987). Serious delinquent behavior as a part of a significantly handicapping condition: Cures and supportive environments. *Journal of Applied Behavior Analysis, 20,* 347–359.

Yeaton, W., & Sechrest, L. (1981). Critical dimensions in the choice and maintenance of successful treatments: Strength, integrity, and effectiveness. *Journal of Consulting and Clinical Psychology, 49,* 156–167.

# Name Index

# Subject Index

# *About the Editor*

Douglas Cheney, Ph.D., has 37 years of experience in special education and has been a teacher, administrator, researcher, and professor. He is currently a professor of special education at the University of Washington (UW), Seattle, where he teaches classes in and directs UW's master's and doctoral programs in emotional and behavioral disabilities. He is a past president (1998–1999) of the International Council for Children with Behavioral Disorders and was Director of the Institute on Emotional Disturbance at Keene State College, New Hampshire, from 1992–1997. While at Keene State, he co-developed, with JoAnne Malloy, Project RENEW, an adolescent transition program for youth with emotional or behavioral disorders, which is featured in this text. Dr. Cheney has also been the principal investigator of multiple research projects funded by the U.S. Department of Education, including Project DESTINY, the BEACONS project, and Check, Connect, and Expect. He is an active member of both the national and Washington State's Positive Behavior Support Network. Dr. Cheney is also the coeditor of *The Journal of Emotional and Behavioral Disorders* and an associate editor for *Intervention in School and Clinic.*

# About the Contributors

KATHLEEN ABATE is the Executive Director of the Granite State Federation of Families for Children's Mental Health. She has over 20 years experience in advocacy, training, and program development, based in the principles of self-determination for people with disabilities. Kathleen is also the parent of a young man with emotional challenges who is now a successful leader in his community.

MICHAEL TODD ALLEN, PHD, is an associate professor in the School of Psychological Sciences and the College of Education and Behavioral Sciences at the University of Northern Colorado. His research interests include the neural substrates of learning and memory, applying findings from psychology and neuroscience to the classroom, and metacognitive tutoring of at-risk students.

HANK BOHANON, PHD, is an associate professor in the School of Education at Loyola University Chicago. He conducts research regarding the implementation of positive behavior support in high schools. He also leads projects that conduct evaluation for statewide initiatives, including response to intervention and social and emotional learning.

PATRICIA M. BRAZIEL is the project coordinator for dissemination and outreach services for the National Secondary Transition Technical Assistance Center (NSTTAC). Her research areas include special education identification practices, school completion, and transition services for students with disabilities.

MICHAEL BULLIS is the Sommerville-Knight Professor and Dean of the College of Education at the University of Oregon. For more than 20 years, he has conducted research on the school-to-community transition of adolescents with emotional disorders and directed model demonstration projects that provide direct transition services to this population.

TIM CANTER is a transition specialist located at the Serbu Youth Campus, Lane County, Oregon, Juvenile Justice Center. He is also employed by the Springfield, Oregon, School District.

ERIK W. CARTER, PHD, is an associate professor of special education in the Department of Rehabilitation Psychology and Special Education at the University of Wisconsin–Madison. His research and teaching address secondary transition services, self-determination, peer relationships, and access to the general curriculum.

HEATHER GRILLER CLARK, PHD, is a principal research specialist at Arizona State University. Her research focuses on issues of transition, gender, and professional development for youth with emotional and behavior disorders in the juvenile justice system.

HEWITT B. "RUSTY" CLARK, PHD, is Director of the National Network on Youth Transition for Behavioral Health and a professor at the Florida Mental Health Institute, College of Behavioral and Community Sciences, University of South Florida. Dr. Clark has innovated and researched numerous programs, has published widely in the areas of individualized interventions for children and youth with emotional/behavioral difficulties, and has developed the Transition to Independence Process (TIP) system, and evidence-supported model.

GAIL M. CORMIER is the Executive Director of North Carolina Families United. She has worked for over 25 years in New Hampshire and North Carolina with at-risk youth who are struggling with mental health issues, helping them get back into their communities, stay in school, and be successful contributing adults and family members.

JONATHON DRAKE, MSW, has been the RENEW Training Coordinator at the Institute on Disability at the University of New Hampshire since

2008 and has worked with over 50 youth using the RENEW model. Mr. Drake has also provided training and technical assistance to high school professionals and mental health clinicians to implement RENEW in various settings.

NICOLE DESCHÊNES, RN, MEd, is Codirector of the National Network on Youth Transition (NNYT), an organization dedicated to improving practice, systems, and outcomes for youth and young adults with emotional and behavioral difficulties. Author of various publications and reports, she is also on the faculty of the Department of Child and Family Studies at the Louis de La Parte Florida Mental Health Institute in Tampa. Her current efforts focus on developing effective transition models for youth.

CINDA JOHNSON, EdD, is an assistant professor in the College of Education and Director of the Special Education Program at Seattle University. Her research areas include secondary transition services and the post-school outcomes of youth in special education, with particular emphasis on youth with emotional and behavioral disorders. She is the principal investigator for the Center for Change in Transition Services for Washington State.

DENNIS A. KOENIG is Chief Clinical Officer for Positive Education Program (PEP). He manages referrals and enrollment and supervises all agency clinical services for children and families. He provides mental health programming and service consultation and crisis intervention and has been instrumental in developing and launching the agency's school-based program for transitional youth ages 16 to 22.

LARRY J. KORTERING, PhD, is a professor of special education at Appalachian State University and a co-principal investigator for the National Secondary Transition Technical Assistance Center (NSTTAC). His research areas include school completion, assessment, and transition services for students with disabilities.

JOANNE M. MALLOY, MSW, is a developer of the RENEW model and has directed six state and federally funded employment and dropout prevention projects, with a focus on intensive services for youth with emotional or behavioral disorders. Ms. Malloy has authored numerous articles and book chapters on employment and secondary transition for youth with emotional disorders and adults with mental illnesses.

SARUP R. MATHUR, PhD, is an associate professor in the College of Teacher Education and Leadership at Arizona State University. Her research areas include social skills, behavioral issues of children and youth, and professional development.

FRANCIE R. MURRY, PhD, is a professor in the School of Special Education at the University of Northern Colorado. Her research areas include positive support and academic and behavioral program development for youth with emotional and behavioral disorders and those at risk for identification of the disability.

FESTUS E. OBIAKOR, PhD, is a professor in the Department of Exceptional Education at the University of Wisconsin–Milwaukee. His research interests include multicultural psychology and special education, self-concept development, school reform, and international/comparative education. In addition, in his works he is interested in how we can reduce misidentification, misassessment, miscategorization, misplacement, and misinstruction of culturally and linguistically diverse learners in general and special education.

AMY M. PLEET, EdD, Secondary Inclusion Consultant at the University of Delaware Center for Secondary Teacher Education, provides professional development to Delaware school districts on topics related to program improvement, instructional strategies, and parent engagement so students with disabilities are better prepared to transition into adulthood.

ANTHONY J. PLOTNER, PhD, is a research fellow in the Department of Special Education at the University of Illinois at Urbana-Champaign. His areas of research interest include transition planning/services and post-secondary outcomes for persons with disabilities.

CHAD A. ROSE, MA, is a doctoral candidate in the Department of Special Education at the University of Illinois. His areas of research interest include bullying and victimization among students with disabilities, with a focus on students with emotional or behavioral disorders.

JAMES G. SHRINER, PHD, is an associate professor in the Department of Special Education at the University of Illinois at Urbana-Champaign. His areas of research interest include issues related to policy implementation and standards-based instruction/assessment/accommodation for students with disabilities, including those with emotional or behavioral disorders.

PATRICIA L. SITLINGTON (1947–2009), PHD, was a professor of special education at the University of Northern Iowa. She wrote extensively in the area of transition services, assessment, and post-school outcomes for students with disabilities and also served as director or co-director of a number of federally and state-funded research projects.

SARAH A. TAYLOR, MSW, PHD, is the CalSWEC-II Mental Health Coordinator and a lecturer in the Department of Social Work at California State University, East Bay. Dr. Taylor earned her MSW in 2002 and PhD in 2007, both from the University of California, Berkeley. Her research interests include transition-age youth, community mental health, disability, and LGBTQ issues.

DEANNE UNRUH, PHD, is a senior research associate in the Secondary Special Education and Transition Research Unit at the University of Oregon. Her areas of research interest include secondary transition services targeting youth in the juvenile justice system and adolescents with emotional and/or behavioral difficulties.

CLAUDIA LANN VALORE is Chief Program Officer for Positive Education Program (PEP). She oversees programming for the agency's early childhood, day treatment, and autism centers, which annually serve nearly 1,000 youth with emotional, behavioral, and/or significant developmental disabilities.

THOMAS G. VALORE, PHD, is Staff Development Director for Positive Education Program (PEP). He oversees the creation and implementation of consultation and training curricula for internal and external audiences of special education and mental health professionals. An educator and psychologist, his training and experience qualify him as an expert in serving troubled and troubling youth.

MIRIAM WAINTRUP, MED, is a senior research assistant in the Secondary Special Education and Transition Programs Research Unit at the University of Oregon. Her work has focused on coordinating research and model demonstration projects on transition for high-risk youth with disabilities.

DONNA L. WANDRY, PHD, Associate Professor and Chair of the Department of Special Education at West Chester University of Pennsylvania, has professional priorities in teacher preparation, family empowerment in transition, school legal issues, and school/agency transition systems change.

LYNN K. WILDER, EDD, is Associate Professor and Program Leader for Special Education and Early Childhood Education in the College of Education at Florida Gulf Coast University. Her research and publications include reliability of assessment for diverse students with emotional/behavioral disorders, positive behavior support for parents of children with challenging behavior, developing culturally responsive faculty, and working with students with low socioeconomic status.